THE GREAT SURVIVORS

How Monarchy Made It
into the Twenty-First Century

PETER CONRADI

ALMA BOOKS

ALMA BOOKS LTD
London House
243–253 Lower Mortlake Road
Richmond
Surrey TW9 2LL
United Kingdom
www.almabooks.com

First published in Great Britain by Alma Books Limited in 2012
Copyright © Peter Conradi, 2012

Cover and plate images © Corbis

Peter Conradi asserts his moral right to be identified as the author of this
work in accordance with the Copyright, Designs and Patents Act 1988

Printed and bound by CPI Group (UK) Ltd, Croydon, CR0 4YY

Typesetting and eBook by Tetragon

ISBN (Hardback): 978-1-84688-209-8
ISBN (Export edition): 978-1-84688-215-9
eBook ISBN : 978-1-84688-213-5

CONTENTS

To Lisa, Alex and Matthew

The Main Branches of Europe's Reigning Monarchies

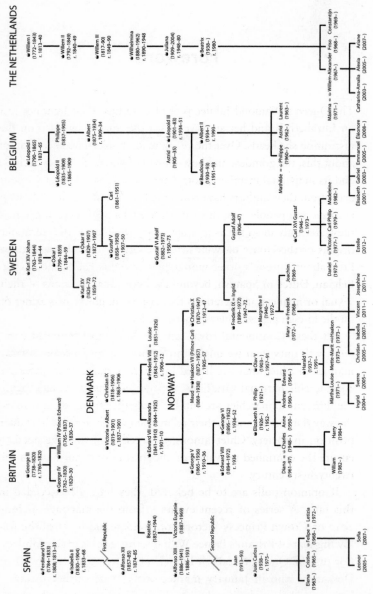

Reigning king/queen

Crown prince/princess

Foreword

The Queen's Diamond Jubilee year of 2012 has shone light not just on Elizabeth II and her sixty years on the throne, but also on the institution she heads. Over the years, many books have been written about this, the grandest and best-known of the world's monarchies, and its individual members, both past and present. Almost without exception, their authors have concerned themselves exclusively with events – and people – on this side of the Channel, venturing across the water only in so far as it is necessary to describe the Germanic origins of the House of Windsor. By contrast, most Britons know little about Europe's other monarchies, whether the Scandinavian, Belgian, Dutch or Spanish, beyond the occasional mentions of their sexual or financial indiscretions that appear in glossy magazines or on the foreign pages of newspapers.

Yet these Continental royal families have much more in common with ours than we might think, and not only because of the manner in which they are linked by intermarriage. True, there are considerable national variations, yet the fundamental issues facing the different monarchies are similar – whether their political roles, the way they are financed, their relationship with the media or their position in society. Chief among these challenges is the need to ensure the continued relevance of the institutions they head in the twenty-first century.

If opinion polls are to be believed, they have all succeeded in this task. A series of recent events – from the marriage in June 2010 of Crown Princess Victoria of Sweden and in April the following year of Britain's Prince William, through to 2012's Jubilees, not just of Queen Elizabeth but also of Queen Margrethe II of Denmark, who in January marked forty years on her throne – have served to underline the continuing importance of Europe's royal families in the lives of their respective countries – as well as to demonstrate the enormous affection they inspire among their subjects.

This book will try to put the Windsors into this broader, European context, comparing and contrasting them with their Continental counterparts. I hope it proves illuminating – and will lead you to look at our own royal family in a different light.

– Peter Conradi, London, April 2012

Introduction

It was just after nine a.m. on a cold and wet January day in 1793 that they came for the King. At his own request, Louis-Auguste, king of France and Navarre, had been woken by his valet, Jean-Baptiste Cléry, four hours earlier and celebrated Mass for the last time in a room of the Tour du Temple, the medieval fortress in what is now the 3rd arrondissement of Paris, where he had been held since the previous August. The ornaments had been borrowed from a nearby church; a chest of drawers served as the altar. His prayers finished, the King gave Cléry a series of objects to pass to his wife and children.

"Cléry, tell the Queen, my dear children and my sister that I had promised to see them this morning, but wanted to spare them the pain of such a cruel separation," he told his valet. "How much it makes me suffer to leave without receiving their last embraces."

Then Louis was led outside, where a guard of 1,200 horsemen stood ready to escort him on the journey to his place of execution. Seated with him in the carriage was Henry Essex Edgeworth, an Irish-born priest brought up by the Jesuits in Toulouse, who had became confessor first to the King's sister, Élisabeth, and then to the King himself. It was Edgeworth who had conducted the service in the fortress.

Louis, then thirty-nine, had been dauphin since the death of his father when he was just eleven, and had succeeded to the throne in 1774 at the age of twenty. Weak and indecisive, he had mishandled the growing political and economic crisis in which he became enveloped. France was declared a republic on 21st September 1792, and in December of that year he went on trial before the National Convention accused of high treason and various crimes against the state. The guilty verdict was a foregone conclusion, but Louis's fate was not. A sizeable minority of members of the Convention argued for imprisonment or exile, but the majority prevailed: the King must die.

When the carriage stopped in the Place de la Révolution (now the Place de la Concorde), Louis knew his end was near. "We are arrived, if I mistake not," he whispered. Edgeworth's silence confirmed it. Surrounded by gendarmes, he was led to the scaffold, brushing off all attempts to tie his hands.

The path was rough and difficult to pass, and the King walked slowly, leaning on Edgeworth for support. When he reached the last step, he let go of the priest's arm, his pace quickened and, with one look, he silenced the ranks of drummers opposite him. Speaking loudly and clearly, he declared: "People of France, I die innocent. It is on the brink of the grave and ready to appear before God that I attest my innocence. I forgive those responsible for my death and I pray to God that my blood never falls on France."

Louis's head was severed with one stroke of the guillotine. The youngest of the guards, who was eighteen, displayed it to the people as he walked round the scaffold, accompanying it with what Edgeworth described as the "most atrocious and indecent gestures". The crowd were first stunned into silence, but then, cries of *Vive la République!* began to ring out. "By degrees the voices multiplied and in less than ten minutes this cry, a thousand times repeated, became the universal shout of the multitude, and every hat was in the air," the priest recalled.

Nine months later, Louis's Austrian-born queen, Marie Antoinette, went to the guillotine too, after a sham of a trial in which she was accused, among other things, of sexually abusing her son. Her last words were more prosaic than those of her husband. "Pardon me, sir, I meant not to do it," she said to the executioner, whose foot she accidentally stepped on before she died.

The revolution of 1789 that led to the death of Louis XVI and Marie Antoinette appeared to signal the beginning of a new age. As Napoleon's armies spread revolutionary ideas across Europe, borders were redrawn, new countries appeared and kings were forced into exile. Yet far from bringing the end of the monarchy, the decades that followed the French Revolution saw the institution flourish – a reaction, in part, to the bloody excesses that had followed. This was the case even in France itself where, in 1814, the Bourbon dynasty returned in the form of Louis's younger brother, Louis-Stanislas-Xavier, who ruled as Louis XVIII for a decade before he was succeeded by another sibling, Charles.

When new nation states came into existence in the years after the Congress of Vienna, it seemed self-evident that they should be headed by kings. The Netherlands, for centuries a republic ruled by a series of stadtholders, became a monarchy in 1815, as did Belgium and Greece when they became independent states in the 1830s. The unification of Italy in 1861 transformed Vittorio Emanuele II, ruler of Piedmont, Savoy and Sardinia, into the king of Italy; a decade later, in the aftermath of his victory over the French, King Wilhelm of Prussia was proclaimed German kaiser in a grandiose ceremony at Versailles.[1] When Bulgaria was established as a state in 1878, it was as a monarchy; the same was true of Norway, which voted to establish its own dynasty when it ended its union of crowns with Sweden in 1905.

The other great monarchies of Europe also survived the upheaval of the Napoleonic wars and the revolutions of 1830 and 1848 – although they reacted to the growing clamour for democracy in different ways. In Russia, the thirty-year reign of Catherine the Great, who came to the throne in 1762, had established the country as one of Europe's great powers – but although she was influenced by the ideas of the Enlightenment, Catherine baulked at turning them into practice, especially after the French Revolution. Her successors followed varying courses: Nicholas I, tsar from 1825 until 1855, was one of the most reactionary of the Russian monarchs, earning the sobriquet of "gendarme of Europe" for the determination with which he suppressed revolution abroad. His son Alexander II by contrast was a reformer who emancipated the serfs, reformed the army and navy and introduced limited local self-government, and would have gone further had he not been assassinated in 1881.

The Austrian kaiser, Franz Joseph I, whose sixty-eight-year reign from 1848 remains the third longest of any European monarch,[2] began by granting his people a constitution, but, after suppressing the Hungarian uprising with the help of Nicholas I, moved towards a policy of absolute centralism. Spain's rulers too oscillated between reform and autocracy: Fernando VII ruled initially according to the liberal constitution of 1812, but later abolished it; his daughter, Isabel II, also often interfered in politics in a wayward, unscrupulous way that made her very unpopular – and led to her enforced exile in 1868.

And then there was Victoria, who ascended to the British throne in 1837 a few weeks after her eighteenth birthday and went on to reign for sixty-three years and seven months, longer than any British monarch before or since, and the most of any female ruler. Victoria's reign witnessed considerable industrial, cultural, political, scientific and military progress; it also saw a doubling of the size of the British Empire, which by the time of her death in 1901 covered a fifth of the earth's surface and was home to almost a quarter of the world's population.

Victoria's significance to the story of European monarchy derives also from the sheer number of her children – nine – and the energy she and Albert devoted to their marriages. Indeed, the majority of European monarchs and former monarchs today from Norway to Romania can trace their ancestry back to the royal pair.

The first years of the twentieth century were the high point of monarchy in Europe. With the exception of France – a republic again since Napoleon III's defeat by the Prussians in 1870 – Switzerland and San Marino, every country was headed by a monarch. At King Edward VII's funeral in May 1910 the procession included nine crowned heads and more than thirty royal princes.

Then, one by one, the monarchies began to fall, starting that October in Portugal: the young Manuel II, who had become king only two years earlier following the assassination of his father and elder brother, was ousted in a coup. Revolution claimed the throne – and then the life – of Nicholas II, the Russian tsar, executed with his family and their servants in a cellar in Yekaterinburg in 1918. Military defeat in the First World War led to the deposing of Wilhelm, the German kaiser, and Karl I of Austria, although both escaped with their lives.

The Second World War and its immediate aftermath also took its toll: in Italy, King Umberto II was forced from the throne after just thirty-four days following a referendum in June 1946 in favour of a republic. His father, Vittorio Emanuele III, discredited by his close relationship with Mussolini, had abdicated in favour of his son, but it was too late to save the house of Savoy. Umberto's counterparts in central and eastern Europe fared no better. Stalin, whose Red Army now controlled the region, had no need for kings, and one by one, colourful King Zog of Albania, Miklós Horthy, who had ruled

Hungary as regent, Petar II of Yugoslavia and King Mihai of Romania all departed the scene.

In Greece, where monarchy had been something of an on-off affair since Otto of Bavaria became king in 1832, a referendum in September 1946 confirmed royal rule, allowing Georgios II to return from exile. His nephew Konstantinos II was forced to flee in 1967, however, following an abortive counter-coup against the junta. Greece finally became a republic, apparently for good, after a plebiscite in December 1974. Spain bucked the republican trend: on 22nd November 1975, two days after the death of Francisco Franco, Juan Carlos, who had been prince of Spain since 1969, was designated king, according to the law of succession promulgated by the late dictator.

And so the royal map of Europe has stayed in the more than three decades since Juan Carlos's inauguration: besides the Spanish monarchy, six other countries in Europe have kings or queens regnant: the United Kingdom, Belgium, the Netherlands, Denmark, Sweden and Norway. Also with royal rulers are the Grand Duchy of Luxembourg and the principalities of Liechtenstein and Monaco.[3]

Together, all ten nations – which are between them home to more than 150 million people[4] – retain a political system in which the head of state owes his or her position to birth alone, and whose lifestyle, funded by the state, is way beyond the dreams of most of his or her subjects. Furthermore, these royal families enjoy a deference and degree of public interest that appear completely unrelated to their personal skills or accomplishments. And all this is at a time when in almost every other sphere of society the idea that someone's lineage should guarantee them a lucrative job for life – especially one that still carries some vestige of political power – would be considered laughable.

It is the aim of this book to look at how this apparent anachronism has survived into the twenty-first century and to understand why these ten families have not been swept aside and replaced by elected heads of state. These are by no means Europe's poorest or more backward countries. The Scandinavian nations, in particular, are some of the most egalitarian, not just on the Continent, but in the world. Nor are they politically conservative. Their democratic credentials are exemplary.

No one setting out to create a constitution from scratch today would seriously suggest such a system. Yet not only are such archaic arrangements tolerated, they are regularly supported by a clear majority of the countries' respective parliaments and by their populations as a whole: call a referendum on the future of the monarchy in any of these ten nations today and you can be sure of a vote in favour of its retention. These, then, are the great survivors.

Attempting to explain this paradox requires a study of these royal families, of their history and of their present; of the gradual diminution of their political influence and of what remains of it; of their education and how their members are prepared for the top job; of their finances and their relationship with the media. And above all, it means examining Europe's royals as ordinary people who are privileged – and sometimes, it seems, condemned – to play such an extraordinary role.

Chapter 1

Who's Who

Queen Elizabeth II is the starting point for any discussion of Western monarchy – and not only because she is Europe's longest-serving monarch and in June 2012, aged eighty-six, celebrates sixty years on the throne. She heads a royal house – the House of Windsor[1] – which, thanks to a combination of its history, influence and sheer glamour, is unmatched in the world, and her remit extends across the widest geographical area. Unlike Victoria, she cannot refer to herself as Empress of India, but besides the United Kingdom she is queen of a further fifteen nations, including Canada, Australia and New Zealand, and head of the fifty-four-member Commonwealth, the modern-day successor to the British Empire.

But while Britain's monarchy is the most influential in Europe, it is not the oldest. That distinction is held by its Danish counterpart. Margrethe II, who became queen on the death of her father Frederik IX in January 1972, can trace her lineage back more than a thousand years to the Viking kings Gorm the Old and Harald Bluetooth. Under its hero kings, Canute the Great and the Valdemars, Denmark conquered not just England but also much of what are now the Baltic states in the eleventh and twelfth centuries. Margrethe I, who married King Haakon VI of Norway at the age of ten, ended up ruling not just Denmark and Norway but Sweden too, ushering in a union of the three Scandinavian kingdoms that was to last from the late fourteenth until the early sixteenth century.

Denmark was ruled from the middle of the fifteenth century by the Oldenburg branch of the family, and then from 1863 by Christian IX, from the junior Glücksborgs, who had been named heir presumptive in 1847 at the age of twenty-nine with the blessing of Europe's great powers. Christian's claim to the throne had been strengthened by his marriage to Princess Louise of Hesse-Kassel, a niece of Christian VIII, the previous monarch but one, after Queen Victoria rejected him. By royal standards, the Danes were neither wealthy nor grand: in comparison with some of their dysfunctional European counterparts, however, they seemed remarkably like a normal family.

The country that Christian IX reigned over for most of the second half of the nineteenth century had only a fraction of Britain's economic or political influence, but he and his German wife, Louise of Hesse-Kassel, were more than a match for Victoria and Albert when it came to finding royal marriage partners for their six children.

As well as bringing together the Danish and British royal families by marrying his eldest daughter, Alexandra, to Victoria's heir, Edward VII, Christian set up his own first son and heir, the future Frederik VIII, with Louise, the daughter of the king of Sweden and Norway. Of his other children, one became tsarina of Russia, one the king of Greece, and another married the ex-crown prince of Hanover. One of Christian's grandsons, Prince Carl, was later to ascend the Norwegian throne as King Haakon VII. The royal families of Belgium and Luxembourg can also trace their lineage back to the King, who became known as the "father-in-law" of Europe.

Christian used to invite his children and their own families back every summer from their adoptive homelands to the Fredensborg Palace, a baroque royal country seat on the island of Zealand. Leaving the cares of state behind them, they would eat, drink, relax – and often play practical tricks on one another. Those present would scratch their names and other messages on the glass window panes – starting a tradition of royal graffiti that has endured until today.

The former King Konstantinos II of Greece tells the story – perhaps apocryphal – of how Christian, who was his great-great-grandfather, was out walking with his family one day in a park near the palace when they came across an elderly man who was lost and asked for directions. Christian told him to follow them. "He noticed this very happy family joking and laughing, and when they came out of the park he thanked them and asked whom he had had the pleasure of talking to," Konstantinos recalls. Christian told him that he was the king of Denmark and proceeded to list his companions, who were members not just of the Danish royal family, but of those of Britain, Greece and Russia. "And the man was very happy," continues Konstantinos, "and he took his hat off and he said, 'My name's Jesus Christ,' and walked off."[2]

Margrethe II, Christian's great-great-granddaughter, was born on 16th April 1940, a week after the Nazis invaded Denmark, providing a substantial morale boost both to the royal family, who had chosen to remain in Copenhagen and sit out the occupation, and to the country as a whole. Her grandfather, Christian X, almost sixty-nine on the outbreak of war, became a highly visible symbol of "mental resistance" as he rode alone through the streets of the city on his horse. When asked by senior Nazis why he shunned a bodyguard, he reportedly replied: "The people of Denmark are my bodyguard."

The eldest of three daughters, Margrethe owes her position to a change in the rules of succession, implemented when she was a child, that removed the bar on women sitting on the Danish throne. As queen, she has proved a firm and popular monarch; she is also an accomplished artist. More controversial has been the role of her husband, Prince Henrik, a former French diplomat, born Count Henri de Laborde de Monpezat. Notorious like Britain's Prince Philip for his gaffes, Henrik has appeared to struggle – on occasions openly – with the role of consort. In 2002, apparently angry at being relegated to third place in the pecking order behind his son, he went off in a huff to the couple's Château de Caïx in Cahors in southern France.

Next in line to the throne is Crown Prince Frederik, who, after providing plenty of fodder for the tabloids as a young man, in May 2004, at the age of thirty-five, married Mary Donaldson, a former estate agent from Tasmania whom he met in a bar during the Sydney Olympics. The union has been widely seen as a success, but the couple have faced media criticism of their lavish lifestyle. The Crown Princess was dubbed a "Nordic Imelda Marcos" in 2006 after an annual report into the finances of the Danish royals showed she and her husband were splurging the equivalent of almost £2,000 a day on clothes, shoes and furniture.

Several months after Frederik's wedding, it was announced that his younger brother Joachim was divorcing Princess Alexandra, his Hong Kong-born wife, after nine years – the first Danish royal divorce in more than one and a half centuries. The palace was applauded for the openness with which it handled the breakup, and both have since remarried.

Most countries in Europe – and indeed the world – have made the transition over the past few centuries from monarchy to republic. The Dutch are unique in having moved in the opposite direction. It was only in the nineteenth century that the country became a monarchy under King Willem I. But his dynasty of Orange-Nassau, whose current head is Queen Beatrix, has exerted influence over the lands that now constitute the Netherlands since they moved there from Germany in 1400.

Until the sixteenth century, this region was ruled by Spain, along with most of present-day Belgium, Luxembourg and some parts of France and Germany. The predominantly Protestant Dutch were pressing to free themselves from their Catholic Spanish overlords, however, and in 1581 the States-General of the Dutch provinces passed an Act of Abjuration declaring that they no longer recognized King Felipe II of Spain as their king. The rebellion was led by Willem, Prince of Orange, and although he was assassinated in 1584 his fellow countrymen fought on in what became known as the Eighty Years' War, eventually defeating the Spanish in 1648.

Under the idiosyncratic system the Dutch devised to rule themselves, their country was divided into provinces, each led by a stadtholder, many of whom were chosen from the House of Orange. Formally, the state remained a confederated republic rather than a monarchy, even when it was decided in 1747 to make Willem IV, Prince of Orange, who was already stadtholder of Friesland and Groningen, into the stadtholder of all the other provinces too. Willem was the first man to have such a position and was given the title of Stadhouder-Generaal, which was made hereditary, turning him into a king in all but name.

The arrival of French Revolutionary forces in 1795 and the creation of the Batavian Republic was bad news for his son and successor Willem V, who fled to Britain and died in exile in Prussia in April 1806 – just two months before Napoleon made his own younger brother, Louis, King Lodewijk I. He reigned for just four years before Napoleon decided to incorporate his kingdom into France. Then, in 1813, the French were swept out, and Willem's son, also Willem, returned, proclaiming himself sovereign prince of the United Netherlands. On

16th March 1815, Willem became king of the Netherlands (and also grand duke of Luxembourg).

Queen Beatrix, his great-great-great-granddaughter, who has reigned since 1980, is the third in a succession of female monarchs. Initially, only men were allowed on the throne, but the rules were changed after the Netherlands faced a potential succession crisis in the late nineteenth century.

Beatrix's grandmother, Wilhelmina, who reigned for fifty-eight years, longer than any other Dutch monarch, came into her own during the Second World War when she fled to London and, thanks to her regular radio broadcasts to her subjects, became a symbol of resistance to Nazi rule of her homeland; Winston Churchill famously described her as the "only real man in the Dutch government in exile". The reign of her daughter, Juliana, was more controversial, however, and marred by controversy during the 1950s over her association with Greet Hofmans, a faith healer said to have exercised a Rasputin-like influence over her, and then, two decades later, by revelations that her German-born husband, Prince Bernhard, accepted more than one million dollars in bribes from the Lockheed Corporation, an American aerospace company. By contrast, Beatrix, who will eventually be succeeded by her son, Willem-Alexander, has rarely put a foot wrong in more than three decades on the throne.

Sweden has been a monarchy for almost as long as Denmark, and has a warlike past that seems out of place for a nation better known today for its neutrality, generous welfare state and flat-pack furniture. During the Middle Ages Swedish warriors terrorized Russia. Then in 1630 the greatest of the country's kings, Gustaf II Adolf, known as "the Lion of the North", invaded Germany too.

The current royal family, the Bernadottes, can trace their lineage back to the early nineteenth century and an adventurous Frenchman named Jean-Baptiste Bernadotte. The son of a petit bourgeois from Pau in the south-west of the country, Bernadotte rose to become one of Napoleon's marshals, his position further strengthened by the fact he was married to Désirée, Joseph Bonaparte's sister-in-law.

During his time as governor of the captured German city of Hanover, Bernadotte had become friendly with some influential Swedish officers taken prisoner during Napoleon's northern campaign. It was to prove a life-changing friendship: these were turbulent times in Sweden and in Europe, and the Swedes needed a strong ruler. King Carl XIII, who had been installed after a coup in 1809, the previous year, was elderly and decrepit and without surviving children – which meant an heir had to be found. The first choice was Carl August of Augustenburg, a minor Danish royal, but a few months after he arrived in Stockholm, he fell off his horse and died, apparently of a stroke.[3] Bernadotte, with his military expertise, seemed like a good replacement.

Napoleon was initially sceptical when Bernadotte went through the motions of obtaining his approval before accepting the throne, but the Emperor gave his blessing a few months later, and Bernadotte was adopted as Prince Carl Johan. Although initially only heir apparent rather than king, he swiftly consolidated his position, defeating Napoleon's forces with an army largely made up of German, Austrian and Russians at the Battle of Leipzig in 1813, before then taking on Denmark and forcing it to cede Norway to Sweden. When the old King died in February 1818, Bernadotte succeeded him, ruling for twenty-four years as Carl XIV Johan.

The former revolutionary soon turned into an authoritarian ruler in a more traditional mould. Queen Désirée – or Desideria as she became known to the Swedes – took a hearty dislike to her husband's adoptive country, especially its bleak weather – and was not that fond of her husband either. As a result she spent more than a decade back in Paris before eventually returning north in 1823; it was not until six years later that she was crowned queen of Sweden (she was never crowned queen of Norway). Swedish cuisine proved a particular disappointment to the royal couple. When nothing that their chefs prepared took their fancy, the King was served a lightly boiled egg – it has been tradition ever since in the palace to place a golden egg cup at the King's place.

Bernadotte once famously described himself to the Tsar as "man of the north", but appears to have suffered the occasional doubt that he had done the right thing. "Of me, you may say that I, who was once a marshal of France, am now only king of Sweden," he declared on one occasion. His subjects do not seem to have shared such doubts. Even though their king never bothered to learn either Swedish or Norwegian, the Bernadotte dynasty became firmly established.

The current monarch, Carl XVI Gustaf, is the great-great-great-great-grandson of the founder of the dynasty and the seventh Bernadotte king. He came to the throne in September 1973, at the age of just twenty-seven, on the death of his grandfather, Gustaf VI Adolf, who, confirming the Bernadottes' reputation for longevity, lived to see his ninetieth birthday. Carl XVI Gustaf never knew his father, Prince Gustaf Adolf, who was killed in a plane crash before his son's first birthday. Although a tragedy for the royal family – and the nation – Gustaf Adolf's death meant that Sweden, which was neutral during the Second World War, was spared the embarrassment of having as its king a man who during the 1930s had openly expressed sympathy towards Hitler's Reich.

Carl XVI Gustaf's designated successor is Crown Princess Victoria – who will become Sweden's first queen regnant in modern times. At her side will be Daniel Westling, her former fitness trainer, whom she married in June 2010 after a courtship that lasted eight years, and who thereafter was styled Prince Daniel, Duke of Västergötland. Queen Victoria's role will be a limited one, however: a constitutional reform that came into force in 1975 after at least two decades of discussion stripped the Swedish monarchy of all but ceremonial and representative duties. Some royalists were appalled; for others this was the perfect compromise and a model other European nations should adopt: a way of keeping all the popular trappings of the institution while removing the last vestige of the hereditary principle from the workings of modern democracy.

The Belgian royal house was also founded by an outsider, Leopold of Saxe-Coburg-Gotha, who, like Bernadotte, took advantage of the frequent redrawing of the map of Europe during the first half of the nineteenth century to secure himself a throne. The current monarch, Albert II, who acceded in 1993, is the country's sixth king and the great-great-grandson of the founder of the dynasty.

The Saxe-Coburgs' realm was a tiny collection of unconnected territories spanning just over four hundred square miles, split between modern-day Bavaria and Thuringia, which was home to a mere fifty thousand people. The family were not just political minnows, they were also virtually bankrupt – and realized that salvation for their dynasty lay in finding good marital partners for their children.

Leopold, born in 1790 as the penultimate of nine children, was an adventurous young man who did his family proud. He became a lieutenant general in the imperial Russian army and won the greatest prize in Europe: Princess Charlotte, the daughter of the future King George IV of the United Kingdom. Charlotte had it all: youth, beauty and above all the prospect of becoming head of one of Europe's grandest monarchies. When they married in May 1816, the couple even seemed in love – a rarity for nineteenth-century royal unions.

Yet Leopold's hopes of becoming consort were dashed just eighteen months later when Charlotte died in childbirth – a tragedy that prompted an outpouring of public grief similar to the hysteria that followed the death of Princess Diana almost two centuries later. "It was really as though every household throughout Great Britain has lost a favourite child," Lord Brougham, the Lord Chancellor, wrote in his memoirs.

Leopold was destined to be more than just a footnote in history – and time was on his side. Although already a widower, he had not yet reached his thirtieth birthday and had a generous pension of £50,000 voted by the British parliament. After being offered – and declining – the Greek throne, he agreed in 1831 to become the first king of the Belgians, after the southern part of the Netherlands broke away to form an independent if fragile nation. Along with his new realm, he acquired an accent on the "e" in his name.

Léopold also had a passion for matchmaking. Thus it was with his encouragement that his nephew, the young Albert of Saxe-Coburg-Gotha, wooed his niece, the then Princess Victoria, paving the way for one of the great royal love stories of all time. Léopold also succeeded in placing other members of his family in other royal houses. Climb your way up through the tangled branches of the family trees of most of Europe's royal families – both of those still on the throne and those that are defunct – and you will get back to the house of Saxe-Coburg-Gotha, memorably described later in the nineteenth century by Otto von Bismarck, the German chancellor, as the "stud farm of Europe".

Many contemporary observers – among them Léopold himself – were sceptical about the prospects of Belgium's survival. The French diplomat Talleyrand described the new country as "an artificial construction" in which the Dutch-speaking Flemings in the north would struggle to exist alongside the French-speaking Walloons in the south. The leading figures of mid-nineteenth-century diplomacy such as Metternich, Napoleon III and Bismarck did not expect it to last more than a generation or so.

They were to be proved wrong, in considerable part thanks to the skills of its first king. During his thirty-four years as king of the Belgians,[4] Léopold I oversaw the transformation of Belgium into an industrial powerhouse. More than 180 years later, his adoptive homeland continues to exist, even though relations between its two main linguistic communities have lurched from crisis to crisis in recent years, provoking the periodic question: "Will Belgium survive?" The dynasty that Léopold founded is still at its head – although since 1920 its members have been known simply as *de Belgique* (or *van België* or *von Belgien*) rather than of Saxe-Coburg-Gotha.

Belgium has hitherto had only male monarchs. Léopold II, who succeeded to the throne in 1865 on the death of his father, was a monster best known for his acquisition of the Congo, which he ran with enormous brutality as a private fiefdom until his own death in 1909, acquiring huge riches in the process. He was also deeply disliked at home for much of his reign. His nephew, who succeeded him as Albert I, was a more popular figure, hailed across the world for spearheading his country's resistance to the Germans during the First World War – but died in a climbing accident in the Ardennes aged just fifty-eight and was succeeded by his son, Léopold III.

Like Edward VIII, Léopold cut a glamorous, youthful figure, although unlike his British counterpart he had the ideal consort: Astrid, the niece of King Gustaf V of Sweden. Their marriage in November 1926 had been an arranged one, but quickly turned into a love match that produced first a daughter, Joséphine Charlotte, and then two sons, Baudouin and Albert. His was an unhappy reign, however: tragedy struck on 29th August 1935, when Astrid was killed in a car accident by Lake Lucerne in Switzerland. The car was driven by the King, who escaped with minor injuries. The loss of the beautiful young Queen provoked an anguished reaction that was to be echoed decades later by the deaths of first Princess Grace of Monaco and then Princess Diana.

Léopold chose to stay with his people when Belgium was occupied during the Second World War but, although he lobbied behind the scenes on behalf of his fellow countrymen, he was seen as a defeatist who was persuaded that the Germans would win the war and that

resistance was futile. His reputation was further damaged by his secret marriage on 6th December 1941 to Mary Lilian Baels, the young,
British-born daughter of a prosperous Belgian fish salesman turned
government minister, after she became pregnant with his child.

Imprisoned by the Nazis in Austria in the latter months of the war,
Léopold was freed by the Americans but delayed returning home. Instead he remained in exile, settling in Switzerland, while his younger
brother, Charles, acted as regent. Léopold's fate was sealed in March
1950, when Belgians were asked to vote in a referendum whether they
wanted him to return. Overall, he won the backing of fifty-seven per
cent, but the country was deeply divided – while seventy-two per cent
of the largely Christian Democrat Flemings supported him, fifty-eight
per cent of the predominantly Socialist-voting Walloons wanted him
to go. When strikes and protests turned violent, raising fears of civil
war, Léopold stepped down in July 1951 in favour of his twenty-seven-
year-old son, Baudouin.

The Belgian monarchy's battered reputation was restored in the decades that followed. However, Baudouin and his Spanish-born queen,
Fabiola, both devout Catholics, failed in their prime responsibility of
producing an heir. And so, when Baudouin died unexpectedly in 1993,
aged sixty-two, he was succeeded by his brother Albert, four years his
junior. Many had expected the throne to pass straight to Albert's son,
Philippe, whom Baudouin had been grooming for many years as his
successor. It was widely felt, however, that the young prince was not
yet ready for the responsibility.

More then a decade and a half later, Philippe, known as the Duke
of Brabant, the traditional title of the heir to the Belgian throne, is
married with four children, and seems ready to assume the role. He
and his younger brother Laurent find themselves in an uncomfortable position, however, and increasingly come under attack from a
resurgent Flemish nationalism that sees the Belgian monarchy as the
only glue binding the country together – and, for that reason, would
like to see it disappear.

The Norwegian monarchy can trace its origins back more than a thousand years to Harald Fairhair, who united the country's various petty
kingships into a single realm in about 885. Its current dynasty dates
back only to 1905, when Norway became a fully fledged independent

nation after centuries of domination, first by the Danes and then, from 1814, as junior partner in an alliance with Sweden forced upon it by Bernadotte.

It was by no means a foregone conclusion that the new Norway would remain a monarchy. An overwhelming majority of the Storting, the country's parliament, were republicans, but at a time when most European nations were monarchies, the Norwegians reckoned their chances of international recognition and long-term survival would be enhanced by having a king of their own. Their choice fell on Prince Carl, the second son of Frederik, the Crown Prince of Denmark. Carl ticked all the boxes: he was a Scandinavian, in his early thirties and the father of a son still young enough to be brought up as a Norwegian. Even more importantly his wife, Maud, was the daughter of King Edward VII, one of the most influential monarchs in Europe. The British King was equally keen on having his son-in-law on the throne, and wrote to Carl urging him to accept the offer.

Carl was more cautious than either Léopold or Bernadotte, however. His family was also unwilling to damage relations with their Swedish opposite numbers, who were unhappy about the loss of Norway. Setting out to establish his legitimacy in the eyes of his new subjects, Carl insisted on a referendum. An overwhelming majority of Norwegians voted for their country to become a monarchy. Carl was formally elected to the throne on 18th November 1905, aged thirty-three, after getting the go-ahead from his grandfather, King Christian IX – endearing himself to his new subjects by styling himself Haakon VII, an old Norse name used by past kings of Norway.

The new king's court was as much British as Scandinavian, thanks to the influence of Maud, who brought with her as her comptroller and private secretary Henry Knollys, whose elder brother, Francis (and later Viscount) Knollys, fulfilled the same role for her father. Initially, the monarchy also had something of a temporary feel; Haakon knew he owed his throne largely to foreign-policy considerations; the reverberations that followed the Russian Revolution added to the feeling of insecurity. A woman who went to high school with Haakon's son, Prince Olav, in 1920 recalled years later that he had bet her ten kroner (about two US dollars at the time) that he would never become king.

Olav turned out to have been too pessimistic – even if he had to wait until 1957 to succeed his father, by which time he was himself

fifty-four. The dynasty had become extremely popular in the intervening years, emerging strengthened from the Second World War, during
which Haakon had refused to surrender to the Nazis. Instead, together
with his son, the King escaped in spectacular fashion to Britain, from
where he headed the Norwegian resistance.

The current King, Harald V, who succeeded Olav in 1991, has
continued to enjoy high approval ratings. The royal family nevertheless found itself under fire towards the end of the last decade of the
twentieth century over the huge amounts of money spent on renovating
the royal palace in Oslo, which had been badly in need of modernization. Another cause of controversy was Crown Prince Haakon's
relationship with Mette-Marit Tjessem Høiby, a single mother with
a son by a man with a conviction for drug-dealing, whom the Crown
Prince had met at a music festival.

After defusing the crisis through deft media management, the
couple married in August 2001 and have since had two children.
While Mette-Marit has flourished in her new role as Crown Princess,
Haakon's elder sister, Märtha Louise, has courted controversy in
recent years both because of her choice of partner, Ari Behn, a flamboyant writer and film-maker, and as a result of her own commercial
activities, centred on claims she can help people to talk to their "inner
angels" – and even the dead.

Juan Carlos, the Spanish king, is a member of the Borbón dynasty
who have ruled the country on and off since 1700, when Felipe de
Borbón, the Duke of Anjou, succeeded his great-uncle Carlos II,
who was the last of the Spanish Habsburgs. Yet when Juan Carlos
was born to his parents in exile in Rome on 5th January 1938 at the
height of the Spanish Civil War, his chances of ever becoming king
of his homeland seemed slim.

Monarchy in Spain has had a chequered history, and the royalists
have been bitterly divided among themselves since the 1830s when the
ailing King Fernando VII set aside the country's Salic laws of succession to name his daughter Isabel as heir in place of his own younger
brother, the Infante Carlos. She came to the throne as Isabel II on
her father's death the following year, but her reign was marred by a
series of wars waged by supporters of Carlos, who over the following
century became a rallying point for the Catholic right.

Isabel, whose scandalous private life became the talk of Europe, responded by becoming more authoritarian herself, which alienated her more liberal supporters. She fled to France in 1868, and after abdicating two years later was replaced briefly by Amadeo, the duke of Aosta, nicknamed King Macaroni because of the Italian accent with which he spoke Spanish, and then, in February 1873, by the country's short-lived First Republic.

A *coup d'état* by the military the following year turned out the parliament and put Isabel's seventeen-year-old son on the throne as King Alfonso XII. He died of tuberculosis just short of his twenty-eighth birthday, however, and was succeeded by his own son, Alfonso XIII, born six months after his father's death. Despite reigning (initially with his mother as regent) for almost half a century, Alfonso XIII too was eventually driven from power in 1931 when a republican majority was returned to the Cortes Generales with a programme to abolish the monarchy. The Second Spanish Republic was declared, and the King went into exile – but didn't abdicate.

General Francisco Franco's victory in the civil war that followed should have been good news for the Borbóns, but Franco depended for his support on the Falangists, who were avowedly republican, and the Carlists, who, although unable to agree on a candidate of their own, were united in their rejection of all Isabel's descendants. And in any case, as long as he was alive, Franco was insistent that he – rather than a king – should be the undisputed leader of the nation.

Despite their history, the Borbóns possessed the tenacity typical of exiled royals and did not give up their dream of one day regaining their throne. Alfonso died in 1941, but a few months earlier had abdicated in favour of his second surviving son, Don Juan. The pretender's relations with Franco were to prove difficult; the *Ley de Sucesión* passed in 1947 declared Spain a kingdom, but gave Franco the right to name his eventual successor. And the dictator made clear he did not want Juan. The Prince's son, Juan Carlos, was far more acceptable to him, however, and so, when the boy was just ten, his father, still living in exile, took the difficult decision to send him back to be educated in Spain. The strategy paid off: in 1969 Juan Carlos was named by Franco as his successor. On 22nd November 1975, two days after the dictator's death, he became king.

Thankfully for Spain – and for Europe – Franco's trust in Juan Carlos as the best man to continue his authoritarian rule after his death turned out to have been completely misplaced. After acceding to the throne, the King horrified Franco's supporters by instituting liberalizing reforms, appointing Adolfo Suárez, a moderate nationalist, to oversee the transition to democracy and accepting the constitution of 1978 that turned him into a constitutional monarch. Any last doubts about Juan Carlos's commitment to democracy were dispelled in February 1981 when he saw down an attempted military coup. In the years since he has proved a model modern king.

Juan Carlos is married to Sofía, daughter of Pavlos, the penultimate king of Greece, and great-great-granddaughter of Christian IX of Denmark. The youngest of their three children, Felipe, prince of Asturias, is next in line to the throne. Married to Letizia, a former television journalist who was already briefly married before, he has two daughters, Leonor and Sofía.

Over the centuries, Luxembourg, which lies on the border between Germanic and Romance Europe, has been variously occupied by the Bourbons, Habsburgs, Hohenzollerns and the French. It became a grand duchy in a personal union with the Netherlands under the terms of the Congress of Vienna of 1815, but then lost more than half its territory in 1839 to recently independent Belgium.

The country's union with the Netherlands was broken in 1890 with the death of King Willem III. While the Dutch throne passed to his daughter Wilhelmina, Luxembourg was governed by semi-Salic law (which allowed inheritance by females or through the female line only upon extinction of male members of the dynasty) under a Nassau family pact dating back to 1783. This meant Willem was succeeded there by Adolphe of Nassau-Weilburg, who had been duke of Nassau but had been left without a job after Prussia annexed his duchy in 1866.

Luxembourg is home to just under half a million people, living in an area of just over 1,600 square miles. The current grand duke, Henri, who was born in 1955, came to the throne in October 2000, when his father Jean abdicated in his favour.

Moving southwards, Liechtenstein, a micro-state of just sixty or so square miles sandwiched between Switzerland and Austria, has been an independent entity since 1719, when Karl VI, the Holy

Roman Emperor, merged the territories of Vaduz, the future capital, and Schellenberg, both of which were owned by the Liechtenstein family, turning them into a *Fürstentum* (principality). The move was essentially inspired by expediency: the territory was given its new status so Prince Anton Florian of Liechtenstein would be entitled to a seat in the Reichstag.

The Prince felt no need actually to live in his principality, though; indeed it was not until 1818 that a member of the house of Liechtenstein, the future Prince Aloys II, bothered even to set foot in the realm that bore the family name. In the century that followed, the royal family preferred to live in cosmopolitan Vienna rather than tiny Vaduz, although that changed when the Nazis annexed Austria in the Anschluss of 1938.

The current prince, Hans-Adam II, who was born in 1945 in Zurich, has had a prickly relationship with the country's politicians since coming to power in November 1989. His resolve was undoubtedly strengthened by a personal fortune estimated at five billion dollars, derived largely from his stake in the LGT Bank – which in 2008 found itself at the centre of controversy after the German intelligence services bought a CD with details of those of its nationals who had made use of accounts at the bank to avoid paying taxes at home. A long-running trial of strength between the Prince and the Landtag came to a head in 2003: the Prince won, turning him into Europe's only absolute monarch. In August 2004, he handed his son, Prince Alois, the power to make day-to-day decisions, but he remains head of state.

Covering a mere three-quarters of a square mile and with a population of just 33,000, the Principality of Monaco is by far the smallest of Europe's monarchies. Since Prince Rainier married Grace Kelly in April 1956 it has also been one of the most colourful, although her death in a car crash in September 1982 deprived it of much of its glamour.

The ruling House of Grimaldi's link with the principality dates back to 1297, when Francesco Grimaldi, dressed as a Franciscan monk, led a force of men who captured the Rock of Monaco. Ruled by both France and the Kingdom of Sardinia, the principality had its sovereignty recognized by the French-Monégasque Treaty of 1861 – although this also obliged it to sell the towns of Menton and Roquebrune, which accounted for ninety-five per cent of its territory, to France for four million francs.

When Rainier came to the throne in 1949 on the death of his grandfather Louis II, gambling accounted for all but five per cent of Monaco's annual revenue. The principality, as the writer William Somerset Maugham put it so memorably, was a "sunny place for shady people". Rainier put his energies into promoting Monaco instead as a tax haven, commercial centre, real-estate development opportunity and international tourist attraction. He also pushed through the constitution of 1962, which turned his realm from an absolute monarchy into one in which the prince shares power with a national council of eighteen elected members.

Rainier's son Albert II, who succeeded him on his death in April 2005, has used his position to campaign for the need to protect the marine environment. He has also backed an ambitious plan to expand the principality, Dubai-style, by building an area of about five hectares out into the Mediterranean. The Prince insisted the entire extension should be built on stilts to avoid upsetting marine life, claiming that it will be a "model of sustainability".

Chapter 2

Coming and Going

In October 2009, John Lindskog, a veteran Danish journalist and royal expert, published a book about his country's royal family that contained a bold claim: Queen Margrethe II – Daisy to her family – was considering doing what none of her predecessors had ever done before her: abdicate. Her French-born husband Henrik was not well and had made no secret of his desire to escape the cold, wet Danish winter and live out his remaining years in the couple's beloved Château de Caïx in the wine district of Cahors in southern France. With her seventieth birthday due the following April, it seemed the ideal time for the Queen, who was also in poor health, to head south with her husband, giving up the throne in favour of her son, Crown Prince Frederik, by then in his early forties and happily married with two children.

"It is no secret that the Prince has long felt tired. He said simply that he has done his duty, and at the age of seventy-five years he feels that he is ready for retirement," Lindskog claimed in the book, *Royale rejser – Bag Kulisserne Hos De Kongelige (Royal Travels – Behind the Scenes with the Royals)*. "A number of events appear to have pushed forward something the Queen has always been against but that certain circumstances seem to suggest she will nonetheless do – be the first Danish monarch to abdicate the throne."[1]

The Danish royal palace denied the claim, as palaces always do, but that did not seem sufficient to dispel Lindskog's theory completely. Yet more than two years later, in January 2012, Margrethe celebrated forty years on the throne – and made clear that she had no intention of stepping down. This was despite opinion polls suggesting a majority of Danes wanted their Queen to abdicate in favour of her son, if not immediately, then before she became much older. "You are handed your job as the old king or queen dies," she said in a television interview to coincide with her jubilee. "It is not a life sentence, but a life of service."

As Margrethe made clear, being king or queen is a job unlike any other – and that goes as much for the manner in which it is given up as that in which the appointment is made. A monarch is not just a head of state, but also, in many cases, head of the Church and army. He or she will be seen as not just the father or mother of the nation but also its very embodiment.

In a world of elected politicians who come and go, the monarch is a constant, his or her status enhanced by each year that passes. For me, as for most Britons alive today, Queen Elizabeth II has always been there, a reassuring symbol of continuity. In times of war or natural disaster, the monarch is the one we turn to. Through judicious management of the media she and her European compeers have even managed to establish themselves as part of our own Christmas or New Year celebrations.

When our monarchs marry or have children, it is like a happy event in our family; when they die, we feel it as a personal tragedy. They are also embedded in the political system: most turn up in person to open parliament every year, formally appoint prime ministers and accept their resignations. Even in the second decade of the twenty-first century there appears little serious pressure to change what is a profoundly undemocratic element in our democracies – perhaps simply because it works. If we bring ourselves to question our monarchs at all, it is to criticize the way they and their families are fulfilling their role; only a minority think to question whether they should have such a role in the first place.

The monarchy is ubiquitous and references to its members, past and present, are woven into the national culture. Past eras are defined by their monarchs. In Britain, houses can be Georgian or Edwardian in style, while the phrase "Victorian values" conjures up thoughts of conservative sexual mores and the covering of the legs of tables and pianos to avoid provoking lewd thoughts among those who gazed upon them.

Enter the word "royal" into Google and you come across a succession of organizations bearing that prefix, from the Royal Mail and the

Royal Society to the Royal Academy of Arts. Visit a British supermarket and you will see a seemingly random collection of products that proclaim themselves to be "By Appointment to HM the Queen" – a mark of recognition extended to some 850 Royal Warrant holders who have supplied goods or services for at least five years to the Queen, the Duke of Edinburgh or the Prince of Wales.

Although dating back more than eight hundred years, this accolade is more than a historical curiosity. The chocolate-maker Cadbury, which received its warrant from Queen Victoria in 1854, revealed recently that every Christmas it delivers several small boxes of a special dark chocolate to Buckingham Palace for the royal family to enjoy. Made by a team of three on specially reserved equipment, it has more cocoa solids than other dark chocolate – and is not sold to the Queen's subjects. Anyone wanting a more direct royal connection can buy a product from Duchy Originals, a company set up by Prince Charles in 1990 in a reflection of his interest in organic and sustainable farming, which now produces a range of more than two hundred products from biscuits and preserves to gifts and garden seeds.

Even more visible is the Queen's head on postage stamps and coins, and the letters ER – Elizabeth Regina – that grace letter boxes and other street furniture, just as GR did during the reign of her father, George VI. When Britain was discussing in the mid-1990s whether or not to adopt the euro, one of the arguments used by opponents was that it would mean the disappearance of the Queen's image from coins and banknotes. To address such concerns the design was modified to provide space for the inclusion of such national symbols – even if Britain, in the event, decided to keep the pound. Indeed, some British Eurosceptics are concerned that ever closer European union will eventually lead to the creation of a superstate that will leave no role for the British monarch (although quite why the EU's six other monarchies would acquiesce in such a plot is not explained).

Cross the English Channel and you will find monarchy equally embedded in society. Many of the streets of Brussels, Stockholm or The Hague contain the word "royal" or the name of a previous monarch. The same is true of Oslo, which continues to extend the courtesy to members of the Bernadotte dynasty who ruled the country before 1905, during the years when Norway was a junior member in an alliance with Sweden. Indeed, a statue of Carl III Johan, the dynasty's founder (known to the Swedes, and to us elsewhere in this book, as Carl XIV Johan), still stands outside the royal palace (situated, of course, at the end of Karl Johans Gate).

Like the British version, most Continental royal families issue royal warrants of their own; Chocolaterie de Monaco, for example, is proud to declare itself a "*Fournisseur Breveté de S.A.S. le Prince Souverain*" ("supplier by appointment to HSH the Sovereign Prince"), and has launched special lines to mark royal occasions such as the marriage of Prince Rainier and Grace Kelly and the accession of Albert II.

Centuries ago monarchs were more than just synonymous with the nation over which they presided: they were considered divine. The ancient Egyptians believed their pharaohs were directly descended from gods. Although such ideas later came to be seen as ridiculous, the notion that kings are mortals, albeit chosen by God, endured longer. The concept of the Divine Right of Kings, which came to the fore in Britain under King James I (otherwise known as King James VI of Scotland) and in France under King Louis XIV, stated that a monarch owed his title to the will of the Almighty, and not to that of his subjects, the aristocracy or any other competing authority. Any attempt to depose him or restrict his powers, therefore, ran contrary to the will of God – a convenient way of dissuading those who might have contemplated rebellion.

Yet supernatural powers were still attributed to them. In England and France in the Middle Ages it was believed the monarch could cure scrofula – a disease known as the "King's evil" – by touching the sufferer. Charles II is estimated to have touched as many as 90,000 people for the evil during his twenty-four-year reign in the late seventeenth century. William III, his successor but one, refused to touch at all, except when one man begged him. Laying his hand on the man's head, the King declared, "God give you better health and more sense." George I, who succeeded to the throne in 1714, ended the practice as "too Catholic". In France, Louis XV stopped soon afterwards.

Old habits die hard, however. When Elizabeth II came to the throne, a quarter of the British still believed that she actually reigned by the grace of God – in other words that she was God's representative on earth – a belief perpetuated by the most important part of the ritual surrounding the coronation of a British monarch, in which he or she is anointed with oil by the archbishop of Canterbury.

But who actually chooses the monarch? The answer, looking around the remaining monarchies of Europe, seems self-evident: the throne passes from the monarch to the oldest son – or, increasingly in this era of sexual equality, the oldest child.

In fact, heredity is only a relatively recent phenomenon. The traditional form of determining succession was military conquest and then acclamation or some form of election. In the eighth century, Pepin the Short, the father of Charlemagne, was elected king of the Franks by an assembly of Frankish leading men. Such a system of election persisted through the Middle Ages. The Germanic peoples continued to cling to the concept of elective monarchies, while the Holy Roman Emperors were chosen by prince-electors, although this often was merely a formalization of what was, in reality, hereditary rule.

Until the demise of the Polish-Lithuanian Commonwealth in 1795, its kings were elected by gatherings of nobles in a field in Wola, now a district of Warsaw. Given that every one of the half a million noblemen was entitled to take part, this was by far the widest franchise of any European country of the time. Not that it was democracy in the way we would understand today. The last king, Stanisław August Poniatowski, owed his election in 1764 largely to the military might of Tsarina Catherine the Great, his Russian patron – and lover.

Such a method became less fitting as kingdoms grew in size and societies became less egalitarian. Gradually, the right to vote would be restricted to local chieftains, the nobility or some other defined group. An elective monarchy also had the disadvantage of creating an interregnum during which the election was held, which provided an opportunity for rival candidates to ignore the rules and try to establish their rights to the throne by force.

Clear rules on succession – normally to the first-born son – provided a solution; it also suited monarchs understandably keen to pass the throne, along with their other possessions, down the generations. And so it was that elected monarchs gradually established dynasties. In Sweden, for example, Gustaf Vasa, although himself elected king by the Riksdag in 1523 after liberating his country from the Danes, was succeeded by his son, establishing a dynasty that would rule for much of the sixteenth and seventeenth centuries.

There is no guarantee, of course, that the heir will actually be up to the job. Often the opposite has been the case, a serious problem when kings ruled rather than reigned. And then there were the cases when there was no legitimate heir, a frequent occurrence in the days of high infant mortality, especially in the many European countries where the succession was governed by Salic law – that is, where it was stipulated that only men could become the monarch.

Flexibility has often been the response. When the Danes found themselves with the childless Frederik VII in the middle of the nineteenth century, the future Christian IX's claim to be named heir presumptive was helped by the fact that his wife, Princess Louise of Hesse-Kassel, was a niece of Christian VIII, the previous monarch. By contrast, there was no attempt to prove even a weak blood link when a reluctant Carl XIII of Sweden was prevailed upon in 1810 to accept Jean-Baptiste Bernadotte as his successor.

Britain was one of the earlier countries both to embrace the principle of heredity and to have queens who reigned in their own right – provided there was no male heir, that is. This should, in theory, have improved the chances of an orderly succession. On many occasions, however, the rule was broken, either because there was no heir or because he was deemed unsuitable. Henry VII, founder of the Tudor dynasty that counted Henry VIII and Elizabeth I among its members, owed his crown to victory over Richard III, the last Plantagenet king, at Bosworth Field in 1485 rather than to heredity. When Elizabeth died childless more than a century later, the calling of James VI of Scotland to London to replace her was due not so much to his claim of descent from Henry VII as to the fact he was invited by the English parliament.

The late seventeenth and early eighteenth centuries brought more departures from the usual rules of succession in Britain: during what became known as the Glorious Revolution of 1688, King James II, who was considered too pro-Catholic, was deposed and replaced by a joint monarchy of his daughter Mary and her husband William of Orange. It proved a short-lived remedy: the couple were childless, leaving Mary's younger sister Anne to succeed them in 1702. Although the unfortunate Anne bore no fewer than eighteen children, none survived her – which meant another imaginative solution was needed. Again, one of the main qualifications for a successor was that he should not be a Catholic – a requirement that had been enshrined in law with the Act of Settlement of 1701. And so the Protestant George, Elector of Hanover, was invited to become King George I, even though he was already fifty-four, spoke no English and fifty-seven other people had a better claim to the throne than he had.

Heredity was not an option when it came to creating a new monarchy, as happened on several occasions in Europe during the nineteenth century and the first part of the twentieth. It was instead a matter of casting around other royal houses in search of a suitable candidate. This was a golden time for second or third sons otherwise faced with the prospect of life as a "spare".

As already seen, Leopold of Saxe-Coburg and Prince Carl of Denmark were both beneficiaries of this, establishing dynasties that still reign over Belgium and Norway, respectively, today. Other countries' experiences of "importing" a monarch have not been so happy: when Greece became an independent country under the protection of the great powers in 1832, Otto, son of the philhellene King Ludwig I of Bavaria, was invited to be its first king, even though he was just sixteen. King Otto's thirty-year reign was stormy, however, and he was deposed in 1862. The following year the Greeks tried again, this time asking Prince Vilhelm, son of the future King Christian IX of Denmark, to be their ruler. Taking the name Georgios I, he reigned until 1913, when he was assassinated by a madman two weeks short of the fiftieth anniversary of his accession. Despite this tragic end, he did succeed in establishing a dynasty that reigned over Greece – with some gaps[2] – for another half a century until they were forced into exile.

Success is not the word to describe the fate of Maximilian, the younger brother of Emperor Franz Joseph of Austria, who was installed as Emperor of Mexico by Napoleon III of France in 1864. He was dependent on French military support for his survival, but when the civil war began, Napoleon pulled out his troops – and advised Maximilian to cut and run too. The unfortunate Austrian failed to do so and died aged thirty-four in front of a firing squad, in June 1867. His widow, Charlotte of Belgium, daughter of King Léopold I, had tried in vain to save him, having sought help in Paris, Vienna and finally in Rome from Pope Pius IX. Her husband's violent death drove her mad, but she lived on for a further sixty years.

Equally curious was the search for a king of Albania, which was proclaimed an independent country in 1912. The crown was hawked around, but in the end was taken by Ahmed Bey Zogu, a mountain chieftain who rose from prime minister to president before becoming King Zog I in 1928. He was chased out by the Italians in 1939 and spent his last years in exile in a sparsely furnished villa on the French Riviera with Géraldine, his Hungarian-American queen, who supported him by writing mystery stories. Despite four abortive assassination attempts and a ferocious nicotine habit – he smoked 150 cigarettes a day – it was stomach ulcers and a liver ailment that eventually did for Zog. "My life is an adventure story," he once claimed.

All of Europe's monarchies – excluding, as we have seen, the Vatican and Andorra – have long since embraced heredity. So have those in the rest of the world, although here too there are exceptions: in Saudi Arabia, for example, succession to the throne, although hereditary, is not determined by a succession law but rather by consensus of the House of Saud as to who should become the next crown prince.

This has not prevented some rewriting of the rules of succession over the years. Appalled by the behaviour of female incumbents of the throne – especially his own mother, Catherine the Great – Tsar Paul of Russia changed the system in the late eighteenth century to ensure that a woman could succeed only in the extremely unlikely case that there were no legitimate male members of the dynasty.

In more recent times expediency has often triumphed over tradition. In the late nineteenth century the Dutch were ready to bend the rules when Willem III outlived all three sons by his first marriage, leaving only a daughter, Wilhelmina, the sole fruit of his somewhat scandalous union with his second wife Emma, who was more than forty years his junior. She became the first of a succession of three Dutch queens regnant – and a far better monarch than her male predecessors.

The Monégasques proved equally flexible a decade later, when the failure of Prince Albert's son Louis to produce a legitimate heir meant the crown might end up in the German branch of the family – which no one wanted. And so the rules were changed to legitimize Charlotte, a bastard daughter Louis had sired by a cabaret singer while serving in the French Foreign Legion in Algeria. Ennobled as the Duchess of Valentinois and married in due course to a French nobleman, Charlotte never reigned in her own name – but did give birth to

Rainier, who made his mark on the principality in the second half of the twentieth century.

After the Second World War, changing the rules of succession in Denmark proved more controversial. The constitution of 1849 declared that "Man shall follow man", ruling out the possibility of a queen regnant. Unfortunately, King Frederik IX, who came to the throne in 1947, had three daughters but no son, and his wife, Queen Ingrid, had been warned by her doctors not to attempt childbirth again. The law seemed clear: next in line to the throne was Frederik's brother Knud, who already had two sons, Prince Ingolf, born two months before Margrethe, and Prince Christian, born in 1942. There were concerns, however, about the suitability of both father and son – especially when they were compared with the intelligent and pretty young Princess. A referendum in 1953 approved a change in the constitution establishing male-preference primogeniture – which meant a daughter should succeed to the Danish monarchy when there was no eligible son.

Knud – reduced at the stroke of a pen from first to fourth in line to the throne – and his wife (and first cousin), Princess Caroline-Mathilde, were not pleased, leading to a bitter rift within the Danish royal family that endured for decades. From then on the two brothers saw each other almost only on official occasions. Knud, who died in 1976, outliving Frederik by four years, "would have liked very much to have those years as king", Ingolf revealed in a magazine interview in 2010. "He died as a bitter man."[3]

Ingolf, then a thirteen-year-old schoolboy, was also disappointed, although with time he came to accept he would never be king. The events of 1953 nevertheless continued to hang for a long time like a cloud over the Danish royal family. It was only after his father's death that Ingolf, much against his mother's will, approached his cousin Margrethe, who was now Queen, with the aim of reconciliation.

The rules of succession were changed again in 2009 to give equal rights to both male and female, but this time it was uncontroversial: Margrethe has two sons and the elder, Crown Prince Frederik, himself produced a male heir, Prince Christian, in October 2005.

In putting men and women on an equal footing, the Danes were following their Scandinavian neighbours. In 1980 Sweden became the first monarchy in the world to introduce equal primogeniture, which put Crown Princess Victoria, the first child of King Carl XVI

Gustaf, next in line for the throne ahead of her younger brother, Carl Philip. The King had made little secret of his opposition to the change, but was unable to prevent it. Norway took the same step a decade later, but this time the change was not made retroactive: this meant King Harald's son Haakon remained first in line to the throne rather than having to stand aside in favour of his elder sister, Märtha Louise.

The trend elsewhere in Europe is also towards sexual equality – the Dutch adopted equal primogeniture in 1983 and the Belgians in 1991 – and in its 2004 election manifesto, Spain's victorious Socialist Party vowed to follow suit, even though it failed to do so in its two terms of office. Luxembourg followed in 2011.

This still left Britain (along with Monaco and Liechtenstein) continuing to give precedence to male heirs. But there was change here, too – prompted by Prince William's engagement to Kate Middleton in November 2010 and their marriage the following April. The prospect of the couple's starting a family made the problem a potentially urgent one: if William and Kate's first-born were a girl, it would provoke complaints of unfairness if she were overtaken by any brother born subsequently. But making such a change to the rules would be potentially more complicated than elsewhere in Europe, given Elizabeth's role as queen not just of the United Kingdom but of fifteen other countries – all of whom would have to agree.[4]

David Cameron set out to tackle the issue after coming to power in May 2010. At the Commonwealth Heads of Government Meeting in Perth, Australia, in October 2011, he won unanimous agreement from the leaders of the fifteen that the daughters of any future monarch should have the same rights as the sons. It was also decided to end the bar on a future king or queen marrying a Roman Catholic. "The idea that a younger son should become monarch instead of an elder daughter simply because he is a man, or that a future monarch can marry someone of any faith except a Catholic – this way of thinking is at odds with the modern countries that we have become," Cameron told them. The changes required the amending of a mass of historic legislation – including the 1701 Act of Settlement, the 1689 Bill of Rights and the Royal Marriages Act 1772 – initially in the United Kingdom but then also in the fifteen other countries.

* * *

The gradual reduction over the centuries of the status of the king from god to mortal has been reflected in ritual: the Byzantine emperors placed the crown on their own heads as a way of demonstrating that their power came directly from God. So did the tsars and also the future Kaiser Wilhelm I when he was crowned king of Prussia in 1861. This went too far for most other European monarchies, though, which made it the task of a senior churchman to crown the king – Napoleon I called on Pope Pius VII to do the honours at his investiture in a highly elaborate ceremony in 1804 in Notre-Dame Cathedral in Paris.

Britain is the only European monarchy that has continued the coronation ritual – and there seems little doubt that Prince Charles will be crowned when he succeeds his mother, Elizabeth II. In a ceremony whose origins date back a thousand years, the sovereign is first presented to and acclaimed by the people. He or she then swears an oath to uphold the law and the Church and is anointed with holy oils by the archbishop of Canterbury, the primate of the Church of England, who places the crown on his or her head.

Although the next in line to the British throne succeeds immediately and automatically on the death of his or her predecessor, the coronation is typically held more than a year later, such is the time and effort that goes into organizing it. Edward VIII, for example, was never crowned, despite reigning for almost a year, as he abdicated before 12th May 1937, the date set for the ceremony. Being practical people, the British didn't put all that preparation to waste: with Westminster Abbey already booked for the day, they made use of it to crown George VI, Edward's younger brother, who had reluctantly succeeded him as king the previous December.

The coronation of George VI's daughter Queen Elizabeth II on 2nd June 1953 was a spectacular pageant that added a dash of colour to grey post-war Britain, drawing hundreds of thousands of people from across the country to the streets of London. It was also to prove an important milestone in the monarchy's relationship with the media as television cameras were allowed into Westminster Abbey to film proceedings. Although marred by heavy rain, the ceremony was perfectly choreographed and went off without a hitch – unlike some previous coronations, which had contained an element of farce: George III's in 1761 was held up for three hours after the sword of state went missing, while his son and successor George IV's was overshadowed by his row with his estranged and hated wife, Caroline of Brunswick.

In terms of pomp, the Dutch come closest to the British, although its monarchs are invested rather than crowned. The ceremony is held in the Nieuwe Kerk in Amsterdam, but proceedings are secular rather than religious and conducted in accordance with constitutional law. Unlike in Britain, the regalia – a crown, the sceptre, the orb, the sword of state, the national standard and vellum-bound copy of the constitution, all of which symbolize royal power and dignity – are displayed on a credence table rather than worn or carried by the monarch.

Elsewhere such ceremonies are more modest affairs. In Belgium the king is sworn in before parliament and seated on a throne more or less knocked together for the occasion.[5] He also has no crown and no sceptre. Similarly, when Juan Carlos became king of Spain he merely swore an oath in the Cortes. The last Swedish king to be crowned was Oscar II, who came to the throne in 1872. His son, Gustaf V, who disliked such ceremonial as much as Britain's Edward VII loved it, decided not to have a coronation at all when he became king in 1907.

Subsequent Swedish monarchs have followed his example. Carl XVI Gustaf, the current monarch, was installed in a simple ceremony in the throne room of the Royal Palace in Stockholm. As in the Netherlands, the crown jewels were displayed on cushions to the right and left of the royal throne, but were never given to the king.

When Margrethe II of Denmark replaced her father in 1972, the formalities were restricted to an appearance on the balcony of the Christiansborg Palace, the seat of parliament, with Jens Otto Krag, the prime minister, shouting three times to the crowds below: "King Frederik IX is dead. Long live Her Majesty Queen Margrethe II." The declaration was followed by the traditional ninefold hurrah. The other symbols of royal power have long since fallen into disuse: the Christiansborg Palace has a *Trongemak* (Throne Room) where the queen receives foreign ambassadors, but although there are two special chairs there they are not used for formal occasions. The crown jewels, meanwhile, are kept in a museum at Rosenborg Castle.

Nevertheless, as is shown by the example of Norway, the youngest of Europe's dynasties, there is sometimes a reluctance to dispense completely with the spiritual. Although many of Norway's politicians considered such ceremonies "undemocratic and archaic", Haakon, the first king of a fully independent Norway, was crowned and anointed in 1906 in Nidaros Cathedral in Trondheim, which had been used as a place of coronation since the fifteenth century. The crown and other regalia had been inherited from the Bernadottes.

Two years later, however, the country's parliament voted overwhelmingly to remove the article in the constitution stipulating the requirement for a coronation. From then on, the monarch needed merely to take a formal accession oath in the Council of State and the Storting, the parliament. Traditions die hard, however, and when Olav succeeded his father in 1957, he insisted on a "consecration" ceremony to mark the beginning of his reign. Held as before in Nidaros, it retained some elements of the old tradition of *konungstekja* – "king-taking" or "proclaiming" in Old Norse – dating back to the Norwegian monarchs of the tenth century.

Significantly, though, even here the crown jewels were displayed, but not bestowed, during the ceremony, reflecting a modern rejection of the medieval Christian concept that a crowned and anointed monarch was God's highest temporal representative in his or her nation. It all went too far for many members of the ruling Labour Party – although several of them attended anyway. By the time Harald, the current Norwegian king, repeated the ceremony on his accession in 1991, it had become an established part of tradition. This – along with the monarch's lying-in-state – remains the only occasion on which the crown and other regalia are used; the rest of the time they are on display in the Archbishop's palace next to the cathedral. The royal coaches and horses have also long since gone – when the King travels to open parliament he does so by car.

But what happens to terminate a monarch's reign? Regicide has brought an end to some: while the killings of Charles I, Louis XVI and Tsar Nicholas II – as well, indeed, as that of the unfortunate Maximilian of Mexico – were executions effectively carried out in the name of a new regime, other kings were murdered for political reasons or simply by madmen. Most far reaching in its consequences was the assassination of Archduke Franz Ferdinand, heir to the Austro-Hungarian throne, and his wife Sophie, on the streets of Sarajevo in June 1914. Gavrilo Princip, the Bosnian Serb patriot who shot them, lived long enough to see the consequences of what he had done, although before dying in jail in April 1918 he reputedly claimed, perhaps with some truth: "If I hadn't done it the Germans would have found another excuse."

The killing of Franz Ferdinand demonstrated the vulnerability of royalty when they were in transit away from the protection of the court. Tsar Alexander II of Russia survived several assassination attempts – including one in which a bomb was placed under the dining room of the Winter Palace in St Petersburg – before the revolutionaries finally got him in 1881. The bulletproof carriage given to him by Napoleon III saved him from one bomb, but when he got out he was mortally wounded by a second. Carlos I of Portugal and his elder son Luís Filipe were shot as they travelled through Lisbon in 1908; the assassination of Georgios I of Greece five years later was as he was walking through Thessaloniki.

The most spectacular royal killing, in terms of pure theatre, was that of Gustaf III of Sweden in 1792 – so much so that it formed the inspiration for Verdi's *Un ballo in maschera* (even though the censors obliged him to shift the action from Stockholm to colonial-era Boston). An absolute monarch who found himself increasingly out of tune with the times, Gustaf had received a number of threats to his life, the most recent of them as he was sitting down for dinner before attending a masked ball at the Royal Opera House. As he entered in the early hours of the morning, he was surrounded by three noblemen wearing black masks, who greeted him in French with the words *"Bonjour, beau masque"*. The lead conspirator, Jacob Johan Anckarström, a military officer, then shot the King in the back with his pistol. Gustaf died almost a fortnight later, the third Swedish monarch in a hundred and sixty years to perish from gunshot wounds.

For every successful regicide, there have been several abortive attempts. Queen Victoria was the victim of eight attacks of varying degrees of seriousness during her reign – the first in 1840 as she was riding through London with Prince Albert in a carriage, and the last in 1882 as she left Windsor railway station. Most of her assailants were unhinged rather than politically motivated. The last, Roderick McLean, was a budding poet who wanted revenge after a poem he had sent the Queen was rewarded with only a standard reply from Buckingham Palace.

Victoria's son, the future Edward VII, almost fell victim to a politically motivated killing in 1900 when he was shot at by a Belgian anarchist angry at Britain's role in the Boer War while he was on his way to Denmark.

As the monarchs' roles have diminished so, thankfully, has the number of assassination attempts. While Queen Elizabeth has had to contend with the odd intruder into the palace, there have been no attempts on her life – although Prince Philip's uncle, Louis Mountbatten, the man responsible for bringing him and Elizabeth together, was killed when the Irish Republican Army blew up his boat in 1979 while he was holidaying in Northern Ireland. Five years earlier, the Queen's daughter Princess Anne had narrowly escaped a kidnapping attempt when she and her then husband Mark Phillips were driving near Buckingham Palace.

More serious, however, was the attempt on the life of Queen Beatrix of the Netherlands during the Queen's Day celebrations on 30th April 2009. Karst Tates, an unemployed thirty-eight-year-old recluse, drove his car at high speed into an open-topped bus carrying Beatrix and other members of the royal family as they were travelling through the streets of Apeldoorn a few hundred metres from Het Loo Palace, the former residence of Queen Wilhelmina. Tates missed the bus, but ploughed into a crowd of spectators at seventy miles per hour, killing seven bystanders and seriously injuring himself. As he lay slumped and bleeding in his car, he confessed that he had intended to kill the royal family, calling Crown Prince Willem-Alexander a "fascist" and a "racist". Tates went into a coma shortly afterwards, dying of his injuries the next day. A four-month investigation by more than two hundred detectives portrayed him as a loner who could not hold down a job and had spent some time homeless – but failed to provide an explanation for the attack.

Accidents, meanwhile, have claimed the life of King Albert I of Belgium, who died in the mountains aged fifty-eight, and Prince Gustaf Adolf of Sweden, the heir to the throne and father of the current king, who was killed in an air crash aged just forty in January 1947. Car accidents killed Léopold III of Belgium's Swedish-born wife, Queen Astrid, and Princess Diana, the estranged wife of Prince Charles. A coronary thrombosis did for Queen Elizabeth II's father, George VI, when he was fifty-six; King Baudouin of Belgium was sixty-two when he died of heart failure.

Some monarchs, though, have chosen to give up their thrones voluntarily, although in recent times the practice of abdication has been confined to two monarchies: the Dutch and the Luxembourgeois. Queen Beatrix of the Netherlands has lived through the abdication of both her predecessors: in September 1948, when she was aged ten, her grandmother, Wilhelmina, stepped down; in April 1980 Wilhelmina's daughter Juliana followed suit, making way for Beatrix.

Surprisingly, Beatrix herself has yet to do the same: born in 1938, she has long since passed any conventional retirement date or indeed the age at which both her predecessors relinquished the throne. Dutch commentators have suggested she is waiting until Willem-Alexander's children are older before stepping aside for her son.

Members of the house of Nassau-Weilburg, who have sat on the throne of Luxembourg since it split from the Netherlands in 1890, have proved even more determined abdicators. Marie-Adélaïde, who became the first reigning grand duchess in 1912, stepped down in favour of her younger sister Charlotte in 1919 after criticism of her over-friendly relations with German occupying forces during the First World War. After a forty-five-year reign, Charlotte abdicated in 1964; her son Jean, who succeeded her, in turn stepped down in favour of his son, Henri, in October 2000.

These are the exceptions, though. The notion of abdication appears anathema to Europe's other monarchs, who, until now at least, have regarded theirs as a job for life. The reluctance of Queen Elizabeth II, in particular, to step down is understandable if one considers the fate of her "Uncle David" – better known as King Edward VIII.

Edward's abdication in December 1936 after just 327 days as king in order to wed Wallis Simpson, a twice-married American divorcee, was in many respects the best thing that could have happened to the House of Windsor and, by extension, the country. During his brief reign – the shortest of any British monarch since that of Jane Grey more than 380 years earlier – Edward showed little appetite for what he once described as "the relentless grind of the king's daily life". To the exasperation of his ministers, he was often late for appointments or cancelled them at the last moment. His red boxes, which contained the state papers on which monarchs are meant to work so diligently, were returned late, often apparently unread or stained by the bases of whisky glasses. George V's warning that as monarch his eldest son would "ruin himself within a year", were prescient.

The contrast with Edward's younger brother Bertie, who reluctantly succeeded him as George VI, could not have been greater. A nervous but diligent character with a debilitating stammer, he became a much respected and loved king, not least because of the fortitude he showed during the Second World War. His brilliant portrayal by Colin Firth in the multi-Oscar-winning film *The King's Speech* brought him to life for a new generation. George's untimely death in February 1952, aged just fifty-six, also paved the way for the accession of the present Queen. Nevertheless, the events of 1936 confronted the British monarchy with one of the greatest crises in its history, and Edward's abdication cast a shadow over the institution during the decades that followed.

Chapter 3

Of Pageantry and Political Power

Every year, in late October or early November, Queen Elizabeth II sets off in the horse-drawn Irish state coach from Buckingham Palace down the Mall, the grand thoroughfare that leads eastwards in the direction of Trafalgar Square. As crowds – many of them tourists – look on, her carriage, painted gold, turns right into Horse Guards, then left across the parade ground, to emerge through Horse Guards Arch and then along Whitehall to the Palace of Westminster, the seat of parliament. When she arrives, the royal standard is hoisted over the building.

Once inside, Elizabeth follows a carefully scripted ritual that has changed little since she first made the journey in 1952. After being helped into the robes of state and the imperial state crown, which has been carried to Westminster earlier in the day on a cushion aboard its own state coach, she proceeds through the royal gallery, with her husband, the Duke of Edinburgh, at her side, to the House of Lords, the upper house of parliament.

Seated on the throne, she tells the assembled lords to sit and motions to the Lord Great Chamberlain to summon the members of the House of Commons. He signals to a parliamentary official known as the Gentleman Usher of the Black Rod, who turns and, escorted by both the doorkeeper of the House of Lords and an inspector of police, approaches the doors to the chamber of the Commons. As he comes near, the doors are slammed in his face. He then strikes three times with his staff (the Black Rod from which he derives his title), and is admitted. At the bar, he bows to the speaker before proceeding to the dispatch box and uttering the following words: "Mr (or Madam)

48

Speaker, the Queen commands this honourable House to attend Her Majesty immediately in the House of Peers."

The Serjeant-at-Arms, essentially the head of security for the House of Commons, who since 2008 is for the first time a woman, picks up the ceremonial mace and then, together with the Speaker, leads the prime minister and leader of the opposition to the Lords' Chamber. By tradition, they do not so much walk as saunter, laughing and joking together as they go. When they arrive, they bow to the Queen and wait by the bar. The Queen then reads out a speech outlining her government's political programme for the year. It is traditionally written on goatskin vellum. Not a single word has been written by her, but the speech, which she delivers in a deadpan voice, is peppered with references to "my government".

Much of the pageantry has its origins in the struggles almost half a millennium ago between the monarch and the House of Commons. The ceremony is held in the Lords rather than the Commons because of a tradition dating back to the seventeenth century that forbids the sovereign from entering that chamber.[1] The closing of the door in the face of the Queen's representative – and the casual manner in which the MPs answer her summons – are further symbolic reminders of how hard their predecessors fought to gain their independence from the crown.

Away from the public eye there are some other strange twists: before the Queen arrives in the Palace of Westminster, its cellars are symbolically searched by the Yeoman of the Guard to prevent a repetition of the 1605 gunpowder plot in which a group of English Catholics were accused of trying – and failing – to blow up the building and kill the Protestant King James I.

Even more bizarrely, before the Queen sets off for the day, a member of the House of Commons, known as Vice-Chamberlain of the Household, is brought to Buckingham Palace and held hostage – a reference to the reign of Charles II, when there was concern that the King would be arrested as he entered the Houses of Parliament and suffer the same fate as his father Charles I, executed in 1649. According to past "hostages", these few hours of luxurious captivity are a pleasant experience. "Prince Philip always greets the Vice-Chamberlain upon their return with the same words: 'I hope you've looked after the shop while we've been away,'" recalled Nottingham North MP

Graham Allen, the son of a former coal miner, who was given the job in 1998.[2]

With its curious rituals, fancy costumes and cast of characters with archaic-sounding names, the ceremony is a reminder of the time when the monarchy, in the words of Walter Bagehot, the prominent British nineteenth-century journalist, editor of the *Economist* and constitutional expert, gave a "vast strength to the entire constitution, by enlisting on its behalf the credulous obedience of enormous masses".

As with much royal tradition in Britain and elsewhere in Europe, however, the impression of continuity is misleading. Despite the frequent references to the seventeenth century, the ceremony took its current form only in 1901 on the accession of King Edward VII, who adored such pageantry and a mere three weeks after the death of his mother, Queen Victoria, processed to the House of Lords in crimson, gold and ermine robes, reading the speech himself. Victoria, by contrast, had refused to come to the state opening for years after the death of Prince Albert, her consort, in 1861, and even when she started turning up again, she and her children and their spouses would sit at the front listening while the Lord Chancellor read the speech. Queen Elizabeth II has opened every session of the parliament since her accession, with the exceptions of 1959 and 1963, when she was pregnant with her second two sons.

In 1998, a year after Tony Blair had become prime minister with a determination to "modernize" Britain, the ceremony was streamlined and speeded up. The changes were modest, however: the number of participants in the Queen's procession that year was cut from fifty-seven to thirty-one – among those missing were such exotically named characters as the Gentleman Usher of the Sword of State and Silver Stick in Waiting – while Lord Irvine, the incoming Lord Chancellor, did without the traditional tights, breeches and buckles. And, after pulling the government's speech from his ceremonial purse and hand-delivering the legislative programme to the Queen, Irvine turned his back on her as he walked away down the carpeted steps, rather than walking backwards as had previously been the case.

The speech the Queen read that year contained a radical proposal to end one of the most undemocratic and archaic provisions in the British constitution: the right of hereditary peers to sit and vote in the House of Lords – even if more than a decade later the country is still without a fully elected upper house. When it came to the ceremony itself, however, the changes were limited. Some traditions, it seems, are too important to tamper with.

The ceremonial surrounding the British state opening of parliament stands out by virtue of its sheer scale and the richness of its spectacle, but it is not unique: some of the Continental monarchies also still mark their sovereign's involvement in the political process with shows of pageantry.

Closest in nature to the proceedings in London is the opening of the Dutch parliament, held on Prinsjesdag (Prince's Day), the third Tuesday in September, in The Hague. Starting shortly before midday, members of various regiments, resplendent in their dress uniforms, march through the streets. Then on the dot of one o'clock, the Gouden Koets (Golden Coach), carrying Queen Beatrix, her son Crown Prince Willem-Alexander and his wife Princess Máxima, sets off from the Noordeinde Palace, where she works, to travel the short distance through the centre of the city to the Ridderzaal (Hall of Knights) in the Binnenhof, the building that houses the parliament. A more modest coach carrying other members of the family precedes her. With their gilded uniforms, the coachmen look as if they have stepped straight out of a fairy tale.

Then, seated on a throne in front of members of both houses of parliament, the Queen reads out the Troonrede ("Throne Speech"), which is written for her by the government and outlines the legislative programme for the year ahead. Unlike her British counterpart, she wears a hat – and often quite a spectacular one – rather than a crown. That afternoon she and her family will make a brief appearance on the balcony of the Noordeinde Palace to the delight of the cheering crowds below.

Beatrix's short journey, during which her coach is accompanied by members of the armed forces in their ceremonial best, is watched by spectators seated on specially erected stands along the route. Unlike the state opening of parliament in London, it is not so much a tourist attraction as an opportunity for the Dutch to display their support for the monarchy and for the ruling house of Orange-Nassau in particular. This is the day of the so-called Orangists, the grass-roots supporters of the monarchy, or rather of the ruling dynasty. Wearing orange coats or football shirts, or with garlands of orange flowers around their necks, they begin to gather as early as seven in the morning to be sure of securing the best places behind the barriers that line the narrow streets of The Hague. The Troonrede itself is broadcast not just on television but also on giant screens erected on the street, but few people seem to pay much attention: they have turned out for the glory of the spectacle, not to hear dry details of laws planned.

In recent years Prinsjesdag has also turned into an occasion for female members of parliament and for women out on the street to sport the most spectacular hats, the more extravagant the better – a tribute to the Queen's own headgear. The creations, reminiscent of the sort seen every June at Royal Ascot, provide a colourful talking point for the Dutch media, which run competitions asking readers and viewers to choose their favourites.

Visiting in 2009, I watched the parade from a stand on Lange Voorhout, one of the oldest and grandest streets in The Hague. My fellow spectators, the majority of whom had obtained their tickets through *Vorsten Royale*, a royal magazine, were mostly in their sixties or seventies. I pointed this out to my neighbour, who would soon be drawing a pension himself. A tour guide by occupation, he was here for work rather than pleasure. "If I think about my own family, my parents were the monarchists, I am not really that bothered either way, while my children just talk about what it costs," he admitted.

The atmosphere has traditionally been relaxed, but this year was different: it was only a few months since a failed attack on the royal family in Appeldoorn during celebrations marking Queen's Day, the other important event in the Dutch royal calendar. The challenge for the authorities was how to tighten security without destroying the character of the event itself. They succeeded with characteristic Dutch aplomb. To protect the parade from a car-borne attack the centre of the city had been completely sealed off, but rather than use conventional crash barriers the authorities opted for concrete flowerpots filled with red and orange flowers. Members of the police, normally in ceremonial uniform, were this year dressed in their usual clothes, while walking alongside Beatrix's coach were men carrying suspiciously large attaché cases. These cases, the Dutch press claimed the next day, contained special shields that would pop up in an emergency to protect the Queen from attack.

And then, at two p.m., it was all over. The Queen returned to her carriage and retraced her route back through the city. A few minutes later she and other members of the royal family appeared on the balcony of the Noordeinde Palace and waved to the crowds packed in the street below. "*Leve de koningin* (long live the Queen)," called out one man, and the crowd broke into applause.

Royal involvement with the workings of parliament continues to varying extents elsewhere. In Norway the King delivers a speech opening parliament on the second working day of October from a throne of gilt wood and red velvet, with his queen on his right and the crown prince on his left. In Sweden too the King makes a speech to the Riksdag, but it is only a short formal one rather than a statement of government policy and he doesn't sit on a throne. In Denmark, by contrast, the Queen and her family are merely spectators – albeit high-profile ones whose every gesture is captured by photographer from the moment they arrive in black vintage limousines. Shots of them appearing to nod off to sleep are particularly prized by the press. The Spanish king appears only after a parliament convenes for the first time after an election, when he makes a speech seated at a normal chair and table rather than on a throne. In Belgium, the only occasion on which the monarch sets foot in parliament is to be sworn in at the beginning of his reign.

However reduced in form, such ceremonials serve as a vestigial reminder of the central role that royalty once played in the political and public life of the nation, when kings not only reigned over their subjects but ruled them. Owed their places often by virtue of military conquest, they maintained control of their realms thanks to a combination of brute force, patronage and clan loyalty. Parliaments, to the extent they existed at all, were purely advisory bodies.

The story of much of the past millennium is one of attempts by other forces in society to curb such powers. In Britain, one of the earliest such attempts was Magna Carta, the document King John was obliged by the barons to sign in 1215 establishing the principle that the monarch should rule according to law and not trample willy-nilly over the rights of his subjects.

It has not been a one-way process. In the centuries that followed Magna Carta, the power of the monarchy in England increased rather than diminished – although the execution of Charles I in 1649 and Britain's brief, and hitherto unrepeated, republican interlude under Oliver Cromwell meant an end to the doctrine of the Divine Right of Kings promulgated by Charles's father, James I.

The monarchy was restored under Charles II, but when his brother, James II, who succeeded him, tried to reassert royal power, he was driven from the throne and replaced by his son-in-law (and nephew) William of Orange. At the formal ceremony in February 1689 at which they were jointly offered the crown, William and Mary were presented with a Declaration of Rights that marked the limits to their powers. This declaration (passed later that year by parliament as the Bill of Rights), together with a package of other laws over the following few years, known collectively as the Revolutionary Settlement, marked an end to arbitrary rule by the monarch in Britain and established the principle of the supremacy of parliament.

Initially, at least, the monarch was still left with considerable powers – even if, from then on, these powers had to be exercised within a framework of constitutional rules. As Vernon Bogdanor, one of Britain's foremost constitutional scholars, has argued, "sovereigns still sought to secure governments which could carry out their policies, but they had to achieve this through methods of political management. They could no longer interfere with elections, but they could seek to influence them... Similarly, sovereigns could no longer ignore parliament, but they could seek to influence it."[3]

As a result, the British in the eighteenth and early nineteenth centuries saw a number of battles between successive kings and their ministers – with mixed results. Power was gradually ebbing away from the monarch, due largely to the emergence of a modern party system, which meant governments would come to depend for their survival on the support not of the King, but instead of the party that had a majority in the House of Commons. The process was reinforced by the extension of the franchise, first in 1832 to the middle classes and then in 1867 to some members of the working class too. The British monarchy had thus become a constitutional one, which, according to Bogdanor, was a term first coined by a Frenchman, W. Dupré, who wrote in 1801 of "La monarchie constitutionnelle" and "un roi constitutionnel".[4]

In his influential book The English Constitution, published in 1867 and widely read since (including, it seems, by the monarchs themselves), Bagehot summed up the role of the monarch thus: "To state the matter shortly, the sovereign has, under a constitutional monarchy such as ours, three rights: the right to be consulted, the right to encourage, the right to warn. And a king of great sense and sagacity would want no others." Yet despite Bagehot's words, Victoria, who had already been on the throne for more than thirty years when his book appeared, had been far from an impartial bystander, initially adopting a highly partisan approach in favour of her beloved Lord Melbourne, a Whig, over the Tories. Her husband Albert, too, began to see the sovereign as an umpire, independent of the parties, who could use his or her influence for the good of the country. Fortunately, perhaps, for the health of the British constitution, Albert died in December 1861. Although Victoria responded to the loss of her beloved consort by withdrawing from public life, she reverted to her old partisan ways in the last two decades of her reign, favouring Benjamin Disraeli, the Conservative leader, who shared her passion for empire.

Kept away from all affairs of state by Victoria while she was alive, her son, Edward VII, intervened vigorously in all aspects of public life during his own brief reign. He was especially active in foreign policy, where he worked hard to build relations with France, creating the atmosphere that led to signature of the Entente Cordiale in 1904. His son, who succeeded him as George V, also found himself embroiled in politics. No sooner had he come to the throne in 1910 than he was caught up in the crisis prompted by the attempts of the House of Lords to block the budget. The fairness with which he treated the first Labour government in 1924 helped to ensure the party remained loyal to the monarchy rather than republican. Then, in 1931, when the nation was in crisis again, George intervened directly to encourage Ramsay MacDonald, the Labour leader, to form a "national government", even though it meant splitting his own party. In 1945, however, his son George VI was unable to prevent the return of Labour, this time with a majority and a programme of radical change.

A similar process was under way over the same period in Continental Europe. Louis XIV, the Sun King, was as much a believer in the Divine Right of Kings as James I. His phrase "*L'état, c'est moi*" ("I am the state") summarizes the fundamental principle of absolute monarchy, namely that sovereignty is vested in one individual.

Absolutism was on the rise elsewhere in Europe too. In Denmark in 1660, riding on a wave of popularity after his successful defence of Copenhagen against Swedish forces, King Frederik III, whose kingdom included Norway and the duchies of Schleswig and Holstein, converted the monarchy from an elective to an absolute, hereditary one. The "Kongeloven" (or "Lex Regia", both meaning "King's Law"), signed on 14th November 1665, declared Denmark the personal property of the monarch, who was accountable only to God. His signature was required for all national business and once he signed a decree it became law immediately. The Danish council was an advisory body that the king could dismiss at will. This, in theory, was the most extensive and consistently defined absolutism in Christendom – even if, in practice, the Danish king's powers and resources were as limited as in other monarchical states and he was just as dependent as other sovereigns on the general acceptance of his subjects.

Across Europe, the aftermath of the French Revolution and the Napoleonic Wars saw monarchs obliged to accept the kind of constraints on power that had followed Britain's Glorious Revolution more than a century earlier. In Sweden, the 1809 constitution that followed the *coup d'état* against Gustaf IV Adolf and his replacement by his elderly uncle, Carl XIII, did away with despotism, bringing in constitutional monarchy in its place. The king, it was decreed, could henceforth only exercise his powers within the government and under the control of the council of state. In the event, Carl, already aged sixty, was decrepit, and any influence he had was swiftly taken away by Jean-Baptiste Bernadotte, the French revolutionary turned marshal who was imposed on him as crown prince. When, largely thanks to Bernadotte's efforts, Norway was united with Sweden under a single crown in November 1814, its people were allowed to keep the liberal constitution adopted that May after the defeat of their former Danish masters. The document remains in force today.

Belgium was a constitutional monarchy from the start after breaking away from the Netherlands in 1830; Spain became a constitutional monarchy in 1837. The Dutch followed in 1848: their king, Willem II, although a conservative, saw a diminution in his powers as the only way the monarchy could survive and charged Johan Rudolf Thorbecke, who became the country's first de-facto prime minister, with drawing up a new constitution that is still in operation today. "I changed from conservative to liberal in one night," Willem declared. The document, passed in June 1849, ended absolute rule, established a bicameral parliament, limited the powers of the monarch and secured basic civil rights. In Sweden, following the replacement of the traditional parliament of the Four Estates with a more modern two-chamber system in 1866, Bernadotte's grandson, King Carl XV, found his influence increasingly constrained by the legislature.

That, at least, was the theory. In practice Continental monarchs were, like British ones, often reluctant to submit to such constraints on their power. Despite his revolutionary origins, Bernadotte began his transformation into an old-fashioned royal autocrat even before he formally acceded to the Swedish (and Norwegian) throne in 1818 as Carl XIV Johan. As time went on, he increasingly chose as councillors loyal bureaucrats who would carry out his will. During the last fifteen of his twenty-six-year reign, the King – who rarely rose before two p.m. – ruled through what became known as his "bedchamber regime", with Count Magnus Brahe, his personal advisor and favourite, acting as a kind of gatekeeper.

Belgium's Léopold I and his son Léopold II also bridled at attempts to control their actions. Queen Isabel II of Spain, who reigned from 1843 until 1868, often interfered in politics, while Willem III, who came to the throne in the Netherlands in 1849, loathed the constitutional changes initiated by his father the previous year. His daughter, Wilhelmina, who was queen of the Netherlands for almost the entire first half of the twentieth century, was often unhappy with her government, and in the aftermath of the Bolshevik revolution of 1917 she managed to see down attempts to turn the country into socialist republic.

The first decades of the twentieth century saw a series of clashes – not all of which were won by parliaments. In 1914, Sweden's Gustaf V, an advocate of rearmament, appealed directly to the people in a battle with the government of Karl Staaff, which had come to power three years earlier on the promise to disarm. That February, more than 30,000 farmers marched to the palace in support of the King, who denounced the government's defence policy in a speech to the crowds gathered in the courtyard. Matters rapidly escalated into a constitutional crisis, prompting some to call for a republic – but the King prevailed, managing to form a conservative administration. The outbreak of war a few months later proved him right.

Yet the tide of history was running against Gustaf and the other monarchs, especially after the extension of the vote to the working classes – and to women – which helped the rise of the British Labour Party and other social-democratic parties. These, by their nature, tended to be less favourable towards monarchy than their conservative rivals. Even so, many leading left-leaning politicians quickly became dazzled by the allure of court once they were allowed to taste its charms, turning the most determined class warrior into a royalist. The victory of left-wing parties in the Swedish elections of 1917 obliged Gustaf to accept a liberal government again, this time in coalition with the Social Democrats, whose programme committed them to a republic. Three years later, Hjalmar Branting, who had led the Social Democrats in their battle against the King, even briefly served as prime minister.

Gustaf's Danish counterpart, Christian X, who became king of that country in 1912, also came into conflict with his politicians. Although a conservative, he had acquiesced in the formation of Denmark's first liberal government in 1901 but never really came to terms with the loss of the monarch's traditional influence. He tried to regain some of it in 1920 during what became known as the Easter Crisis, when he sided with nationalists against his own government in a dispute over the return of Schleswig, a former Danish fiefdom lost to Prussia sixty years earlier. The King, who rode over the border on a white horse with a young girl on his knee, initially prevailed, forcing the prime minister to resign and replacing him with a more conservative figure. The political crisis that followed threatened the monarchy, however, and it was Christian who was eventually forced to back down: he learnt his lesson, as did his successors who, despite the formal powers still granted them in the constitution, have not tried to exert direct political influence.

Christian's younger brother, who had become King Haakon VII of Norway in 1905 after it broke away from Sweden, trod more carefully, conscious perhaps of his own potentially more vulnerable position. During a government crisis in 1928, he took the bold move of inviting the Labour Party, whose platform included a provision to abolish the monarchy, into the government for the first time. The administration lasted only twenty-eight days, but the point had been made: the king was above politics. From that time on, the Norwegian left was not as antagonistic towards monarchy as its Swedish equivalent, although it took the outbreak of war for the Danish-born monarch to become a truly national figure.

In Belgium, Léopold I's successors proved unwilling to accept the constraints imposed on them by the constitution. Indeed, the premature end to the reign of Léopold III was the result in part of the way in which he tried to ignore the wishes of his ministers in the 1930s. When the King himself came under fire over his war record, few politicians were prepared to support him – which, in the end, was to leave him little choice but to abdicate.

Although the general tendency was towards a reduction in royal power, Russia remained a glorious exception. The experiment with a limited constitutional monarchy after the 1905 Revolution proved a brief one. The Tsar had absolute state power, delegating it to persons and institutions only as he saw fit. He was, in a popular metaphor, the father of Russia, and the subjects of his empire were his children. It all came to a bloody end in 1917, however, when the Bolshevik revolution replaced absolute monarchy with an even more brutal form of authoritarian rule that was to endure for more than seven decades.

So what, if anything, is left of royal power today? Are Europe's kings and queens mere figureheads or do they still play a role in the political process?

The most obvious place where royal influence can be felt is in the formation of governments, especially in those countries where coalitions are the norm. In both Belgium and the Netherlands, for example, the monarch is charged with appointing first a so-called *informateur* after an election to assess the political landscape and then a *formateur* who, all being well, will go on to become prime minister. In theory, the monarch should play a neutral role – but the larger the number of parties and the more possible combinations capable of generating a majority there are, the greater the influence of the monarch will be. That influence will also tend to grow the longer he has been on the throne.

Belgium's fragmented political system, with the parties split not just along left-right lines but also between Flemings and Walloons, provides further scope for royal influence, by increasing the number of potential coalitions. When these administrations fall apart, as they do regularly, the king also has the power either to accept or to reject a prime minister's resignation and allow a dissolution.

During his forty-two-year reign, King Baudouin made what some critics saw as rather too much use of such powers. In October 1991, just under two years before his death, when Belgium was in the midst of one of its periodic political crises, he refused to accept the resignation of Wilfried Martens, the prime minister, which had the result of bringing forward the general election. He is also said to have routinely struck out the names of proposed cabinet ministers of whom he didn't approve. His younger brother, Albert, who succeeded him in August 1993, was by nature less keen to intervene, but has been obliged to do so, especially as the growing polarization of Belgium along linguistic lines has made it more difficult to form governments – as was shown after the Flemish nationalist Bart De Wever's New Flemish Alliance won the largest number of seats in the June 2010 election.

Britain's first-past-the-post political system, in which either Labour or Conservatives typically obtains an absolute majority, leaves considerably less room for royal intervention. There were nevertheless several occasions during the twentieth century – including during Elizabeth's reign – when the monarch exercised discretion over the choice of leader. This was particularly the case with the Conservative Party, which traditionally did not elect a leader but clung to a curious system under which the leader "emerged" – leaving scope for royal involvement. These days, however, the Conservatives, like Labour, formally elect their own leader, which meant the appointment of Tony Blair and Gordon Brown, and of Margaret Thatcher and John Major before them, was automatic rather than an example of the Queen exercising her discretion.

The general election of May 2010, which did not give an overall majority to either Labour or the Conservatives, seemed on the face of it to create a situation in which the Queen could play an interventionist role, as in Belgium or the Netherlands. This was not the British way: Buckingham Palace was careful to avoid giving the impression of any involvement, with the Queen remaining for five days at Windsor Castle while the party leaders back in London found a solution – a Conservative-Liberal Democrat coalition. The contrast with the active role played by her grandfather, George V, in the formation of the National Government in 1931 could not have been greater.

Behind the scenes, however, Christopher Geidt, the Queen's private secretary, was monitoring events closely from the Cabinet Office. Geidt, it subsequently emerged, warned Brown not to resign until a formal pact between his two rivals had been concluded – in part by giving the defeated Labour leader the false impression he might yet be able to cling to power.[5] This averted a situation in which the country was left for a few days without a government; this is fairly commonplace for Belgium and the Netherlands, where coalition-building can sometimes take weeks or even months, but would have been an alarming constitutional novelty for Britain. It was therefore only once the Conservatives and Liberal Democrats had done their deal that Brown went to the palace to tender his resignation and the Queen invited Cameron to form a new administration.

Royal influence is not restricted to coalition-building. Between elections it can also extend to the day-to-day running of government. In the Netherlands, Queen Beatrix, as one of her former premiers revealed, would often be quite forthright as far as ministerial appointments were concerned. Monarchs have also occasionally given political direction at crucial moments: Baudouin, for example, suggested after the outbreak of troubles in the Belgian Congo in the late 1950s that independence for the African nation was becoming inevitable. In the late 1980s, a royal speech signalled acceptance of the country's move towards federalism as the only way of reconciling warring Flemings and Walloons – even though the transfer of power from Brussels to regional and communal levels means ultimately a diminution of royal influence.

In most countries the prime minister holds weekly meetings with the monarch. Such meetings are not minuted and what goes on is known only to the participants, but as Margaret Thatcher wrote in her memoirs, "Anyone who imagines that they are a mere formality or confined to social niceties is quite wrong; they are quietly businesslike and Her Majesty brings to bear a formidable grasp of current issues and breadth of experience."[6] As Bogdanor puts it, "it is a good thing that those who have political power should give some account each week to those who do not."[7] The number of years that Elizabeth has spent as queen, and the dramas and crises she has lived through along the way, inevitably add to her influence. After all, she was already on the throne when David Cameron was born.

In Denmark, the Queen meets the prime minister once a week, usually on a Wednesday, unless either has a pressing engagement. She also holds a separate meeting with the foreign minister. Around once a month, she presides over the Council of State, a body that contains all the members of the cabinet. The crown prince becomes a member once he reaches eighteen. As elsewhere – with the exception of Sweden – the Queen also signs bills, laws and other documents.

Norway goes further: every Friday at eleven a.m. the members of the government assemble in the cabinet chamber of the Royal Palace in Oslo for a meeting of the Council of State, presided over by the King, seated in the original 1848 golden and red-velvet throne chair. One by one the various cabinet ministers read out their bills, which are then signed by the King. Often Crown Prince Haakon will also attend. Although the King's signature is required, the meeting, which typically takes just half an hour, is largely symbolic these days. All the decisions have already been taken at a conventional cabinet meeting the day before – to which the King is not invited.

The nature of royal influence these days means that it is inevitably exerted behind the scenes: monarchs are as aware as everyone else that political power wielded by virtue purely of birth is an anachronism. The king or queen is not meant to have opinions – or at least they must keep them to themselves. In one notorious case in Belgium in 1990, however, King Baudouin broke this principle over the question of abortion. While other European countries had been liberalizing the law one by one, Belgium had been holding back, in part, it has been claimed, thanks to manoeuvring by the King. Baudouin's main motivation appeared to have been his strong Catholic faith; a role may also have been played by his own personal experience: attempts by him and Queen Fabiola to have children ended in five miscarriages.

By the end of the 1980s, however, with Belgium, along with Ireland, almost alone in forbidding abortion, the popular mood was turning against him. After a bill approving terminations under certain circum-stances was passed by the Senate in November 1989, the King vented his anger in public by devoting his New Year speech to a homily on the sanctity of human life. Despite his intervention, the bill was passed by an overwhelming majority in the Chamber of Representatives that spring, leaving the monarch in the invidious position of having to sign it into law. Instead he took advantage of a law that allowed him to step down if illness or "other reasons" prevented him from fulfilling his duties – but was allowed to resume his constitutional powers forty-eight hours later.

Although this did not allow Baudouin to block the measure, the republican lobby was angered by such an unusual constitutional manoeuvre. By putting his own religious faith ahead of his political neutrality, the King had clearly broken the rules – although opinion polls suggested his act of conscientious objection had actually increased rather than reduced his popularity.

The move nevertheless set a curious precedent that could have caused problems several years later when the parliament passed laws authorizing homosexual marriages and euthanasia – both of which Baudouin's faith would have made him uncomfortable with. By then, however, he had already been succeeded by his more liberal younger brother, Albert, who signed both measures into law without objection.

A similar crisis was looming in Luxembourg in December 2008, when Grand Duke Henri, a devout Catholic, said he would refuse to sign into law an act on euthanasia voted on earlier that year by the Chamber of Deputies. The constitution was swiftly changed, making royal assent, which had been a requirement in the constitution since 1848, no longer necessary. But calls arose for a broader reform of the constitution, to reduce the powers of the grand duke, bringing his role more into line with that of Europe's other monarchs.

Less dramatically, monarchs have also made use of their annual Christmas or New Year addresses – which, unlike the speeches to parliament, are their own rather than their government's words – to express opinions. In the case of Queen Elizabeth II, the sentiments expressed are usually far from controversial: musings on the nature of Christianity and of family. Yet her words can also contain a more political message: in 2004, for example, she signalled support for a multicultural society – and opposition to the British National Party – by telling the story of an overseas visitor who had spoken approvingly of a trip he had taken on the Tube from Heathrow during which he had encountered children of different ethnic and culture groups, all of whom seemed to get on well with one another. "Some people feel that their own beliefs are being threatened," she said. "Some are unhappy about unfamiliar cultures. They all need to be reassured... that diversity is indeed a strength and not a threat." Significantly, the first stop in March 2012 on her five-month Diamond Jubilee tour of the United Kingdom was Leicester, a city with a mixed population. The Queen's frequent references in her messages to the Commonwealth are also effectively a political statement of the importance of that organization.

Multiculturalism is a theme that has been seized on by Queen Beatrix of the Netherlands too. After the murder of Theo van Gogh, the controversial Dutch film-maker, by an Islamic extremist in November 2004, she appealed for tolerance during an unannounced visit to a multicultural workshop set up by young people in Amsterdam. In June 2006, Beatrix won praise from Jan Peter Balkenende, the prime minister – but anger from the far right – over her behaviour during a state visit to the Mubarak Mosque in The Hague to mark its fiftieth anniversary. Contrary to her usual practice she agreed not to shake hands with the leaders in deference to their belief that Islam forbids men from touching women other than their wives. Critics noted that such tolerance appeared to extend only to Muslims: the Queen had refused to meet an Orthodox Jewish group in 1982 because they also didn't shake hands with women.

In contrast to the rest of European royalty, the Swedish monarch is almost completely devoid of formal political power, as a result of the new constitution that came into force in 1975, two years after King Carl XVI Gustaf, the current monarch, succeeded his nonagenarian grandfather, Gustaf VI Adolf. Swedish politicians had been arguing for years about how to modernize the monarchy – and indeed, whether to continue to have a king at all. The Social Democrats, who dominated Swedish politics from the 1930s, had always been committed to turning their country into a republic, even if they proved reluctant to take any concrete steps in that direction, for fear of upsetting their core voters, many of whom were ardent royalists. The right, by contrast, were determined to keep the king.

Almost as soon as Gustaf VI Adolf succeeded his father in 1950, work began on a new constitution in which everything – including the retention of the monarchy – was up for discussion. Indeed, the Bernadotte dynasty's days looked numbered in 1966 when a bill introduced by some thirty Social Democratic MPs calling for the abolition of the monarchy won a majority in both houses of parliament. "Monarchy can only be regarded as an irrational system, with its future in its past," they asserted. "Feelings in its favour are waning."[8] Yet concerns about the reaction from the public prevailed, and the same majority rejected calls to put the proposal to a referendum. It was decided instead to hand the delicate matter to a constitutional commission.

After much deliberation, the commission hammered out a compromise in August 1971 at a meeting at Torekov, an exclusive summer resort on Sweden's south-western coast: the king would remain as head of state but be stripped of all but his ceremonial and representational functions. The 1809 constitution had begun its definition of the monarch's powers with the words "The King alone has the right to govern the realm" – a right that, for the first decades, had been limited only by a duty to ask the opinion of a council that he had himself appointed.

The current document starts instead with the words "All public power in Sweden derives from the people" – which is then conferred on parliament and government. However, in deference to the old King, who was due to celebrate his ninetieth birthday in November the following year, it was decided that the change, if agreed, would not come into effect until after his death.

By removing the monarch entirely from the political sphere, the Swedes were taking to a logical conclusion the gradual reduction in royal influence that had been taking place across Europe for the previous two centuries. This new document was, to a great extent, merely adapting the constitutional text to fit reality: real political power had long since drained away from the palace. But it also meant concrete changes in the way the system functions. Since 1975, it is the speaker of the Riksdag rather than the king who acts as a broker in the formation of government coalitions and appoints the prime minister. The monarch no longer presides over cabinet meetings, rubber-stamps bills or takes the title of commander-in-chief of the armed forces, though he does chair a committee on foreign policy. In the words of Olof Palme, the then prime minister, the reforms reduced the monarchy to a feather in the hat. Sweden, he declared, could easily be turned into a republic "with a stroke of the pen".

This Swedish model is attractive to those who want to cling to the ceremonial trappings of royalty but whose democratic sentiments are affronted by having anyone granted political powers merely on the basis of heredity. It also obviates the need for a president, who could become a divisive party-political figure. Yet some critics are not satisfied, claiming the accident of the monarch's birth still automatically gives him an authority denied other citizens, especially when he chooses to speak out on issues. Carl XVI Gustaf has certainly chosen to do so on various occasions in recent years, often provoking controversy, whether criticizing neighbouring Norway's seal culls or upsetting environmentalists at home by calling for the killing of some of his country's wolf population. A Christmas speech in which he urged his subjects to work harder was also seized on by critics who wondered if a hereditary monarch was best placed to express such sentiments.

Despite the attractions of the Swedish model, it has not so far been emulated elsewhere in Europe. Indeed, in May 2011, Mark Rutte, the Dutch prime minister, wrote to parliament explicitly opposing any formal restrictions to the powers of the monarch. "The monarch is certainly the symbol of power, but does not herself possess any power," he said. Many in parliament were not convinced, however. In recent years, the Dutch monarchy's traditional critics on the left and in the centre have been joined by Geert Wilders's Freedom Party (PVV), which has been angered by the Queen's calls for social cohesion and what it sees as her excessive respect for Muslim sensibilities. In September 2011, Wilders put forward a proposal in parliament to remove the monarch from the political system, but the move foundered on the requirement for a two-thirds majority to implement constitutional change. Yet, with relations between the Queen and the PVV set to remain poor, further attempts to limit royal power seem likely.

Alone of Europe's monarchies, tiny Liechtenstein has bucked the trend towards a reduction in royal power. In a referendum in March 2003, nearly two thirds of the electorate backed a new constitution, proposed by Prince Hans-Adam II, which instead added considerably to his influence. The vote represented the culmination of a long and messy battle between the Prince and his parliament. The Prince Hans-Adam, who had been effectively running the principality since his ageing father transferred executive powers to him in 1984, had threatened that he and his family would move to Austria if the referendum failed, and even joked about selling Liechtenstein.

"We might indeed decide to leave the country," Hans-Adam said in an interview in 2000 that reflected the unique relationship between the ruling family and their tiny country. "But that would not be the end of the principality, because until 1938 my ancestors also lived in Austria and came down here only once a year or so. My ancestors bailed out Liechtenstein when it was bankrupt and thus acquired sovereign rights. If ever the people decided time is up for this ruling family, they would have to find someone else rich enough to take our place. But I am confident it won't come to that."[9]

Despite opposition led by Mario Frick, a former prime minister, the people backed their prince. He is not only able veto any law he dislikes, he can also dismiss the government or any minister at will. The result has been to make him effectively Europe's only absolute monarch.

Chapter 4

An Ordinary Day at Work

The 10th of December has a special significance for Sweden and its royal family. On this day in 1896, at the age of sixty-three, Alfred Nobel, a rich and highly successful Swedish chemist, died of a stroke in the Italian Mediterranean resort of San Remo, where he had made his home five years earlier. A pacifist and poet, the eccentric Nobel had intended that dynamite, his most famous invention, should be used only for peaceful purposes. To his dismay it proved even more useful for warfare. And so, partly to assuage his conscience – and partly to burnish the family name – when he sat down in 1895 to write his will, Nobel pledged the bulk of his fortune, equivalent to around $250 million today, to establish a series of awards to recognize excellence in science, literature and peace. In 1901, after some wrangling with both Nobel's heirs and the French tax authorities, the first Nobel Prizes ceremony was held. To add prestige to the event, the awards were handed out by Crown Prince Gustaf.

More than a century later, what began as a relatively low-key Scandinavian event has turned into the most prestigious prize-giving ceremony in the world – and the high point of the Swedish royal calendar. When the laureates in literature, medicine, physics, chemistry and economics – the last of which was added in 1969 – gather for the gala ceremony in Stockholm's concert hall, it is currently Gustaf's great-grandson, Carl XVI Gustaf, who hands them each a diploma and medal. The King and his family also have pride of place at a sumptuous banquet for 1,300 people – including 250 students – held later that day in the Stockholms Stadshus (Stockholm City Hall). To add to the lavishness, both venues are decorated with flowers flown in from San Remo.

Sweden's media wallow in the spectacle: newspapers record the number of pigeon breasts and lobster tails eaten and bottles of wine and champagne drunk, while these days their reporters blog and tweet a running commentary from their tables. Invariably, attention focuses less on the elderly men and women honoured for their worthy but often incomprehensible academic achievements than on the glamorous guests – chief among them the King's daughters, Crown Princess Victoria and her beautiful younger sister, Madeleine. Which ball gowns are the princesses wearing, which jewels have they selected from the Bernadotte family collection and (at least until Victoria's wedding in June 2010) which men are on their arms?

The same day, 250 miles to the west, a similar ceremony takes place. The Nobel Peace Prize, the most prestigious of the awards, is awarded not in Stockholm but in Oslo – and here Carl XVI Gustaf's fellow monarch, King Harald V, plays his part. In the richly decorated reception hall of the City Hall, in front of a thousand guests, the prize is handed over – although by the chairman of the Norwegian Nobel Committee rather than by the King, who together with his immediate family is seated in the place of honour. That evening there is a glittering banquet in the Grand Hotel.

For the Kings of both Sweden and Norway, what has become known as Nobel Week is merely the most high-profile of a series of engagements – from the glamorous to the humdrum – that fill their year. There was a time when the role of monarchs was to rule, with ceremonial activities such as handing out prizes or medals little more than a public manifestation of such power. Yet, as was seen in the previous chapter, such political power has almost completely drained away, leaving today's kings and queens in search of another role, which they have found in representational engagements such as the Nobel ceremonies. It is these functions, whether trips to obscure provincial factories or glittering state visits to important trading partners, that have come to constitute the bulk of their work. Europe's royal families have become part of the public-relations wing of Great Britain plc, Nederland BV or Sverige AB.

The various events attended by members of the royal families are laid out in their official reports and websites. Take Sweden's Carl XVI Gustaf. A visit to www.royalcourt.se reveals that during March 2012 he took part in no fewer than twenty-one events, ranging from a formal gathering of the Royal Swedish Academy of Sciences, an audience with the President of the Royal Swedish Academy of Agriculture and Forestry and hosting the Prince of Wales and Duchess of Cornwall on an official visit to a trip to the Cross-Country Skiing World Cup Final. King Harald, meanwhile, was listed as having more than one hundred and forty engagements over the year, from audiences with foreign diplomats to cultural and sporting events – as well as chairing the weekly meeting of the cabinet. Harald's son Crown Prince Haakon and other members of the family also make their fair share of outings. And then there are the various ceremonial events, chief among them the 17th of May, Constitution Day, marked in Norway not with shows of military force but with children's parades – including one in Oslo, drawing up to 100,000 people, who are greeted by the royal family from the balcony of the palace, as well as the state opening of parliament every October.

When it comes to public appearances, however, it is the British royal family who are the most active. The journalist Robert Hardman, who followed the Windsors for a year for a BBC documentary, estimated Queen Elizabeth II and thirteen members of her family would perform 4,000 engagements over the twelve months. And although now well into her eighties, our monarch is showing little signs of slowing down. All are reported in a document issued by Buckingham Palace every day known as the Court Circular. Established in the early nineteenth century by George III, frustrated at the inaccurate reporting of his movements, it is now published by the *Times*, the *Daily Telegraph* and the *Scotsman*. In keeping with the palace's enthusiastic embrace of new technology, a searchable version is also included on the website.

Queen Elizabeth II's calendar each year includes the usual regular meetings with politicians and audiences with diplomats, as well as the more routine dinners and openings. She must also present some 2,500 honours, handed out at twenty or so investitures. In addition there are also high-profile fixed events, rich in the pageantry that characterizes the British monarchy: besides the state opening of parliament there is the Trooping of the Colour, a military parade marking the Queen's "official birthday" on a Saturday in June,[1] the closest Britain comes to a national day. The Queen also presides for the third week of June over the Royal Meeting at Ascot Racecourse, west of London. In a tradition dating back to the 1820s and the reign of King George IV, she and her party begin each day with the Royal Procession, during which they parade along the track in front of racegoers in horse-drawn landaus. This is more than just duty for the Queen: a keen horsewoman, she has owned more than twenty winners at Royal Ascot.

Other members of the royal family, meanwhile, have similar duties of their own, often chosen to reflect their own interests. Prince Philip has been active in science, conservation and youth welfare; the Duke of Edinburgh's Award scheme for the under twenty-fives has been imitated across the world since he created it in the 1950s; Prince Charles is especially interested in farming and the built environment. As they have come of age, Princes William and Harry, although both in the armed forces, find time to devote to various charities. In part, these reflect their own interests: William, for example, works with Tusk, a small British charity devoted to African wildlife, while his brother helped create Sentebale, a charity to help deprived children in Lesotho, where he spent several months after leaving school. William has also taken over some of the charity work of the late Princess Diana, and is a patron of Centrepoint, a charity that works with homeless young people. It is the princes' aunt, Princess Anne, though, who notches up the most engagements – more than six hundred a year, including at least three major overseas tours.

The extent to which participation in such events, or other "duties" such as visits to the ballet, an art exhibition or cinema festival, constitutes work – at least in the sense that the rest of us understand the term – is a matter for debate. Yet whenever there is media discussion in Britain of the sums paid to minor members of the royal family, the question of whether they are "worth it" is conducted largely in terms of how many such appearances they make. Purely by their presence, monarchs and their families arguably provide a public service to their subjects who treasure any contact with them, however fleeting or superficial.

The possibility of such a royal contact is the entire *raison d'être* of the royal garden parties, invitations to which have turned into a form of reward for public service. The first events were first held in the 1860s when Queen Victoria instituted what were known as "breakfasts" (even though they were held in the afternoon). These days, four are held each year – three in Buckingham Palace and one at Holyroodhouse in Edinburgh – attended by more than thirty thousand guests, whose names are put forward by government, the armed services or other bodies. The British monarchy is justly proud of the precision with which such events are choreographed. In more than half a century and what must be tens of thousands of public appearances, the Queen has never made a mistake.

An important category of such spectacles are the intrinsically private occasions – such as marriages, births and deaths – that have been transformed by first the newsreels and then television into huge public media events. When the future King George V married Princess May of Teck (later Queen Mary) in 1893 in the Chapel Royal, St James's Palace, there was room for only a hundred people. When his great-great-grandson Prince Charles wed Lady Diana Spencer in the considerably grander setting of St Paul's Cathedral in 1981, there were three thousand five hundred people in the congregation, another six hundred thousand on the streets of London and an estimated television audience across the world of seven hundred and fifty million. More recently, the marriage of Crown Princess Victoria and Daniel Westling in June 2010 was the culmination of two weeks of celebration in which Stockholm was transformed into a "capital of love" with flowers and performances throughout the city – and rival functions organized by republicans who saw this as the perfect occasion to try to drum up support for their cause. The wedding of Prince William and Kate Middleton in April 2011 was an even bigger international media event.

The media wedding par excellence was undoubtedly that between Prince Rainier of Monaco and Grace Kelly in April 1956. In a fore-taste of the kind of deals now commonplace between celebrities and magazines such as *Hello!* or *OK!*, MGM studios negotiated the rights to film the ceremony for its documentary, *The Wedding of the Century*, turning Monaco cathedral into a film set. In return, not only did the couple receive a $7,226 wedding gown designed by MGM's head costume designer, Helen Rose, the services of an MGM hairdresser and publicity executive and a substantial share of the proceeds, but the film, seen by an estimated thirty million television viewers across the world, also meant valuable publicity for a principality keen to expand its tourist business.

A similar function is served by royal births. Court officials may no longer be crowded into the delivery room – or in an adjoining room as was until quite recently the case – but hoards of photographers are sure to be waiting outside, hungry for an image of the newest addition to the royal family. Funerals can also play an important role in strengthening the monarchy; the sight of the coffin of a beloved elderly king or queen borne through the streets in a lavish cortège can unite a nation in grief. The effect is even stronger in the case of those such as Britain's Princess Charlotte, Belgium's Queen Astrid or Monaco's Princess Grace, who were cut down in their prime. There has been one important exception, though: following the death of Princess Diana in 1997, the royal family was pilloried by the media for maintaining a traditional stiff upper lip despite the near-hysterical public reaction. And during the funeral itself, comments made by Diana's brother, Earl Spencer, were interpreted as a thinly veiled attack on the monarchy itself.

Although many such events – both joyful and sad – take place in the respective countries' capitals, royal families have to avoid falling victim to accusations of metropolitan bias. Over the years the tradition has become established that the monarch and other members of the family should tour the realm and meet their subjects. Such tours have a special significance for the British monarchy: not only must due attention be paid to the Scots, Welsh and Northern Irish, the fifteen other countries of which Elizabeth II is queen must be kept loyal with visits, if not from the monarch herself, then from other members of her family. Beyond that are the remaining countries of the Commonwealth. Composed of fifty-four nations, it has a combined population of 2.1 billion, almost a third of the world, representing twenty-one per cent of the surface of the globe.

The monarchy under Victoria and her successors was closely identified with the British Empire – as was symbolized by her proclamation as Empress of India at the Delhi Durbar of 1877. Although Victoria never actually travelled to India (or indeed anywhere further east than the Alps), her successors have more than made up for that, embarking on a number of far-flung tours. It was fitting perhaps that when the then Princess Elizabeth heard of her father's death, she was in the middle of one such visit to Kenya.

Of Europe's current monarchies, the Netherlands, Spain and Belgium also had considerable possessions abroad. Their experiences have differed from one another, though – with varying implications for relations between former rulers and subjects in the post-colonial era. The acquisition by Belgium of what was initially known as the Congo Free State (and then the Belgian Congo, Zaire and now the Democratic Republic of Congo) was essentially a private venture by King Léopold II pursued for financial gain – and it was not until 1908, following reports of the appalling abuses committed there, that it was formally annexed by the Belgian government. When the country won independence in 1960, King Baudouin personally attended the festivities, but a speech he gave there was widely seen as insensitive to the atrocities that had been carried out there. Belgium's relations with the country have been somewhat unstable since, leaving little role for the royal family.

The Netherlands' relationship with Indonesia, the largest of its former colonies, has also been difficult. Queen Wilhelmina's decision to abdicate in favour of her daughter Juliana in 1948 was inspired in large part by the economic blow her country suffered when what had been known as the Dutch East Indies fought its way to independence. Nevertheless, Juliana visited in 1970 and her daughter Beatrix, the current queen, followed in 1995. The Dutch monarchs also pay special attention to the former colonies of Aruba, Curaçao and Sint Maarten, which today form autonomous countries within the Kingdom of the Netherlands. Spain, by contrast, lost its considerable Latin American possessions much earlier, and by the early twentieth century was left with only a handful of territories in Africa. But it still retains a special link with its former colonies.

Trips made by royalty can by their nature be gruelling, especially the foreign ones, even though they provide suitably exotic photo opportunities for television news bulletins. Some of the monarchs' domestic engagements, in particular, can be downright tedious, with their endless meetings – but woe- betide a royal who were to let slip they were anything but delighted to be at the event in question.

In a newspaper interview in 2003 Denmark's Queen Margrethe provided a rare insight into the realities of her job. "Being Queen involves a lot of repetition – the same ceremonies, the same functions, the same routine, every year," she told her interviewer, Gyles Brandreth. "Sometimes you think, 'Here we go again!' but my parents taught me something useful that I have tried to pass on to my two boys. Whatever you are doing, be aware of it and stay involved. For example, I have to listen to a lot of boring speeches, but I have discovered there is nothing so boring as not listening to a boring speech. If you listen carefully, the speech is very rarely as boring as you thought it was going to be. You can disagree with the speech in your head. You can think, 'He's saying it very badly,' but don't switch off. Somehow listen. It is much better that way."[2]

There are two institutions in particular with which monarchy has a special relationship: the Church (at least in those countries that are not Roman Catholic by tradition) and the armed forces.

In England, King Henry VIII broke with Rome in the 1530s after the Pope excommunicated him for divorcing Catherine of Aragon and putting himself at the head of the newly created Church of England. In 1559, under his daughter Elizabeth I, the monarch's title was changed from Supreme Head to Supreme Governor, to assuage critics who said this was usurping Jesus Christ, identified by the Bible as the head of the Church. Half a millennium later, Queen Elizabeth II remains the head of the Church, appointing its high-ranking members. This leadership is largely symbolic, however. She does so on the advice of the prime minister, who in turn takes his cue from Church leaders. The monarch also retains the title of Defender of the Faith. Originally granted by Pope Leo X to Henry VIII in 1521 for his early support for Roman Catholicism, it was taken away after the break with Rome, but then reconferred by parliament during the reign of Edward VI.

Although there is no doubting Elizabeth's own Christian faith, she is becoming something of an exception in today's multicultural Britain. The Church of England is just one of a number of religious faiths competing for souls – albeit one which, for historical reasons, continues to enjoy a privileged status. These days it probably counts fewer active churchgoers than the Roman Catholics. Muslims, Hindus and Sikhs are also present in growing numbers.

Acutely conscious of such sensitivities, Prince Charles has argued for a change when he comes to the throne, but it is a treacherous subject: an initial suggestion that he would like to be known as "Defender of the Faiths" after he becomes king alarmed some within the Church of England. As a compromise, it has since been mooted that he instead be termed "Defender of Faith" – a more abstract-sounding job description that avoided the need to choose between the singular and plural. Even this might not be easy: constitutional experts have warned that removal of that single word would nevertheless require parliament to agree to amend the 1953 Royal Titles Act, which came into law after changes were made for the Queen's coronation in the same year.

There are other, even more complicated issues relating to the British monarch's relationship with the Church. Under the terms of the Act of Settlement, passed in 1701 (and extended to Scotland in 1707), a relic of a very different age that is still in force, the monarch "shall join in communion with the Church of England". Catholics are explicitly prevented from becoming monarch or indeed marrying into the royal family. Its provisions extend well beyond those who have any realistic chance of succeeding to the throne: when the Queen's cousin, Prince Michael of Kent, married Baroness Marie-Christine von Reibnitz, a divorced German Catholic in 1978, he had to give up his right to the throne – even though he was so far down in the order of succession that the right was little more than theoretical.

Following the marriage of Prince William in April 2011, the question of what seemed unfair and outdated discrimination against Catholics also looked likely to be tackled, and, as was seen earlier, at the Commonwealth Heads of Government Meeting in Perth in October 2011, it was agreed that the laws of each of the sixteen countries of which Elizabeth is queen would be amended in order to ensure that daughters of future sovereigns would not be passed over in favour of elder sons, and that successors to the throne would no longer be barred from marrying Catholics.

Elsewhere in the Protestant world, the Norwegian, Danish and Swedish monarchs are heads of their respective Lutheran state Churches.[3] In the Netherlands, the Dutch Reformed Church was put under the direct control of the state when the Kingdom of the Netherlands was formed in 1815, but Church and state were formally separated as early as 1853. However, persecution of Dutch Protestants during the period in which they were ruled by the Catholic Spanish ensured that religion continued to be a touchy subject.

Although the Netherlands has long had a substantial Catholic minority, it has become a tradition that monarchs are members of the Dutch Reformed Church (which was merged in 2004 with three other institutions to form the Protestant Church in the Netherlands). For this reason, the monarchy was plunged into crisis in 1963 by the decision of the future Queen Beatrix's younger sister, Princess Irene, secretly to convert to Catholicism and get engaged to a Spanish Catholic, whom she married the following year. Beatrix's youngest sister Marijke also fell for a Catholic, this time a Cuban exile whom she met in New York, but in an attempt to avoid a repetition of the scandal she renounced her and future children's rights to the throne before converting to Catholicism and officially announcing her engagement in 1975.

Times have changed, however. Princess Máxima, the Argentinian-born wife of Crown Prince Willem-Alexander, is a Catholic and has shown no inclination to change her faith, which would make her the first Catholic queen of the Netherlands when her husband becomes king. Even so, she did study the Protestant faith and, crucially, agreed that their eldest daughter, Princess Catharina-Amalia, who is destined herself to become queen one day, and her two younger sisters should all be brought up as Protestants.

The armed forces too have traditionally enjoyed a special relationship with monarchy, a reflection of their position as the defender of the nation that has the king or queen at its summit. In modern European societies the army and other services are also a repository of deference, service, hierarchy and discipline, values with which royalty has traditionally been associated.

English history is full of stories of royal derring-do on the battlefield: Henry V's courage against the French at Agincourt in 1415 was celebrated by Shakespeare, while Henry VII became the last English king to win the throne in battle after defeating Richard III at the Battle of Bosworth Field in 1485. Two centuries later, William III's victory over James II at the Battle of the Boyne in 1690, in which the Protestant Dutchman personally led his forces, is still celebrated to this day by the Protestants of Northern Ireland – and remains a source of often violent friction with the Catholic community.

Elsewhere in Europe many kings over the centuries have reigned thanks to military conquest – or at the very least continued in power thanks to the success of their armed forces in seeing off enemies who would have overthrown them. The overwhelming majority of monarchies that fell in the twentieth century did so as a result of defeat in the First and Second World Wars.

No European monarch these days would lead his or her army into battle; for a start, most would not have the know-how. And then there is the fear of the possible consequences if they were killed or, worse, captured by the enemy. George II was the last reigning British monarch to fight, with not very impressive results: on 27th June 1743, during the War of the Austrian Succession, the King, then aged sixty, personally led his forces against a French army commanded by the Duc de Noailles at the Battle of Dettingen, in Bavaria. The British won, although it almost ended in disaster for the King: at one point his horse ran off and had to be halted by Ensign Cyrus Trapaud, who received a promotion as a reward.

By the nineteenth century monarchs were increasingly leaving military matters to those who knew what they were doing. This did not stop them trying to play a role. Under the Belgian constitution, the King was both required to "maintain the national independence and the integrity of the territory" and made the commander of territorial and maritime forces. Belgium's Léopold I personally commanded his troops against the country's former Dutch rulers in 1831–32; his grandson, Albert I, in turn, led Belgian forces when the Germans invaded in 1914; heavily outnumbered, they were, inevitably, defeated. But while the Belgian government moved across the French border to Le Havre, Albert and his little army stayed in De Panne, on the Flemish coast, maintaining a foothold in the country.

By that Christmas, the legend of the Roi-Chevalier was born – and the King was hailed as a hero around the world – even if evidence since uncovered by revisionist historians has somewhat undermined his image. The King led his army during the Courtrai offensive of autumn 1918 and on 22nd November entered Brussels in triumph on horseback flanked by the Queen, his children and the Duke of York, the future King George VI of Britain.

Other royal involvement in military affairs ended less happily; Germany's Kaiser Wilhelm II, a great lover of the culture and trappings of militarism, revelled in the title of Supreme War Lord during the First World War, but as the conflict continued it was increasingly his generals who took the decisions. His arch-foe, Tsar Nicholas II, meanwhile, insisted on appointing himself commander-in-chief in 1915 when the war started going badly for Russia, in the mistaken belief it would inspire his troops. The effect was disastrous: the country's military performance went from bad to worse while the Tsar, based at Mogilev, some 370 miles from St Petersburg, failed to grasp the seriousness of the crisis unfolding in the capital.

During the Second World War, it was Léopold III's attempts, in his role as commander-in-chief, to emulate his father's behaviour during the previous conflict that led to his subsequent undoing. Other monarchs played less of a direct role in military affairs, acting as symbols of national resistance in exile – such as Queen Wilhelmina of the Netherlands or King Haakon VII of Norway – or within their country, in the case of the Danish and Swedish monarchs. In Britain too, military strategy was a matter for the government and the generals. The main contribution of George VI – who had served in the Royal Navy during the First World War – and his wife, Elizabeth, was instead his morale-boosting visits to munitions factories and the scenes of bombings as well as to military forces abroad. His daughter, the future Queen Elizabeth II, meanwhile, although only thirteen on the outbreak of war, joined the Women's Auxiliary Territorial Service in 1945, becoming number 230873 Second Subaltern Elizabeth Windsor. Training as a driver and mechanic, she drove a military truck, rising to the rank of junior commander.

When Elizabeth became queen seven years later, she also became nominal head of the armed forces – a position she still occupies. Long-standing constitutional convention, however, has vested de facto executive authority in the office of the prime minister and the cabinet. The Queen nevertheless remains the "ultimate authority" of the military and retains the power to prevent its unconstitutional use.

Europe's other monarchs also remain commander-in-chief, in name if not in practice – with the exception of Sweden: when the constitution was changed in 1975 to strip the king of political power, he also ceased to be titular head of his country's military. He nevertheless remains a four-star general and admiral à la suite in the Swedish army, navy and air force and is by convention the foremost representative of the Swedish armed forces.

In Britain, where the links between royalty and the armed forces are particularly strong, soldiers fight for "Queen (or King) and country", not "prime minister" or "government" and country. It is to the Queen that they swear allegiance, rather than the constitution, which in the case of Britain is anyway a set of laws rather than a single document – and it is the Queen's portrait that hangs on mess-hall walls. The country has a *Royal* Navy and *Royal* Air Force, although strangely not a *Royal* Army – even though many individual regiments have "royal" as part of their name. The defence of the Netherlands, meanwhile, is in the hands of the Koninklijke Landmacht, the Royal Army. Europe's palaces are also home to a disproportionate number of retired army and naval officers, perhaps because they are seen to possess precisely the necessary qualities of obedience, discipline and discretion required for royal service.

Indeed, across Europe the link between royalty and the armed forces remains an enduring one, right down to regimental level. Monarchs and their families have wardrobes full of different military uniforms – whether army, navy or air force – to be worn as the occasion demands. At the last count, Queen Elizabeth was colonel-in-chief of – or held some other formal military position in – some thirty-five British regiments or other formations, as well as a further two dozen in Canada, Australia and New Zealand. The Duke of Edinburgh and their children hold similar positions at several others. Princess Diana became colonel-in-chief of the Princess of Wales Royal Regiment when it was formed in 1992. Since her death five years later, her place as colonel-in-chief has been taken by Queen Margrethe II of Denmark.

Not surprisingly, a spell of military service has traditionally been considered de rigueur for young royals – and this remains the case today in all Europe's royal houses. In Sweden, this goes for the girls too. And so, in March 2003, Crown Princess Victoria, the twenty-five-year-old eldest daughter of King Carl XVI Gustaf, was among a group of forty-two men and women learning combat skills, marksmanship, first aid and chemical-warfare safety as part of their basic military training. Dressed in army fatigues and with camouflage paint on her face, the Crown Princess took time out after a course at the Swedish armed forces' peacekeeping training ground south of Stockholm to meet the press, handling her AK-5 assault rifle with practised ease as she posed for pictures. While some of the other forty students in the course were expected to go on to international assignments in Swedish peacekeeping units, a posting to a foreign war zone was not on the cards for Victoria.

Although obligatory at the time for men, military service in neutral Sweden was optional for women – and only a relatively small number signed up. For Victoria, however, her time at the camp was a highly symbolic part of her preparation for her future role as queen, which had also included stints as an intern at the United Nations in New York and at Swedish foreign-trade offices in Berlin and Paris. It also provided spectacular photographs published by newspapers and magazines across the world.

Crown Princess Mary, the Australian-born wife of Denmark's Crown Prince Frederik, has also been seen to be doing her part for the defence of her adoptive homeland – in 2008 she joined the Danish Home Guard, a volunteer unit of the country's military responsible for domestic security, and after receiving basic training in, among other things, weapon use, she was awarded the rank of lieutenant in February of the following year.

While such involvement was largely symbolic, the forces have continued to play a more significant part in the life of the current male heirs to the throne. After leaving school, Frederik served in the regiment of the Royal Life Guards and then, in 1988, joined the Royal Hussars as a First Lieutenant. After graduating he returned to the Danish military in 1995, this time to the navy, where he was chosen from among three hundred applicants to become a member of the elite Frømandskorpset unit, the Royal Frogmen Corps, modelled on America's Navy Seals and Britain's Special Boat Service.

The three-year training course, centred on the unit's base in a village an hour's drive outside Copenhagen, is legendary for its toughness. Among the various tests of physical fitness on both land and water, aspiring Frogmen must be able to run one and a half miles in hilly terrain in full uniform with boots and gun in less than eleven minutes – Frederik managed it with seven seconds to spare – and swim six miles in open sea and fifty yards with hands and feet bound. "The whole time they think up imaginative ways of punishing people," said Jesper Lundorf, the Crown Prince's secret-service protection officer, who did the course alongside Frederik.[4] One of the greatest challenges recruits face during their training is "Hell Week", when they are dropped in small groups with an inflatable boat into the water. After weighing down the boat and hiding it underwater, they must then survive in an exercise designed to simulate life behind enemy lines. The week also includes a seventy-five-mile march.

Although Europe's other heirs to the throne have not submitted themselves to quite such a gruelling schedule, they have also earned their stripes in the military. Following in the footsteps of his father, grandfather and two of his great-grandfathers, Prince Charles joined the navy after graduating from Cambridge University, and qualified as a helicopter pilot before becoming a member of 845 Naval Air Squadron, which operated from the commando-carrier HMS *Hermes*. Two years later he took command of the coastal mine-hunter HMS *Bronington* for the last nine months of his naval career.

Belgium's Prince Philippe rounded off his secondary education with a spell at the Royal Military Academy, before qualifying as a fighter pilot and a paratrooper. Willem-Alexander, the Dutch crown prince, also gained his military pilot's licence. Spain's Prince Felipe is a qualified helicopter pilot, while Norway's Crown Prince Haakon spent a year aboard missile torpedo boats and other vessels of the Royal Norwegian Navy.

The absence of war in Western Europe for over six decades has helped ensure that none of those mentioned above have been involved in anything more dangerous than exercises. Prince Andrew, the second son of Queen Elizabeth II, is the exception: he served for twenty-two years in the Royal Navy, and when Britain set out to reclaim the Falkland Islands from Argentina in 1982, the Prince was a member of the task force.

The question of how much danger members of the royal family can be exposed to still remains a sensitive one, especially in Britain, which in the years since the Falklands has been involved in a number of military interventions and peacekeeping missions ranging from Bosnia and Kosovo to Afghanistan and Iraq. While Andrew has long since returned to civilian life, his nephews William and Harry are both serving officers.

It was initially planned to send Harry to Iraq but, much to the young Prince's frustration, General Sir Richard Dannatt, head of the British army, announced in May 2007 that it would be too risky, as it would turn the Prince and his comrades-in-arms in the Household Cavalry into too much of a target for insurgents. Deeply disappointed, Harry considered leaving, but agreed to stay on to retrain as a battlefield air controller. Several months later a plan was hatched: the Prince would be sent to Afghanistan, but in conditions of absolute secrecy. In an extraordinary arrangement, the editors of Britain's major newspapers and broadcasting organizations were told of the plan but signed an agreement to maintain a news blackout. It was the Queen who told Harry of his mission.

That December, the Prince, who had just turned twenty-three, was deployed to Helmand, spending time at bases deep in a Taliban-infiltrated area in the far south of the province. Although his work meant he was in regular radio contact with pilots from several countries, they knew him only by his call sign. Then, after just over two months, his secret posting was revealed in two little-noticed articles in an Australian magazine. On 28th February the Drudge Report, the American website best known for revealing Bill Clinton's relationship with Monica Lewinsky, broke the news to the world. Harry was immediately recalled to Britain for his own safety.

Despite its abrupt ending, the Prince's posting appeared to have been a success, especially in the way it allowed him to serve alongside other officers. "It's very nice to be a normal person for once," he declared in a television interview that was recorded in Afghanistan and broadcast after his cover was blown. "I think this is about as normal as I'm ever going to get."[5]

This desire, on the part not just of Harry but of the army, for him to be treated as much as possible like an ordinary officer is a familiar one. But it is difficult to achieve, because princes will often have official royal duties that they will have to discharge while in the service. Various aspects of Harry's and his elder brother William's military service have brought this into sharp relief. In the early years, commentators questioned how the party-loving pair, although supposedly full-time officers, were able to spend so much time on the dance floors of fashionable London clubs. Further embarrassment came after it emerged that William used a Royal Air Force helicopter on which he was training in April 2008 to pick up his brother in London and then fly to the Isle of Wight to attend a stag party for his cousin, Peter Phillips. Nor was this an isolated incident: William reportedly made use of other training flights at the time to practise landings in a field owned by the parents of his future wife, Kate Middleton, to attend a wedding in Northumberland and to fly over Highgrove, his father's estate.

The Ministry of Defence initially justified William's flight to the stag party as an exercise that "tested his new skills to the limit". This was not the whole story, however. Republic, a republican pressure group, used the Freedom of Information of Act to demand the release of internal documents to get to the truth. Not only had the nine training flights cost taxpayers £86,434, it also emerged that the Prince's station commander had not been told about the "true nature" of the flights and would certainly not have approved the one to the Isle of Wight if he had known. Several senior officers were taken to task over the affair – as was William himself.

Military helicopters were a sensitive issue at the time, because of the acute shortage of them being suffered by the armed forces fighting in Afghanistan. What looked to have been a deliberate attempt to cover up the incident only added to the embarrassment both for the royal family and the government.

Chapter 5

Pomp, Circumstance and Paying the Bills

At first sight she could have been any elderly lady heading out of London for her Christmas holidays. Dressed in a long grey coat, with a bunch of flowers in one hand and a Hermès scarf tied firmly over her head, Queen Elizabeth II walked down platform 11b of King's Cross station. After boarding the 10.45 First Capital Connect train to King's Lynn in Norfolk, she took her seat in a first-class carriage next to a middle-aged man with closely cropped hair who was dressed in a smart suit.

The photographs, which appeared in the press in December 2009, did not tell the whole story. A few minutes before the Queen had arrived at the station, one of Britain's busiest, the platform had been cleared and swept by security men. And, rather than mingling with other passengers, Elizabeth was seated in an eight-seat section at the back of the carriage. The man beside her was a plain-clothes royal-protection officer; his four colleagues standing by the door of the compartment turned away any other passengers who tried to join her. Then, at 12.20, when the train arrived at its destination a hundred miles to the north, the Queen was whisked away by a waiting Range Rover to Sandringham House, where she and her family traditionally spend the Christmas holidays. Yet the point had been made – and was rewarded with approving headlines that will have brought cheer to Buckingham Palace and its spin doctors. As one newspaper pointed out, the Queen could have chosen instead to make the journey by the royal train – which costs taxpayers £57,142 each time it is used. In comparison, the regular first-class tickets cost £44.40 each for the monarch and members of her entourage.[1]

However unusual the image, it was not the first occasion on which the Queen had taken public transport. A spokesman for the palace said members of the royal family frequently use scheduled train services when security allows. The difference this time was that the press had been tipped off in advance.

In Britain, as in the rest of Europe, the cost of maintaining the monarchy is a complicated and highly emotive issue. In medieval times the monarchy and state were indistinguishable from one another: the king received revenue from taxes, but this had to pay for the workings of the government and for fighting wars – as well as fund his own court. The country was like a family-run firm, and the treasury was what its name suggested: the chest that contained the king's personal wealth.

A medieval monarch would demonstrate his power in part through the splendour of his court. By wearing finer clothes or owning more luxurious palaces than those of rival rulers, he was not merely indulging himself or even showing off on a personal level. He was also showing off on behalf of his nation. When Henry VIII of England and King François of France met near Calais in 1520, both monarchs tried to outshine each other with the magnificence of their tents, clothes, feasts, music and games. Such was the splendour of the occasion that their meeting place became known thereafter as Le Camp du Drap d'Or – the Field of the Cloth of Gold.

Such traditions of conspicuous consumption are still maintained by the ruling families of the Gulf states; visitors to Muscat, the capital of Oman, will see the Sultan's splendid five-hundred-foot yacht – large enough to accommodate a fifty-piece orchestra – anchored conspicuously off the Corniche. Yet different rules apply to constitutional monarchs, whose economic power has dwindled over the centuries along with their political influence.

The modern-day European monarch has much in common with a civil servant: in return for the duties outlined in the preceding chapters, he or she is paid a fixed sum each year from the public purse. Yet this is clearly a civil servant with a difference. For a start, the amount paid, variously described as a "civil list" or an apanage, is, in most cases, several times higher than that received by the prime minister or any other public figure – even though it may be dwarfed by the sums earned by the more successful banker.

Nor does it stop there: in most cases, there are also allowances for the monarch's spouse, children and, in the British case, even cousins. Typically there are several palaces and other residences that need maintaining – and staffing – as well, perhaps, as a royal yacht, train or plane.

Blurring the picture, monarchs can also rely on vast personal wealth, accumulated over the centuries; such fortunes usually have their origins in military conquests or other confiscations, but have grown in recent years thanks to successful investments. Special tax concessions, especially on inheritance, have also helped.

Writing in the middle of the nineteenth century, Walter Bagehot contrasted the relatively modest nature of Queen Victoria's court with the splendour of Napoleon III of France's surroundings. "Refined and original observers," he said, believed that "there are arguments for not having a court and there are arguments for having a splendid court, but there are no arguments for having a mean court. It is better to spend a million in dazzling when you wish to dazzle, than three quarters of a million in trying to dazzle and yet not dazzle." Yet while conceding this argument might hold true for Napoleon's realm, Bagehot was not sure how appropriate it was for his own country. If the British court were to be as lavish as its French counterpart, he warned, "it would do evil if it added a new example to our many examples of showy wealth – if it gave the sanction of its dignity to the race of expenditure."[2]

In today's more egalitarian, meritocratic age, public opinion has shifted further in Bagehot's direction: we are much more likely to disapprove of such displays of royal wealth, which, although acceptable among film stars or footballers, are less easy to stomach when indulged in by those who have inherited rather than earned their fortunes. There are limits, however: while some may grumble at the sight of some or other act of royal extravagance, few – at least among those who support the idea of monarchy – would want to see their king or queen living in a modest home, travelling regularly by bus or train or dressed in high-street clothes.

But how wealthy are Europe's royal families? How much are they paid – and, indeed, how much *should* they be paid – and how lavish should their court be? The answers have varied from country to country.

Sandringham, the estate to which Queen Elizabeth II was heading on that December day, is one of a series of residences that the monarch occupies at different times of the year. Home to four generations of sovereigns since 1862, it is here, close to the north Norfolk coast, that Elizabeth and her family traditionally spend the period from the Christmas holidays until February. In August and September, by contrast, their home is Balmoral Castle – a property beloved of Queen Victoria and Prince Albert, which lies on a 17,400-acre estate in the Scottish Highlands. Both are the private property of the royal family.

And then there are the official residences. Windsor Castle, west of London, the largest occupied castle in the world and a royal home and fortress for more than nine hundred years, is usually used by the Queen at weekends and is her official residence for a month over Easter and again for a week in June, when she attends the service of the Order of the Garter and the Royal Ascot race meeting.

The most famous royal residence of them all – and indeed in the world – is Buckingham Palace, a massive structure 335 foot wide, with 775 rooms and almost 830,000 square feet of floor space. Bought by George III in 1761 for £21,000 as a private retreat, it was only in 1837 on the accession of Queen Victoria that it became the principal royal residence. Very much a working building, it has since become firmly established as the centrepiece of Britain's constitutional monarchy. There are a series of other palaces too, among them Clarence House, the former London home of the late Queen Elizabeth the Queen Mother, which provides an official residence for the Prince of Wales, the Duchess of Cornwall and Princes William and Harry.

Despite the obvious scale of the palaces, life within them cannot always be described as opulent. The Buckingham Palace into which the future Queen Elizabeth and her younger sister Margaret moved in 1937 after their father became king was a curious mixture of luxury and decrepitude. As Marion Crawford, the girls' governess found, the upper floors had been little changed since Victoria's days. Shortly after they arrived, Crawford – or "Crawfie" as she became known – recalled sitting down for tea on a pink-and-gold chair in the magnificent Belgian Suite, only for it to dissolve beneath her with an ominous splitting sound. The chair, it seemed, had not been recaned. The first night that the housemaid came to pull down her bedroom curtains, the whole thing – curtains, pelmet and heavy brass rods – came down with a clatter, narrowly missing their heads. In a nod to modernity, electric light had recently been installed, but the switch to operate the bedroom light was two yards away down the corridor.

And then there were the mice. Crawford described a meeting with the vermin man, who offered her his secret weapon for her bedroom: the so-called sticky trap, a piece of cardboard with a lump of aniseed in the middle surrounded by a sea of treacle. Crawford declined. "People think that a royal palace is the last word in up-to-date luxury, replete with everything the heart could desire, and that people who live there do so in absolute comfort," she recalled later. "Nothing could be further from the truth. Life in a palace rather resembles camping in a museum. These historic places are so old, so tied up with tradition, that they are mostly dropping to bits, all the equipment there decades behind the times."[3]

Life at Buckingham Palace became considerably grimmer during the Second World War as the royal family made a great show of sharing rationing and other privations endured by their subjects. Hot water was available for only a few hours a day, and black lines were painted on the side of all the royal bathtubs to indicate the five inches of water allowed. President Franklin D. Roosevelt's wife Eleanor, who stayed there for two days in 1943, was struck by how tough life was: she was allocated the Queen's bedroom; it was cold and draughty, with wind whistling through the bombed-out windows, while the fishcakes offered for dinner were of poor quality. Roosevelt's hosts may have been exaggerating the hardship they were suffering for dramatic effect: the royal family's rations were, in reality, bolstered by the large numbers of deer, pheasants, grouse and rabbits caught on the royal estates. One member of the staff at Balmoral recalled eating so much venison during rationing, "it's a wonder we didn't grow antlers".[4]

Buckingham Palace has been considerably updated in the decades since, largely thanks to Prince Philip. After his wife became queen in 1952, Philip had wanted them to remain living in Clarence House. The palace, recalled Mike Parker, Philip's private secretary, "seemed to him the coldest and most unfriendly place to raise a young family and the Queen quite agreed. She was delighted with the idea."[5] Winston Churchill, the prime minister, was opposed, insisting that Buckingham Palace was the centre of empire and this was where the royal family should live. Philip was forced to back down, but in the years that followed he devoted considerable energies to making it a more modern and comfortable place.

Various insights into the day-to-day reality of royal life in the decades since have been provided by latter-day "Crawfies", the various servants or royal hangers-on who have attempted to cash in on their connections, or from the occasional tabloid stunt. In 2003 for example, an undercover reporter from the *Daily Mirror* spent two months working as a footman at Buckingham Palace, taking photographs of royal bedrooms and other private areas which revealed a rather dubious royal taste in interior design, as well as some curious insights, such as that the royal cornflakes and porridge oats are put on the breakfast table in Tupperware containers. Further amusement was provided for the press a few years later by the publication of a photograph of an old white plastic tray on which, it was claimed, the Queen's breakfast of tea, white toast, butter and jam is brought to her bedroom every morning at eight o'clock.[6]

The conclusion is obvious: despite the Queen's vast wealth, her lifestyle has little in common with that of a Russian oligarch or a Hollywood star. She and Prince Philip instead exhibit the kind of parsimony traditional to the British upper classes, who think nothing of sitting down on a broken chair or wearing a worn jacket. Philip, for example, seems quite happy to be seen in public in trousers more than fifty years old – albeit taken in by his tailor to reflect current fashion – or a Royal Naval uniform, vintage 1947. It is merely important that such items, however old, should have been of good quality to start with. "Counter-intuitive as it may seem, and notwithstanding the vast excesses of luxury into which they were haplessly born, the Queen and her kind specialize in a kind of inconspicuous non-consumption," commented one observer. "Understand this, and everything else about the Queen makes perfect sense."[7]

Such thrift does not extend to the size of the royal staff, however – a legacy of the past when servants were cheap. In all, the royal household comes to 1,200. A glimpse of the scale of Prince Charles's entourage was provided by evidence at the trial in 2002 of Paul Burrell, long-serving butler to Princess Diana, on charges of theft – which then collapsed. The heir to the British throne, it emerged, had a team of four valets so that one is always available to lay out and pick up his clothes, a servant to squeeze his toothpaste onto his brush, and another who once held the specimen bottle while the Prince gave a urine sample after he broke his arm. Such revelations were acutely embarrassing at a time when the royal family was trying to present itself as reinvented, modernized and scaled down. Even Queen Elizabeth was said to have been appalled at the degree of Charles's profligacy, reportedly believing the "amount of kit and servants he takes around is grotesque".[8] The Queen might be better off looking to her own household: the previous Christmas, during separate trips to Sandringham, Charles took three butlers and four cooks, while his mother brought along eleven butlers and twelve chefs.

More embarrassment for Prince Charles came from a book on royalty by Jeremy Paxman, a well-known BBC current-affairs presenter, published in 2006, which claimed the heir to the throne was so fussy about the boiled egg he eats after a day's hunting that his staff cooks seven and has them arranged in a row, in increasing order of hardness, so if one proves too runny, he can choose the next one along.[9] Clarence House usually refuses to comment on what it considers "personal matters". This particular accusation of profligacy must have hit home, however: within hours of the allegation appearing in a newspaper serialization of the book, a spokeswoman for the prince declared, "The story about lots of eggs being boiled is not true."[10]

Living on such a scale – even if eating only one boiled egg at a time – costs a lot of money, which means the financing of the monarchy both in Britain and elsewhere in Europe is a complex and often controversial issue that over the course of the years has regularly been tied up with broader political questions.

In Britain, whose monarchy is by far the costliest to maintain in Europe, the publication of the royal accounts every June is typically accompanied by pronouncements by palace officials of the good value that the institution represents. The year 2011 was no exception: the cost of maintaining the Queen and the rest of the royal family in the year up to that April had fallen by £1.8 million to £32.1 million – a total cost of 51p per person, down 3p from the previous year, it was announced. "The Queen is very keen that the royal household should continue to reduce its expenditure in line with public-expenditure reductions," declared Sir Alan Reid, keeper of the privy purse,[11] though there were limits to what more was possible after a nineteen-per-cent fall in expenditure in real terms over five years. There was a difference, however: the release of the figures coincided with the drawing up of a new formula that would change fundamentally the way in which the monarchy is financed.

For the past two and half centuries, the main element of royal financing has been the Civil List, which is intended to cover expenditure related to the Queen's duties as head of state. About seventy per cent of this is spent on staff salaries, although it also meets the cost of official functions such as garden parties, receptions and entertainment during state visits. Its origins lie in a deal done by George III on his accession to the throne in 1760. The King agreed to surrender the considerable revenues from the Crown Estates – vast royal landholdings dating back to 1066 that still today include Regent Street and large parts of St James's in central London, as well as forest, farmland and half the foreshore – and to receive in return a flat fee of £800,000 a year for the duration of his reign. (Any money that the Estates earned beyond that was to go to parliament.) Unlike today, the Civil List was not purely for the King's own expenditure: he also had to use it to fund the civil, but not military activities of the state – hence the name.[12]

The arrangement became increasingly unworkable during the late eighteenth and early nineteenth centuries, as Britain turned into a world power and the size of the state and scope of its activities grew. Rather than simply increase the Civil List – and with it the economic clout of the monarchy – parliament began to fund an increasing share of expenditure directly itself. In 1830, when William IV acceded to the throne, this process reached a logical conclusion: a new reduced Civil List was introduced, allotted purely for the benefit of "the dignity and state of the Crown and the personal comfort of Their Majesties".[13] The government's civil expenditure, like the money it spent on the military, would henceforth be financed by parliament.

Over the years since, British monarchs have done well out of the Civil List – while all the while pleading poverty. Queen Victoria's German-born husband, Prince Albert, who always felt himself especially badly done by, led the way in the early 1850s, calling for a more than doubling of his £30,000 annuity to £80,000 to pay for "the ordinary establishments and pursuits of an English gentleman". These he listed as "a hunting establishment, a pack of hounds, a breeding stud, shooting establishment, a moor or forest in the Highlands of Scotland, a farm, etc. etc. etc.".[14]

Yet at the same time Albert and Victoria had managed to buy Osborne House, a substantial property on the Isle of Wight, in 1845. The initial cost was £45,000, but the total bill, once they had rebuilt the place in Italian Renaissance style, came to £200,000.[15] Then, in 1852, the royal couple found the £31,500 necessary to buy the freehold on Balmoral. After Albert's death in 1861, Sandringham was purchased for their son, the future Edward VII, in the vain hope it would encourage him to spend more time away from his unsuitable London friends.

And so it went on: when Edward came to the throne in 1901 he was deeply in debt after years of lavish living; when he died nine years later, he left £2 million – the equivalent of about £150 million today – in his will, thanks to all the money he had managed to set aside over the years out of the Civil List. His son, George V, saved a net £487,000 during his quarter of a century on the throne.[16] This did not prevent Sir Frederick Ponsonby, the keeper of the King's privy purse, in 1920, at a time when the post-war boom was turning to bust, from asking for an increase of at least £103,000 in the Civil List from the £470,000 at which it had been fixed a decade earlier. In trying to make the case for royal penury, Ponsonby conjured up the rather fanciful image of "the King going to open parliament in a taxicab". The request was declined. The Treasury instead initiated a study of the expenditure of the royal household, recommending a series of economies that saved £40,000 a year.

Such a build-up of wealth has been facilitated by the extraordinarily favourable tax status enjoyed not just by British monarchs but also by the extended royal family over the years. When income tax was introduced for the first time in peacetime in 1842, Sir Robert Peel, the prime minister, made great play of Queen Victoria "volunteering" to pay it on her income, including on the bulk of her £385,000 Civil List. Yet from 1910 onwards, even as the general income-tax burden on the rest of the population grew, so the royals were progressively freed of tax.

That changed as a result of 1992, the present Queen's "*annus horribilis*", which saw the marriages of three of her four children fail very publicly, followed by controversy over who – the royal family or the government – should fund the £37 million bill for repairing the damage to Windsor Castle caused by a massive fire. With the royal family's popularity plunging, John Major, the prime minister, announced in February 1993 that the Queen had "voluntarily" decided to pay income, capital-gains and inheritance taxes on her personal income and wealth, starting from the start of the next tax year that April.

Yet the Queen was not quite subjecting herself or her family to the same rules as her subjects. For a start, the Civil List would not be taxed, as it had been under Victoria, on the grounds that it was used to cover official expenses. Furthermore, "special arrangements" would be made to exempt the royal palaces and certain other assets from inheritance tax when they pass directly to her successor – presumably Prince Charles.

Quite how much tax the Queen would have to pay depended on how wealthy she was, which palace officials were understandably reluctant to reveal. At a press conference, Lord Airlie, the Lord Chamberlain and head of the Queen's household, nevertheless tried to downplay the extent of her wealth, saying that the monarch had authorized him to describe estimates of £100 million as "grossly overstated". Some experts estimated the value of the Queen's private investments at roughly £75 million, which, provided that she was earning a reasonable rate of return on her money, would have equated to between £1.5 and £3 million a year in tax.

As part of the package of reforms it was also agreed that henceforth only the Queen, Prince Philip and the Queen Mother would benefit from the Civil List. This left the question of the more than £1 million a year in allowances paid not only to the Queen's three younger children, Anne, Andrew and Edward, but also – in a unique feature of British royal financing – to her cousins, the Duke and Duchess of Gloucester, the Duke and Duchess of Kent and Princess Alexandra. It was decided they would continue to be paid, but the Queen would then give an equivalent sum back to the Treasury out of income she earned from the Duchy of Lancaster, a portfolio of 46,209 acres of farmland, urban developments and historic buildings across England and Wales.[17]

It was in this climate that Elizabeth suffered what was one of the most symbolic blows to her prestige – the loss of the Royal Yacht. In a reflection of its seafaring past, Britain has a long tradition of such vessels. *Britannia*, built in Clydebank in Scotland and launched in April 1953 by the young Queen, was the eighty-third such yacht since the Restoration of King Charles II in 1660. By the late 1990s, however, the yacht was badly in need of replacement: while Major's Conservatives vowed, after some hesitation, to replace it, Tony Blair's Labour Party was opposed, claiming that the £60 million it would cost could be better spent elsewhere. When Blair won the May 1997 general election, *Britannia*'s fate was sealed. The yacht was decommissioned that December and moored in Leith, Edinburgh, where it was turned into a tourist attraction and luxurious venue for corporate events. The move, the former prime minister was later to lament, was "such a mistake".

In the years that followed there were proposals for the construction of a new royal yacht, financed perhaps through a loan or the Queen's own money, but they made no headway. Then, in January 2012, in the run-up to her Diamond Jubilee, Michael Gove, the monarchist education secretary, suggested a replacement as an "excellent" way of thanking the Queen "for her long and untiring service to this country" – although how to raise the money to build it was not clear. Cameron described the proposal as a "truly inspirational initiative" but made clear that the government would not finance it at a time when public spending was being cut.[18] This left open the possibility of public donation – anathema to many, especially on the left – or that it should be paid for by big business. But then there was the question of how to fund its upkeep and running costs.

Although deprived of her yacht, the Queen still has use of aircraft from No. 32 (The Royal) Squadron, based at RAF Northolt, northwest of London, and of a Sikorsky S-76 C+ helicopter operated by the royal household from Blackbushe Airfield in Hampshire. And there is the Royal Train, a pair of two special diesel locomotives that can pull up to eight royal carriages, including sleeping, dining and support cars, all painted in a distinctive maroon with red-and-black coach lining and a grey roof.

Traditionally the Civil List was revised every ten years – which would have meant an increase in 2000. Unusually, it was left unchanged by Blair. The previous settlement of £7.9 million a year, set a decade earlier, had turned out to have been too generous, as inflation had been below the predicted 7.5 per cent a year, leaving the palace with a massive surplus of £35 million by the beginning of the new millennium, which was only gradually eaten away over the following years as expenditure rose.

As 2010 approached, palace officials began again lobbying behind the scenes for an increase in the Civil List, on the grounds that the £7.9 million, adjusted for inflation, was worth only a quarter of what it had been twenty years earlier. On the other hand, the Civil List Reserve, although much depleted, still amounted to more than £20 million. Aides, meanwhile, were calling for an increase in the grant-in-aid that covers the maintenance of Buckingham Palace and the other royal residences. These buildings, it was claimed, were in a poor state, as demonstrated by an incident in 2007 when Princess Anne narrowly avoided being hit by a piece of loose masonry that fell off the roof. The palace's staterooms, where the Queen entertains foreign leaders, hadn't been redecorated since 1952 and were also said to be in urgent need of repair. A palace audit in 2009 put the cost of meeting the backlog of repairs at £40 million.

The economic climate was not a good one for the Queen or anyone else to demand a pay rise, however. After becoming prime minister in 2010, David Cameron was committed to cutting the deficit, and so when his government unveiled its budget the following month, it was announced that the Queen, like many of her subjects, would have to accept a pay freeze – and continue to dip into the Reserve, which contained enough money to keep her going through 2012, the Diamond Jubilee year.

In the meantime, George Osborne, the chancellor of the Exchequer, was working on a more radical solution. From April 2013, it was announced, the Civil List would be combined with the various other payments made to the monarch covering the cost of building and travel into a single payment, to be known as the Sovereign Grant. This would be set at the equivalent of fifteen per cent of the profits of the Crown Estate, which reached £210.7 million in 2010 – thereby restoring the link between the monarch's income and the revenue from her traditional lands that was broken more than two hundred and fifty years ago.

If such a formula had been in place in 2010, the Queen would have received £31.6 million, slightly more than the £30 million she was actually paid. Critics also pointed out that Crown Estate's profits were expected to grow substantially thanks to a planned expansion of wind farms on its coastal land. Faced with an outcry over this potential windfall for the monarchy at a time when everyone else was being forced to live more frugally, the government swiftly announced that a cap would be imposed on the formula.

In the event, the net effect in the short term was expected to be a slight decline – rather than rise – in royal income; an official Treasury briefing document deposited in the House of Commons Library for the second reading of the Sovereign Grant Bill warned that the levels of support provided under the new system would, in real terms, in the early years be "below what the royal household spent in every one of the last twenty years", indicating that the Queen could not expect a rise in her real pay until April 2015 at the earliest.[19]

Under the new formula, it is also expected that for the first time Elizabeth will be forced to lay her account books before parliament to promote "clear accountability" and "strengthen public confidence". Whether such scrutiny will lead, in turn, to a reduction in the main item of expenditure, namely the vast number of staff employed to look after the Queen and her family, remains to be seen.

Prince Charles, as the heir to the throne, does not receive an allowance from the Civil List as such, but like previous princes of Wales before him he is funded by income from the Duchy of Cornwall, a predominantly agricultural estate of 134,724 acres that has been passed down the generations since it was created in 1337 by Edward III for his son and heir, Prince Edward, the Black Prince. Part of the income finances Charles's public and charitable work, while the remainder goes on meeting his costs and those of his wife Camilla and Princes William and Harry. Bills run up by the Prince while carrying out his official duties are also reimbursed out of the grants-in-aid.

In 2010, following repeated criticism of Charles's spendthrift ways, it was reported that he too had been cutting back, with his total official expenditure, including that which he funds himself, down by fourteen per cent to £10.72 million. The British press were amused to note that the Prince slashed £275,000 from his entertainment bill by feeding his 9,396 official visitors with finger buffets rather than banquets.

Such cost-cutting was all relative, however. The £17.1 million salary the Prince pocketed from the Duchy was four per cent higher than the previous year. The annual report from Duchy of Cornwall, published a few days after the royal pay freeze, revealed that while the monarch appeared to have been tightening her belt and cutting back on staff, her son had been hiring extra housekeepers, valets and gardeners. By

2010 his official household stood at 125, a sharp rise from ninety-four five years earlier.

The Prince's income rose even further in 2011, with the proceeds from the Duchy of Cornwall up by almost another four per cent to £17.8 million and the amount he was paid from grants-in-aid increasing by £298,000 to £1.96 million. The size of his household, too, grew – to 132 – after he took on five new aides, three of them to work for Princes William and Harry.[20]

A major omission from British royal accounts is the cost of security provided by the police and the army and ceremonial duties performed by the armed forces, which, although not officially disclosed, has been estimated at more than £100 million a year. Republic, an anti-monarchy group, has put the true cost of maintaining the Queen and her extended family at as much as £200 million a year – if you add not just security costs but also the loss to the public purse of revenue as a result of royal ownership of the Duchies of Lancaster and Cornwall and various other property enterprises.[21]

Provision of a royal yacht was one of the conditions set out by Prince Carl of Denmark when he agreed to become King Haakon VII of Norway of 1905. Also essential for the modern monarch, he felt, were a palace and a country house. The new king got his palace – albeit a relatively modest nineteenth-century one in the centre of town. He and his successors have also had use of the summer palace of Oscarshall, located on the peninsula of Bygdøy in Oslo, and the Bygdø Royal Manor nearby. There is also Skaugum, an estate fifteen miles south-west of the capital, which has been passed to subsequent crown princes since Haakon's son, the future King Olav, moved in after his wedding in 1929.

Haakon did not push for his yacht, though – and it was not until more than forty years later that a national appeal was launched to raise money to buy him one to express gratitude for his heroic resistance to the Nazis during the Second World War. Built in 1937 in Gosport, Hampshire for Sir Thomas Sopwith, the aviation pioneer, the yacht, *Philante*, measures just over 260 feet and was one of the largest vessels of its type. Extensively refitted and renamed KS *Norge*, it has been used by Haakon, his son and his grandson, although major repairs were needed in 1985 after it caught fire while being worked on at the navy shipyard in Horten. A Royal Decree of 1947, the year the ship was acquired, provides that it shall be manned, operated and maintained by the nation's defence forces – a substantial expense given that it has a crew of more than fifty when it is used by the King and his family from May until late September each year.

Haakon's reluctance to press his demand for a yacht is typical of the modesty that has always characterized the Norwegian monarchy – making it in many respects the polar opposite of its British equivalent. While the British monarchy has evolved over the centuries, the Norwegians, ruled first by Danes and then in a union with Sweden, were free to create their own modern version from scratch in 1905. The result has been a kind of stripped-down "monarchy-lite", which remains true to its modest origins even today, when Norway's vast oil and gas reserves have turned the country into one of the wealthiest in Europe.

Since the Second World War the Norwegians have been without the royal stables and carriages that are such an important part of British royal ceremonial. For special occasions they have a black 1939 Cadillac – which the royal drivers are wary of because of its unreliability – and an open-back Lincoln Continental dating from the 1960s. Most of the time, King Harald makes do with a Lexus instead or, when travelling abroad, uses the Airport Express. For longer journeys, though, they do have a set of royal carriages maintained by Norwegian State Railways. There is a throne, but it is brought out only once a year for the opening of parliament and remains for the rest of the time in a closet next to the office of the vice-speaker.

Harald, the current monarch, seems happy with such a low-key style: "The King is very much a middle-class chap," says Carl-Erik Grimstad, a former court official turned writer and critic. "He has a nice country house, he has got middle-class friends, he's into musicals and likes to watch sport – any sport."[22] He is also a keen yachtsman. The Queen, by contrast, is more interested in modern art.

Annemor Møst, a veteran Norwegian royal reporter who has been watching her country's royal family since the late 1950s, is also struck by the King's lack of airs. "He's a very nice person, intelligent and with a sense of humour," she says. "He takes his work very seriously, but not himself very seriously."[23]

The Swedish and Danish monarchies share something of this Norwegian simplicity. The Swedes make great play of the fact that King

Carl XVI Gustaf drives himself from home to work every morning like an ordinary subject. The only difference is that his office is located in a magnificent eighteenth-century baroque royal palace. The Danes also put the emphasis on informality: alongside her official duties, Queen Margrethe II is a gifted artist whose various endeavours have included designing sets for theatre and film. Her special interest is découpage – a technique of making images from photographs cut out from magazines.

While working on a version of Hans Christian Andersen's 'The Wild Swans', released in 2009, the Queen regularly joined Jacob Jørgensen, the head of JJ Film, and his team at their studio in Valby, in the suburbs of Copenhagen, to work on the project. A heavy smoker, she was often spotted popping outside for a cigarette. However informal her behaviour, no one ever forgot she was the Queen: when her colleagues addressed her, it was not as "Margrethe" but as "Your Majesty". The Queen's eldest son Crown Prince Frederik and his Australian-born wife Crown Princess Mary have tried to cultivate the image of a modern couple having a normal life in which they raise their own children – inspired, in part, by Mary's own middle-class upbringing in Tasmania. Yet they reportedly employ twenty-five staff including maids, nannies for their three children, private secretaries, footmen and Mary's *hofdame* (lady-in-waiting), Caroline Heering.

When it comes to residences, both the Danish and Swedish royal families are well supplied: Margrethe has a string of palaces between which she and her family, like their British compeers, move according to a long-established ritual. Thus winters are spent at Amalienborg, spring and autumn in Fredensborg and the summer at Marselisborg or Graasten. The palaces were historically the property of the royal house, but following the introduction of the 1849 constitution they passed to the state.

The Queen and her consort, Prince Henrik, also have a home in his native France, Château de Caïx, near the latter's family estate of Cayrou. Since buying the property in 1974, the royal couple have carried out an extensive renovation of the house, which has been rebuilt several times since the fourteenth century. It is to this residence, overlooking a curve in the River Lot, that they traditionally repair in summer and also where they used to host an informal press conference each August – until the practice was halted, without explanation, in 2009.

For Henrik, it is a chance to spend time not just relaxing but also indulging his passion for wine-making – the chateau's website even contains a poem that the Prince, an artistic soul, has composed about his vineyards:

Cahors de Cœur
Des vins seigneurs
Du Lot la fleur
De Cayx l'honneur.

Beloved Cahors
Lord of wines
Flower of the Lot
Honour of Cayx.

The wine is not just for royal consumption. Just as Prince Charles has turned his passion for organic farming into a food business, so Henrik markets his wines – all marked clearly with a Danish crown and large H, lest anyone be in doubt of their royal origins. One is known as "La Royale", the other as "Le Rosé du Prince de Danemark". There is also a shop and the chance for visitors to tour the estate.

Critics in the Danish media have not been impressed. Figures published in January 2009 that cast doubt on the profitability of the Prince's wine-making operations were seized on by *Ekstra Bladet*, an anti-royal tabloid, which complained the whole operation was kept afloat only with subsidies from the Queen – and so, effectively, from the country's taxpayers. "Henrik must be thanking his wife and her position as Denmark's head of state with an associated salary that he can live a life that none of the other growers in the region can match," it claimed. The newspaper also noted how the Amalienborg Palace effectively propped up Henrik's venture by being a major buyer of his wines, which are often on the table at official dinners.[24]

Sweden has no fewer than eleven royal palaces, although the King and Queen use only two: Drottningholm Palace, dating from the seventeenth century, west of Stockholm, where they live in rooms in the southern wing; and the six-hundred-room Royal Palace, on Stadsholmen (City Island), in Gamla Stan, the old town of the capital, which remains their official residence and the place where they work and official receptions are held. Even these two are open to the public. Since their marriage in June 2010, Crown Princess Victoria and Prince Daniel have moved into Haga Palace, just outside Stockholm. Once home to Victoria's grandparents – and the place where her father was born – it was used as a government guest house for foreign dignitaries from the mid-1960s and then restored for her and Daniel at a cost of more than 40 million kronor (£3.7 million).

Officially, Queen Beatrix of the Netherlands has three palaces: Noordeinde Palace and Huis ten Bosch Palace, both in The Hague, and the Royal Palace in Amsterdam. All three, though, belong not to the Queen but to the state and, as the official jargon puts it, "have been placed at her disposal by Act of Parliament". King Albert II of Belgium makes do with just two: his official residence, the Palais Royal, in the centre of Brussels, and the eighteenth-century Château de Laeken, which has been home to Belgian monarchs since the time of Léopold I.

Although the Spanish monarchy is almost Scandinavian in its modesty, the country has the largest royal palace in Europe – a throwback to the glorious past of the Borbóns. Built from 1738 until 1755 and first occupied by Carlos III in 1764, the Palacio Real de Madrid, in the western part of the city centre, has more than 2,800 rooms and a combined floor area of 1.5 million square foot. But although deemed the official residence, it is used only for state ceremonies.

Juan Carlos and his family have lived instead since 1962 in the more modest Palacio de la Zarzuela, built in the seventeenth century as a hunting lodge. For symbolic reasons they refused after the death of Francisco Franco in 1975 to move into El Pardo Palace, where the dictator had lived, using it instead for foreign state guests. Another former royal property, the Moncloa Palace, meanwhile, became the residence of the prime minister. The King's son Prince Felipe has lived since summer 2002 in a 34,000-square-foot palace in the grounds of La Zarzuela.

Although the British monarchy remains by far the most expensive in Europe to run, the finances and financing of its Continental counterparts remain a highly complex and controversial subject. The systems used vary from country to country, but two factors are common to all: firstly, not just the sovereigns but also, in most cases, other members of the royal families are paid considerable sums of money each year by their subjects. Secondly, the precise amount that they cost the state and the extent of their private wealth are shrouded in mystery.

Not surprisingly, such arrangements came under growing scrutiny in the aftermath of the financial crisis of 2008; while many of their subjects had to cut their spending or lost their jobs, the monarchs and their families continued to enjoy not just absolute job security but also a generous pay and benefits package that, in most cases, has been steadily increased year in, year out.

The debate in Belgium has been especially intense, in part because of the hostility towards the Crown of substantial parts of the Flemish political establishment. Matters have not been helped, however, by the behaviour of the royal family themselves – whether it was Prince Laurent, the younger son of the King, at the wheel of a brand new €87,000 Porsche Carrera, or King Albert himself, paying €4.6 million for a ninety-foot yacht in summer 2009 while his country was still only slowly emerging from recession – especially since it was just two years since he had spent €1.5 million on another vessel.

The Belgian system is one of the least transparent in Europe. Or so says Herman Matthijs, a professor at the Vrije Universiteit Brussel, who has made a study of the financing of Belgium's royals.[25] According to Matthijs, under an arrangement dating back to 1853, the king receives a payment from the state known as the *liste civile* (or *civile lijste*). The amount is fixed on the accession of each monarch and, like much else in Belgium, automatically increased each year in line with the cost of living. Out of the total, fixed at €10,673,000 for 2011 (£8.89 million), King Albert was expected to cover both his personal needs and the expenses required to run his various palaces. How he divides the money is up to him. "He is completely free with the money to do what he wants," says Matthijs. "There is no control system whatsoever, not from the government or from the parliament."[26]

Another four members of the royal family – the King's children, Philippe, Laurent and Astrid, and his late brother's widow, Fabiola – received a further €2,989,547 (£2.46 million) in 2011. For the second year running, the figure was actually cut – albeit by a modest 1.4 per cent – after the royal family was called on to take on its fair share of belt-tightening in response to the financial crisis.

Curiously, Laurent is only a relatively recent addition to the payroll: it was only in 2001, when he was thirty-seven, that he began to receive an allowance of his own, after complaining publicly about being left out. Questions have also been asked about the generous treatment enjoyed by Fabiola, the Queen Dowager, now in her eighties, whose *dotation*, set for more than €1.46 million (£1.18 million) in 2011, has long been almost as much as her niece and two nephews' allowances put together. This, according to the news magazine *Le Vif*, seemed "even so rather a lot for an elderly woman... living piously in her Château du Stuyvenberg (also put at her disposal by the state)".[27] The palace's explanation that much of the money went on paying Fabiola's twenty-strong staff – including driver, *valet de chambre*, hairdresser and secretary – did not silence the critics.

Fabiola's *dotation*, like the money paid to the other members of the Belgian royal family, is tax-free, since it is not considered income as such – a valuable perk in a country that has long been one of the most highly taxed in Europe. Members of the family also pay little or no property taxes, since the official royal residences in which they live technically belong to the state.

As in Britain, however, the official figure of almost €14 million (£11.5 million) substantially understates the true cost of maintaining the Belgian royal family. About the same amount again goes on security, which includes around 240 police assigned to royal-protection duties. Albert also has the salaries of a number of his staff paid for him: many of those working at the palace are on secondment from the armed forces or the civil service and their salaries are covered by their employers (although the King has to make a small contribution towards them). Royal trips, too, must be funded. Matthijs estimates the true total cost of the Belgian monarchy at about €30 million a year.

Amid growing criticism of the royal family, especially among Flemish politicians, there have long been calls to reform the system. In July 2009, a cross-party senate committee proposed that in future only the monarch, his or her spouse and the heir to the throne would receive money from the state. The reform will only come into effect after Albert's death, however; in the interests of fairness, it was decreed that Princess Astrid and Prince Laurent, each paid more than €300,000 a year at present, will continue to receive the money for life.

This did not go far enough for some, however, among them Pol Van Den Driessche, an outspoken former journalist turned Christian Democrat senator from the CD&V party, who wants greater transparency over the manner in which the royal family spend their money. "The King's Civil List is there to cover the costs of the royal house," he said. "But besides that, resources are provided in the budgets of different government departments for that same royal house. The result is an impenetrable tangle where no democratic control is possible."[28]

Van Den Driessche and his allies are also keen to shed more light on the Donation Royale, an opaque organization that owns a considerable amount of land and buildings in Brussels and beyond – some of which are used by members of the royal family. The foundation has its origins in the last days of Léopold II, who, following the death of his only son as a child, was determined not to let any of his fortune fall into the hands of his three daughters, who had all married foreign princes. He instead left it to the foundation – much to the fury of the daughters, who fought several unsuccessful court cases after their father's death in 1909 to receive what they considered their rightful share of their inheritance.

It remains to be seen whether such proposals will eventually see the light of day. Even if they do, it will not be enough for some, such as Ben Weyts, a member of the Chamber of Representatives for Vlaams Belang, a party whose ultimate aim is an independent Flemish republic; in the meantime he and his fellow party members would like to see the King paid just a salary. So how much would the monarch be paid? "The same as the prime minister," replies Weyts[29] – a generous salary by Belgian standards, but a fraction of the amount that he gets at present.

Conscious of such criticism, King Albert has been keen to show he is sharing some of the suffering of his hard-pressed subjects. In January 2012 the palace announced that he would voluntarily renounce a three-per-cent inflation-linked pay rise – roughly €350,000 – to which he was automatically entitled under the constitution, and use the money to pay some of the property-maintenance costs normally borne by the government. The King "had the intention to contribute voluntarily to the [government's] austerity measures", it said.[30]

For critics of the opaque nature of Belgian royal financing, their Dutch neighbours offer a more acceptable model. That country's rules restrict payment to four members of the royal family: the monarch and his or her spouse and the next in line to the throne and his or her spouse. Given that Queen Beatrix is a widow, this means that just she, Crown Prince Willem-Alexander and Crown Princess Máxima qualify. Rather than receiving a single lump sum, however, each of them is given two distinct payments – the first part, which reached €7.16 million (£5.81 million) in 2011 and is effectively a salary, and the second, considerably larger part – amounting to €26.41 million (£21.95 million) – which pays for the 260 or so people who work in the Amsterdam, Noordeinde and Huis ten Bosch palaces, and other maintenance and travel costs. This spending is laid out in accounts that can be monitored – making the Dutch royal family commendably transparent, if not especially cheap. According to official figures, the total cost of maintaining the monarchy in 2011 reached €39.17 million (once another €5.61 million to cover work by the government information service and the cost of ceremonial military activities had been added) – though it was due to fall slightly in 2012. This makes it the second most expensive monarchy in Europe, after the British.

The Scandinavian monarchies, not surprisingly, are also relatively transparent and less costly for taxpayers. King Haakon VII, first king of Norway's current dynasty, got off to a good start in 1905 with a civil list fixed at a generous 700,000 Norwegian kroner a year – the equivalent of about £30–33 million a year today. In order to avoid unpleasant discussions every year about money, it was decided to fix the sum for the duration of his reign. No one, though, had foreseen the inflation of the 1920s, which reduced the real value of the royal couple's income to a third of what it had been when he came to the throne.

Fortunately for Haakon and his wife Maud, they could also benefit from the generosity of her father, Edward VII. When they married in 1896, the British King gave his daughter a generous allowance of £5,000 a year – understandable given that her husband, then Prince Carl of Denmark, was a second son with little prospect of his own throne and the wealth that would bring. Curiously, the sum was increased to £7,000 – more than half a million pounds in today's money – and continued to be paid for the rest of her life.

Haakon and his successors did receive steady inflation-linked increases in the post-war years; as elsewhere, however, the figures were deceptive: as the years passed, there was growing concern at what were called "camouflaged supplements" – that is, the hiding-away of expenditure on the royal family into broader government spending. Harald, the present monarch, also faced criticism of the cost of a renovation of the palace – the first major one for many years – that was begun after he succeeded his father in 1991. Decades of neglect took their toll: the final bill by the time they had finished in 2000 was 400 million Norwegian kroner (almost £43 million), far exceeding the original budget of 150 million kroner.

A report was commissioned from Dag Trygsland Hoelseth, a Norwegian historian specializing in royal history, and in 2002 a new system was introduced: under its terms, the King in 2010 was paid nine million kroner as an *apanasje* (salary), intended to cover his personal expenses and official clothes, with a further 142.5 million kroner for the costs of the court, 15.7 million kroner for the renovation of palaces and 20.9 million kroner to mark his and the Queen's seventieth birthdays, which goes to a foundation to support humanitarian activities. Crown Prince Haakon and his wife also receive their own *apanasje* of 7.5 million kroner, with a further 15.7 million kroner to cover their operating costs. Taken together, this takes the cost to the state budget to 232.2 million kroner (about £25.2 million).

The Danish royal family, subject to a more transparent accounting system since 2001, appears considerably better value. As of October 2011 the total annual bill came to 97.4 million Danish kroner (just under £11 million). The Queen receives the overwhelming majority of this – 75.5 million Danish kroner – but is required to give ten per cent (7.5 million kroner) of it to her husband Henrik and 1.5 per cent (1.1 million kroner) to her sister Benedikte. The money is intended to cover costs incurred during the carrying-out of their official duties as well as the upkeep of the interior of their palaces – although the state covers external repairs. Crown Prince Frederik meanwhile receives 18.6 million kroner, 1.86 million kroner of which he must give to his wife, Crown Princess Mary. A relatively modest 3.3 million kroner goes to his younger brother, Joachim. The Prince's former wife, Alexandra, whom he divorced in 2005, has continued to receive about 1.9 million kroner a year, although since she remarried in 2007 she has had to start paying tax on it.

The Swedish royal family, at just over 122 million Swedish kronor (£11.4 million) in 2011, comes in at about the same cost as the Danish version. Under an agreement between the King and the government made in 1996, fifty-one per cent of this goes on *Kungliga hovstaten* (court administration), which covers the official duties, travel, administration and personal expenses of King Carl XVI Gustaf and Queen Silvia, Crown Princess Victoria and Prince Daniel, and the King's elderly aunt, Lilian. (The royal couple's two other children, Carl Philip and Madeleine, are not included.) The remaining forty-nine per cent, under the heading of *Slottsstaten* (palace administration), finances the royal palaces, their grounds and the various royal collections – although about as much again is obtained in entrance fees and other revenues from the palaces which are open to the public.

Cheapest of all the seven major monarchies is the Spanish one; under article sixty-five, paragraph one of the country's constitution, the King is entitled to an annual sum from the state budget, which he is free to spend on himself and members of his family. For 2011 the sum was fixed at €8.43 million (£7.01 million) – 5.2 per cent less than the previous year, after spending on the monarchy was cut in line with the funding of other constitutional bodies such as the parliament. The sum is intended to cover the costs incurred by the monarch in carrying out his duties as head of state, but not to pay for official visits, receiving foreign delegations or security. The King is also not required to pay for the upkeep of the Zarzuela Palace or any other royal domains, which is funded by a body known as the Patrimonio Nacional (National Heritage).

In December 2011 the palace revealed for the first time how the money was divided between members of the royal family. Of the €8.43 million, the King received €292,000 (€140,000 in the form of salary, and the remainder to cover expenses) – taxed at forty per cent, while Prince Felipe was paid €146,375 (compared with the mere €78,185 earned by the prime minister). Queen Sofía and her daughters Elena and Cristina and daughter-in-law Letizia did not receive an official salary as such, but were paid up to €375,000 between them in expenses.

Concentrating on civil lists and apanages risks ignoring another element in the equation: the private wealth accumulated by the various royal families, which dwarfs anything they receive from the state. Not surprisingly, determining precisely who is worth how much has proved difficult – although this has not prevented people trying.

During the 1970s, for example, it was widely assumed that Queen Juliana of the Netherlands was the wealthiest woman in the world – surprising perhaps given that her public image was of a rather homely lady more comfortable on a bicycle than on the back seat of a limousine. This impression was strengthened by the publication in 1979 of the biography *Queen Juliana: The Story of the Richest Woman in the World*, by William Hoffman. Such estimates appear to have been exaggerated: after the death of her husband Prince Bernhard in December 2004, the Dutch royal fortune was evaluated at about €200 million – a huge sum by most people's standards, but certainly not enough to give Juliana a place in the top ten.

When *Forbes*, the American business magazine, attempted a study of the world's richest royals in 2009, its list was headed by King Bhumibol Adulyadej of Thailand, with an estimated net worth of $35 billion. The rest of the list was dominated by oil-rich Arabs, with only two European monarchs: in sixth place was Prince Hans-Adam of Liechtenstein, whose wealth *Forbes* put at $6 billion, and ninth was Prince Albert II of Monaco, with an estimated $1.4 billion. Queen Elizabeth II, meanwhile, was down in twelfth place, with an estimated $650 million fortune, ahead of Queen Beatrix of the Netherlands, whose estimated $300 million – less than one hundredth of her Thai counterpart's – placed her fourteenth.[31]

The source of Hans-Adam's wealth is not difficult to explain: Liechtenstein's princely family owns LGT Group, a lucrative private-banking, wealth- and asset-management concern, which is headquartered in Vaduz, the capital, and has more than two dozen branches across Europe and beyond. It also owns RiceTec, a Texas company that develops hybrid rice. Much of the Monégasque royal family's money, meanwhile, comes from its holdings of real estate in the tiny principality.

The sources of wealth of the heads of Europe's larger monarchies are more complex. As discussed above, Queen Elizabeth has considerable land, property and other financial holdings. The Dutch royal family, meanwhile, owns a substantial slice of Royal Dutch Shell. Despite its absence from *Forbes*'s analysis, the Belgian royal family has accumulated a considerable fortune over the years, with some calculations published in the late 1990s putting it at more than €1 billion. At the time, a spokesman for the Royal Palace, Françoise Gustin, described the figures as grossly exaggerated, but would not give any alternative sums to prove them wrong.[32]

The foundations of the royal family's wealth were laid by Léopold I, thanks, initially at least, to his brief marriage to Princess Charlotte, heir to the British throne. The £50,000 a year he was paid by the British government after her death was a colossal sum – equivalent to more than £3 million today, and double the amount received by Prince Frederick, Duke of York, the heir presumptive to the throne, and eight times the £6,000 a year that his sister-in-law, the Dowager-Duchess of Kent, was left with to bring up the future Queen Victoria after the death of her husband. To this should be added his substantial inheritance from his wife. He was also allowed to keep Claremont House, the mansion where they had lived.

Even after he became king of the Belgians – which earned him a generous annual sum of 2.7 million francs (or about £108,000) – Léopold insisted, extraordinarily, on continuing to receive his British pension, partly because of the doubts about the long-term viability of Belgium as a country. After some haggling, a compromise was struck: he would still receive his allowance but reimburse the British Treasury with any money left after he had covered the upkeep of Claremont House and paid off any debts accumulated while living in England.

Not surprisingly, Léopold did not return a penny until April 1834, when the British parliament threatened him with an official investigation into the £150,000 he had received since ascending the Belgian throne. In his book, *A Throne in Brussels*, Paul Belien estimates Léopold received a total of £1.4 million from 1818 until his death in December 1865, a sum equivalent to more than £80 million today. "His marriage to Charlotte was by far the most expensive royal marriage the British have had to finance in their entire history," Belien concludes.[33]

Determined to ensure the financial future of his dynasty, Léopold was also a keen investor, buying real estate across Europe and shares in a number of companies, including, most significantly, Société Générale de Belgique, a holding company set up by the Dutch King Willem I in 1822 to encourage investment in what had then been the southern provinces of his realm. Rather than buy the shares out of his own fortune, Léopold did so with money the company itself lent him, under an advantageous arrangement with Ferdinand de Meeûs, its corrupt governor – who was later rewarded with the hereditary title of Count de Meeûs d'Argenteuil.

His son, Léopold II, also devoted considerable attention to boosting the family fortune; indeed the motivation behind his attempt at the end of the nineteenth century to turn the Congo into a personal colony was as much personal enrichment as a desire for national glory. Quite how much found its way to Léopold II's descendants remains unclear, given his determination to disinherit his daughters and his establishment of the Donation Royale. More recent Belgian monarchs do not appear to have been quite such successful accumulators of wealth as the country's first two kings.

The Scandinavian monarchs are believed to be considerably poorer. Norway's King Harald, for example, once claimed his inheritance was two figures in millions of Norwegian kroner – the equivalent of a maximum of about £10 million. Spain's Juan Carlos is also not thought to have much of a personal fortune – not that he could be said to live frugally: a book published in 2009 claimed the King, renowned for his penchant for fast cars, luxury yachts and expensive ski resorts, has a fleet of seventy vehicles, including an extremely rare Rolls-Royce Phantom IV, once owned by General Franco, and a Harley Davidson given to him by the billionaire publisher Malcolm Forbes – as well as a team of sixty-five people to look after them.[34] Juan Carlos does not have much need of chauffeurs, however, preferring to drive himself whenever possible – on one occasion, with an almost fatal result: it is claimed that he came close to death in 1990 when he skidded out of control while driving a Porsche 959 on icy mountain roads in the Pyrenees.

Chapter 6

Kings Behaving Badly

King Carl XVI Gustaf, Sweden's bespectacled monarch, has long been known for two passions: fast cars and hunting elk. In November 2010 his subjects learnt of a third, rather more risqué interest.

Rumours had long been circulating about the private parties that the monarch organized with a small group of close male friends in the exclusive clubs and restaurants around Stockholm's Stureplan. Affluent and aged, like him, in their early sixties, these are mostly people the King has known for years and in whose company he feels safe. During a visit to the country that summer I was told by a member of parliament of an incident involving a friend's twenty-something daughter who had been approached on the street in Stockholm by two young men and told that the King would like to "invite her to a party".

A few months later the rumours were splashed all over the pages of the newspapers not just in Sweden but across the world. In their book, *Carl XVI Gustaf: Den motvillige monarken* (*Carl XVI Gustaf: The Reluctant Monarch*), Thomas Sjöberg and two fellow journalists painted a vivid picture of the King and his friends' constant partying and playing around with young women. It was "girls à la carte for the King gang", wrote the authors, who relied largely on anonymous sources to detail their monarch's many supposed indiscretions.

Many of Carl XVI Gustaf's alleged liaisons appeared to have been fleeting encounters. But the book alleged he had also had a year-long affair at the end of the 1990s with Camilla Henemark, a half-Nigerian, half-Swedish singer turned actress. Its authors claimed that Queen Silvia, Carl Gustaf's German-born wife of thirty-four years, knew about the affair but could do nothing because her husband had fallen in love "like a teenager" with Henemark and the two were talking about escaping to a distant island to "live on coconuts".

Ultimately more damaging, though, were claims that the King was putting himself in danger by partying at dubious clubs, including one owned by Mille Markovic, a feared figure in the Stockholm underworld. The King and his friends were said to have regularly had the club to themselves on Mondays for nights filled with elaborate meals and capped with liaisons in a whirlpool with scantily clad would-be models. Markovic was allegedly keen to have the monarch as his patron because it minimized the chances of unwanted visits by the police. Agents from Säpo, the Swedish security service, the book claimed, snooped around in various flats and otherwise pressured women who had partied with the King, ordering them to hand over rolls of film, negatives and photographs – or else face unpleasant consequences.[1]

Anticipation ahead of the book's release had been building for weeks, with vague rumours of its content circulating but few actual details leaking out in advance. Its publication was timed to coincide with the annual elk hunt at the Halle- och Hunneberg reserve on the shores of Vänern in western Sweden, which traditionally ends with the King addressing a press conference.

The number of journalists who turned up that year was considerably higher than usual. "I have seen some headlines that have not been so nice, and of course I have talked to the family and the Queen," the King told them. But he declined to comment on a book he had not read. "We will turn a page and move on now because, as I understand it, this is about things that happened a long time ago," he added. In an interview a few days later with *Expressen*, the leading Swedish tabloid, Henemark distanced herself from the book's description of her as a courtesan, but said "we played and had fun".[2] The book sold out almost its entire initial print run of 20,000 copies on the first day.

The King initially appeared not to have sustained much damage from the claims. A poll by SVT, the public broadcaster, found just a quarter of Swedes thought journalists were right to investigate his private life. But the scandal did not go away, amid reports that Markovic claimed to have photographs in his possession showing the King in a sex club in the same shot as two naked women. To add fuel to the fire, Anders Lettström, one of the King's friends, admitted contacting underworld figures in an apparent attempt to track down the pictures – although insisted he was acting on his own rather than the King's initiative.

As the crisis deepened, Carl XVI Gustaf took the unprecedented step on 30th May of giving a long interview to TT, the Swedish national news agency – the first time a monarch had deigned to answer such direct questions about his private life. The King flatly denied allegations he had visited sex clubs or had indirect contact with organized crime, and said such incriminating photos could not possibly exist. He seemed uncomfortable, however, did not always speak clearly and seemed confused about what he had – or had not – already admitted the previous November.

The Swedish media were not impressed: if the claims were not true, why had it taken the King so long to issue a denial? they demanded. In a commentary in the Swedish newspaper *Dagens Nyheter*, Peter Wolodarski drew parallels with the disastrous attempts by Bill Clinton to cover up his relationship with Monica Lewinsky during the mid-1990s that almost cost him the presidency.[3]

Carl XVI Gustaf is not the only one of Europe's monarchs to have his private life subjected to scrutiny, however. Spain's journalists had long gossiped in private about Juan Carlos's private life, but when French and Italian magazines published stories in the early 1990s linking the Spanish King to Marta Gaya, a Catalan interior decorator, the stories were dismissed by Felipe González, the prime minister, as an international plot to undermine his country. Most of Spain's newspapers and magazines – with the exception of the republican-minded *El Mundo* – agreed.

Such a united front broke down in 2008, however, when Jaime Peñafiel, a leading royal expert and former editor of *¡Hola!* magazine, published a book, *Juan Carlos y Sofía. Retrato de un matrimonio* (*Juan Carlos and Sofía: Portrait of a Marriage*), in which he claimed that the King had had a series of affairs during his married life – including an eighteen-year relationship with Gaya. In his book, the contents of which were eagerly seized upon by the media, Peñafiel claimed that Gaya's former husband, an engineer, had once complained to a friend about his wife's affair. "Go and give the guy a couple of punches," the friend replied. "I can't," the cuckolded husband reportedly said.

"We're talking about the King." The book also claimed the royal couple had blazing rows, which ended with Sofía, his Greek-born queen, in tears. "I hate you, I hate you," the King is quoted as shouting at her on one occasion – to which Sofía reportedly replied, "Hate me, but you can screw yourself because you can't get divorced."⁴

Further embarrassing revelations followed in January 2012, in a biography of the Queen written by Pilar Eyre, a veteran commentator on Spanish royal affairs. According to the book, *La soledad de la Reina* (*The Solitude of the Queen*), Juan Carlos and Sofía's marriage had broken down as early as 1976, when the Queen discovered her husband with his mistress at a friend's country house near Toledo. Sofía, Eyre claimed, had wanted to leave Juan Carlos but was persuaded by her mother, the exiled Queen Frederika of Greece, not to do so. Instead the couple led separate lives, with the King embarking on affairs with a series of *amigas* while his wife devoted herself to bringing up their children.⁵ The palace maintained a dignified silence in response to the allegations, although a woman named as having been one of the King's lovers denied she was anything more than a friend. Soon after the book was published, Eyre was fired from her job at the television station Telecinco – the result, she claimed, of pressure from the royal family.

The love life of Albert II of the Belgians has also provided fuel for the tabloids – and here as well it was laid open to public scrutiny by a book: in this case, an unauthorized biography of his wife, Queen Paola, published in 1999. Entitled *Paola: van la dolce vita tot koningin* (*Paola: From la Dolce Vita to Queen*), the book claimed that back in the 1960s, when his elder brother Baudouin was king, Albert had fathered an illegitimate child, who was now living in London, where she worked "in the arts". "During a troubled period, [the King] carried out an extramarital relationship," it claimed. "Paola, distressed, refused to receive [in the palace] the half-sister of their children."⁶ And that was that. Curiously, its author, Mario Danneels, was no seasoned royal commentator, but rather an eighteen-year-old unknown writing his first book.

Danneels did not name the royal love child, nor did he provide any further details, but within a few days of the book coming out the tabloid *La Dernière Heure* named her as Delphine Boël, an artist. Alongside its article it printed a photograph of one of Boël's typically provocative artworks: a montage featuring Brussels's celebrated

Manneken Pis with a huge penis in the Belgian national colours of black, yellow and red.

Despite the revelations of such alleged infidelities, the three kings' marriages have survived. For the three monarchs – and also for Europe's fourth king, Harald of Norway, and its three queens regnant – marriage is an institution to be entered into for life. Whatever the ups and downs they have experienced during married life, divorce has never seemed a realistic option.

When Juan Carlos and Sofía celebrated their fiftieth wedding anniversary in May 2012, it was only the latest in a long line of events that demonstrate the longevity of the unions of Europe's current generation of monarchs: in 2007, Queen Margrethe of Denmark celebrated her fortieth wedding anniversary and Queen Elizabeth of Britain her sixtieth. Harald V of Norway has been married for more than forty years and Carl XVI Gustaf more than thirty. Even Belgium's Albert and Paola made it to their fiftieth in 2009, by which time the marital difficulties that had brought them to the verge of divorce in the 1960s seemed like ancient history. Beatrix of the Netherlands is the only current European monarch without a partner, and she was married for more than thirty-six years before her husband, Claus, died in 2002. For the kings at least, though, that has not necessarily meant absolute fidelity.

When it comes to their private lives, today's monarchs are to a great extent a product of their time. During the 1950s and 1960s, when they were coming of age, European society was changing, and arranged marriages seemed like an anachronism. Like their subjects, they wanted to marry whom they wanted rather than someone chosen by their parents. In their case, however, a series of rules, some written, some informal, stipulated who was suitable royal-marriage material and who was not. This went not just for those expected to accede to the throne, but also their brothers, sisters and even cousins. If they insisted on pressing ahead with an unsuitable match, there was a risk it could cost them their place in the line of succession to the throne.

In most cases, the preference remained for a member of another ruling family, but this was far more difficult than it had been half a century earlier, because of the small number of monarchies that had survived the upheavals of the First and Second World Wars. A member of an ousted house – or one of the innumerable German princes or princesses – was often a good substitute or, failing that, a member of the country's own aristocracy.

In the case of male royals, when it came to choosing a bride the rules were simple: the younger the better. Not just because she would tend to be more fertile – which is of vital importance to a monarchy based on heredity – but also because it made it less likely that a parade of former lovers would emerge with embarrassing stories to tell. Other factors, such as formal educational achievements, were of far less importance, especially in Britain – all of which explained why the twenty-year-old Lady Diana Spencer, widely thought to have been "without a history", seemed such a perfect match for Prince Charles, who was almost thirteen years her senior and with a long string of much publicized sexual conquests behind him.

In most cases, approval for a royal marriage continues to be required both from the monarch and from parliament – which in many cases over the years has proved anything but a formality. To this have been added some other rules – both formalized and unwritten. In Britain, for example, it was, as mentioned previously, only at the Perth summit of October 2011 that it was agreed to repeal the provisions of the 1701 Act of Settlement that barred the heir to the throne from marrying a Catholic. Furthermore, the Royal Marriages Act, passed after two of George III's brothers married unsuitable women, decrees that no member of the royal family under the age of twenty-five may marry without the permission of the monarch. Members of the Dutch royal family have also traditionally been prevented from marrying Catholics, although this was not stipulated in the constitution, but was rather a practice born out of the country's past domination by Catholic Spain – and did not appear to be an obstacle to Crown Prince Willem-Alexander's marriage to Máxima Zorreguieta in 2002. Until relatively recently the Scandinavian monarchies observed the practice that members of the royal house should marry only foreigners.

Queen Elizabeth, the oldest of Europe's current reigning monarchs, was also the first to marry. Her husband Prince Philip, the Duke of Edinburgh, a member of the junior branch of Greece's royal family, was like his bride a great-great-grandchild of Queen Victoria, but the drama of his early life in Greece could not have been more different from the comfort of Elizabeth's upbringing in London.

Known as Philippos to the Greeks, he was born on 10th June 1921 on the dining-room table of Villa Mon Repos, a rented house on the island of Corfu. He was the fifth child, but first son, of Prince Andrew of Greece and Denmark and the British-born Princess Alice of Battenberg. The first years of his life were turbulent: in September 1922 his uncle King Konstantinos was forced to abdicate, and Andrew was among those arrested by the military government and blamed for the defeat of his country at the hands of the Turks. Andrew was taken to Athens and put on trial in the Chamber of Deputies by a jury of junior officers.

Found guilty of disobeying orders and abandoning his position in the face of the enemy, Andrew was sentenced to death. Alice was determined to save her husband's life and telegraphed her younger brother, Louis Mountbatten, who was a junior officer in Britain's Royal Navy. Although only twenty-one, he not only secured an audience with King George V but managed to persuade the monarch to intervene to rescue his distant relative. When Greece's dictator Theodoros Pangalos refused such interference in his country's internal affairs, the HMS *Calypso*, a British warship, arrived in the bay and trained its mighty guns on the government offices.

The following day Andrew was brought before the court again, stripped of his military rank and royal titles and banished from Greece for life. That night, Pangalos himself drove him to the warship, where his wife was waiting. The ship then steamed to Corfu to pick up the rest of the family and took them to the Italian port of Brindisi – from where they continued by train to France. The baby Philip was carried on board the ship in a makeshift cot made out of a fruit box.

As he grew up, Philip was taken under the wing of his Uncle Dickie, as Louis Mountbatten was known in the family, an extraordinarily well-connected character who was to become Admiral of the Fleet, like his father before him, and also the last viceroy of India. Although he began his education in France, Philip was sent, aged seven, at his uncle's insistence, to Cheam School, living partly with his maternal grandmother Victoria at Kensington Palace, and partly with his other uncle, George Mountbatten, Marquess of Milford Haven, at Lynden Manor, Berkshire. In 1933 he was sent to Schule Schloss Salem, in Germany, which was owned by one of his brothers-in-law, Berthold, Margrave of Baden. With the rise of Nazism, however, Kurt Hahn, the school's Jewish founder, fled Germany and founded a new school, Gordonstoun, in Scotland. After two terms, Philip moved there.

Philip left in 1939 and joined the Royal Navy, graduating the next year from the Royal Naval College, Dartmouth, as the top cadet in his course. It was on 22nd June 1939, twelve days after his eighteenth birthday, that Philip had what, without hyperbole, could be described as a life-changing experience – and, inevitably, it was thanks to his "Uncle Dickie".

King George VI and his wife Elizabeth had travelled aboard the royal yacht to visit the naval college, and someone had to look after their two daughters, Elizabeth, then aged thirteen, and nine-year-old Margaret. Mountbatten, who was there in his role as the King's aide-de-camp, made sure that of all the young men present, it was his nephew, Philip, a tall, strikingly good-looking man, who was given the task. Elizabeth was smitten. "She never took her eyes off him," observed Marion Crawford, her governess, even though Philip did not seem to pay the Princess special attention.[7] The couple nevertheless soon began to exchange letters.

Philip had a successful war; as the prince of a neutral power, he was initially posted as midshipman to a battleship in Ceylon (Sri Lanka), safely out of the way of the action. But after appealing to Mountbatten, by then a captain in the Royal Navy, Philip was posted to HMS *Ramillies* in the Mediterranean, and then in October 1942, at the age of twenty-one, he became one of the youngest first lieutenants in the navy, serving on board HMS *Lauderdale*, a Hunt-class destroyer. In 1944 he left for the Pacific and was in Tokyo Bay in September of the following year, when the Japanese finally surrendered.

During this time, Philip and Elizabeth continued to write. While Philip was, by all accounts, enjoying shore leave in various ports, the young Princess was knitting him socks and, every night, before going to sleep, would kiss the black-and-white photograph she kept of him beside her bed. The relationship was fed by the ambitious Mountbatten: he would tell Elizabeth where Philip was serving and how he was doing, and would do all he could to ensure that the couple met whenever he was back in Britain on leave.

As one of Queen Elizabeth's biographers put it: "The courtship of Elizabeth by Philip seemed more like a game of chess, with the grandmaster Mountbatten in control of half the board, advising Philip how to conduct himself. For the marriage Uncle Dickie wanted to secure for Philip was of vital importance, such was his determination to cement the Mountbatten family to the house of Windsor."[8]

It was not until 1943, when Elizabeth turned seventeen, that Philip let it be known that he was indeed courting her. The King was not happy when told by his wife, Elizabeth, the future Queen Mother, but she persuaded him to let the romance take its course. As long as the war continued, she reasoned, there was not much danger of her daughter's relationship going further. With the outbreak of peace, however, the problem became more acute. Philip was seen by many at court – the King included – as an unsuitable consort for the future Queen. Her mother reportedly referred to him as "the Hun". Hoping their daughter might find someone else, the King and Queen organized a series of balls packed with eligible men over the following months, to which Philip, to his great annoyance, was not invited. Yet Elizabeth remained devoted to her prince.

Eventually, in 1946, Philip asked the King for his daughter's hand in marriage. George agreed – but still had one last trick up his sleeve, insisting any formal announcement be postponed until after their Elizabeth's twenty-first birthday the following April. By 18th March 1947, at Mountbatten's suggestion, Philip had renounced his Greek and Danish titles, as well as his allegiance to the Greek crown, converted from Greek Orthodoxy to the Church of England and become a naturalized British subject. He also adopted the surname Mountbatten (an Anglicized version of Battenberg) from his mother's family.

The couple married on 20th November 1947 in Westminster Abbey in a ceremony attended by representatives of various royal families – but not Philip's three surviving sisters, who had married German royals with Nazi connections. On the morning of the wedding, Philip was made Duke of Edinburgh, Earl of Merioneth and Baron Greenwich of Greenwich in the County of London; the previous day the King had bestowed on him the style of His Royal Highness. Elizabeth's mother was still not convinced.

The war had ended only two years earlier and times were tough. Rationing was still in place, but Elizabeth, like other brides, was allowed two hundred extra clothing coupons to buy her dress, made of silk from China rather than from former enemy Japan. Women across the country also sent in their own coupons but, since the rules stipulated they were non-transferable, they were all returned. The day of the wedding was bitterly cold, and when the newly-weds left Buckingham Palace for Waterloo Station in an open landau to begin their honeymoon, they had hot-water bottles and blankets on their knees. For extra warmth, the Princess had one of her beloved corgis by her feet.

Albert, the second son of King Léopold III, was the next of the current generation of monarchs to tie the knot. He met Paola Ruffo di Calabria, an Italian aristocrat, in October 1958 while they were both in Rome to attend the coronation of Pope John XXIII. After the ceremony the Belgian embassy held a ball at which Albert, then Prince of Liège, was the guest of honour. Paola, also among those invited, claimed later she had not really known who Albert was. "I had a vague idea of who Baudouin was, but I didn't really know anything about Belgium or Prince Albert. Only Tintin," she said.[9] They clearly made an impression on each other – so much so that Albert came up with various reasons to prolong his stay in the Italian capital and see Paola again. And so, as one commentator put it, began a "fairy-tale romance in the least erotic place in the whole of Europe. During the official inauguration of the most jovial pope of the twentieth century, the most bourgeois of all the royal princes got to know the most flamboyant of all princesses."[10]

By the time Albert arrived back in Belgium, he had already made up his mind to marry Paola. Two months after their meeting, he introduced his wife-to-be to his family, and four months later to the press. On 2nd July 1959, only eight months after their first meeting, they married in Brussels. Thousands of people turned out for a glimpse of the bride, a vision of beauty in a white satin dress with a fifty-foot train by Concettina Buonanno, a Neapolitan designer, and a lace veil that had belonged to her Belgian grandmother.

The couple's whirlwind romance and marriage had little in common with traditional royal pairings. "It was passionate love between Albert and Paola," claims Erik Wellens, another of the King's biographers. "There are even stories of hotel visits during which discarded clothing was found strewn from the lift to the door of the room."[11] Two weeks after Paola walked down the aisle, she was already pregnant with Philippe, born the following April. A daughter, Astrid, was born in June 1962 and a second son, Laurent, in October 1963.

The Belgians fell in love with "*la dolce Paola*", and she and Albert became a prime target of the paparazzi, who chased them during their engagement and their honeymoon in Mallorca. Like Princess Diana two decades later, she was often obliged to leave shops through the back door to avoid their lenses.

In common with many royal second sons, Albert was faced with the challenge of finding a role: by the mid-1960s he was leading economic missions on behalf of Belgian industry, which involved considerable foreign travel. At first Paola went with him, but as their children grew older she stayed behind in Brussels. For a young woman bought up in the *dolce vita* of Rome, the Belgian capital must have seemed a grey place. Paola was lonely, homesick and chafing under the protocol of the Belgian court.

Relations were also often strained with Queen Fabiola, the rather severe Spanish aristocrat whom Baudouin had married in December 1960. Fabiola had little time for such frivolities as make-up or designer clothes – unlike her Italian sister-in-law, who during an official visit to Luxembourg was said to have worn no fewer than twelve outfits in four days. Fabiola and Baudouin used to drink water rather than wine and organized few parties. Like the King, Fabiola was deeply religious: indeed, according to one account, the couple first met thanks to the clerical matchmaking of Cardinal Leo Suenens, Belgium's most senior churchman, and Sister Veronica O'Brien, an Irish nun, who had visions of the Virgin Mary. Given her five miscarriages, Fabiola may also have been a little jealous of Paola with her three healthy young children.

Rumours began to spread about Albert's alleged extramarital escapades; there were reported sightings at Paris nightclubs; more fancifully, at sex parties. Paola, meanwhile, was also spotted in male company.

Then in 1966 Albert met Sybille de Selys Longchamps, a Belgian baroness. She was married at the time to Jacques Boël, an industrialist, but they were already separated. Albert appears to have fallen in love with her as quickly as he had with Paola: in February 1968, they had a daughter, named Delphine.

Albert and Paola went their separate ways – the children staying with their mother – but such were the preoccupations of the day that they still tried to present a united front to the outside world, even allowing television cameras to film them on their tenth wedding anniversary in 1969. This show of marital unity was somewhat undermined the following year when Paola was photographed arm in arm with Albert de Mun, a journalist from *Paris Match*, on holiday in Sardinia.

In the early years Albert was a regular visitor to the house in Uccle, an affluent suburb of Brussels, where Sybille lived with Delphine. The little girl didn't know who the man was – but liked him and nicknamed him *papillon*. "He was a fun guy with a good sense of humour and I liked him," she said in an interview published in 2008 to coincide with the publication of her autobiography. "I understood that I had to remain in the shadows, that he had another life with his wife and three children."[12]

According to Delphine's account, as early as October 1969 Albert talked to her mother about the possibility of divorcing, but it was made clear to him that if he did so, he would have to renounce his claim to the throne. He was also told that Sybille would be prevented from seeing his other children.

In the years that followed, the couple continued to see each other clandestinely, but in 1976 Sybille told Albert she couldn't go on. Again, the subject of divorce was raised, and again the conditions were the same. This time Sybille acted, moving to London, taking Delphine, aged six, with her.

A distraught Albert bowed to the inevitable, but continued to visit for several years and, according to Delphine, used to talk to her mother almost every day on a specially installed telephone line. Delphine, who attended a series of schools before ending up at the Chelsea School of Art, had since learnt the identity of *papillon*, but still assumed he and her mother had been merely friends – rather than lovers. Then, in 1986, when she was eighteen, her mother revealed the truth over dinner one evening in the Foxtrot Oscar restaurant on Royal Hospital Road in Chelsea. Delphine was delighted.

Albert and Paola, meanwhile, were finding themselves again, thanks in part to the intervention of Cardinal Suenens, who recommended they went on a Christian-inspired Marriage Encounter weekend course. The couple were impressed – so much that they even invited

Spain's King Juan Carlos and his wife Sofía to their castle in Ciergnon to attend one. Albert and Paola also got into religion – becoming members of the Charismatic Movement. The marriage of their daughter Princess Astrid to Lorenz, an Austrian archduke, in September 1984 seemed to have helped their reconciliation.

Then, on 31st July 1993, Baudouin died unexpectedly of heart failure while on holiday with Fabiola at Villa Astrida, their estate in Motril in southern Spain. He was just sixty-two and childless. It had been widely expected that Albert – four years younger and next in line – would renounce the throne, and his son, Philippe, then aged thirty-three, would become Belgium's sixth king. But instead it was Albert who on 9th August swore the constitutional oath. No explanation was given, even though it was felt by many – including apparently Jean-Luc Dehaene, the prime minister – that the still unmarried Philippe, whose main interests appeared to be fast cars and aeroplanes, was not yet ready to assume the role.

The revelations, six years later, of Albert's love child came at an unfortunate moment. Danneels's book appeared just as Philippe, the King's eldest son, was setting off on a prenuptial tour of Belgium, the so-called Joyeuse Entrée, with his fiancée, Jonkvrouwe Mathilde d'Udekem d'Acoz, whom he was due to marry on 4th December that year.

As experience across Europe has shown, there is nothing like a royal wedding to boost the standing of a royal family – and this looked a good one, so good in fact that when Philippe and Mathilde's engagement had been announced that September there was speculation that it was an arranged marriage – an assertion Philippe angrily denied. The bride, whose striking beauty, grace and social skills inevitably drew comparisons to the late Diana, Princess of Wales, would become the first Belgian-born queen in the country's history. More significantly, she also had rare credentials to act as a binding force between the country's two warring linguistic communities, the French-speaking Walloons and Dutch-speaking Flemings. Mathilde's family was originally from Poperinge in West Flanders, and her uncles were Flemish Christian Democrat politicians, but the family chateau in which she grew up was in Wallonia, at Villers-la-Bonne-Eau, near Bastogne. By then she was working as a speech therapist in Brussels.

Philippe's marriage was a suitably grand affair, courtesy of €1 million of taxpayers' money. It began with a civil wedding at the town hall on the gothic Grand-Place, a two-hour Mass at a nearby cathedral, a lunch for twelve hundred people at the royal palace, and a reception for two thousand five hundred at the Château de Laeken, the royal family's sprawling estate in the northern outskirts of Brussels. Work to spruce up the roads around the royal palace and the cathedral had been going on for two months; the fifteen-hundred-man security detail included 132 gendarmes on horseback and another twenty-five who formed a motorcycle escort. There was a ceremonial fly-by of F-16 fighter jets over the royal palace.

Yet the scandal of the King's alleged love child was not going away. The initial reaction of the royal palace was to dismiss the matter as "gossip" – but that changed a few months later when Albert made his traditional Christmas speech to the nation. Straying from the usual pleasantries, he noted how the season gave the opportunity to look back not just on happy times but also unhappy ones – in particular, on a crisis that he and Paola had undergone in their marriage thirty years earlier. "Together we were able to overcome these difficulties and rediscover a deep understanding and love," the King declared. "We were reminded of this period of crisis recently."

Albert's words were vague, yet few of those gathered around their television sets were in much doubt about what the King meant – nor of the significance of his apparent willingness, if only obliquely, to tackle it.

But what of the reminder of these difficulties the couple had left behind them? Delphine had remained in contact with Albert even after he had become king, but accepted his insistence that he could not publicly acknowledge her existence. He would often call, though, and send her "little presents" on her birthday.

This changed after Danneels's revelations. Delphine's first reaction was one of relief that she would no longer have to keep her secret, but that quickly became apprehension after the paparazzi tracked her down to the house in fashionable Notting Hill in west London where she had made her home. Delphine and her mother were besieged with requests for interviews, but refused to comment. When they turned to the palace for help, they received a cool reaction. "At the palace one had imagined there would be a solution to my problems," she wrote in her book *Couper le cordon*. "It was suggested to us that it would be desirable for me to disappear, that I leave England for a distant location, where the press would no longer always be after me. What would have been, according to them, the ideal place of exile? Zanzibar or the North Pole."

For a contemporary artist who compares herself with Britain's Tracey Emin, Delphine's sudden celebrity brought distinct benefits: she exhibited at the Venice Biennale and at galleries in London and Belgium. Her exhibits seemed intended to shock – among them a sculpture of a crowned pig and cow. Yet she could not help wondering whether the new-found fame was due to her parentage rather than her talent. In the feverish world of Belgian politics, meanwhile, some saw her as a willing – or unwilling – part of a plot by Flemish nationalists to destabilize the monarchy, seen as the last piece of glue that holds Belgium together – charges she was later fervently to deny.

Two years later, when her mother's heart problems worsened and were aggravated by nervous depression, Delphine wrote to Albert. When he failed to reply, she found his number, called him and asked him to contact her mother. Although he did so, Sybille still seemed dissatisfied, and Delphine called him again. This time, she claims, he was furious. "You must never call me again... I do not want to hear any more about this matter. And by the way, you are not my daughter." A horrified Delphine told him not to be ridiculous, saying she had the same blue eyes as his mother, the tragic Queen Astrid, but that only made Albert angrier. "Stop! Do not say that you resemble my mother. Never say that again! How dare you!"[13]

In 2003, when she was about to give birth to her first child, Joséphine, Delphine decided to move back to her homeland, determined that her daughter should grow up in the country of her birth. Jim O'Hare, her American-Irish businessman partner, followed her a few months later.

As for Albert and Paola, they appeared to have become completely reconciled to one another. "We had our difficulties but now we say that we were made for each other," Paola declared in a television documentary broadcast on Belgian television in 2006 for which she granted the cameras unprecedented access.

* * *

The marriage of Juan Carlos and his queen, Sofía, three years after Albert and Paola's, was something of a throwback to an earlier age when dynastic considerations predominated. When the couple walked down the aisle in Athens in 1962, it represented the coming-together of two of Europe's leading royal families, the Borbóns and the House of Schleswig-Holstein-Sonderburg-Glücksburg.

True, Juan Carlos's family had not sat on the Spanish throne since his grandfather Alfonso XIII had been forced into exile just over thirty years earlier, yet there was still the hope that the House of Borbón would be restored – which came a step closer to realization seven years later when the young prince was finally confirmed by General Francisco Franco as his successor.

Sofía, by contrast, was the daughter of King Pavlos, who had been on the Greek throne since 1947. Members of the dynasty had ruled the country since 1863, when the seventeen-year-old Prince Vilhelm of Denmark had become King Georgios I. Few would have foreseen that the family's reign would end as soon as 1967, when Sofía's brother, who had succeeded their father as King Konstantinos II three years earlier, was forced into exile.

In making his choice of bride, Juan Carlos was even more constrained than his other European counterparts: not only did his choice have to be acceptable to his own parents, he also had to take into account the views of Franco, who had ruled Spain since his victory in the Civil War. Choosing someone whom the Caudillo rejected ran the risk of prejudicing his prospects of ever being named the dictator's successor.

The future Spanish royal couple first met in 1954 during a cruise, when Juan Carlos was sixteen and Sofía fifteen. It was organized by the latter's mother, Queen Frederika, the German-born wife of King Pavlos, who had invited ninety members of European royal families past and present to set sail from Naples on a cruise through the Greek islands aboard the brand-new 5,500-ton liner, the *Agamemnon*. Among them were representatives of the ruling houses of not just Greece but the Netherlands, Denmark, Sweden, Norway and Luxembourg. There were also recently disinherited princelings from Italy, France, Spain, Romania, Yugoslavia and Bulgaria and relics from defunct kingdoms such as the Bourbon-Parmas, Thurn und Taxis and the Hohenlohe-Langenburgs. The event, recalled Juan Carlos's mother, Doña María de las Mercedes, was organized "with Prussian efficiency".[14] The cruise was ostensibly to promote tourism; it also seems to have been about royal matchmaking.

Those on board had a jolly old time, according to one contemporary account.[15] Since they were all related, Frederika insisted on informality: there was a ban on formal dress and protocol, and lots were drawn to decide on the seating arrangements. Frederika's uncle by marriage, Prince Georgios of Greece, aged eighty-five, known as Uncle Goggy to the family, was the only one allowed to bring along a personal servant on account of his advanced age. During their daily island stops, the guests enjoyed the sights and generally behaved as tourists. In the evening there were films on board and sometimes they danced the mambo and the rumba. During one especially boisterous evening, Christian of Hanover was tossed fully clothed into the swimming pool by some of the other young royals, who then jumped in after him. After that, Frederika ordered the pool emptied each evening at two a.m.

As Juan Carlos recalled later, his meeting with Sofía was not an especially auspicious one. The young princess told him she was learning judo.

"That won't do you much good," he commented.

"You don't think so? Give me your hand," she replied, and proceeded to fling him onto the ground with an expert judo throw.[16]

That was not the only drama during the cruise. Some time afterwards Juan Carlos started to complain of stomach pains. Fortunately his mother had trained as a nurse and realized her son was suffering from appendicitis. Their ship stopped in Tangiers, where the Prince was treated by Alfonso de la Peña, a leading Spanish surgeon who happened to be in the city when they landed.

For the time being, though, nothing more happened between Juan Carlos and Sofía. His first love was instead Maria Gabriella of Savoy, the middle daughter of the short-lived King Umberto II, who had reigned in Italy for just a month in 1946 before going into exile, as the ousted Spanish royals had done, in Portugal. In December 1956, while back in Estoril with his family for the holidays, Juan Carlos met another Italian, Contessa Olghina Nicolis di Robilant, a beautiful minor screen actress. The Prince was infatuated and they began an affair that lasted for almost four years – yet, conscious of his position and his loyalty to the dynasty, he made clear their relationship could never be permanent.

His relationship with Maria Gabriella was not to last either. Despite persistent rumours late in 1960 that the couple were about to announce their engagement, both Juan Carlos's father Don Juan and Franco were opposed, and the Prince eventually succumbed to pressure to drop her. In any case, his attentions had turned in the meantime to Sofía – even though this apparently did not prevent him from indulging in one impromptu last night of passion with Olghina di Robilant in a Rome hotel room.

Juan Carlos and Sofía's paths had crossed again in 1958, four years after the cruise, when they were both invited to the wedding of the daughter of the duke of Württemberg, held at Schloss Altshausen near Stuttgart. Their relationship really appears to have taken off in 1960, however, when Sofía's brother, Konstantinos, was a member of the Greek sailing team at the Rome Olympic Games, and both the Greek and Spanish royal families found themselves staying in the same hotel. By June the following year, when Juan Carlos was Sofía's escort at the wedding of the duke of Kent and Katherine Worsley in Westminster Abbey, their relationship was becoming an open secret. Sofía subsequently claimed that during this time in London they effectively became engaged.

There were obstacles, however: first and foremost one of language, despite the fact that both of them were polyglots. Juan Carlos spoke French, Italian and Portuguese in addition to his native Spanish; Sofía had German as well as Greek. The only tongue they had in common was English, which Sofía spoke well, but, initially at least, Juan Carlos struggled with. Other problems appeared more serious: Juan Carlos was Catholic; Sofía had been brought up Greek Orthodox. For either of them to convert would have been a serious matter.

Sofía's family could also have been forgiven for wondering how much of a catch Juan Carlos was. While their daughter was a member of one of Europe's ruling dynasties, Juan Carlos was merely the son of the pretender to the throne of a country that had long since ceased to be a monarchy. Little did either realize that within a further two decades the respective fortunes of their two dynasties would have been reversed. Sofía's parents were enthusiastic, however, and Juan Carlos and his parents were invited to join the Greek royal family for the rest of the summer in Corfu.

On 13th September 1961, news of the engagement appeared on the front pages of newspapers in Greece and in Portugal. As part of his continuing battle of wills with Franco, Don Juan had not informed the Caudillo in advance about his son's intentions. The dictator was furious, but there was little he could do, and his fondness for the young Prince eventually won him over.

Juan Carlos and Sofía married on 14th May 1962 in Athens with ceremonies both at the Catholic Cathedral and the Greek Orthodox Metropolitan Cathedral. Until two days before the wedding the Prince had his arm in a sling: three weeks earlier he had broken his collarbone while practising judo with Crown Prince Konstantinos, his future brother-in-law.

Other European royal princesses, meanwhile, were finding it more difficult to secure a suitable partner. As *Time* magazine pointed out in 1962, the *Almanach de Gotha*, the directory of Europe's highest nobility and royalty, listed twenty-six spinster princesses, but only sixteen unattached princes of the right generation.[17] The biggest imbalance was in the Netherlands and Denmark, where the countries' future queens regnant, Beatrix and Margrethe, were both of marriageable age. Beatrix had three younger sisters; Margrethe had two. Matters were further complicated by the legacy of the Second World War: the various German families that had hitherto provided a disproportionate share of Europe's royal brides and grooms had lost much of their lustre – especially those with members who had joined the Hitler Youth or, God forbid, the SS.

And so, following Frederika's example, other European queens began to play matchmaker. Queen Juliana of the Netherlands threw a ball in 1960 to help her eldest daughter Beatrix, by then in her early twenties, find a suitable mate. It didn't work. Five years later, though, Beatrix did find her man: Claus-Georg Wilhelm Otto Friedrich Gerd von Amsberg, a German aristocrat and diplomat. Early in July 1965, just as Wilhelmina had done three decades earlier, Juliana made a broadcast to the nation announcing her daughter's engagement. "I assure you, it is a good thing," she said.

The Dutch were not so easily convinced. Both Juliana and her mother Wilhelmina had married Germans – with mixed success. Wilhelmina's spouse, Duke Heinrich Wladimir Albrecht Ernst of Mecklenburg-Schwerin, who died a decade before Beatrix was born, was an uninspiring character. "Henry was a taxidermist's dream of a German princeling," according to one contemporary account, "a beady-eyed, mean-spirited fellow, of whom the best that can be said is that he learnt his place (considerably below the throne) and that, after eight years of marriage, he fathered Princess Juliana."[18]

The former American president Theodore Roosevelt described in a letter after a visit to their home how Wilhelmina "ruled her fat, heavy, dull husband with a rod of iron", snapping at him if he failed to do as he was told. When Roosevelt congratulated him on the birth of Juliana, born after three miscarriages, the unfortunate Prince replied: "Yes, I hope she has a brother; otherwise I pity the man that marries her!"[19] Not surprisingly, perhaps, he sought solace in other women's arms, reportedly fathering several children out of wedlock. Beatrix's father, Bernhard, as will be seen in the next chapter, was also a serial womanizer – and, more seriously, was to drag the Dutch royal house into a murky financial scandal. This, however, was still a decade ahead.

Claus's problem was far simpler: he was a German. Although Bernhard had won over the Dutch after more than twenty-five years of marriage, thanks in part to his role during the war, the Dutch had suffered badly under the Nazis, and by the 1960s anti-German feelings were still strong. Claus's case was not helped by his past member-ship of both the Hitler Youth and the Wehrmacht. Crowds marched through the streets of Amsterdam chanting "*Claus raus*" ("Claus out"), and orange swastikas began to appear all over the country; one was even daubed on the Royal Palace. Rotterdam's *Nieuwe Courant* newspaper spoke for many when it asked: "Can a German put flowers at our memorials for heroes he fought against?" Some commentators suggested Beatrix should renounce her claim to the throne.

If anything the criticism was directed more at Beatrix's mother, Juliana. In fact, despite her public support for the marriage, the Queen had been privately opposed to it because of the damage she feared it would do to the royal family. Unable to persuade her daughter to change her mind, she had asked the German foreign minister to post Claus, who was based at the time in Bonn, out of Europe. Beatrix heard about the scheme and went on a three-day royal hunger strike in protest. Juliana's plan was dropped.

The wedding, set for 10th March 1966, was held in Amsterdam. It was a high-risk choice: the city had probably suffered more than any other in Holland from the Nazi occupation and by the mid-1960s was a hotbed of radical opinion. Juliana would have preferred her daughter to follow the Dutch royal tradition, according to which monarchs were married in The Hague, inaugurated in Amsterdam and buried in Delft. Yet Beatrix seemed determined to make a point. "I could be married in The Hague or Rotterdam and win over either city," she declared. "But if I win the hearts of the Amsterdammers, I will win the heart of all the Netherlands."

The Amsterdammers were not so easily won over. As Beatrix and Claus rode out from the Royal Palace in their golden coach, accompanied by eight footmen in bulletproof vests, a smoke bomb rolled underneath and exploded, and the royal couple disappeared momentarily from view. Other bombs were thrown and a dead chicken with a swastika painted on its body thumped against the door. The police responded heavy-handedly, wading into the crowd, clubbing a number of innocent bystanders to the ground. Beatrix tried to smile and wave but the smoke made her eyes water. When police staged a photographic exhibition of their handling of the riots nine days later, demonstrators again took to the streets, damaging buildings and setting fires in front of the Dam Palace.

It was at about the same time that Margrethe, two years Beatrix's junior, was meeting her husband to be. Born Henri Marie Jean André Count de Laborde de Monpezat, the future prince consort was, like Claus, a diplomat, albeit a fairly lowly one in the French embassy in London, and on one occasion found himself seated at a dinner at the right hand of the then Princess Margrethe, who was studying at the London School of Economics. He was immediately smitten – apparently by her intellect as much as by her looks. "I fell under the charm of her turn of mind and her granite intelligence," he wrote in his memoirs. "My attraction was immediate."[20] Margrethe reciprocated his feelings. Henri proposed marriage in the summer of the following year during a secret visit to Denmark. Although the news was meant to be secret, it was leaked – apparently by a politician – and splashed on the front page of *Ekstra Bladet*, a Danish tabloid, leaving the palace with little alternative but to confirm that the couple would, indeed, wed.

They married on 10th June 1967; Margrethe's groom had to change not just his name – henceforth he was to be known as Henrik rather than Henri – but also his nationality and religion. Such sacrifices were a foretaste of what was to come. At a wedding reception for four hundred guests in a huge marquee in the garden of Fredensborg Palace, the Prince charmed guests with a speech in heavily French-accented Danish in which he sung his praises of his bride.

Given the surfeit of eligible young princesses, finding a bride should have been simpler for Beatrix and Margrethe's male peers, the future King Harald V of Norway and King Carl XVI Gustaf of Sweden. Yet unlike Albert and Juan Carlos neither of them went for the royal – or even the noble – option. It is difficult to overestimate the significance of their choices: both men's fathers and grandfathers before them had married foreign princesses, and it had been expected that they, like Juan Carlos, would follow suit. Instead Harald and Carl Gustaf married middle-class girls, inadvertently paving the way for their children's unions several decades later, which have pushed the boundaries of what is acceptable even further.

Harald was just twenty-two in 1959 when he stunned his father King Olav by announcing his choice of bride. Her name was Sonja Haraldsen, and her father, Karl August, recently deceased, had owned an upmarket ladies' apparel shop in Oslo. Although affluent, with a comfortable villa in one of the western suburbs of the capital, the Haraldsens were commoners – and Norwegian monarchs were meant to marry royalty, or at least nobility – which meant a foreigner, since the country had long since dispensed with nobles.

There was a precedent, but not a very happy one: in 1953, Harald's eldest sister Ragnhild had married Erling S. Lorentzen, a highly successful businessman and army officer who had served as her bodyguard immediately after the war, but the union caused a controversy. She was the first Norwegian royal to marry a commoner, and the newly-weds, encouraged to keep a low profile, moved to Brazil, where Lorentzen's family had business interests. Their initial plan was to stay for a short time – in the event they were still there more than half a century later. Then in 1961, Harald's other sister, Astrid, married Johan Martin

Ferner, owner of an upmarket men's clothing store. Ferner, a former Olympic medallist in sailing, was also a commoner – and worse, divorced – which did not go down well with many Norwegians.

Harald was heir to the throne, though, and different rules applied. His grandfather, Haakon, had married King Edward VII's daughter, Princess Maud, while his father, Olav, had concluded an equally traditional royal union by wedding his cousin, Princess Märtha of Sweden, who had died of cirrhosis of the liver in 1954, three years before her husband had come to the throne. During his youth Harald had been linked with all manner of Scandinavian and other European princesses. Queen Frederika of Greece had high hopes that he would marry her youngest daughter, Irene. It was not to be, however.

Haraldsen, four months Harald's junior, had met the future King as a thirteen-year-old child at a sailing camp in Hankø in 1950. Their first encounter as adults was nine years later at a party organized by Johan Stenersen, a friend of the Crown Prince's from his time at school. It was surprising that their paths had not crossed before: they moved in similar circles and had a number of friends in common.

Sonja had recently come back to Oslo after taking a diploma in dressmaking at the École Professionnelle des Jeunes Filles in Lausanne and a year in Cambridge learning English, where she worked behind the bar of the celebrated Eagle pub, pulling pints and calculating change in pounds, shillings and pence. Her father had just died unexpectedly, and Sonja spent most of her time at home with her mother, Dagny. She didn't feel in the mood to go to parties, but when Stenersen's invitation came, her mother had persuaded her to accept.

Harald was due to graduate a few weeks later from the Krigsskolen, the Norwegian military academy, and a few days after their meeting at Stenersen's party, he telephoned Sonja and invited her to go with him to the graduation ball. She said later she was struck by his sense of humour and how shy he was.

While they were at the ball, Bjørn Glorvigen, a journalist and photographer, took the first press image of the two together, although it was some time before Sonja was identified. In the months and years that followed their romance continued, even though they spent considerable time apart: while Harald was pursuing royal duties, Sonja was studying at the Bjørknes private school in Oslo.

While the couple's friends and the Norwegian press were discreet, the same was not true of the foreign media. "It was not very private," Sonja recalled later. "A classmate told me that he had been offered a good sum of money by a foreign publication to allow interviews about me. There was also a foreign reporter and a photographer who pretended that they wanted to make a report on the school. The rector said yes to them – and realized too late what the two were really looking for."[21] Eventually, after the photographers got too much for her, she escaped to France.

King Olav, meanwhile, was opposed to the match, refusing even to meet Sonja. "Norwegians are not ready for this," he told his son. Most Norwegian royal watchers also doubted it would last. "No one took it seriously," recalls Annemor Møst, a Norwegian journalist who began to cover the royal family in the late 1950s. "Everyone thought it would be impossible that he would marry a commoner – especially because there were so many princesses around."[22] As the relationship began to look serious this disbelief turned into disapproval, both in parliament and the media. "The End of the Kingdom?" asked a front-page headline in the newspaper *Verdens Gang* in 1967.

The couple, too, were beginning to despair. "There were periods when we lost hope that we would get King Olav's consent for our marriage, and we saw no other way but to break off our relationship," Queen Sonja recalled later.[23] It did, however, give them time to be sure they were serious about each other. "Nobody could accuse us of marrying head-over-heels. And we learnt to know each other very well indeed."[24] The situation was equally hard on the future king, who was finding it difficult to hide his feelings. "He used to look very sad as he went about his duties," recalls Møst.[25]

Eventually, according to a biography of the King by Per Egil Hegge, the Crown Prince presented his father and Per Borten, the prime minister, with an ultimatum: if he was not allowed to marry Sonja then he would never marry anyone, which would have meant the end of Norway's brief monarchy: his sisters were both prevented by the constitution from inheriting the throne. And so, despite powerful objections, politically, publicly and within the palace, the engagement was announced in March 1968.

In the few months that followed, the public mood shifted in favour of this unconventional match. Their marriage, on 29th August that year in a Lutheran ceremony in the Cathedral of Oslo, was a spectacular affair. It was the first grand wedding since Harald's parents had married in 1929, and the streets of the Norwegian capital were packed with well-wishers. Guests included the monarchs of Sweden, Denmark, Belgium and Luxembourg and the Presidents of Iceland and Finland. In what was a clear sign of the completeness of Sonja's acceptance by the royal family, she was given away by the King rather than by her brother.

In a speech at their wedding banquet, Harald reflected on their nine-year courtship. "Allow me to thank you, Dagny," he said, addressing himself to his new mother-in-law, "for the trust you showed in believing that I, through my feelings for your daughter, might be allowed to have her in the end and that the fact that I was with her would not ruin her life. But today she is at my side as the country's Crown Princess."[26]

Just over a decade later, the future Carl XVI Gustaf also fell in love with a commoner, Silvia Sommerlath, the glamorous daughter of Walter Sommerlath, a German businessman, and his Brazilian wife, Alice. They met at the 1972 Munich Olympics, where Silvia was working as chief assistant to the head of the German Olympic Committee. Silvia was sitting in the VIP area of the stadium and the then Crown Prince Carl Gustaf was two metres behind her, when she turned around and their eyes met. "It clicked," he declared. He was twenty-six; she was twenty-eight.[27]

Over the few days that followed, the two of them came across each other at various events, greeting each other warmly. Then one day a young man came to Silvia and told her that His Royal Highness, the Crown Prince of Sweden, wanted to invite her to dinner. They were not alone, of course: various other members of the Swedish royal family were also present. But that dinner nevertheless marked the beginning of a friendship that quickly turned into a long-distance love affair after the Olympics ended and Carl Gustaf returned to Sweden.

Just as had been the case with Harald, however, there was a serious problem that initially prevented Carl Gustaf's relationship from turning into something more serious. Members of the Swedish royal family who wanted to marry had first to obtain permission from King Gustaf VI Adolf, Carl Gustaf's grandfather. And there was little doubt how the old King, due that November to celebrate his ninetieth birthday, would react to the prospect of his grandson and heir marrying a commoner. Gustaf Adolf had himself married a princess, Margaret of Connaught, a granddaughter of Queen Victoria, and tradition dictated that his five children should follow suit.[28] The eldest, Prince Gustaf Adolf, Carl Gustaf's father, had done his duty, marrying his second cousin, Princess Sibylla of Saxe-Coburg-Gotha, while the King's only daughter, Ingrid, spoken of at one time as a possible bride for Britain's future Edward VIII, instead married Frederik, the then crown prince of Denmark. Their three siblings were less obliging, however, and all had lost their titles after marrying commoners.

Although embarrassing to the dynasty, none of this would have been so serious if it had not been for the death of Crown Prince Gustaf Adolf in 1947 in an air crash. Fortunately for the Bernadotte dynasty his wife had given birth to Carl Gustaf nine months earlier. But he was their only boy: before that the couple had had four daughters, who were not allowed to reign in their own right under the laws of succession that prevailed in Sweden at the time. What if King Gustaf VI Adolf, already sixty-seven when he came to the throne in 1950, died before his grandson came of age – or if something happened to the boy before he was old enough to have children of his own?

The old King did have one more son, Prince Bertil, who could potentially act as the Bernadottes' insurance policy. The problem was that he too seemed in danger of writing himself out of the succession by falling in love with a commoner – Lilian Craig, a Welsh model and singer whom he had met in London in 1943 while he was posted there as a naval attaché at the Swedish embassy. Bertil had become fascinated by her and they soon became lovers. Marriage, though, was out of the question, and not only because Lilian, the daughter of a Welsh coal miner, was herself married to Ivan Craig, an actor. To ensure the continuation of the Swedish royal house, Bertil promised he would not marry his commoner sweetheart until the new crown prince grew up.

But nor did he want to give up Craig – and so he came up with a bizarre plan, which his father tolerated: he placed an advertisement in a Swedish newspaper seeking a housekeeper: more than two hundred women responded, among them, of course, Lilian Craig. She was hired. Thus they were able to live as man and wife under one roof, even though the unfortunate Lilian was not allowed to accompany her lover to official events.

As the future monarch, Carl Gustaf was to be spared such a fate. For as long as his grandfather was alive, he was highly discreet about his relationship with Silvia. By the summer of the following year, however, the old King's health was deteriorating badly and on the evening of 15th September 1973 he died in his sleep. When his grandson stood on the balcony of the royal palace four days later to be acclaimed King Carl XVI Gustaf, he was accompanied by his four sisters and his loyal uncle Bertil. Silvia, the woman he loved, was not among them: she watched the proceedings on the television news from her home in Innsbruck.

As monarch, Carl Gustaf was now the only person in the Swedish royal family free to marry whom he wanted, but he hesitated. His relationship with Silvia had remained a secret: although his four sisters knew about it, the media and the country as a whole did not, and he was wary of how they would react. For her part, Silvia was naturally apprehensive about what life as a queen would be like. In the meantime, apparently vying with Britain's Prince Charles for the title of Europe's most eligible bachelor, Carl Gustaf provided fuel for the gossip columns by associating with a variety of society beauties.

But he and Silvia continued to meet, in Stockholm and also in the south of France, where Uncle Bertil lent them his villa on the seafront in Sainte-Maxime. Yet the press still knew nothing of the relationship, instead linking their young king with every woman who crossed his path. That all changed when the pair met again on Öland, the island in southern Sweden where the royal family has its summer residence. While out driving one afternoon with Silvia in his metallic-blue Porsche Targa, Carl Gustaf stopped to refuel. As they were pulling out of the petrol station, a photographer snapped them. The picture, printed in newspapers across Europe, was a sensation. Who was this young woman travelling alone with the King? Forty-eight hours later she had been identified as Silvia Sommerlath.

What happened next was entirely predictable, as least as far as royal love affairs were concerned. Palace officials in Stockholm tried to downplay the significance of the relationship, while journalists did not believe them and besieged the Olympics office in Innsbruck where Silvia was working for the 1976 winter games. Wearing a wig and dark glasses, she would slip unnoticed into Sweden to visit him. Or they would meet in Munich, where Carl Gustaf's sister, Birgitta, lived with her German husband Prince Johann Georg in a villa in the upmarket suburb of Grünwald.

As the Games drew to a close, rumours grew stronger that they would become engaged. Then on 12th March 1976, it was official. "This is the woman whom I love, whom I will marry and with whom I will spend the rest of my life," Carl Gustaf told a press conference at the palace in Stockholm.

They married on 19th June that year. It was the first wedding of a reigning European monarch since King Konstantinos of Greece married Princess Anne-Marie of Denmark in 1964 – and the first of a Swedish king since Gustaf IV Adolf in 1797. At a televised gala in the couple's honour held the day before at the Royal Swedish Opera in Stockholm, members of Abba, dressed in baroque outfits in a tongue-in-cheek attempt to blend in, performed their forthcoming single 'Dancing Queen'.

There was a poignant postscript to the royal love affair: that December, after obtaining permission from his nephew, Prince Bertil, now aged sixty-four, was finally able to marry his beloved Lilian – more than thirty years after their first meeting in London. How could Carl Gustaf have refused him? They had another twenty years together as man and wife before he died, aged eighty-four.

Chapter 7

Mistresses, Bastards and Maris complaisants

With their extramarital dalliances, Kings Carl XVI Gustaf, Juan Carlos and Albert II were following a long-established practice. Traditionally, royal marriages were not about love, lust or friendship – they were instead about producing heirs and cementing alliances, and were carefully arranged by parents and ministers. It is because of the usefulness of the royal marriage as a tool of foreign policy that unions were invariably with those from other countries – even if, as the experience of the First World War showed, it was perfectly possible for countries linked by close family ties to go to war against each other.

When the future King George VI, the father of Queen Elizabeth II, married Elizabeth Bowes-Lyon in April 1923, she became the first Briton to make a legitimate marriage to a prince of the royal house since Anne Hyde became James II's first wife in 1659. The Continental monarchies have clung even longer to the tradition of seeking wives and husbands abroad – often in Germany. The future King Harald V of Norway's marriage to Sonja Haraldsen in 1968 made him the first future head of a Scandinavian nation to choose a compatriot. Crown Prince Philippe of Belgium's wedding to Mathilde d'Udekem d'Acoz just over thirty years later was the first domestic match involving the heir to the throne of one of the three Benelux monarchies.

With so much at stake, relatively little attention was traditionally paid to the personal suitability of the couple – which in the Middle Ages, at least, would lead to some bizarre matches. Take Richard, Duke of York, the younger of the two princes murdered in the Tower of London. He was already a widower when he disappeared at the age of ten in 1483; he had been betrothed to Anne de Mowbray, a rich heiress, when he was four and she was five.

In the days before photography, the potential for disappointment presented by such long-distance unions was considerable. England's Henry VIII was dismayed when he caught his first glimpse of the German-born Anne of Cleves, destined to become his fourth wife. When the King went to the water's edge to meet her on 3rd January 1540, he discovered she looked little like the portrait that Hans Holbein, the court's most prominent artist, had painted of her. By then, however, it was too late to call off the union with a woman whom he dubbed his "Flanders mare". "If it were not that she had come so far into my realm, and the great preparations and state that my people have made for her, and for fear of making a ruffle in the world and of driving her brother into the arms of the Emperor and the French king, I would not marry her," Henry complained. "But now it is too far gone, wherefore I am sorry."[1] He claimed he could not consummate the marriage because he "could not overcome his loathsomeness" of her "nor in her company be provoked or stirred to the Act". At Henry's instigation, the marriage was annulled, but Anne received a generous settlement including Richmond Palace and Hever Castle, home of Henry's former in-laws, the Boleyns, and became known as "the King's Beloved Sister". And, unlike Anne Boleyn and Kathryn Howard, she also kept her head.

In many cases, a royal couple would marry "by proxy" before even meeting at all. Under a curious procedure that endured until the nineteenth century, each would separately undergo a marriage ceremony in their home country in which a stand-in, usually a relative, would play the part of the spouse to be. The "couple" would even go to bed afterwards, although there was a limit: the union would be deemed to have been consummated once their feet had touched. As well as preventing any last-minute hitches, this would ensure the bride's honour was protected, since she would be travelling abroad as a married rather than a single woman.

The practice was famously depicted in Rubens's painting, *The Wedding by Proxy of Marie de' Medici to King Henri IV* (1622–25), which shows the marriage of the Florentine princess to the French King, which took place in the cathedral of Florence in 1606. Henri himself is not present – instead it is the bride's uncle, Grand Duke

Ferdinando of Tuscany, who is pictured slipping the ring on Marie's finger. As late as 1810, when Archduchess Marie Louise of Austria became Napoleon's second wife, the initial marriage ceremony, held in Vienna, went ahead without him. He did, however, deign to turn up for a second ceremony held three weeks afterwards in the chapel of the Louvre.

Even without such a ceremony, parental pressure was such that bride and groom would do their duty. If the two felt some kind of attraction to their spouse to be, then this was a bonus. Indifference, dislike or even physical revulsion were not reason enough to abandon the process.

With marriages viewed this way, it is no surprise that the bride and groom were individually interchangeable. Take the case of Princess Dagmar, the brown-eyed second daughter of Christian IX of Denmark. Having set himself the task of finding his children partners in Europe's most important dynasties, Christian wanted Dagmar to marry into the Tsar's family. The Russians, keen for an alternative to the all too common German option, were in favour of the match too. Tsarevich Nicholas seemed the perfect husband.

The young heir to the Russian throne had been given a photograph of the girl destined to be his bride when he was just twelve. Fortunately for their families, he and Dagmar hit it off when he travelled to Copenhagen to meet her. In 1864, when Dagmar was sixteen and Nicholas – or Nixa as she called him – was twenty, they were betrothed. Dagmar prepared herself for her future role, learning her future husband's language by reading Hans Christian Andersen in Russian.

In April the following year, tragedy struck: while Nixa was holidaying in the south of France at the Tsar's villa in Nice, he was struck down with meningitis. When Dagmar received a telegram from his father saying he was being given the last rites, she rushed to Frankfurt where she met the Tsar. Together they travelled on the Russian leader's special train at high speed; Emperor Napoleon III ordered all the normal services off the track to speed their passage southwards.

A small matter such as death could not be allowed to stand in the way of such dynastic considerations, however, and so it was decided to marry the unfortunate princess to Nixa's younger brother, the future Tsar Alexander III instead. After a year of mourning, he travelled to Denmark and, three weeks later, proposed.

A bear of a man who had shocked his parents by bending the family silver, Alexander was very different from his intellectual elder brother. He would not have been Dagmar's choice, but she did as she was told and, in November 1866, after converting to Russian Orthodoxy and taking the name of Maria Fyodorovna, she married him in the Imperial Chapel of the Winter Palace in St Petersburg. She went on to bear him six children, including the future Tsar Nicholas II, and became Tsarina in 1881 after her father-in-law Alexander II was mortally wounded by a terrorist bomb.

Fear of a similar assassination attempt against her husband was to oblige Maria Fyodorovna and Alexander III to move thirty miles away from St Petersburg to a palace in Gatchina, considered more secure. Respite from such fears came every summer when they travelled to the more relaxed atmosphere of Denmark for family gatherings; they made the journey on board one of the royal yachts, accompanied by more than a hundred courtiers, large amounts of baggage and a cow to provide milk for the children along the way.

There was a happier outcome for Princess Mary of Teck, a British-born minor royal of German descent, who found herself in the same unfortunate situation as Dagmar almost three decades later. The Princess, known to her family as May, was betrothed in December 1891 at the age of twenty-four to her second cousin, once removed, Prince Albert Victor, Duke of Clarence and Avondale, the eldest son of the future Edward VII and Alexandra. The Prince – known to his family as Eddy, was expected one day to become king. But he was also a sleazy character who frequented prostitutes of both sexes and had a penchant for the low life: rumours circulated that he was associated with – or even was – Jack the Ripper, the notorious serial killer blamed for a series of brutal murders in the impoverished East End of London in the late 1880s.

Six weeks after their engagement was announced, Eddy died unexpectedly of pneumonia. For the royal family she was too good a catch to miss and so, the following year, May became engaged to Eddy's younger brother, the future George V. They were to remain happily married until his death more than forty years later.

A few other royal marriages, although arranged, also turned into genuine love matches – most notably Queen Victoria's union with Albert. The attraction was not just physical, but also intellectual.

When Albert died of typhoid fever in 1861 at the age of just forty-two, Victoria was devastated and wore black for the rest of her life. Her grandfather George III too had been devoted to his wife, Princess Charlotte of Mecklenburg-Strelitz, whom he met for the first time on their wedding day, in 1761 – the year after he became king. They remained married – happily by all accounts, apart from George's later bouts of madness – until her death in November 1818, and she bore him no fewer than fifteen children.

These were the exceptions, however: many other royal unions quickly degenerated into indifference or downright dislike. Even so, few had got off to quite as disastrous a start as that between Victoria's uncle, the future George IV, and Princess Caroline of Brunswick in 1795 – not least because he was already married to Maria Anne Fitzherbert, a beautiful twice-widowed Roman Catholic, with whom he had fallen in love at the age of twenty-one a decade earlier.

The Prince, believed to have lost his virginity with one of the Queen's maids of honour when he was sixteen, quickly acquired a reputation for philandering that clung to him throughout his life. In the spring of 1779, at the age of seventeen, he fell passionately in love first with Mary Hamilton, one of his sister's ladies-in-waiting, who was six years his senior; then, more scandalously, with Mary Robinson, a married actress with whom he became infatuated after he saw her appear as Perdita in *A Winter's Tale* at Drury Lane.

His father, George III, was appalled, not least because his son's dalliances were calling into question the monarchy's reputation for moral probity. "Your love of dissipation has for some months been with enough ill nature trumpeted in the public papers," he declared on his son's eighteenth birthday. For that reason, when George was given his own residence in 1780, he was required to continue living with his parents so they could keep an eye on him.

The tactic failed badly. Despite being kept under a virtual curfew, the Prince proved adept at evading those trying to watch over him. By the summer of the following year he had been seen "riding like a madman" in Hyde Park, been involved in drunken brawls at Vauxhall and Ranelagh Gardens and seduced a number of women.[2] He also embarked on another ill-advised affair with a married woman, this time with Countess von Hardenberg, the wife of a Hanoverian diplomat, who began to talk of "running away together". George was tempted, but when he confided in his mother she had her husband send the von Hardenbergs back to Germany, where the Countess then tried her luck with George's younger brother, Prince Frederick.

Then George met Mrs Fitzherbert, who like Mary Hamilton was six years his senior. It was love at first sight – at least on the part of the Prince, who pursued her relentlessly, on one occasion stabbing himself to draw blood and having her brought to him so she could see his state of despair. George, who appears to have been genuinely in love, realized the only way to have his way with her was to marry – which was triply problematic: Mrs Fitzherbert was a commoner, and thus unsuitable by tradition; she was a Roman Catholic, but the Act of Settlement of 1701 stated that the heir apparent would forfeit his right to the crown if he married a follower of Rome; and, under the Royal Marriages Act of 1772, every marriage contracted by a member of the royal family under the age of twenty-five without the King's consent was invalid. George was just twenty-three.

He was undaunted, however, and on 15th December 1785 they wed secretly in the drawing room of her home in Park Lane. The service was conducted by Robert Butt, a one-time vicar of Twickenham who was in prison for debt and who agreed to do the deed in return for his discharge. They left afterwards for a honeymoon at Ormeley Lodge, near Richmond.

The couple made a token attempt to keep their marriage secret: rather than move in with George, Mrs Fitzherbert rented a house nearby. Rumours spread about their relationship, however, and they increasingly lived together as man and wife. And so it might well have continued, had it not been for the huge debts being run up by the spendthrift Prince. By the early 1790s his finances were in such a parlous state that he was obliged yet again to turn to his father to bail him out. By this time he had also fallen out with Mrs Fitzherbert and had taken Frances, Countess of Jersey, as his mistress. So, in August 1794, George told the King that he was ready to make a suitable marriage, in return for a considerable financial settlement. His cousin, Princess Caroline of Brunswick, six years his junior, was chosen as his bride. The Prince agreed, even though he had never met her.

The match was in part thanks to lobbying by Lady Jersey who, according to one contemporary observer (the Duke of Wellington), had chosen the Princess, a woman of "indelicate manners, indifferent character and not very inviting appearance from the hope that disgust for the wife would secure constancy to the mistress".[3] To further strengthen her own position, the Countess insisted on becoming a lady-in-waiting to the Queen.

When Caroline, a blonde, high-spirited woman who paid little attention to fashion or personal hygiene, arrived at St James's on 5th April 1795, it was revulsion – rather than love – at first sight on both sides: after giving her the obligatory kiss, George retreated to the corner of the room where he was fortified by a dram of brandy. The wedding ceremony, held on the evening of the 8th in the Chapel Royal of St James's, proved even more of an ordeal; Caroline, who complained that her husband was "nothing as handsome as his portrait", claimed afterwards he had been dead drunk for most of the wedding night.

The couple parted company almost immediately after their brief honeymoon – but not before conceiving a daughter, Charlotte, born on 7th January the following year. His duty done, George wrote his wife a letter on 30th April renouncing further cohabitation, and their separation became final.

In the years that followed, the Prince made it difficult for Caroline to see their daughter; exasperated, she left for the Continent, returning to Britain only after George III died in January 1820 and her husband succeeded him. Any hopes that Caroline may have had that she would be welcomed back as his queen were swiftly dashed. George banned her from his coronation, held at Westminster Abbey on 19th July 1821, and when she turned up regardless, she was sent away by prizefighters dressed as pages. This was like a death blow to the unfortunate Caroline: she was taken ill while watching a performance at Drury Lane Theatre a few days later and, to George's apparent delight, died on 7th August.

In addition to his well-documented liaisons with Fitzherbert and Robinson, and Ladies Jersey, Hertford and Conyngham, George had at least thirteen other mistresses as well as very many other short-lived affairs. Yet Fitzherbert appears to have been the only woman to whom he was ever sincerely attached: when he died in 1830, it was with her portrait around his neck.

Many of George IV's Continental contemporaries also had unhappy marriages, even if they did not go quite as disastrously wrong as his.

An example was Léopold I, the first king of the Belgians. Although devoted to the unfortunate Princess Charlotte and distraught at her death in childbirth, relations were far cooler with his second wife, Louise, daughter of Louis Philippe, the king of France, whom he married, largely out of dynastic considerations, in 1832. Some twenty-two years his junior, the young Princess, who was aged just twenty when they married, found sex with her husband a terrible chore. "I am indifferent to his caresses, and to his familiarity... I put up with them, I allow it to happen, but I find it more repugnant than pleasing."[4] Although this did not prevent the couple from having four children over the following eight years, Léopold sought his pleasure elsewhere.

The marriage of his son, also called Léopold, was even more of a disaster. The Duke of Brabant, as he was known at the time, was most likely still a virgin when his father married him in August 1853 at just eighteen to Marie-Henriette de Habsburg-Lorraine, the daughter of Archduke Joseph of Austria. Again, the motivations were dynastic, but they were a poor match: a tall, scrawny adolescent with a large nose, who was likened somewhat cruelly by some contemporaries to a "stick of asparagus", the future Léopold II was quiet, solitary and sullen. Beautiful, if a little plump, Marie-Henriette was an extrovert tomboy who loved music, especially wild Gypsy tunes, playing cards and horses, which she rode Magyar-style at great speed.

Léopold would have preferred her elder sister, Elisabeth, but was not given the choice. Writing to his parents from Vienna, he described his future wife as "a bit fat and not very pretty, though without being ugly". Marie-Henriette, who had been dreaming of a very different Prince Charming, told her half-brother, Stephan, before leaving for Brussels, that she felt "like a nurse going to tend a patient with consumption". It was, said Madame Metternich, a match between "a stable boy and a nun, the nun being the Duke of Brabant".[5]

The marriage got off to a predictably poor start after the couple set up home together in Brussels. Like her mother-in-law before her, Marie-Henriette quickly lost her gaiety and spontaneity. Withdrawing into herself, she established a menagerie of ponies, horses, dogs, parrots and even camels and llamas. "If God hears my prayers, I shall not go on living much longer," she wrote to a friend in Vienna a month after her marriage.[6]

The couple's incompatibility was immediately obvious to all. The Duchess of Dino commented that Marie-Henriette had a "very sad manner": "I pity also the young Duke, for they are two children who only got married reluctantly."[7] Léopold and Marie-Henriette's failure to do their duty and produce an heir also became a matter of concern – especially to Queen Victoria, who took an interest in the family. "Leo does not demonstrate the slightest feeling of *love* or admiration for Marie, or *any woman*," she wrote despairingly to the young Prince's father. To try to improve matters, she had her husband, Albert, write to the future Belgian king to encourage him to be a better husband. In one letter, written in April 1857, almost four years after they had married, he urged the young couple "to love each other with greater passion than displayed so far".[8]

It seemed to work: the following February, Marie-Henriette gave birth to the first of four children. Unfortunately, the only boy among them – also named, of course, Léopold – died aged just nine after falling in a pond at Laeken. Léopold was forced to accept that it would be his brother Philippe's son who would eventually succeed him – and like many monarchs before him, he knew who was to blame: his wife. Marie-Henriette was understandably upset. "What can we do against the will of God?" she asked in a letter to Adrien Goffinet, a confidant.[9]

Their marriage effectively over, Marie-Henriette, now aged thirty-six, withdrew almost completely from court life, spending most of her time at a house she bought in the health resort of Spa in the Ardennes, where she devoted herself to breeding dogs and horses – and to Pierre Chazal, the minister of war. He was as fond of animals as she was; he had once owned a park with zebras and kept a monkey in his living room – and so presumably did not much mind the smell of animals that observers reported hung around the Queen. After Chazal returned to his native south of France in 1871, he was replaced in her affections by Henri Hardy, the young royal veterinarian, who looked after her when she was ill. "Treat me as if I were a horse," Marie-Henriette used to tell him.[10] The full misery of her life was revealed only in letters published a few weeks after her death in September 1902 in the *Neues Wiener Tagblatt* and reproduced in the *New York Times*. "I am an unhappy woman," she had written in September 1853, just a month after her marriage. "God is my only support. If God will hear my prayer, I will not live longer."[11]

There were similar tales of marital woe elsewhere in Europe. Especially unhappy, even by royal standards, was the Dutch king Willem III's first marriage in June 1839, to his cousin Sophie, daughter of King Wilhelm I of Württemberg and Grand Duchess Catherine Pavlovna of Russia. The problem was not just her husband's much publicized philandering, which led the *New York Times* to brand him after his death as "dissolute and lustful" and "the greatest debauchee of the age",[12] but also the fact that, intellectually, Sophie was far superior to the King, who was described by Queen Victoria, with whom she corresponded, as an uneducated farmer. Sophie made this widely known, suggesting she should be regent in his place. Although half-Russian herself, she also had a prickly relationship with her Russian mother-in-law, Anna Pavlovna, who had been completely against the marriage. After bearing her husband three sons – none of whom lived long enough to become king – Sophie tried to separate from him – but was refused permission. From 1855 the couple lived apart and she spent much of her time in Stuttgart with her own family. When Sophie died in 1877, she was buried in her wedding dress, because, in her own view, her life had ended on the day she married.

Willem, by now aged sixty, wasted little time mourning his late wife. A few months after her death, he announced his intention to marry Eléonore d'Ambre, a French opera singer, whom he ennobled as Countess d'Ambroise – without government consent. When the Dutch government objected, he settled instead for Princess Emma of Waldeck and Pyrmont, a small German principality, who was forty-one years his junior. Despite the age difference the marriage appears to have been a happy one, enduring for the remaining eleven years of his life.

While death was, in most cases, the only way of getting rid of an unwanted spouse, divorce, as Henry VIII had shown with two of his wives, was occasionally a solution – at least in Denmark. The future King Christian VIII learnt three years after marrying his cousin, Charlotte Frederikke of Mecklenburg-Schwerin, in 1806 that she was having an affair with her voice teacher, the composer Édouard du Puy. Retribution was swift: the marriage was dissolved, and Charlotte Frederikke was banished to Jutland and forbidden from ever seeing her son Frederik again.

The boy, who was to reign as Frederik VII from 1848 until 1863, grew up to have his share of marital difficulties. When he was twenty, long before coming to the throne, he married his second cousin, Vilhelmine, youngest daughter of the then king, Frederik VI. It was not a happy union: he was unfaithful and ruthless towards his wife and finally crossed the line one evening when he got drunk in her bedroom and threatened her. It was too much for the King, who banished him to Jægerspris Castle and demanded a divorce for his daughter. It came through in 1837. Frederik's second marriage, with Duchess Caroline of Mecklenburg-Strelitz in 1841, was also a failure, ending in divorce five years later. Such divorces were the exception, though; most royal couples remained married, at least in name.

Once a royal marriage had taken place, the aim was clear: to produce a legitimate heir, preferably a male one. The birth itself became an official occasion, governed by its own rules and procedures.

In Britain, following the so-called "warming-pan incident" of 1688, when Mary of Modena, second wife of King James II, was accused of substituting a changeling smuggled in a warming pan for her own stillborn child, a minister of the crown was required to attend all royal births as an independent witness. The practice survived well into the twentieth century and was not abolished until the time of the birth of Prince Charles in 1948.

One son was not enough, especially in those countries – the majority – that did not allow queens regnant. In those days of high infant mortality, several were needed to be sure of producing a male heir who would survive through childhood. Léopold II was not the only king to bury his son and see the throne pass instead through his brother's line. Carl XV of Sweden and Norway, who reigned from 1859 until 1872, lost his only son Prince Carl Oscar to pneumonia at just fifteen months, after doctors prescribed a cold bath as a cure for his measles. Carl XV was then succeeded by his younger brother, Oscar. His Dutch contemporary, Willem III, meanwhile, buried three sons before siring the future Queen Wilhelmina at the age of sixty-three – even though the rules of succession had to be altered in order to allow a woman to come to the throne.

The most unfortunate was Denmark's Frederik VI – or rather his wife, Marie Sophie Frederikke of Hesse-Kassel, who bore eight children only to lose six of them as babies. The two who survived were girls and therefore barred from the throne – as were the four children the King had by his mistress, Frederikke Dannemand. So when Frederik died in 1839, he was succeeded by his cousin, Christian VIII.

Once the heir was born and succession assured, most monarchs lived separate lives from their wives, almost certainly sleeping in a different bedroom or even palace. Often a glowering and unhappy presence, she could not be removed without threatening a diplomatic incident with the country of her birth.

Kings would then seek solace in the arms of other women, some of whom then became permanent features at court. The heyday of the mistress was undoubtedly pre-revolutionary France. François I, who ruled from 1515 to 1547, is believed to have been the first monarch to appoint his favourite as *maîtresse-en-titre*, a quasi-official title that came with expectations of an apartment in the palace, jewels and a steady income. Some of the women who went on to assume the title accumulated considerable power: Françoise-Athénaïs de Rochechouart de Mortemart, better known as Madame de Montespan, was widely considered the true queen of France for the influence that she exerted over Louis XIV in the late 1660s and 1670s – which came to an end when she was accused of involvement in a series of suspicious poisonings. Almost a century later, Madame de Pompadour and Madame du Barry exerted an equally powerful influence over Louis XV.

Far from a dirty secret, a mistress was an essential trapping of royal life elsewhere in Europe too. Louis XIV's cousin, Charles II of Britain, was one of the few monarchs to have several mistresses simultaneously – among them Nell Gwynn and Lady Castlemaine – who between them bore him at least a dozen children (while his marriage with Catherine of Braganza of Portugal remained without issue). When Augustus the Strong of Saxony became king of Poland in 1697, he was advised that in order to become a "complete monarch" he should take a mistress in Warsaw to complement the one he already had in Germany. Failure to do so, he was told, would upset his new Polish subjects.

Presumably with Charles's example in mind, George, the elector of Hanover, brought two mistresses – one tall and thin, the other short and fat, and both surprisingly ugly – with him from Germany when he succeeded to the British throne in 1714. His son, who was to succeed him as George II in 1727, also took a mistress, although more out of a sense of duty than passion. The King, wrote the memoirist Lord Hervey, "seemed to look upon a mistress rather as a necessary appurtenance to his grandeur as a prince than as an addition to his pleasures as a man, and thus only pretended to distinguish what it was evident he overlooked and affected to caress what it was manifest he did not love."[13]

By the nineteenth century changing sexual mores meant that such a formal system of mistresses no longer seemed appropriate. Yet princes were still forced by their parents, often at an early age, into a love-less marriage for the sake of the dynasty, and only a few could bring themselves to embrace monogamy completely. A particular favourite for short dalliances were actresses, who were invariably beautiful and often available. And if the relationship became more serious they could be married to a suitable husband in order to provide a veneer of respectability. Other royal males preferred high-born women who were already married.

In both cases the husbands of such royal conquests – who became known as *maris complaisants* – were required to turn a blind eye to their wife's extramarital adventures. The reward for playing the cuckold could be a job or an honour or a curious kind of prestige that came from the knowledge among fellow aristocrats that your wife was being bedded by the King. Often, they were simply too busy with their own affairs to be worried about what their wife was up to.

It proved an enduring model. There is no better modern-day example of such a triangle than the romance that Prince Charles carried on with the then Camilla Parker Bowles while he was married to Diana, Princess of Wales, and she to Andrew Parker Bowles. Diana minded considerably, but Parker Bowles, pursing his own relationships with other women, apparently did not.

Léopold I of Belgium took several mistresses, most of them much younger than himself: the most celebrated among them was Arcadie Claret, the beautiful eighteen-year-old daughter of a French army officer whom the King met in 1844 when he was fifty-four. Infatuated with her from the start, Léopold married her to Frédéric Meyer, a young army officer, and installed her in an *hôtel de maître* in the Rue Royale in Brussels, close to the royal palace.

The King made little attempt to hide his relationship, appearing with his young mistress at the theatre and other events, much to the anger of the Belgian public, who whistled and even pelted the windows of her home in Brussels with rotten vegetables. In November 1849 she bore him a son, who was named Georges-Frédéric – Georges being the King's second name. Matters became simpler in October the following year when his wife Louise died of tuberculosis, aged just thirty-eight; Léopold could now be more open about his relationship with Arcadie, installing her in the Château du Stuyvenberg near Laeken, which he bought for her. It was here on 25th September that she gave birth to his second child, named Chrétien, Léopold's third name. When the King died in 1865 after a long illness, the last word he uttered was not Arcadie but Charlotte – although it was not known whether he meant his English first wife or his daughter of the same name.

Léopold's son, meanwhile, had already started seeking pleasure elsewhere early during his unhappy marriage with the unfortunate Marie-Henriette. Although introduced to carnal pleasures only relatively late, Léopold II soon developed his father's passion for sex, which vied with his obsession with the Congo and with money. "My nature requires manifold encounters with the fair sex," he confided to his diary. "I do not understand how clerics can live."[14]

Among his many mistresses was Marguerite d'Estève, known as "Margot, the Queen of the Congo", who kept a salon on Brussels's prestigious Avenue Louise. There were others in Nice and other fashionable resorts of the time. The King had a particular passion for chambermaids, shop girls and *chocolatières*, the young women who sold chocolate in *salons de thé*, all of whom were sent away weighed down with presents.

In later life Léopold was also a frequent visitor to Paris nightclubs, where expensive prostitutes with pseudo-aristocratic names catered to the needs of affluent clients. He was especially fond of Émilienne d'Alençon, who, along with Liane de Pougy and Caroline "La Belle" Otero, were known as the "Trois Grâces" or, more appropriately, the "Grandes Horizontales". More shocking were the allegations of paedophilia made during a court case in London in 1885. A former servant at a "disorderly house" owned by a Mrs Mary Jeffries testified that the King paid £800 a year for a supply of young virgins, aged ten to fifteen, to be sent to him in Brussels.[15] William Stead, the editor of the *Pall Mall Gazette*, then wrote a series of articles in which he claimed a hundred girls were sold each year. Mrs Jeffries herself admitted having had a young girl delivered to the royal yacht *Alberta* when it was moored on the Thames during one of the King's visits. Léopold did not seem troubled by the affair, which was barely mentioned in the Belgian press.

Then, in the summer of 1900, Léopold began what was to prove a highly controversial relationship with Blanche Delacroix, a young French woman. He was already sixty-five and Blanche just seventeen: he was taken by her youth and beauty; she was dazzled by his wealth and position. She had been living with Antoine-Emmanuel Durrieux, a sea captain eighteen years her senior whom she had met during her voyage from Argentina, where she had been living for the previous few years, but was quick to see the attraction of a royal liaison. Léopold, feeling unloved by his own family and needing someone to nurse him in old age, made her his permanent mistress. He shared his vast fortune with her, showering her with expensive jewels – including a diamond necklace worth 75,000 francs – and properties: he renovated for her Villa Vandenborght, near his palace in Laeken – even building a special walkway over the road to link the grounds of their two homes – and bought her the Villa Caroline, in Ostend, which was connected to his Chalet Royal by an underground tunnel, and the Château de Balincourt, in Arronville in the Val-d'Oise, which had silver bathtubs and a bed adorned with gold under a vast canopy of handmade Belgian lace.

Léopold wooed his young mistress in Cap Ferrat, a spectacularly beautiful but still wild area on the Côte d'Azur, where he bought more than a dozen plots of land after visiting his daughter Clémentine in 1895. It was here in 1902 that he was to build the Villa Léopolda, an extraordinary home whose later owners were to include the Fiat boss Gianni Agnelli and the Jewish-Lebanese financier Edmond Safra – and, after his death in a suspicious fire in Monaco in 1999, his widow Lily.

Far from prying eyes, this was the ideal place for an illicit affair. Léopold installed Blanche in a villa called Radiana, deep in the middle of lush vegetation, where she was effectively his prisoner. Every evening, equipped with a dim lantern, he would make his way to the house along a little path hidden by the trees. Officially he went to play cards, but the gardener of the Léopolda had orders to deliver a basket of fresh flowers every day.

Although Léopold was by now a widower, the relationship earned wide disapproval – and provided fodder for the caricaturists – much as his father's liaison with Arcadie Claret had done sixty years earlier. Such criticism intensified after Delacroix had two children, both sons: Lucien, born in February 1906, and Philippe, born in October the following year. Whether the King, now aged seventy-two, was actually Philippe's father is not clear – even though he was encouraged to see that the newborn baby had a deformed hand, something of a hereditary trait of the Coburgs. Blanche was rewarded for the birth of Lucien by being ennobled as the baroness de Vaughan. The two boys were to be treated rather more generously than Delphine Boël would be by King Albert II almost a century later: Lucien became the duke of Tervuren and his younger brother the count of Ravenstein.

By this time Blanche, who had begun to dominate the ageing King, had resumed her relationship with Durrieux, her former boyfriend and pimp; on one occasion Léopold came across the two of them together during a visit to Villa Vandenborght. Blanche tried to explain Durrieux away as his brother. Whether or not Léopold believed her is not clear, but he tolerated the man's presence near his mistress and at court, prompting Socialist pamphlets to talk of "an indecent triangular relationship". Catholic opinion was also outraged: on one occasion the King was confronted in Ostend by a priest. "Sire, I have heard rumours that you have a concubine," he told him. "Good Heavens, Father," Léopold replied. "I have heard the same rumours about you, but I *don't* believe them."

Léopold contemplated abdicating in favour of his nephew Albert and spending the last of his days with his mistress, whose ennobling had brought more criticism. Then, in December 1909, moments before he had a serious operation on his intestine, which he feared he might not survive, he married Blanche in a secret religious ceremony, with the benediction of Pope Pius X. Léopold was dressed in white; his bride wore a black silk robe. The King called her "*ma veuve*" ("my widow").

Such a ceremony – similar to his great-nephew Léopold III's clandestine wartime marriage to Lilian Baels – may have made it possible for the King to make peace with the clergy, but still did not make Blanche his queen or allow either of their sons to succeed him. That would have required a civil ceremony. In any case, he died just two days after the operation. Nevertheless, Blanche, who remained with him until the end – just as his father's mistress, Arcadie, had done six decades earlier – still enjoyed a substantial inheritance. The following

August she married Durrieux, who had wisely remained in touch and even allowed himself to be registered as the father of her sons. The ceremony was held at the unusual hour of 6.30 in the morning to shake off the paparazzi. They divorced three years later.

There were similar goings-on elsewhere in Europe: Oscar I, who ruled Sweden and Norway from 1844 until his death fifteen years later, effectively led parallel lives. Although initially happily married to his Italian-born queen, Joséphine, who bore him five children in rapid succession, he was unfaithful to her almost from the start – chiefly with Emilie Högquist, a prominent actress whom he set up in a luxurious apartment close to the royal palace. Oscar was said to spend alternate nights with his wife and with Emilie, who bore him two sons – who became jokingly known as "the princes of Laponia" (Lappland). Before marrying, he had fathered another child with a lady-in-waiting to the former queen.

Joséphine, a devout Catholic who risked the displeasure of her husband's subjects by refusing to convert to Protestantism, was deeply wounded by such infidelity. In her diary she wrote of her bitterness that a woman was expected to suffer a husband's unfaithfulness "in silence". Their eldest son, who succeeded Oscar as Carl XV in 1859, shared his father's predilection for actresses, having a brief affair with Elise Hwasser, the leading theatre star of her age, before moving on to another actress, Hanna Styrell, who had a daughter by him. Carl's younger brother, who succeeded him as Oscar II in 1872, had similar tastes.

In Britain, the future King Edward VII, a decade Oscar's junior, notched up an even more impressive record of romantic conquests in his long stint as prince of Wales, earning himself the nickname of Edward the Caresser – much to the lasting displeasure of his mother, Queen Victoria, who contrasted the debauched behaviour of her son, known in the family as Bertie, with the moral probity of her beloved late husband, Albert.

At the insistence of the Queen, who was keen her son should settle down, Edward married in 1863, at the age of just twenty-two, Princess Alexandra, the daughter of the future King Christian IX of Denmark, who was elegant and beautiful but increasingly deaf. In the eight years that followed Alexandra bore him six children, but this did little to prevent the Prince of Wales from seeking his pleasures elsewhere; he was a frequent visitor to Le Chabanais, an exclusive brothel in Paris – one room contained a large copper bathtub with an ornate figurehead, half woman and half swan, in which he liked to bathe in champagne with prostitutes. The increasingly overweight prince also had himself built a special *siège d'amour* that allowed easy access for oral sex and other forms of entertainment with several partners.

While Le Chabanais was far from the prying eyes of the press, Edward also took a number of mistresses back in Britain – at least thirteen of them, by one count – many of whom were married. Prominent among his early loves were two well-known actresses: the French-born Sarah Bernhardt and the British Lillie Langtry, known as the Jersey Lilly, whose portrait by Millais in 1878 drew crowds to the Royal Academy. Another liaison was with Winston Churchill's mother, Jennie. In 1889 he met "Daisy" Greville, Countess of Warwick, his "Darling Daisy" and perhaps the first real love of his life, with whom he had a relationship that lasted a decade. Unknown to the Prince, however, the Countess, who was married, was also having an affair with Lord Charles Beresford, Edward's former aide-de-camp, by whom she became pregnant. When she wrote to the Prince to inform him of this, she was swiftly replaced in his affections by Alice Keppel, twenty-eight years his junior, whose daughter, Sonia, was widely believed to be a product of the relationship.

The discreet Keppel was widely considered a positive influence on Edward, and this continued after he became king in 1901. Such was the enduring nature of their romance that she was with him in Biarritz in March 1910 when he suffered the heart attack that precipitated his death two months later. Although less keen on Keppel than on some of her husband's other mistresses, Alexandra reluctantly agreed to allow her to Buckingham Palace to take her final leave of him.

A quarter of a century later, on hearing that her late lover's grandson Edward VIII was renouncing the throne to marry Wallis Simpson, Keppel remarked "things were done much better in my day". In one of those neat twists of history – or an illustration perhaps of the narrow circles in which royalty moved – Keppel was the great-grandmother of Camilla Parker Bowles.

Alice's husband, George Keppel, the consummate *mari complaisant*, appears to have accepted his wife's liaison with the King, who used to visit their home at teatime when George was out – thereby avoiding potential embarrassment all around. The husbands of his other married mistresses were equally accommodating – with the notable exception of Sir Charles Mordaunt, who arrived home unexpectedly early from a salmon-fishing trip in Norway in summer 1869 to find his twenty-one-year-old wife Harriet entertaining the Prince of Wales at the family seat, Walton Hall, in Warwickshire. The result was an uncomfortable divorce case in which Edward was called as witness – though thankfully not a co-respondent. Even so, it was the first time for centuries that a member of the royal family had been required to give evidence in court.

The naming of the Prince in connection with such a murky affair was immensely damaging – and provided useful fuel for a rapidly emerging republican movement. Harriet's family, keen to protect their good name, had her certified insane and committed to an asylum, where she spent the remaining thirty-six years of her life. For his part Edward was free to continue his philandering, although he had to endure boos from the crowds and a severe telling-off from his mother.

While Edward VII's tastes were strictly heterosexual, several kings also took male lovers – though such was the imperative of producing an heir that most also had sex with women, albeit with varying degrees of enthusiasm. Willem II of Holland, beaten to the tragic Princess Charlotte of Britain by Léopold I, certainly appears to have been in this category, and in 1819 was blackmailed over what Cornelis van Maanen, the Dutch minister of justice, described as his "shameful and unnatural lusts".

Even more curious was the case of King Gustaf V, who reigned in Sweden for most of the first half of the twentieth century. Several years after his death in October 1950 came a bizarre postscript: Kurt Haijby, a petty thief who had killed a policemen during a jailbreak, said that in 1912, when he was a fifteen-year-old boy scout, he had been seduced by the King during an audience. Furthermore, Haijby claimed to have been the King's lover between 1936 and 1947 – a tribute if nothing else to the sexual powers of Gustaf, who would have been in his late eighties at the end of their relationship.

A subsequent investigation found it was not impossible for the incident to have taken place, but that it could not have occurred in the way described by Haijby – at neither the 1912 audience nor another twenty years later had he ever been alone with the King. Intriguingly, though, it emerged that the royal court had paid Haijby one hundred and seventy thousand Swedish kronor for his silence in the 1930s and then, in 1938, after he was arrested for child sex abuse and put into custody at the asylum of Beckomberga, he was offered four hundred kronor a month if he left Sweden and kept quiet about his accusations. Haijby accepted the deal – only to return after the war.

Gustaf's German-born wife Victoria appears to have had long since given up on her loveless marriage. In the early 1890s she had had an affair with Gustaf von Blixen-Finecke, her husband's equerry. Later she developed a close relationship with her personal physician Axel Munthe, with whom she used to winter on Capri.[16]

There were also instances of other, more complicated domestic set-ups – though few could compare with that of Christian VII, who became king of Denmark in 1766, a few weeks before his seventeenth birthday, and lived for a few years in a bizarre *ménage à trois* with his wife Caroline Matilda, the sister of George III, and her German doctor Johann Friedrich Struensee.

Married a few months after he came to the throne, Christian, who showed early signs of mental instability, exhibited little interest in his wife, preferring a twenty-one-year-old prostitute nicknamed Støvlet-Cathrine ("Boots"-Catherine) with whom he had a number of adventures before she was arrested and deported to Hamburg. Then in 1767, while travelling in the Duchy of Schleswig, he met Struensee, who at thirty was more than a decade his senior. Christian was impressed by the doctor – especially by his ability to cure his hangovers and depression – and brought him back to Copenhagen with the promise of a minor post at court. The dashing German doctor made even more of an impression on Caroline Matilda, becoming her lover, and used his power over the royal couple to become increasingly influential at court. By the summer of 1771 he had acquired dictatorial powers and appointed himself minister of state, whereupon, inspired by the Enlightenment thinkers of the day, he embarked on a programme of reforms intended to modernize Denmark.

Scandalizing opinion, the three of them would often walk or ride in a carriage together and Struensee would eat several times a week with the King and Queen in the royal apartments. To avoid stiff court etiquette, they moved to the palace of Hirschholm, on an island not far from Copenhagen. The King, whose mental state was deteriorating sharply, appeared happy with the arrangement – even after his queen gave birth to a daughter who was almost certainly her lover's. Their unusual relationship was doomed, however. Struensee's reforms, although potentially beneficial to Denmark, were often hastily introduced and upset a number of vested interests. The German had also made a powerful enemy in Christian's stepmother, Queen Juliane Marie, who had one goal in life: ensuring that her own son, Prince Frederik, Christian's younger half-brother, should one day inherit the throne.

Armed with evidence of Caroline Matilda's infidelity collected by several of her servants, Juliane Marie organized a group of conspirators, many of them nobles unhappy at Struensee's reforms. They struck in January 1772 in the early hours of the morning after a masked ball at court, arresting both Struensee and Caroline Matilda. Both lovers were tricked into confessing their adultery: Struensee was sentenced to death and was executed, together with Count Enevold Brandt, one of his allies, at Øster Fælled on 28th April in front of thousands of Copenhageners. Both Struensee and Brandt first had their right hands cut off and then, after the execution, their severed heads were held up for the crowd. Then the bodies were cut into parts and put on wheels, and the heads and hands impaled on stakes.

Caroline Matilda was allowed to live, but barred from seeing her children. She had hoped to return to her native England, but her sister-in-law, Queen Charlotte, refused to welcome back an adulteress and she was sent into exile in a palace in George III's dominion of Hanover. Christian, unaware of what had happened, demanded to see his wife and friend – only to learn to his horror that he had divorced Caroline Matilda and personally signed Struensee's death warrant.

Caroline Matilda died in 1775. Nine years later, her son, now sixteen, forced his father to sign a document under which he would become regent, taking from Juliane the powers she had plotted so hard to acquire for herself. He finally came to the throne in 1808 as Frederik VI, going on to become one of the country's best-loved monarchs.

Complicated marital set-ups seem to have been something of a Danish speciality. After his second divorce, Frederik VII, the next monarch but one, shocked society in 1850, at the age of forty-one, by concluding a morganatic marriage with Louise Rasmussen, a ballet dancer later ennobled as Countess Danner. Their relationship may also not have been entirely what it seemed: both the King and Rasmussen appeared to have been involved in a love triangle with Carl Berling, founder of the newspaper *Berlingske Tidende*, by whom she had a son. Berling later became chamberlain and all three lived in the palace until 1861. In a further twist it has also been claimed that Frederik, long assumed to have been infertile, actually fathered a son in 1843 by Else Maria Guldborg Pedersen, with whom he had an affair after the breakdown of his first two marriages.

The future King Carlos IV of Spain was also apparently tolerant of the sexual peccadilloes of his wife, Maria Luisa of Parma, who was aged just fourteen when he married her in 1765. She went on to have a series of affairs with courtiers, most notably with Manuel de Godoy, the tall, strongly built son of an aristocratic but impoverished army colonel, who had an enormous appetite for women. Godoy did not confine his attentions to the Queen, however: he married María Teresa de Borbón, the King's cousin, had a mistress, whom he obliged the Queen to take on as a lady-in-waiting, and embarked on a string of other casual affairs. Maria Luisa made little attempt to hide her relationship with Godoy – baffling contemporary observers. "The thing that must strike those most who watch Carlos IV in the bosom of his court is his blindness where the conduct of the Queen is concerned," observed the French ambassador.[17] The King, it seemed, was almost the only one at court who didn't recognize the striking resemblance of two of Maria Luisa's fourteen children to Godoy.

Obsessed with hunting and collecting clocks, Carlos, a timid character dominated by his wife, may simply not have cared. Either way, far from being punished, Godoy was made prime minister, and accompanied the royal couple when they went into exile in France in 1808. Carlos and his wife lived with Godoy, his daughter Carlota Luisa, his mistress Pepita and their sons – although Godoy's wife, María Teresa, presumably despairing of her husband's infidelities, had long since left him.

More than a century later, when another Spanish king, Alfonso XIII, the grandfather of Juan Carlos, the current monarch, went into exile, initially in Paris, he became concerned by the closeness of his queen, Victoria Eugenie, to the Duke of Lécera and his wife, the Duchess, thought to be a lesbian. When Victoria Eugenie remonstrated with him over one of his affairs, he taunted her over her relationship with the couple, declaring, "I choose them and never want to see your ugly face again."[18]

Queens did not generally enjoy the freedom for such amorous adventures. Few monarchs went quite as far in punishing infidelity as Henry VIII, who executed two of his six wives, but male pride meant it was a rare king who knowingly allowed himself to be cuckolded – even if he was indulging himself with his own mistress. As the case of Struensee showed, a man who dared to lay his hands on the Queen could be severely punished for what was considered treason.

That was certainly the experience of Tsar Peter the Great's chamberlain, William Mons, who earlier in the eighteenth century was foolish enough to have an affair with Catherine, the Tsarina. Peter was not a man to cross: he had already thrown his first wife, Eudoxia, into a convent and, when she subsequently had an affair, had her tortured and her lover impaled, even though he had long since lost interest in her. When Peter found out what Mons was up to, he had him beheaded – although to preserve the Tsar's honour the official reason given for his punishment was that he had been caught stealing from state coffers. Peter allowed his wife to keep her freedom but ordered that no one should obey her commands and cut her off from all her funds. Returning to her room on the evening after the execution, Catherine found her late lover's newly severed head staring at her from a jar of alcohol on her table.[19] Fortunately for Catherine, Peter died shortly afterwards.[20]

Different rules applied to queens regnant, who ruled in their own name rather than owing their titles to marriage. Although, like the men, often forced by parents into unsuitable unions, they were free, as sovereigns in their own right, to take lovers as they wished without fear of punishment. Elizabeth I, England's "virgin queen", had several favourites, among them Robert Dudley, Earl of Leicester – whom she came close to marrying – and, in later life, his step-son Robert Devereux, earl of Essex, who was more than two decades younger than the Queen.

In Russia, Peter and Catherine's daughter, Elizabeth, who crowned herself empress in spring 1742 after leading a bloodless revolt with the support of the royal guards, had an eventful love life, complicated by her difficult relationship with her aunt, Anna, who ruled the country from 1730 to 1740. Described as "content only when she was in love", the young Elizabeth got through a succession of men, among them Alexis Shubin, a handsome sergeant in the Semyonovsky Guards regiment – who was banished to Siberia and had his tongue cut off on Anna's orders. Elizabeth eventually consoled herself with Alexei Razumovsky, a tall, muscular Ukrainian peasant with a good bass voice who had been brought to St Petersburg by a nobleman for a church choir. Razumovsky, who was a few months older than Elizabeth, was showered with titles and honours and became an increasingly important figure at court; the pair may even have married secretly. This did not prevent the Tsarina from taking other lovers: by the time she reached her forties, she had enjoyed the attentions of several virile young men in their twenties.

This was nothing compared to the sexual antics of Catherine the Great, who disposed of her husband Tsar Peter III after he had spent just six months on the throne and became Tsarina in her own right. The couple had married when they were both still teenagers, but after seven years Catherine was still a virgin. Frustrated, she embarked on an affair with the dashing Count Sergei Saltykov; a series of other lovers followed, chief among them Stanisław August Poniatowski, the Polish count later rewarded with his country's crown, Gregory Orlov, Alexander Vasilchikov, Gregory Potemkin and Peter Zavadovsky.

By the time she reached her forties, Catherine had reduced the process of finding a suitable lover to a fine art: a potential candidate would first be checked out by a doctor for possible signs of venereal disease; he would then spend a night with Countess Prascovya Bruce, Catherine's friend and lady-in-waiting, who would act as "*éprouveuse*", rating the candidate on his appearance, his sexual technique and the size of his penis. Only those who passed such a stringent test would be passed on to the Tsarina.

Catherine remained sexually active until her death in November 1796, aged sixty-seven. A few years earlier, a barrel-shaped toothless grandmother, she had taken her last lover, Platon Zubov, who, at the age of twenty-two, was thirty-eight years younger than her. "The Empress wears him like a decoration," noted one observer.[21]

Nineteenth-century Catholic Spain was a very different country, but this did not prevent Isabel II from playing the field. Although proclaimed queen regent when she was three, on the death of her father,

Isabel was not free to choose a husband for herself. Instead, at the age of sixteen, she was obliged to marry her cousin, Don Francisco de Asís de Borbón. Slightly built, with a shrill falsetto voice and an unusual fascination with perfume, jewels and bathing, he was widely assumed to be gay. "What shall I say of a man who on his wedding night wore more lace than I?" the Queen recalled later.[22]

Understandably, Isabel went on to have a number of lovers, most of them officials and military men, a practice which helped contribute to her political downfall. After ruling for more than thirty years, she was forced to flee to France in 1868 and abdicate. Of her twelve children – only four of whom reached adulthood – few, if any, were thought to have been fathered by her husband. Her son, Alfonso XII, who became king in 1874, for example, was believed to have been the product of a liaison with either Enrique Puigmoltó y Mayans, captain of the Spanish Royal Guard, or General Francisco Serrano. This did not prevent Francisco from holding aloft the infant on a silver salver at each baptism, the traditional gesture of acknowledging the child as his own.[23]

Given that Isabel was a queen in her own right, the true identity of her heir's father – at least from a dynastic point of view – was something of an irrelevance. Of more dynastic significance is the curious case of Olav, the only child of King Haakon VII, the Danish prince who went on to found the current Norwegian dynasty, and his English wife, Queen Maud, the daughter of Edward VII. The couple married in 1896, but it was not until seven years later that their only child, the future King Olav, was born – a suspiciously long time given the importance traditionally attached by all royal families to producing an heir.

Various reasons have been given for the delay. Maud certainly spent a lot of time in Sandringham rather than her adoptive homelands of Denmark and then Norway. There were even rumours – put about by republicans – that Haakon was gay. Then in 2004 came another and rather more bizarre explanation: in the second volume of *Folket*, his voluminous history of the royal couple, Tor Bomann-Larsen, a Norwegian writer, claimed that Olav, who went on to become king in 1957, may not have been Haakon's son at all.[24] The strange assertion was based on examination of the royal couple's travel records, which Bomann-Larsen said showed that Olav had not been with his wife at the time the baby was thought to have been conceived. The book also claimed that medical records suggested the future king may have contracted a sexually transmitted disease during a particularly "debauched" naval tour to the West Indies, which could have left him sterile.

So who was Olav's father? Bomann-Larsen claimed Maud might instead have been artificially inseminated – perhaps without her knowledge – with sperm from her Harley Street doctor, Sir Francis Henry Laking, or his son, Guy Francis. Photographs included in the book certainly showed a remarkable resemblance between Olav and the Lakings – and a lack of one between the future monarch and his father. "At the time when the fertilization normally would have taken place, King Haakon was on a marine vessel in Denmark and Queen Maud was lying in hospital in England," Bomann-Larsen told a news conference to launch the book. "One cannot say precisely who knew what. Maud might not even have known herself."[25]

Not everyone was convinced. Odd Arvid Storsveen, a historian at the University of Oslo, claimed in a review of the book published in *Historisk Tidsskrift* that he couldn't find adequate evidence for Bomann-Larsen's hypothesis. "King Olav's descendants can take it easy," he declared.[26] A spokesman for Norway's royal family said the King had no information suggesting that Olav had not been Haakon's son.

Chapter 8

In Search of the New Princess Grace

It was a turnout worthy of one of the greatest style icons of the twentieth century. When the Victoria & Albert Museum in London held a reception in April 2010 to mark the opening of an exhibition showcasing the fashion of the late Princess Grace of Monaco, the guests were an appropriate mixture of show business and royalty. The Hollywood actress Joan Collins, the model Erin O'Connor and the former Beatles drummer Ringo Starr were there; so, too, were Prince Edward, third son of Queen Elizabeth, and his wife the Countess of Wessex.

On show was an extraordinary collection of forty dresses that charted the journey of the woman born Grace Patricia Kelly from Philadelphia socialite and Hollywood star to princess, via a fairy-tale marriage to Prince Rainier III of Monaco. There was the satin number that Grace wore when she collected her Oscar for *The Country Girl* in 1955, and across the aisle a black chiffon evening dress in which she appeared in *Rear Window*. There was the rather modest "easy to sew" floral outfit from a McCall's pattern book she wore when she first met the Prince (a power outage at her hotel prevented her ironing any of her other more formal gowns) and a gorgeous cream frock she sported that December when her engagement was announced. And an emerald-green wool dress by Givenchy in which Grace met that other fashion icon of the age, Jackie Kennedy, at the White House. There were accessories, too, such as the Hermès bag that was so closely identified with Grace that its designers nicknamed it "the Kelly bag".

Unfortunately, her wedding dress – with its twenty-inch waist (a result of understandable nerves) – was not on display. It was deemed too fragile to travel from the Philadelphia Museum of Art, where it is by far the most popular attraction. As part of the show, scheduled to run for five months, there were film clips, posters and photographs – including one of Grace in a stunning pink ball gown, caught halfway up the marble staircase of Monaco's Princely Palace, almost as if she were in flight.

More than a quarter of a century after her premature death, Grace was on the cover of magazines again. "At a time when it can be difficult to find that rare quality known as class, it is refreshing to see Grace Kelly back in the limelight," observed the *New York Times*.[1] Reviews of the exhibition itself were mixed, but there was no doubting the enduring appeal of its subject. "She's one of the few people who deserves this title of style icon," said Jenny Lister, who curated the exhibition for the V&A. "It's very hard to find anyone else today who can be remembered in the same way fifty years from now."

Guest of honour at the reception was Grace's son, Prince Albert II, head of the royal house of Grimaldi since his father's death in 2005, who spoke of his mother's "exquisite taste", which had remained timeless since her death. Long seen by the media as a confirmed bachelor, the Prince, now balding and with his fiftieth birthday behind him, had been linked over the years with a series of glamorous actresses and models – most of them many years his junior, including Naomi Campbell, Claudia Schiffer, Gwyneth Paltrow and Brooke Shields.

At his side on this occasion, however, was a glamorous thirty-two-year-old woman, who some said looked uncannily like his mother. Her name was Charlene Wittstock and she used to be a teacher and Olympic swimmer. They had first met almost a decade earlier when Charlene had been swimming for her native South Africa at a competition in Monaco; since the couple appeared side by side at the Turin Winter Olympics in 2006, she had been his permanent companion. In contrast to Albert's many previous relationships, this one seemed serious.

The name of Grace Kelly, star of films such as *Dial M for Murder*, *Rear Window*, *To Catch a Thief* and *High Society*, has been synonymous with Monaco since April 1956, when she turned her back on a glittering Hollywood career to marry Rainier, who had become ruler of the pocket-sized Mediterranean principality on the death of his grandfather seven years earlier.

But it was a royal wedding quite unlike any other. The ceremony in the Cathedral of St Nicholas was attended, among others, by the actors David Niven, Gloria Swanson and Ava Gardner – but not by members of any of Europe's reigning royal families, who were unwilling to be seen at the marriage of a prince of a country associated with sleaze and gambling to the actress daughter of a self-made millionaire who had begun his professional life as a bricklayer. The closest among the guests to "real" monarchy were the Aga Khan and ex-King Farouk of Egypt. Aristotle Onassis arranged for fifteen thousand carnations to be dumped on Rainier's yacht from a plane.

Grace, born on 12th November 1929, grew up in a Philadelphia mansion; her family were wealthy and broadly middle-class, but they were also Irish and Catholic, which meant they were scorned by the east-coast Wasp establishment. The third of four children, Grace struggled for acceptance at home too: her father, a triple Olympic-gold-medal-winning sculler and man of enormous ambition, never expected her acting to come to much.

After starting as a stage actress at the age of eighteen, Grace appeared in her first film, *Fourteen Hours*, which was released in April 1951. It was a tiny role – she appeared on screen for just two minutes and fourteen seconds – but it was long enough for her to be spotted by Gary Cooper. It was only after she appeared alongside him the following year in Fred Zinnemann's *High Noon* that her career really took off. In January 1955, she made it to the cover of *Time*. In a profile the magazine described how Kelly, still only twenty-five, had within eighteen months been paired with six of Hollywood's biggest male stars – Clark Gable, Ray Milland, James Stewart, William Holden, Bing Crosby and Cary Grant – and had been transformed in the process from a promising newcomer (generally thought to be English) to the "acknowledged 'hottest property' in Hollywood".[2]

"From the day in 1951 when she walked into Director Fred Zinnemann's office wearing prim white gloves ('Nobody came to see me before wearing white gloves'), the well-bred Miss Grace Kelly of Philadelphia has baffled Hollywood," *Time* noted. "She is a rich girl who has struck it rich. She was not discovered behind a soda fountain or at a drive-in. She is a star who was never a starlet, who never worked up from B pictures, never posed for cheesecake, was never elected, with a press agent's help, Miss Anti-aircraft Battery C. She did not gush or twitter or desperately pull wires for a chance to get in the movies. Twice she turned down good Hollywood contracts. When she finally signed on the line, she forced mighty MGM itself to grant her special terms."

Rainier, like many a royal prince, had a penchant for actresses, and for several years during his twenties had lived openly with Gisèle Pascal, a French performer, in his villa in Cap Ferrat – prompting complaints among some of his subjects that he was neglecting his official duties. Pascal had caught the Prince's eye when he was a student at Montpellier University during the Second World War and she was appearing in boulevard plays. Pascal was not marriage material, however, and was reported (erroneously, it subsequently emerged) to be infertile – a major drawback for a royal bride. When Rainer succeeded to the throne in 1949, it became clear he had to find himself a wife.[3]

Rainer met Grace in May 1955 at the Cannes Film Festival. An executive of *Paris Match* had thought up a new angle for photographing the Prince's palace at Monaco: he asked the actress to pose in the foreground. Grace did so only on condition that she be granted an audience with its owner – who was only too happy to oblige.

After a whirlwind romance conducted largely by letter, Rainier flew to New York that December and proposed. Grace accepted and went back to Hollywood to finish *The Swan*, a film, appropriately enough, about a princess from the minor branch of a European royal family whose mother is trying to set her up with the heir to the throne, played by Alec Guinness. Rainier went to Florida to take a rest. The American press went wild at this union of Hollywood royalty with the real thing. There were some notes of humorous dissent, though. "He's not good enough for a Kelly," claimed the *Chicago Tribune*. "She is too well bred a girl to marry the silent partner in a gambling parlour." A columnist for the United Press news agency claimed executives at MGM were worried "she will fly off to Monte Carlo and be seen henceforth only on postage stamps".[4]

However unlikely a pair, the couple seemed genuinely in love. Like many marriages, though, theirs was also underpinned by some rational calculations on both sides. Grace was not just beautiful, she would also bring a much needed dose of glamour to Monaco and bear Rainier, now in his early thirties, the heir he needed. For Grace, marriage would turn her from screen goddess to real-life princess. She had been determined not to marry a man who would be belittled by her screen success and turned into a mere "Mr Kelly" – there was no danger of this happening with Rainier.

There was a price to pay, however: at her husband's insistence, Grace had to give up her film career; he even banned any screening of her films in the principality. The new first lady of Monaco, ensconced in her two-hundred-room pink palace overlooking the Mediterranean, instead confined her energies to charitable works, garden clubs and the narration of inoffensive child-friendly documentaries, as well as to bringing up her own three children, Caroline, Albert and Stéphanie.

The fairy tale came to an abrupt end on the morning of 13th September 1982. Grace suffered a stroke while driving her ten-year-old Rover down a winding road. The car tumbled a hundred feet down a ravine, turning over several times before coming to rest in a garden. Grace died of her injuries the next day after the life-support system was turned off. Stéphanie, who was with her in the car, escaped with only minor injuries.

Tens of thousands of people from around the world sent cards and letter of condolence; the funeral was watched by an estimated one hundred million people across the world. "Grace brought into my life, as she brought into yours, a soft, warm light every time I saw her, and every time I saw her was a holiday of its own," declared the actor James Stewart in his eulogy.

The funeral was held, as her wedding had been, in the cathedral. But this time Europe's other royal families were out in force, a reflection of the transformation not just of Grace herself but of the principality over the previous twenty-six years. Among the mourners was Diana, Princess of Wales, whose life – and premature death – was to have so many parallels with that of Grace. The two women had met in London in March the previous year just after Diana's engagement had been announced; Grace gave her advice on how to cope with all the media attention that was already beginning to overwhelm her.

Rainier, who lived for another twenty-three years, never got over the loss of Grace, filling his principality with reminders of her. "Twenty years after her disappearance, Princess Grace is always present in our hearts and in our thoughts," he wrote in the preface to a book

published by the palace in 2002 filled with pictures of the couple, praising her for "carrying out to perfection her role as spouse and mother".

Long before Rainier, the tiny principality of Monaco was already
proving a glorious exception to the stuffy rules that have governed
the love lives of the members of other European royal families. For
several generations members of the princely family have married and
divorced – or more often, as good Catholics, managed to have their
marriages annulled – with apparent abandon, prompting talk of a
"curse of Grimaldi" said to hang over their relationships.

Rainier's great-grandfather, Albert I, who reigned from 1889 to
1922, was married twice: his first union with the British-born Lady
Mary Douglas-Hamilton was annulled, while his second, with the
Dowager Duchess de Richelieu, born Marie Alice Heine, the daughter
of a New Orleans building contractor of German-Jewish descent,
ended in separation: the Princess was having an affair with Isidore de
Lara, a British composer and singer, while her husband, like Léopold II
of Belgium, enjoyed the favours of "La Belle Otéro".[5]

The turbulence of Albert's own love life did not make him any more
tolerant of his son Louis's peccadilloes. Louis was not deterred: after
his father made clear he could not marry Marie Juliette Louvet, the
cabaret singer he met in Algeria in the 1890s (and by whom he had
an illegitimate daughter, Charlotte), Louis remained single for several
more decades before marrying Ghislaine Dommanget, an actress, in
1946, when he was seventy-six and she was just forty-five.

In the meantime Louis had arranged for Charlotte – who had been
turned into a legitimate heir – to be married to a French count, Pierre
de Polignac, by whom she had two children: Antoinette and Rainier. It
was an unsuccessful match: Charlotte, a headstrong character, found
her husband too formal and pompous. "To make love he needs to put
a crown on his head," she complained.[6] Soon after her son's birth
Charlotte ran off with Del Masso, an Italian doctor, whom she later
tried to shoot during one of their many heated arguments – leading
the media to brand her the "Madcap Princess of Monaco". She and
her husband divorced in 1933 and the unfortunate Pierre was banned
by his former father-in-law from the principality.

In later life, after renouncing the throne in favour of her son, Charlotte retired to the family estate at Le Marchais outside Paris, which

she turned into a rehabilitation centre for ex-convicts. The rest of the family was not impressed – especially not by suggestions Charlotte had become rather too close to one of her "patients", a legendary gentleman jewel thief named René Girier or "René la Canne" ("René the Cane").

Girier caused something of a sensation by turning up at Rainier and Grace's wedding dressed in a tight-fitting white uniform in the guise of her chauffeur. When Matthew McCloskey, an old friend of Grace's father and publisher of the Philadelphia *Daily Inquirer*, announced that $50,000 of his wife's jewellery had disappeared from their rooms at the Hotel de Paris, and Maree Frisby, a bridesmaid, also claimed $8,000 of her jewels had gone missing, fingers immediately pointed at Girier, who was out on parole from a jail sentence for robbery. For the countless American newspaper men gathered there, the parallels were just too good to be true with *To Catch a Thief*, in which Grace had played alongside Cary Grant, who was cast in the role of a retired cat burglar living on the French Riviera. To the fury of his mother, Rainier ordered her "chauffeur" out of his realm.

Rainier and Grace's two daughters Caroline and Stéphanie made even more colourful marital choices. Caroline, born in January 1957, was just twenty-one when she married Philippe Junot, a Parisian banker seventeen years her senior. They divorced after just over two years, however, and after a brief relationship with Robertino Rossellini, the son of the film director Roberto Rossellini and his actress wife Ingrid Bergman, Caroline married Stefano Casiraghi, the sportsman heir to an Italian industrial fortune. The couple had three children, but Casiraghi was killed in a powerboat accident in 1990, aged just thirty.

After a long affair with Vincent Lindon, a French actor, Caroline was married for a third time in January 1999, this time to Prince Ernst August of Hanover, a third cousin of Queen Elizabeth. Despite Ernst August's royal parentage, his behaviour has, on occasion, been anything but regal: over the years he has been involved in a variety of legal disputes ranging from issues over privacy and assault charges to allegedly being drunk and urinating in public. In the autumn of 2009, media reports began to appear suggesting that the couple had split up. The Princely Palace released a statement dismissing such stories as untrue and saying the couple had no plans to divorce, but Ernst

August's absence during key public appearances appeared a further sign that all was not well.

Stéphanie, younger than Caroline by eight years, has provided the glossy magazines with even more material. After an alleged affair with Miguel Bosé, a Spanish singer, when she was just thirteen, she went on to become involved with a string of well-known men including Paul Belmondo, son of the actor Jean-Paul, Anthony Delon, son of the actor Alain, and, later, the record producer Ron Bloom and the actor Rob Lowe.

In 1992 she embarked on an affair with Daniel Ducruet, her body-guard, bearing him two children before they married in July 1995. The marriage proved short-lived: after photographs were published of Ducruet in a naked embrace with Muriel Houtteman, Miss Topless Belgium, Ducruet was banished from the Monégasque court – despite his insistence it had been a drunken set-up. Stéphanie was awarded a "quickie" divorce in October 1996, although the couple seemed to remain on friendly terms and from time to time were photographed on holiday with their children.

In the months that followed, Stéphanie's love life appeared to become even more complicated: she was romantically linked with several men, including Fabien Barthez, the footballer, Jean-Claude Van Damme, the action-movie star, and Jean Raymond Gottlieb, a former French gendarme and ski instructor who had became her head of security. Then it was announced she was pregnant: Camille Marie Kelly was born in July 1998. The identity of the baby's father was never revealed, but there was widespread speculation it was Gottlieb.

In any case, Stéphanie had moved on, reportedly romancing, among others, Pierre Pinelli, a Corsican barman, whom she met at a the ski resort of Auron, Richard Lucas, her father's butler, and even Junot, her elder sister's first husband. Most unusual of all was her relation-ship with Franco Knie, the Swiss owner of Cirque Knie, whom she first met in 1999 at the International Circus Festival of Monte Carlo while presenting him with the award for Best Animal Trainer. Their affair became public two years later when Knie, who worked with elephants, announced he was leaving his wife, Claudine, for the Prin-cess. Stéphanie spent several months touring Europe with the circus and apparently loved the elephants so much that she was included in one of the acts.

They parted in 2002, and more equally colourful romances followed; then in September 2003 Stéphanie announced she had got married again, this time to Adans Lopez Peres, a Portuguese-Spanish trapeze artist. At the time of writing, she is going out with Merwan Rim, a French actor and musician.

In stark contrast to his sisters, Albert, who became sovereign prince of Monaco in April 2005, had for a long time failed to give the paparazzi anything much to get their teeth into – so little that at one stage he felt himself obliged to deny persistent rumours that he was gay. "At first it was amusing," he declared in an interview published in 1994, "but it becomes very irritating in the long term to hear people say that I am homosexual."[7]

As it turned out, the statement was somewhat superfluous. In 1992 Tamara Rotolo, a divorced Californian real-estate agent, had filed a paternity suit against the Prince, claiming he was the father of her daughter, whom she named Jazmin Grace Grimaldi and who had been born in March that year. It was not until May 2006, after DNA tests confirmed the child's parentage, that Albert admitted, in a statement from his lawyer, that he was the girl's father. He also extended an invitation for the girl to study and live in Monaco.

A hereditary monarchy requires a legitimate heir, however. With Albert well into his forties and apparently a confirmed bachelor, this was beginning to look increasingly unlikely. The simplest solution would have been to recognize one of Albert's two illegitimate children – effectively a repetition of what had happened with his grandmother Charlotte. Indeed, unusually for a monarchy based on the principle of heredity, the rules of the Monégasque royal house explicitly allowed the reigning prince to adopt an heir to succeed him if he died without legitimate heirs – in his case, this could have been one of his nephews or someone completely unrelated.

In 2002, however, amid mounting concerns over the future of the dynasty, the rules were changed to allow the throne to pass to his elder sister, Caroline, if he died without a legitimate heir and then on to her eldest son, Andrea. The law came into effect in October 2005 after it was ratified by France.

Albert claimed his reluctance to settle down was due in large part to the press intrusion he suffered. "Life will not be easy for my future wife," he declared. "I became accustomed at an early age to the incessant presence of photographers. Some of my girlfriends who have been exposed, even for a very brief time, to this sort of life were not at all pleased."[8]

The arrival of Charlene Wittstock raised hopes that there would be no need to change the succession law. Charlene was born in January 1978 to South African parents in the southern Zimbabwean city of Bulawayo. Her father, Michael, was a computer-business operator; her mother, Lynette, had been a competitive diver.

Charlene inherited her mother's prowess in water sports, and at the age of sixteen gave up her studies to devote herself full-time to swimming. At eighteen she won South Africa's junior championships, and was selected to represent her country at the Sydney Olympics in 2000. She reached her peak at the World Cup in 2002, when she won three gold medals, but her career ended in disappointment; a shoulder injury kept her out of the sport for eighteen months and she was unable to realize her dream of swimming for her country at the 2008 Beijing Games.

Charlene met Albert in May 2000, when she went to Monaco to take part in a swimming competition; she won the fifty-metre breaststroke and the Prince presented her with a bunch of flowers. According to an account that appeared in South Africa's *Sunday Times*, they met again in June the following year when she was back in the principality for the Mare Nostrum championships. Charlene was queuing for food in the Tulip Hotel along with swimmers from Sweden and Canada when the Prince saw her and, apparently remembering her from the previous years, asked her to go out with him.

"I wasn't exactly sure what I should say," she told the newspaper. "I was more worried about my curfew and whether I would be allowed to go out so late at night. So I said he should ask the team management for permission. He said he wouldn't take no for an answer and proceeded to escort me to the table where the rest of our team was enjoying their lunch. Of course, when I introduced the Prince there was a frozen silence. He had no problem getting permission to take me out and promised to bring me back himself."[9] This left Charlene, who had been travelling light, to embark on a frantic search with a teammate for something suitably glamorous to wear for a date with a prince.

At the agreed hour, Albert, accompanied by bodyguards, knocked on Charlene's hotel door and escorted her to a waiting stretched Rolls-Royce, whereupon they set off for a nightclub and then a tour of Monaco. Along the way, according to her account, he told her of his love of sport – and how he had once almost married a swimmer – and also mentioned his concern that if he didn't soon marry and produce a legitimate heir he would have to adopt his nephew.

Rather than take Charlene back to her hotel, Albert brought her instead to his three-bedroom apartment overlooking Monte Carlo. "I knew it was a date, but I didn't expect much," she said. "We were not entirely alone. One of his assistants made us coffee as we stared out into the night. I think he liked me because I made him laugh." Around five o'clock that morning, the playboy Prince escorted his date back to her hotel as promised. "He gave me his phone number and said when I'm ever in Monaco again I should give him a call. I was so exhausted that I fell onto my bed."

How their relationship progressed from there was not clear. In the interview, Charlene expressed the hope she would see Albert again during the competition the following year. The Prince appeared keen to see her too, even though a woman who gave an interview with such explicit details of a date would have been anathema to most of his royal counterparts.

In the meantime, Albert was continuing to see other women: in May 2005, the principality was rocked by claims by Nicole Coste, a former Air France flight attendant from Togo, that her youngest son, Alexandre, born two years earlier, had been fathered by Albert. The French weekly *Paris Match* published a ten-page interview with Coste, which included photographs of the Prince holding and feeding the child. Coste also told the magazine that she was living in the Prince's Paris apartment and receiving an allowance from him while pretending to be the girlfriend of one of his friends in order to maintain privacy. The palace initially declined to comment, but on 6th July – six days before Albert was due to be enthroned – his lawyer Thierry Lacoste confirmed the boy was indeed his. In what must have been a small consolation for the Prince, a third paternity suit, brought against him by a German topless model, had failed.

In February the following year Albert and Charlene went public: they were photographed laughing and snuggling up together at the opening ceremony of the Winter Olympics in Turin. In the eyes of the world they were now a couple – an impression that appeared to be confirmed when Charlene moved later that year to the Principality. She kept her own apartment, but also began to appear increasingly at Albert's side.

Back in South Africa, Charlene had the image of a gawky, tomboy-ish "girl next door" – an outgoing figure who was always cracking jokes. After a few gaffes, she also acquired something of a reputation as a dumb blonde. David Isaacson, a sports writer for South Africa's *Sunday Times*, who met Charlene on several occasions, described her as always bubbly, smiling and down to earth. "She told me in an interview once that it was important to treat everyone with respect," he wrote in a profile. "She had already met Albert by that time – though she hadn't started going out with him – but she made it clear that she wouldn't tolerate even him talking down to people." In the same interview, Charlene admitted to relishing her dumb-blonde role: "Anyway, I think you have to be really clever to be a dumb blonde," she told him – but, according to Isaacson, she promptly burst into tears the next day when she saw the headline on his article.[10]

Gradually, however, the dumb blonde was evolving into a polished, sophisticated princess-to-be, as she made an increasing number of public appearances at Albert's side at events such as the Red Cross Ball, the Rose Ball and the Cannes Film Festival, where she was photo-graphed by *Paris Match* in a designer dress alongside famous actresses. Although clearly warming to life with one of the world's most eligible bachelors, Charlene could be forgiven for being frustrated with the role of "*fiancée non-officielle*".

According to those who know the Prince, however, the transition from girlfriend to fiancée and wife could not be hurried. Given the inevitable comparisons with his mother, Albert knew he had to make sure Charlene would be able to withstand the huge media attention to which she would be subjected. In the meantime, she had been preparing for her new role, including taking an accelerated course to improve her French.

By the time Charlene joined Albert for the exhibition dedicated to his mother in London, it was clear she had passed the test, even though the palace repeatedly denied reports by what the French call the *"presse people"* that an engagement was about to be announced. In June 2010, in the ultimate sign of acceptance, Charlene accompanied Albert to the wedding of Crown Princess Victoria of Sweden, which gave him the chance to introduce her to prominent members of Europe's other royal families.

Three days later her engagement to Albert was announced – but only after the Prince had telephoned her father in Johannesburg to break the news. Michael Wittstock, who described the Prince as a "nice chap", said he received the call just as he was settling to watch South Africa's World Cup football match against France. "He phoned me so that I could give him the blessing to put the ring on her finger," he joked. "I wanted to get the whole thing over and done with before the game."

The ring in question was clearly visible in an engagement photograph released by the palace that showed Albert in a dark-blue suit and Charlene in an elegant halter-neck dress. Supplied by the jeweller Alberto Repossi, who was summoned specially to the palace, it was in white gold, with a pear-shaped diamond in the centre, paved with brilliant-cut diamonds. "If she takes up swimming again, she won't be able to wear her engagement ring in the pool – she'd surely sink," quipped Britain's *Daily Mail*.[11]

The wedding, set for the weekend of 1st July 2011, was to be a suitably grand affair. A civil ceremony on the Friday in the throne room of the Prince's palace in Monaco was to be followed on the Saturday by a religious service in the palace courtyard. Yet signs began to emerge in the days before the ceremony that all was not well with the couple.

Albert, it was claimed, was facing allegations that he had fathered a third illegitimate child and, understandably, Charlene was said to be having second thoughts about marrying him. According to reports in the French media, she had tried to flee to her native South Africa three times: the first attempt had been in May when she went to Paris to try on her wedding dress and allegedly attempted to "take refuge" in the South African embassy; the second was supposedly during the Monaco Grand Prix later the same month; the third had been a few days before the wedding, when royal officials were said to have confiscated her passport as she took the helicopter shuttle to Nice airport with a one-way ticket home to South Africa in her handbag.

Albert described the stories as "completely fabricated" and an attempt to destabilize his forthcoming wedding. Charlene's father, Mike, told a South African radio station that the only time his daughter had come close to an aircraft over the previous weeks had been to fly to Paris to buy a hat and shoes for her wedding. Royal officials nevertheless confirmed that the Prince would face a paternity test.

Fears that Albert would be left alone at the altar proved to be unfounded. Charlene turned up on the day, looking stunning in an off-the-shoulder Armani silk dress, covered with 40,000 Swarovski crystals and with a sixteen-foot train. The groom was smart in the cream summer uniform of Monaco's palace guards. Giorgio Armani himself was among the 850 guests, who also included Nicolas Sarkozy, Karl Lagerfeld, Naomi Campbell, Roger Moore and senior members of Europe's royal families. Dinner was prepared by Alain Ducasse, the celebrated French-born chef. Although Charlene laughed as she placed the ring on her husband's finger, the tears she shed after the ceremony seemed to be of despair rather than joy.

The couple left as planned on honeymoon to South Africa, but much of their time seemed taken up with official meetings, including a conference of the International Olympic Committee, of which Albert is a member. Although the Prince tried hard to appear affectionate towards his bride, the South African media claimed they stayed in separate hotel suites.

Yet even if Charlene really had attempted to escape, she did not try a second time. In the months that followed the couple was seen repeatedly by each other's side, both within Monaco and on visits abroad. So had Charlene forgiven her husband his sexual indiscretions? Not necessarily. The couple, it was said, had drawn up a pact: they would stay together for as long as it took Charlene to produce the legitimate heir that Albert needed, and then they would go their separate ways. Had the curse of the Grimaldi family struck again?

Chapter 9

Marrying into the Family

Any message that is received from beyond the grave has a particular poignancy, but the posthumous confession made by Prince Bernhard, the German-born consort of Queen Juliana of the Netherlands, in December 2004 was an especially dramatic one. During the late 1990s, under conditions of great secrecy, Bernhard, then well into his eighties, had given a series of interviews to the journalist Martin van Amerongen, the editor of the weekly *De Groene Amsterdammer* and an avowed republican. There was one important precondition for their meeting: that the interview be published only after Bernhard's death. Its contents were to prove explosive.

Bernhard, who died at the age of ninety-three, outliving his wife by nine months, was a celebrated bon viveur and lover of fast cars, planes and women, who enjoyed considerable popularity in his adoptive homeland, largely thanks to his heroic role during the Second World War and his subsequent founding of the World Wildlife Fund and peacetime role as a champion of Dutch business. A shadow had been cast over the latter part of his life, however, by claims that during the 1970s he had taken a one-million-dollar bribe from the Lockheed Corporation, a US aeroplane manufacturer, in exchange for providing contacts and helping the firm win a contract from the Dutch government. Such was the weight of evidence *against* him that the Prince had been forced to resign his business, charitable, political and military posts. Yet he had steadfastly refused to admit his guilt.

In his interview with van Amerongen, published on 3rd December, two days after his death, however, Bernhard finally confessed that he had indeed taken the money. "I had earned so much money that I didn't need that million from Lockheed," he said. "How can I have been so stupid?" Most of it, he claimed, he had given away, but he knew this would make little difference. "I have accepted that the word Lockheed will be carved on my tombstone," he declared.[1]

That was not the only secret Bernhard had kept up his sleeve. It had long been rumoured that, besides his four daughters with Juliana, he had fathered another daughter, Alexia, in 1967 by Hélène Grinda, a French socialite and fashion model. But Alexia, it now emerged, had not been the only fruit of his extramarital dalliances.

In another series of interviews, this time with *de Volkskrant*, published in a twenty-four-page special three days after his funeral, the Prince revealed that he had had another daughter, Alicia, in the 1950s, at a time when his marriage with Juliana was going through a crisis. Bernhard declined to give more details – beyond that the daughter had been an accident and was now living in America. It subsequently emerged that her mother had been a German pilot based in Mexico, with whom Bernhard had had a long affair.

But was there also a third daughter? In August 2011, Mildred Zijlstra, born in February 1946, was named in a book as another of Bernhard's illegitimate children. *De Vrouwen van Prins Bernhard* by Marc van der Linden, a Dutch royal expert, claimed Zijlstra's mother had been a member of the resistance group Binnenlandse Strijdkrachten – and became one of the many women who became pregnant out of wedlock in the months immediately after the end of the Second World War. The girl was adopted and did not start questioning her background until she had children of her own. It was only then, the book claimed, that Zijlstra first found her biological mother and then learnt the identity of her alleged royal father. Van der Linden did not offer hard proof of the allegation, only statements from Zijlstra's mother and friends of the family – but it was enough for the Dutch media to seize on the story, even though not everyone was convinced.

Being married to a queen or, indeed, a king is not an easy task – especially for someone uncomfortable with a status subordinate to that of his or her spouse. Yet while other consorts have been prepared to adapt to such a role, Bernhard was a far more uncompromising, larger-than-life figure – which largely explains his downfall. So who was this German prince and how did his life come to be so mired in scandal?

* * *

Queen Wilhelmina began the search for a suitable husband for her daughter when Juliana was twenty-six, but it was not easy: the successful candidate had to be a Protestant and meet the high standards of the strictly religious Dutch court. The future Edward VIII and his younger brother, the Duke of Kent, were among those cited as possibles, but nothing came of the idea. It was then during a visit to the Winter Olympics in Bavaria, chaperoned, of course, by her mother, that Juliana met Bernhard Leopold Friedrich Eberhard Julius Kurt Karl Gottfried Peter zu Lippe-Biesterfeld, to give him his full name, the man she would marry.

The couple became unofficially engaged during a meeting at the Weissenburg-Bad hotel in western Switzerland, twenty miles from Gstaad, presided over by Wilhelmina. The terms of their union were set out in a mixture of business contract and early prenuptial agreement that stipulated, in detail, what Bernhard could or could not do, how much money he would be given by the state and how their children should be educated. The Treaty of Weissenburg, as it became known, even set out when the engagement should be made public and contained the requirement that Bernhard give up his job with IG Farben in Paris and get a job with a Dutch bank. When it came to her daughter's future, Queen Wilhelmina was determined not to leave anything to chance.

In the event, the announcement was brought forward because of fears the press would find out; Wilhelmina broke the news to her subjects in a radio broadcast on 8th September 1936. "I fully approve my daughter's choice," she announced, "and consider it a wise one, seeing the excellent qualities which my future son-in-law possesses." Juliana and Bernhard followed her on air. They married the following January in The Hague.

Bernhard proved a controversial choice; relations between the Netherlands and Germany were very different from how they had been in 1901 when Wilhelmina had married Heinrich of Mecklenburg-Schwerin, Juliana's father. The Dutch Nazi party was delighted. Liberal opinion and the country's sizeable Jewish opinion was not. "It would be better if the future Queen had found a consort in some democratic country rather than in the Third Reich," commented *Het Volk*.[2]

Matters were not helped when the former Kaiser, allowed by Wilhelmina after the First World War to go into exile in the Dutch town of Doorn, sent his congratulations, while Hitler suggested the union was a sign of closer ties between the two countries. Bernhard's past employment with chemical giant IG Farben, whose reputation was permanently damaged by its association with Hitler and the Nazis, counted against him. So too did his brief membership of the SS, although years later he said he had joined only to be able to continue his studies.

The couple married in January 1937 in a civil ceremony in The Hague Town Hall – with a blessing in the city's Great Church (St Jacobskerk) – and moved into the Soestdijk Palace in Baarn. Their first child, the future Queen Beatrix, was born in January 1938. Irene, Margriet and Maria Christina, known as Marijke, followed over the next nine years.

As has already been seen, the Dutch royal family – and Bernhard among them – emerged favourably from the war, and by 4th September 1948, when Wilhelmina abdicated in favour of her daughter, Bernhard was already beginning to carve out a role for himself. The position of Inspector General was created for him, and he served as advisor and non-executive director of a number of companies and institutions, becoming an informal ambassador extraordinaire for Dutch business. In 1954 he was instrumental in setting up what was to become the Bilderberg Group, a forum for the business elite and intellectuals of the Western world.

At the same time, Bernhard's marriage was coming under strain after Juliana became increasingly influenced by Greet Hofmans, a faith healer who had claimed to be able to cure Marijke, who was born almost blind. Hofmans, who was also a militant pacifist, did not succeed, but she developed a close relationship with the Queen, who became sympathetic to her views.

At a time when the Cold War was at its peak, this did not go down well with Prince Bernhard or the government, who were in favour of more armament to counter the threat of communism. The affair turned into a full-blown constitutional crisis in 1956, when *Der Spiegel*, the German news magazine, published an article about divisions in the palace.[3] A commission was set up and Hofmans banished. The result was considered a victory for Bernhard – who, it subsequently emerged, had leaked the story himself.

It was about this time that the Prince fathered Alicia von Bielefeld – who was to learn her father's identity only seventeen years later.

Juliana and Bernhard came close to divorce – but eventually pulled back from the brink, realizing the damage it would inflict on the monarchy. Yet Bernhard was continuing to stray, having affairs, including the one that led to the birth of his second illegitimate daughter, Alexia, in 1967.

Juliana appears to have taken such infidelities in her stride. According to Alicia, Bernhard revealed her existence to his wife in the mid-1970s; from 1994 onwards she would visit the royal couple at the Italian home where they spent their summer holidays as well as the Soestdijk Palace. She called Juliana a "nice, sweet woman; very straightforward, too". When Alicia was with Bernhard, she had to say that he was a friend of her father's. "When others were there, I couldn't call him dad," she added. The contrast with the relationship between Albert II of Belgium and his illegitimate daughter, Delphine Boël, could not have been greater.

Bernhard's indiscretions outside the bedroom were to prove a more serious matter, however. In December 1975, Carl Kotchian, a vice-chairman of Lockheed, gave testimony to a Senate sub-committee in which he admitted paying a one-million-dollar bribe to a "high Dutch government official". Ernest F. Hauser, a former company employee, was more explicit: the money, he said, had gone to none other than Prince Bernhard to guarantee sales to Holland of Lockheed's F-104 Starfighter, a supersonic interceptor aircraft.

As inspector general of the Dutch armed forces and a member of the board of Fokker Aircraft, which had a licence to assemble the planes in the Netherlands, the Prince was clearly in a key position. Yet the allegation seemed an unlikely one: Bernhard had a tax-free salary of £190,000 a year and a private fortune estimated at £7.5 million, while his wife was one of the richest women in the world. There was also his presidency of the World Wildlife Fund, his role in setting up the Bilderberg Conference and his membership of some three hundred national and international boards and committees. The suggestion that he should stoop to take a bribe seemed unthinkable.

Bernhard, however, was reluctant to respond to the allegation. Rather than denying it, he simply refused to address it. "If you say four words, 'It is not true,' I will print it," declared a reporter from *Newsweek* who confronted him. "I cannot say that," Bernhard replied.

"I will not say it; I am standing above such things." The explanation for his behaviour was simple: "He thought he was a nineteenth-century prince, that he could do whatever he wanted, that he was above the law," said an associate of Joop den Uyl, who as prime minister from May 1973 until December 1977 had to deal with the crisis.[4]

Such a tactic did not work in the twentieth-century Netherlands, however. A commission of "three wise men" was set up and gradually the story began to emerge: Bernhard, it appeared, had been paid $300,000 by Lockheed in 1960, followed by the same amount again in 1961 and $400,000 in 1962. The money was said to have been channelled through Colonel Alexis Panchulidzev, a former member of the Tsarist Imperial Guard, who for many years had been a companion of Bernhard's mother. Kotchian and Daniel Haughton, another Lockheed official, were in no doubt the money had been paid; they told the US Senate committee they were "absolutely" sure of it.

It is difficult to overestimate the severity of the accusations against Bernhard and its implications for Juliana and the House of Orange. Determined to fight both for her husband and for the royal house, Juliana said she would consider abdication if her husband was not cleared of the accusations against him – something neither she, the Dutch people nor the prime minister wanted.

In the meantime, Bernhard faced more allegations: it was claimed he received another $100,000 from Lockheed in 1968 after a meeting with a company representative on a Utrecht golf course. The Prince, it was alleged, had also paid a bribe of more than a million dollars to Juan Perón, the Argentinian president, to secure a one-hundred-million-dollar order for Dutch railway equipment. As part of the deal, there was also some expensive jewellery for Evita Perón and a deluxe private train for the pair.

Questions were also asked about the Prince's financial and personal relationship with Tibor Rosenbaum, a Swiss banker, whose Geneva-based International Credit Bank was accused of being linked with organized crime, before it went broke in 1975. The previous year Bernhard had sold Warmelo, a castle belonging to him in eastern Holland, to a company owned by the bank for well under the market price, prompting suspicions in the Dutch press that he had squirrelled away some of the money.

As far as the media on both sides of the Atlantic was concerned, it was open season on Bernhard, whose behaviour seemed rather out of place in the Calvinist Dutch court. In a report in April 1976, *Newsweek* claimed the Prince would "sometimes mix his old 'drinking pals' with the nabobs of European business" – a blend that sometimes worked and sometimes didn't. "On one bright morning, I found myself on his private plane en route for Paris, with the champagne already flowing freely on board," a prominent Dutch businessman told the magazine. "After we arrived, we went to a plush hotel where more cold champagne and oysters were waiting. At eleven a.m. I was seeing stars, and at two p.m. I passed out." The businessman also recalls a supply of attractive women, who, he claimed, were a frequent feature of Bernhard's parties.[5]

The findings that the "three wise men" presented to Prime Minister den Uyl were damning. Despite overwhelming evidence against Bernhard, the Queen insisted that he be cleared. For den Uyl this was impossible, however, not least because of all the testimony on a record against him in the United States. When Juliana threatened to abdicate, den Uyl countered by warning her that Bernhard would then probably face prosecution – which would have been the ultimate disgrace for the House of Orange.

And so a deal was struck: in August 1976, the "three wise men" released their report, which immediately became a best-seller in the Netherlands. The Prince's actions, they wrote, had "damaged the national interest". He had been open to "dishonourable requests and offers" and "was the intended recipient of the one million dollars [from Lockheed], which was meant for his benefit alone". It also suggested that some of the many corporate donations given to Bernhard for charitable purposes never found their way to their ultimate destination. "To sum up," the report said, "the commission has come to the conclusion that HRH the Prince, in the conviction that his position was unassailable and his judgement was not to be influenced, originally entered much too lightly into transactions which were bound to create the impression that he was susceptible to favours."

The day the report was made public, Bernhard resigned his various posts. On the insistence of den Uyl, he also issued a statement, but it was carefully worded and admitted the minimum. His relationship with Lockheed, he admitted, had "developed along the wrong lines" and he had failed to observe the caution "which is required in my vulnerable position as a consort of the Queen and Prince of the Netherlands". He stopped short, however, of any admission that he had actually received the one million dollars. That was going to have to wait more than another quarter of a century.

Although no other royal spouses in recent times have been embroiled in such murky matters as Bernhard, the role of male consort has proved a difficult one, not least because of the relatively small number of role models – a result of laws of succession that have either prevented queens from reigning in their own right or have put them on the throne only when they have had no brother. Nor are they likely to become more common, at least for one more generation, despite the drive towards equal primogeniture led by the Swedes. At the time of writing, that country's Crown Princess Victoria is the world's only female heir apparent.

Britain has had the most women on the throne, since unlike the majority of the Continental monarchies its rules of succession have never been governed by Salic law. Previous incumbents have essentially made of the role what they wanted. In the sixteenth century, Mary Tudor's husband Philip of Spain rarely visited Britain at all, because he had a prosperous kingdom of his own that occupied much of his attention. Just over a century later, William of Orange, who declared he could never "hold on to anything by apron strings", gently elbowed Mary Stuart, his wife and co-sovereign, aside in order to rule alone. By contrast, Prince George of Denmark, the husband of Queen Anne, who reigned in the first decade of the eighteenth century, took almost no interest whatsoever in the affairs of state of his adoptive country.

Far more vivid in British memories is Victoria's consort, Prince Albert, who, in a reflection of the traditions of royal intermarriage, was the great-great-grandfather of both Queen Elizabeth and her husband, Prince Philip. Although devoted to his wife, Albert found it difficult to play second fiddle to her. "I am very happy and contented, but the difficulty in filling my place with the proper dignity is that I am only the husband, not the master in the house," he complained in a letter to William von Lowenstein in May 1840, shortly after his marriage.[6]

Matters were not helped by Albert's low standing with the British public, who were not impressed by the impoverished and undistinguished German state from which he came, which was barely larger than an English county. Parliament refused to make him a peer – partly because of anti-German feeling and also out of a desire to exclude him from exercising any political role. The besotted Victoria wanted him to be crowned king (or king consort), but Lord Melbourne, her avuncular prime minister, urged her not to. It was only in June 1857, after he had spent seventeen years as HRH Prince Albert, that he was formally granted the title of Prince Consort by his wife. Albert was also given a relatively modest annuity of thirty thousand pounds – substantially less than the fifty-thousand-pound pension that had been awarded to his uncle Léopold. Albert was aware of the wariness of his wife's subjects towards him and acted in an appropriately self-effacing manner. "The position of prince consort requires that the husband should entirely sink his own individual existence in that of his wife," he wrote.

Over time, however, Albert succeeded in carving himself out a role: he ran the Queen's household, estates and office, was heavily involved with the organization of the Great Exhibition of 1851 and also adopted many public causes, such as educational reform and the abolition of slavery. At a time when the monarch could still conduct diplomacy independently of her government, he carried the key to Victoria's dispatch boxes, serving as advisor and confidant and drafter of her state orders. "He is king to all intents and purposes," one disgruntled critic muttered.[7] Yet he also helped the development of Britain's constitutional monarchy by persuading Victoria to show less partisanship in her parliament – even though he actively disagreed with the interventionist "gunboat" diplomacy of Lord Palmerston while he was foreign secretary.

Recent times have seen two other royal consorts who, to varying degrees, have struggled with the same problems as their predecessors: Prince Claus, the German-born husband of Juliana's daughter, Queen Beatrix of the Netherlands, and Prince Henrik, the French diplomat who married Queen Margrethe II of Denmark.

Despite the outburst of anti-German feeling prompted by his marriage, Prince Claus was to prove a popular member of the Dutch royal family. He became involved in trade and industry as well as the preservation of historic buildings, nature conservation and the environment. More importantly, in April 1967, he and Juliana produced a baby boy, Willem-Alexander, the first male Dutch royal in one hundred and sixteen years. As the guns boomed one hundred and one times, the country went crazy. Bells tolled, bars were packed with revellers and ten thousand people signed a register at the Soestdijk Palace. The animosity towards their wedding just the previous year seemed forgotten. The couple went on to have two more sons, Johan Friso and Constantijn.

Claus displayed a humility that appealed to the unassuming Dutch, which was a sharp contrast with the flamboyance of his father-in-law. In 1997 he asked the public to refrain from marking his birthday because it coincided with the funeral of the Princess of Wales. At an African fashion show the following year he expressed admiration for Nelson Mandela's casual style of dress. In what he called the Declaration of Amsterdam, he ripped off his own necktie and tossed it at his wife's feet, calling it "a snake around my neck". His act briefly touched off an open-necked fashion craze among normally conservative Dutchmen, but the Prince was unable to escape royal decorum for good and, before long, was knotting his tie again.

Claus appears to have found it difficult to adjust to life as a royal consort, however, and suffered a serious nervous breakdown in the early 1980s. In later life he suffered a string of maladies, including Parkinson's disease and prostate cancer, and had to have a kidney removed. Although well enough to attend Willem-Alexander's wedding in February 2002, he spent the following few months in and out of intensive care with respiratory and heart problems. He died that October of Parkinson's disease and pneumonia, aged seventy-six, his three sons at his bedside.

Denmark's Prince Henrik also seems to have struggled to come to terms with his role as first gentleman in his adoptive land, claiming that the Danes have never accepted him. The French accent – and his preference for his native tongue, with which he speaks to the Queen – counted against Henrik in the eyes of many of his subjects. So too did his robust attitudes towards parenting; on one occasion he urged parents to "bring up children like dogs", on the grounds that "both need a strong hand" – a sentiment that may have been accepted in French aristocratic circles, but did not go down well in liberal Denmark where corporal punishment has long been discouraged. He was also unhappy about being financially dependent on his wife and in 1984 asked that he too receive an official allowance, which he was eventually granted.

Henrik reflected his frustration with remarkable frankness in his memoirs, *Destin oblige*, published in 1996. "I said recently that to be prince consort requires the sensitivity of a seismograph under the skin of a rhinoceros," he wrote. "To be tough, but to feel the slightest vibration. To expect to be the preferred target of any head-hunter."[8]

These frustrations came to a head in an extraordinary outburst in January 2002, when Queen Margrethe was forced to miss the annual exchange of greetings with the foreign ambassadors at the staterooms of Christiansborg Castle, the Danish parliament, after falling and breaking two ribs. Henrik hosted the social part of the event, but Søren Haslund-Christensen, the lord chamberlain, arranged it so that it was Crown Prince Frederik who replied in French to the speech by the doyen of the diplomatic corps.

Henrik was livid, especially when he read the praise that the Danish newspapers heaped on his son the next day. The court was a social event where he and Margrethe received greetings, he felt, and therefore he should have replaced the Queen in her absence. Unusually, however, he did not try to keep his feelings to himself.

A couple of weeks afterwards, Henrik left Denmark for France, where he attended a music festival before going home to his estate to oversee production of that year's vintage. While he was there the palace agreed that he should grant an interview to Bodil Cath, the respected royal correspondent of *BT*, a Danish tabloid. Completely at ease on his home turf, he vented his frustrations with the way he had been relegated overnight from second to third in the hierarchy. "I feel that after more than thirty years' service I have been put on ice," Henrik said. "I have been trying to do everything in my power for my country. I am happy in Denmark. I care very much for Denmark. Why this constant degradation of me? Why this need to disappoint me? Why step on my toes and make me lose my self-respect? Something like this would not happen in the United States," he added. "There you have the expression 'The First Lady'; why not 'The First Man'? The First Man is me, not my son." The only reaction from the royal family was provided by Crown Prince Frederik, who told the paper: "My father is not well at the moment. He needs to remain calm."[9]

Henrik's comments caused a media storm. The Danish television news led with his remarks, and other newspapers weighed in with their analysis. The Amalienborg Palace responded to the blizzard of press enquiries with a simple "No comment" but swiftly shifted into damage-control mode. The Queen and Frederik, who had been in the Netherlands at the wedding of Crown Prince Willem-Alexander, flew immediately to France to be with Henrik. Their second son, Joachim, followed soon afterwards.

The next day, Henrik posed with Margrethe and Frederik outside the chateau for photographers. "As you can see with your own eyes, we are very happy to be together," Henrik told them. No questions were allowed.

Predictably, this was not enough to calm the media. "The Prince's comments are incomprehensible, and we need a more profound explanation of what is happening now," declared the conservative daily *Jyllands-Posten*. Speculation was rife that the couple were heading for a divorce. Amid the torrent of criticism, it was up to Anders Fogh Rasmussen, the prime minister, to defend the Prince and voice appreciation for his work for Danish society. Henrik's "period of reflection" over, he finally returned home the following week. The divorce never happened.

The Queen provided her view of events in *Margrethe*, an authorized biography made up of a series of interviews she gave to journalist Annelise Bistrup, which was published in 2005. "At times it has been more difficult for my husband than I realized," she admitted. "And I did not help him sufficiently. I have not been aware of how best to help." She insisted, however, that the couple had overcome the crisis. "When you have been married for so many years as we have, you should be able to cope with some rough seas once in a while," she said. "Actually, I think we have fewer crises than many other married couples. This particular thing had a happy ending. I think my husband feels the same way."[10]

Now in his seventies, Henrik has suffered increasingly from ill health. A lover of food and fine wine, he put on weight after a health scare prompted him to give up smoking in 1997. Ten years later, a royal trip to South Korea had to be cut short after he went down with bronchitis on the flight out there. Arthritis has forced him to cut down on two of his passions – sculpting and playing the piano – and he has also given up horse riding. He devotes himself increasingly to writing poems, in

French of course, which he reads at private gatherings. Some are apparently quite erotic. "He certainly does not beat around the bush when he writes," said a friend who had attended several such gatherings. "It is not that he uses dirty words, but yet, you are in no doubt of the meaning of his poem. His language is very flowery, very verbose."[11]

Prince Philip, husband of Queen Elizabeth II, provides a model for the modern consort – even though he too found it difficult to adapt to his position during the early years of his marriage. As long as his father-in-law George VI was alive, the Duke of Edinburgh, as he became known when he married, was able to continue his career in the Royal Navy. Stationed in Malta from 1949, he spent much of his time away at sea.

The Duke's life changed for good in February 1952, however, when Elizabeth became Queen and he was required to return to Britain to be at her side. Her elevation also confronted him with what he was to perceive as a series of slights – the first over the name of the royal house. Philip's uncle, Lord Mountbatten, who had played such an important role in bringing the couple together, suggested the House of Windsor should be renamed the House of Mountbatten on the grounds that Elizabeth, had she been any other woman, would typically have taken her husband's surname – or at the very least ensured that it was carried by their children. Elizabeth's paternal grandmother, Queen Mary, was appalled, and told Winston Churchill, recently returned to power as prime minister, who advised Elizabeth to issue a proclamation declaring the royal house was to remain the House of Windsor.

The Duke was angry. "I am nothing but a bloody amoeba," he complained. "I am the only man in the country not allowed to give his name to his own children."[12] In a concession to her husband, the Queen did, however, announce that the Duke was to have "place, pre-eminence and precedence" next to her "on all occasions and in all meetings, except where otherwise provided by Act of Parliament".

By nature, Philip loved to be in command, whether of a Royal Navy ship, a polo team or his own family. That could no longer be the case now his wife had become Queen. His role was to support her in her duties as sovereign, accompanying her to ceremonies such as the state opening of parliament, to state dinners and on tours abroad. "Until that point, I was head of the family," he wrote later. "Within the house,

Britain's Queen Elizabeth II with Prince Philip in the House of Lords during the state opening of Parliament in 2003.

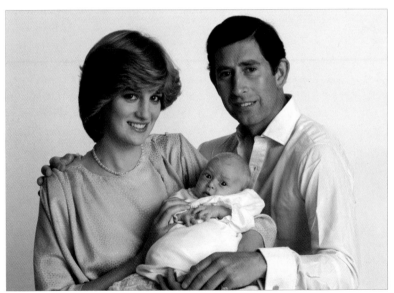

Prince Charles and Princess Diana sit with their new-born son, Prince William, at Kensington Palace in 1982.

Prince Charles and Camilla Parker-Bowles (centre) at Windsor Castle on the day of their wedding in April 2005. Also pictured, from left to right, back row: Prince Harry, Prince William, Tom and Laura Parker-Bowles. Front row: Prince Philip, Queen Elizabeth II and Camilla's father Major Bruce Shand.

Prince William and Catherine, Duchess of Cambridge, at Buckingham Palace just after their wedding in April 2012.

King Juan Carlos and Queen Sofía of Spain with Crown Prince Felipe,
Princess Letizia and their new-born baby, Princess Leonor,
at the Zarzuela Palace in Madrid in 2005.

King Albert II and Queen Paola of Belgium
visiting the city of Geraardsbergen in 2008.

Queen Beatrix of the Netherlands (centre), Crown Prince
Willem-Alexander (left) and Princess Máxima (right) after
the opening of the Dutch Parliament in September 2011.

Princess Madeleine, King Carl Gustaf, Queen Silvia, Prince Carl Philip
and Crown Princess Victoria of Sweden at the Royal Palace
in Stockholm on the King's sixtieth birthday in 2006.

Crown Princess Victoria of Sweden and her husband Prince Daniel
in Stockholm on their wedding day in June 2010.

Queen Margrethe (second from the left) on her sixty-second birthday at Amalienborg Palace in 2002. Also pictured, from left to right: Crown Prince Frederik, Prince Consort Henrik, Princess Alexandra and Prince Joachim, with young Prince Nikolai in the foreground.

The Norwegian Royal family at the Royal Palace in December 2005. From left to right: Princess Märtha Louise with daughter Maud Angelica, Queen Sonja with granddaughter Leah Isadora, Crown Prince Haakon with daughter Ingrid Alexandra, Crown Princess Mette-Marit with sons Sverre Magnus and Marius and King Harald.

Princess Caroline, Prince Albert, Prince Rainier and Princess Stéphanie
of Monaco at the Royal Palace in 1998.

Prince Hans-Adam II of Liechtenstein and Princess Marie Aglaë
on Liechtenstein's National Day in Vaduz in 2008.

Luxembourg's Prince Sebastian, Princess Alexandra, Hereditary Grand Duke
Guillaume, Grand Duchess Maria Teresa, Grand Duke Henri, Prince Louis
and Princess Tessy on Luxembourg's National Day in 2011.

whatever we did, it was together. I naturally filled the principal position. People used to come and ask me what to do. After the King's death the whole thing changed very, very considerably."[13]

Matters were not helped by the attitude of the royal household, ministers and other members of the establishment, for whom Philip, with his foreign origins, was something of an outsider. For some, he was too Teutonic – not a helpful attribute in country that had just spent six years at war with Germany. Some members of the aristocracy nicknamed him "Phil the Greek".

Lord Charteris, who became Elizabeth's first private secretary in 1949, suggested Philip had not made things easier with his own attitude. "I think Philip might have tried a little harder to accommodate the views of the royal household," he wrote. "Because of the way he was treated, especially before his marriage, he had a certain amount of prejudice against the old order. He thought it was stuffy and needed shaking up. He became the consort of the sovereign as opposed to the husband of a princess, with a certain amount of antipathy and impatience. He sulked quite a lot."[14]

Elizabeth quickly realized she would have to find a way of keeping her hyperactive husband occupied; so she put him in charge of modernizing Buckingham Palace, Windsor Castle and Sandringham, as well as making him chief ranger of Windsor Great Park. Philip began with Buckingham Palace: he set to with gusto, coming up with a flurry of proposals to update both the structures of the buildings and the way they were run. Not surprisingly, many of his plans were blocked by staff, but he succeeded in pushing some through. Lower, false ceilings were put into some of the rooms, the central heating was upgraded and an intercom system installed. There were also mass sackings and redundancies among the staff, many of whom were pensioned off.

While the Duke makes a point of walking two steps behind his wife in public, theirs is apparently a far more traditional relationship when they are alone together. "They have worked out an interesting modus operandi," says one senior royal official. "In public, as you might expect, the Queen is very much in the lead, and the jokes about him always being one step behind her are entirely accurate. But in private, he is very much in the lead. He takes the initiative on their conversations and what they will do. So their private and public worlds are entirely different." Gyles Brandreth, author of the joint biography

Philip and Elizabeth: Portrait of a Marriage, who knows the couple well, agrees: "They are typical of their generation. She wears the crown but he wears the trousers. Interestingly, she doesn't really feel safe except with the Duke of Edinburgh."[15]

Sir Michael Oswald, an old friend of the Queen, claims the royal couple also share a sense of humour, teasing each other when they are away from the spotlight. "It helps them deal with stressful situations," he says. "It is part of their mutual support, part of their camaraderie." This is confirmed by Brandreth, who recalls being in a car behind theirs on the night of the Queen's Golden Jubilee in 2002 and seeing them having an attack of the giggles. "You don't think of the Queen really letting go, but she was actually rocking back and forth with laughter," he says. "It was a wonderful sight. They will have been sharing some anecdote about the day."[16]

Unlike many of their royal predecessors, the couple apparently share a bed, even if they have necessarily always spent a considerable time away from each other – which has helped fuel persistent rumours about Philip's philandering. There seems no doubt the Duke enjoyed a number of romantic dalliances during his courtship with Elizabeth. Young, good-looking and a prize catch, he was sought after by beautiful women and reciprocated their attentions. After the end of the war and his return he was a fixture on the London party scene, often together with Mike Parker, who had been a close friend since their time in the navy together. Together they would frequent the capital's drinking clubs and nightclubs.

The partying continued after they married, although no convincing evidence has been produced for any of his supposed liaisons. Nor, following royal tradition, has the Prince ever responded to the claims – to the apparent frustration of some of the women concerned. Pat Kirkwood, an actress who lived for six decades under the suspicion of having been his mistress after they spent an evening together in 1948, wrote bitterly to Philip in May 1993, "I think if there had been some support from your direction, the matter could have been squashed years ago instead of having to battle a sea of sharks single-handed."[17]

Pressed on the subject of his marital infidelity, the Duke replied, jokingly: "For the past forty years I have never moved anywhere without a policeman... so how the hell could I get away with anything like that?"

* * *

In some respects matters have been somewhat simpler for those women who have married into the royal family – the job of a queen (or queen to be) has traditionally been to act as an elegant accompaniment to her husband on public occasions, to bear his children and supervise their upbringing. Provided she gave birth to the all-important son, the queen's position, in most cases, was assured.

In most cases drawn from foreign royal houses, these women have been obliged to adapt to life in a different country with a different language and culture and within a court with different traditions from those they knew at home. A long way from friends and relatives, they often suffered badly from homesickness; until the building of the rail-ways and invention of the aeroplane, visits home were arduous and rare. Matters were not helped by the jealousy – and often downright hostility – that they encountered from their new compatriots. Their life would became even more uncomfortable when a shift in alliances meant their adoptive country found itself at war with the land of the birth. And then there was the humiliation that many suffered on ac-count of their husbands' serial infidelities. Although a brave few took their husbands to task – or took lovers of their own – most had little alternative but to suffer in silence.

Désirée, the eccentric French wife of Jean-Baptiste Bernadotte, founder of Sweden's current royal dynasty, disliked the country so much that for more than a decade after her husband became crown prince in 1810 she refused to live in the country at all, claiming that she caught cold at mention of the word "Stockholm". (Although her pursuit of Duc de Richelieu, the French prime minister, was another reason for her refusal to go north.) A century later, the English-born Queen Maud, wife of King Haakon VII of Norway, also spent much of her time on the British royal family's Sandringham estate rather than in chilly Norway.

When Princess Alexandra of Denmark married the future King Edward VII of Britain in 1863, she was forbidden from bringing with her any of her ladies-in-waiting; it was argued that they could be plotting among themselves in Danish and no one else would be able to understand them. Given its size and splendour, the British court was also daunting to someone used to the smaller, cosier Danish one. Alexandra's isolation was increased by her deafness, which got worse as the years went on, and by her husband's many mistresses.

Like many queens before and after her, Alexandra's response was to devote herself to her five children – and her pets. In the garden of Marlborough House, her London home until Edward became king, are the graves of her three dogs, Tiny, Muff and Joss, and of Bonny, her "favourite rabbit". For Alexandra, as for her siblings scattered across Europe, the high point of the year was the regular family gatherings at the Fredensborg Palace presided over by her father Christian IX and her mother Louise.

In more recent times, queens have been able to play a more active role. The gradual transformation of the monarch's function from a political one to a representational one, which was largely complete by the second half of the twentieth century, has put more emphasis on the royal family as a unit – turning the queen from someone subordinate to the king into an equal partner with an independent public profile and an identity of her own.

Queen Ingrid, the mother of the current Danish Queen, Margrethe II, did much to modernize the monarchy through the positive influence she exerted on her husband, Frederik IX, in the years after their marriage in 1935. "Queen Ingrid was one of the last royals from the world of yesterday, but also the one who, together with King Frederik IX, created the modern Danish monarchy as we know it today," claims Trond Norén Isaksen, a Norwegian historian and expert on Scandinavian royalty. "King Frederik IX was the first non-political monarch in Denmark, and what he and Queen Ingrid did was to transform the monarchy into an institution which, although not democratic itself, lives in harmony with the democracy." As Isaksen argues, Ingrid also helped establish the concept of kingship "as a partnership between the King and the Queen".[18]

Such a partnership was already a given when King Carl XVI Gustaf of Sweden married Silvia Sommerlath in June 1976. The German-born Queen had little chance to ease herself gently into her role, as her husband, unlike the other European monarchs of his generation, was already king when they married. Thus she was faced almost immediately with the need not just to secure the succession – which she did admirably, by bearing two daughters and a son within the first six years of marriage – but also to fulfil the representational functions required of a queen. In addition she has plunged into charity work, with special emphasis on children and on the disabled. In 1999 she founded the World Childhood Foundation, which works towards better living conditions for children across the world. She also chairs the Royal Wedding Fund, which supports research in sports and athletics for disabled young people. The Queen has studied sign language in order to be able to communicate more effectively with those with impaired hearing.

Norway's Queen Sonja, by contrast, had a considerable time to prepare for her role. It was only in June 1991, more than two decades after she married, that her husband Harald became King. Yet it was not easy for her either: for a start, she was moving into a very male-dominated environment. Her father-in-law Olav V had been widowed before he came to the throne in 1957. The only other queen since the establishment of the Norwegian monarchy in 1905 had been Olav's mother, the British-born Queen Maud, who lived in a very different society and also predeceased her husband by nineteen years.

As the product of a middle-class Norwegian family, Sonja had to contend with the snobbery of some court officials who, like King Olav, would have preferred Harald to have married a foreign princess. She also faced a long struggle to be allowed to set up her own office. And then, when her husband became king, she had to put her foot down with Jo Benkow, the president of the Storting, the Norwegian parliament, in order to be allowed to accompany him to the annual state openings of parliament.

Sonja's role has been to expand the royal family's area of activities to reflect, in part, her interest in the arts and culture, while making sure not to overshadow her husband or get in the way of his constitutional tasks. This has helped by her considerable energy – which led to the nickname "Turbo Sonja". She has also been active in the inevitable charitable ventures, like Queen Silvia, with special emphasis on the most vulnerable in society: the young, the disadvantaged, refugees and immigrants and people with psychiatric problems.

The Norwegian queen has been a strong influence on her husband too. King Harald was effusive in praise of his wife when they celebrated their fortieth wedding anniversary in August 2008 with a cruise in the Adriatic aboard the royal yacht *Norge*, accompanied by their children, their children's spouses and their grandchildren. "I was a completely different person when I married forty years ago," he said to Norwegian reporters as he gazed fondly at his wife. "Apart from everything else I was extremely shy, but with her help, I got over it."[19]

Just as Sonja struggled initially with her role, so Britain's Princess Diana found that becoming a member of a royal family, with rituals and traditions that have become established over the centuries, can be daunting even for someone who is not facing a language or cultural barrier. In Diana's case the challenge was made greater by the very messy and public collapse of her marriage with Prince Charles. Unlike generations of previous royal brides who suffered in silence, Diana proved ready to go public with her grievances – with highly damaging results, for herself as much as for the British royal family.

But Diana broke the mould in a more positive way too. After having produced the requisite heir and spare with commendable speed, she fashioned for herself a role that went beyond that of mere consort – becoming a public figure in her own right. Whether hugging HIV-positive children or lepers in a hospital ward or campaigning against Angolan landmines, she threw herself into a range of charitable causes – arousing the jealousy of her increasingly estranged husband.

Diana's opposite numbers on the Continent have learnt from her example, identifying themselves with causes for which their backgrounds appear to suit them. Crown Princess Máxima of the Netherlands has become involved in the issue of providing finance for countries in the developing world, even being appointed the UN Secretary General's Special Advocate for Inclusive Finance. Mette-Marit of Norway has worked on international development and HIV-AIDS as well as youth and mental-health issues, while Denmark's Crown Princess Mary has set up the Mary Fund, which aims to help adults, children and families who are "socially isolated or excluded".

But what fate awaits the queen when her king dies? Higher female than male life expectancy – accentuated by a tendency by many monarchs to marry younger women – has meant most queens have outlived their husbands, leaving them to live out their remaining days playing the largely undefined role of dowager queen or queen mother.

To some extent theirs is merely a more extreme form of the fate of any stay-at-home mother who has devoted her adult life to husband and family and then suddenly finds herself alone. Royal life brings some specific extra humiliations, however: the next monarch will almost certainly have married by then, forcing his mother-in-law to cede the glamour and prestige that comes from being "First Lady" to a woman in the bloom of youth. She will also most likely be obliged to leave the principal palace for more modest accommodation. The financial arrangements – although certainly more generous than those enjoyed by the majority of her subjects – will also most likely be scaled back.

Some, such as George VI's wife Queen Elizabeth – mother of the current Queen Elizabeth II – more than rose to the challenge. Widowed in 1952 at the age of just fifty-one, the "Queen Mother", as she became known, lived on for another half a century, becoming something of an institution. Partly thanks to her discretion – an interview she gave when she was twenty-two and newly engaged was the only one made public during her lifetime – and also her longevity, she established herself as the nation's favourite grandmother. She also became close to her grandchildren. Such was the Queen Mother's enduring appeal that when an authorized biography of her by William Shawcross was published in 2009 it jumped to the top of the best-seller list.

Queen Margrethe's Swedish-born mother, Ingrid, also succeeded in redefining herself during her twenty-eight-year widowhood, especially as a surrogate mother for Crown Prince Frederik, whose own parents were often distant towards him during his childhood.

The position of Fabiola, the widow of King Baudouin of Belgium, has been more difficult, not least because she had no children of her own. Her husband's untimely death and his succession by his younger brother, Albert, meant she had to give up her role not to her daughter but to her sister-in-law, Paola. While she was Queen, the conservative and deeply religious Fabiola was disapproving of Paola's more flamboyant lifestyle. To find their roles suddenly reversed will have come as an uncomfortable shock.

In her old age Fabiola has also not been accorded the same reverence as Britain's Queen Mother by the media. Questions have been asked about the extent of her allowance and size of her entourage, while she has suffered the ignominy of seeing at least one Belgian newspaper erroneously report her death. Bizarrely, she has also had anonymous threats against her life, including one in July 2009 by someone threatening to kill her with a crossbow. Fabiola's response was to appear at Belgian National Day celebrations later that month waving an apple to the crowd – a witty demonstration of her unwillingness to be intimidated by any would-be William Tell. Yet such threats, repeated in early 2010, have undoubtedly weighed on her.

Chapter 10

Learning to Be a Monarch

Situated deep in the countryside of north-eastern Scotland, Gordonstoun was founded in 1933 by Dr Kurt Hahn, a German Jew with some unusual ideas. Hahn had been headmaster of Salem Castle School in southern Germany, but fled after being threatened by the Nazis. As a young man he had visited Morayshire to recover from illness and so the following year chose to establish his international school in two seventeenth-century buildings there.

Hahn set out to blend the traditional British public-school ethos with a philosophy derived in part from Plato's *Republic*. Thus the head boy was known as "Guardian", the school's emblem was a trireme and the regime was Spartan. Hahn believed young people were "surrounded by a sick civilization… in danger of being affected by a fivefold decay: the decay of fitness, the decay of initiative and enterprise, the decay of care and skill, the decay of self-discipline, the decay of compassion", and set himself the task of combating such a situation.[1]

The four hundred boys wore shorts the whole time, regardless of the weather, and began each day with a run in the grounds, followed by hot and then cold showers. They slept in crude wooden beds in dormitories, where the windows were always left open at night – which meant wet sheets or a light dusting of snow for those unfortunate enough to sleep next to them. Emphasis was put on militaristic discipline and physical education, including sailing and hill-walking. It was intended, said Hahn, to be a place where "the sons of the powerful can be emancipated from the prison of privilege".

It was into this curious world that Prince Charles, a rather shy young thirteen-year-old and heir to the British throne, stepped in April 1962.

Charles, the first child of the then Princess Elizabeth, was born in the Buhl Room at Buckingham Palace on 14th November 1948 just after eleven p.m. Outside, a crowd, three thousand strong, celebrated until the early hours of the morning, ignoring the entreaties of the police to quieten down.

In the autumn before her son was born, Elizabeth had declared, "I'm going to be the child's mother, not the nurses." Yet, inevitably, duty intruded, especially after she became queen, and Charles, not yet four, like other royal children before him, was brought up by nannies. "He was very responsive to kindness," recalled his Scottish governess, Catherine Peebles, "but if you raised your voice to him he would draw back into his shell and for a time you would be able to do nothing with him."[2]

Prince Philip wanted his son to come out of his shell and so, at the age of eight, after three years of Peebles's lessons, he was sent to school – making him the first heir to the British throne to be educated with other children. This being class-based Britain, where the children of the affluent are educated separately from everybody else, it could not be just the local primary school. Charles was sent instead to Hill House, a private preparatory school (where the fees now reach more than £12,000 a year) in Knightsbridge, just behind Harrods and a short drive from Buckingham Palace.

After a year at Hill House, it was decided he was ready for that quintessentially British upper-class institution: the boarding school, a place where parents would pay large amounts of money to have their children brought up in some of the harshest conditions possible and with the strictest discipline, in the belief that it strengthens the character. So in September 1957, two months before his ninth birthday, Charles was sent to his father's old school, Cheam – England's oldest preparatory school, founded in 1645 "for the sons of noblemen and gentry".[3] Cheam, which had moved from Surrey to Berkshire since Philip's day, was in many respects typical of such places: it had metal beds in austere dormitories, cold showers, compulsory chapel, Latin and sports – and, of course, corporal punishment.

The Queen insisted that Charles be treated in the same way as the other boys – which was not easy given who he was: she and the Duke of Edinburgh turned up with him in a chauffeur-driven car on the first day of term, while his movements were monitored by his personal detective, who lived in the school grounds. Charles, young for his age and extremely shy, described the first few weeks of his life at the school as the loneliest of his life. He especially disliked the rugby – and was often mocked by the other boys for being overweight.

Although idiosyncratic enough in their own ways, neither Hill House nor Cheam School were quite as curious as Gordonstoun, where he was sent in 1962. Charles, who slept with fourteen other boys in a prefabricated hut, suffered a special kind of hardship there. He was picked on mercilessly by the other boys, in scenes reminiscent of William Golding's *Lord of the Flies*.[4] The rugby field held special tortures for him. After one outburst of especially bad bullying, the novelist William Boyd, a contemporary of Charles, recalls hearing the cry: "We did him over. We just punched the future king of England."[5] Charles subsequently called the school "hell" and "a prison", and described, as part of an initiation ceremony, having been once caged naked in a wicker fish basket and left under a cold shower until he was rescued by a housemaster.

Such bullying was perhaps inevitable. "How can you treat a boy as just an ordinary chap when his mother's portrait is on the coins you spend, the stamps you use?" asked one former schoolmate.[6]

Charles himself remembered the nights as the worst. "I don't get any sleep practically at all nowadays," he wrote home in his sixth term, when he was fifteen. "The people in my dormitory are foul. Goodness they are horrid. I don't know how anybody could be so foul. They throw slippers all night long or hit me with pillows or rush across the room and hit me as hard as they can, then beetle back again as fast as they can, waking everyone else in the dormitory at the same time. Last night was hell, literal hell. I still wish I could go home. It's such a HOLE this place!"[7]

The media were also watching him. As long as Charles remained within Gordonstoun, he was largely free from the prying lenses, but once he stepped outside he became far more vulnerable. Quite how vulnerable became clear in 1969 when, aged fourteen, he became involved in what was to become known as the "cherry-brandy incident".[8] On an excursion on the school yacht to the Outer Hebrides with classmates, he and a few other boys went ashore at Stornoway on the Isle of Lewis, where they stopped off for a meal at a hotel.

Annoyed at tourists staring at him through the windows, Charles fled to a bar and, although he had never been in one before in his life, ordered a drink. "It seemed the most sensible thing," he recalled later. While most boys his age would have gone for a beer or cider, he ordered a cherry brandy. And that might have been it, had it not been for a freelance journalist who was also in the bar and sent the story round the world. "I was all ready to pack my bags and head for Siberia," he declared. Punishment awaited him on his return to school.

Charles, who also spent two terms at Timbertop School in the bush north-east of Melbourne, which was in many respects an Australian version of Gordonstoun, did respectably, if not brilliantly – achieving five GCE O levels and two A levels. He has said subsequently that the school helped him develop willpower and self-discipline – and also taught him curious habits he still follows, such as following a hot bath with a cold shower. He nevertheless claims not to have enjoyed his time there and when he left it was with apparent relief. Tellingly, he did not send either of his own sons to the school. They were educated instead at the prestigious, but rather far more conventional Eton College.

Before Charles, the heirs to the British throne had been educated at home. After early childhoods spent largely in the care of governesses, the royal children were entrusted to a variety of scholars selected from the universities, the army or the Church. The academic results were mixed, and they suffered from their deliberate isolation from other children. Matters were not helped during the eighteenth century by an almost uniformly hostile relationship between father and son.

The future Queen Victoria had an especially strange preparation for her role. The death of her father the Duke of Kent when she was just eight months old left her to be brought up by her German-born mother, Victoria, and Sir John Conroy, an army officer who became comptroller of the Duchess's household and most probably the Duchess's lover.

Together the pair developed a strict set of rules that became known as the "Kensington System": it isolated the young Princess from other children and made her totally dependent on them. Victoria was never allowed to be apart from her mother, tutor or governess and was even obliged to sleep in the Duchess's room. She and Conroy hoped to wield power through the young Princess if her uncle, King William IV, died before she came of age. They failed, however: when Victoria became Queen less than a month after her eighteenth birthday she swiftly turned against both of them. One of her first acts on becoming Queen was to remove her bed from her mother's room. Conroy was banned from her apartments and relations with her mother became cool.

When it came to educating Victoria's own nine children, it was her husband, Albert, who took charge, drawing up a plan outlined in a memorandum that he and the Queen signed in January 1847. His approach was motivated largely by his determination – bordering on obsession – that they should not grow up with the character defects of his wife's uncles, George IV and William IV, whose wayward pasts haunted the royal family. Victoria just wanted them to be little replicas of her beloved Albert – especially when it came to her second-born child and first-born son, whom she christened Albert Edward and who was eventually to rule Britain as Edward VII.

They were to be sorely disappointed. The Prince of Wales – or "poor Bertie" as his mother used to refer to him – proved difficult to teach and was prone to fits of sulkiness and anger, during which he would throw objects around the room. As a result he was frequently beaten. Then, as he got older, it was his sex life that caused his strait-laced parents most concern. Matters came to head when the Prince was studying at Cambridge and invited Nellie Clifton, an actress, to spend the night with him in his rooms. Albert was so appalled at such debauchery that he went to Cambridge to lecture his son. Albert died several weeks later, apparently of typhoid fever, but the Queen blamed it on a cold he caught walking around the city with their son. "That boy – I never can or shall look at him without a shudder," she wrote. Not surprisingly, Bertie was to take a more relaxed attitude to the upbringing of his own three girls and two boys.

Like her predecessors, Queen Elizabeth II did not enjoy anything like a normal childhood, even though she became heiress presumptive only in December 1936 at the age of ten, after her uncle Edward VIII abdicated and her father, Albert, took his place as George VI. Known in the family as "Lilibet" because of her inability as a small child to pronounce her own name, she was educated at home. Because she was a girl, though, the practice of the day dictated that the intellectual demands on her should be smaller.

This was made clear to Marion Crawford, the young Scottish woman who became governess to both Elizabeth and her younger sister, Margaret, during her first meeting with the girls' grandfather,

King George V. "For goodness' sake, teach Margaret and Lilibet to write a decent hand, that's all I ask you," the King told her in his loud, booming voice. "Not one of my children can write properly. They all do it exactly the same way."[9]

Later, after Crawford had started giving them lessons – which were held in a boudoir off the main drawing room of 145 Piccadilly, the tall narrow house just beyond Hyde Park Corner where they lived – Queen Mary, the young princesses' grandmother, was to intervene more directly, asking for a copy of their timetables. The Queen came back with some suggestions: more history and geography – or at least the parts relating to Britain's dominions and India – and learning poetry by heart, but Crawford could cut back on the arithmetic, on the grounds that "these two would probably never have to do even their own household books".[10]

To counter the isolation suffered by previous royal children, Crawford tried to bring the princesses as much as she could in touch with the outside world, taking them out for walks in nearby Hyde Park. On one occasion, to Elizabeth and Margaret's delight, they even went for a ride on the Underground to Tottenham Court Road and took tea at the YWCA. A plain-clothes detective travelled with them at the end of the carriage but, Crawford noted, "looked so very obviously a detective that people began to look round to try to discover what he was detecting." Another time they went for a ride on the top deck of a bus. Such jaunts came to a sudden end, however, when the Irish Republican Army began a letter-bomb campaign to draw attention to their demands for full independence and an end to the country's dominion status.

A further change came after their father became King George VI. For the children this meant leaving the cosiness of 145 Piccadilly for Buckingham Palace, with its vast rooms and long draughty corridors. Crawford likened it to "camping in a museum" and complained of the crumbling furniture and large mouse population. The sheer scale of the place made it a curious experience; outside there were often crowds, apparently waiting for something – although the girls never worked out what. On wet winter afternoons, they used to amuse themselves by staring back at them through the lace curtains. The enormous gardens were also a joy to the two young girls.

George was keen for his daughters to have as normal and happy a childhood as possible; as long as he was duke of York, with relatively light official duties, this had been easy. Nothing was allowed to stand in the way of various family sessions, which ended with the children's bath hour and bedtime. This necessarily became more difficult after he became king, and official engagements intruded, but they would always begin the day with their girls and have lunch with them if they were at home. Even after they moved to Buckingham Palace, few restraints were put on them and they were allowed to race around its corridors.

By now it was becoming clear that the girls were not going to have a younger brother, which meant that Elizabeth would one day be queen. This, it was felt, meant more attention should be paid to her education in order to prepare her for her future role. And so twice a week, until the war started, her mother would take her to Eton College, where Sir Henry Marten, an eminent scholar and vice-provost of the school, would give her lessons in constitutional history.

Home schooling was also the norm elsewhere in Europe for royal children. Queen Wilhelmina of the Netherlands, who became Queen at the age of ten in 1890 after the death of her elderly father Willem III, was given a bespoke education designed to prepare her for her future role. Under the guidance of her disciplinarian mother, Emma, who acted as regent until her eighteenth birthday, she was given private lessons in history, constitutional affairs and foreign languages by the country's finest teachers. Admirals and generals came to the palace to teach her the basics of military science, while economic instructors taught her finance. The curriculum was rounded off with Bible study.

It was an extraordinarily lonely existence, in which Wilhelmina, the only surviving child of Willem III, was prevented from having even the most minimal contact with her future subjects. She later described it as "the Cage". Dolls became a substitute for other children. "If you are naughty I shall make you into a princess and then you won't have any other little children to play with," the young Wilhelmina reportedly told them on one occasion.[11] From the start, Emma tried to instil in her a sense of duty. When, aged ten, Wilhelmina looked down on the cheering ranks of her subjects, she asked her mother, "Mama, do all these people belong to me?" "No," came the reply. "It is you who belong to all these people."[12]

For all her loneliness, the result was an extraordinarily self-confident young woman. As a little girl she visited Kaiser Wilhelm of Germany, one of the most powerful men in Europe. "See, my guards are seven feet tall and yours are only shoulder high to them," the Kaiser told her.

"Quite true, Your Majesty," she replied, "your guards are seven feet tall. But when we open our dykes the water is ten feet deep."

At the age of thirteen she travelled to England to meet Queen Victoria, a formidable figure then in her seventies. The young Wilhelmina returned impressed by the policemen, the pipers at Windsor, but most of all by Victoria herself. "She took me for a drive and I've never seen anyone sit so straight. I couldn't believe she was smaller than me." Five years later, when she was invested as Queen – the first in the history of the Netherlands – she seemed remarkably unfazed by the whole affair and even apparently insisted on writing her own speech.

Wilhelmina was determined that her only child, the future Queen Juliana, should not suffer the same isolation. And so she arranged for a small, carefully selected group of children to be brought to the Huis ten Bosch, the magnificent summer palace just outside The Hague that was Juliana's home for most of her childhood. Wilhelmina may not have been quite as stern as her own mother, but the court in which Juliana grew up was strict and humourless – and one in which she was made aware of her own status from an early age. "Even when I was a tiny girl, if I came into a room old ladies would leap to their feet and give me a tottering curtsy," she remembered. "It was so embarrassing I almost died."[13] It was also deeply spiritual. Wilhelmina took charge of her daughter's religious education, instilling in her from an early age the notion that a good earthly ruler was merely an agent of God's will.

Juliana tried to be more liberal with her own children – a determination apparently reinforced by the time they spent in exile in Canada during the Second World War – even though this brought her into conflict with her more conservative-minded husband. Bernhard was appalled by what he saw when they sat down for their first family dinner together at Soestdijk Palace after returning to the Netherlands in August 1945. Two-year-old Margriet beat a spoon on her plate, Irene sat with a leg curled underneath her and Beatrix, seven, talked incessantly with her mouth full and said she would prefer the steak and ice cream her mother had given her in Canada to the Dutch food on their plate.

The war also had an impact on the lives of others of the current generation of rulers. Like the future Queen Beatrix, the then Prince Harald of Norway was still a child when he fled his native country with his parents after the Germans invaded, going first to Sweden and then to Washington DC with his mothers and sisters, while his father, Crown Prince Olav, and his grandfather, King Haakon, stayed in London with the Norwegian government-in-exile. After the war he was enrolled in the third grade of Smestad Skole, the first member of the Norwegian royal family to attend a public school.

The Danish royal family, by contrast, remained in Copenhagen – although the future Queen Margrethe, born in 1940, would have been too young to understand much of what was going on. She had a mixture of private lessons at the Amalienborg Palace and public schooling, which included a year at a boarding school in Hampshire, something that helps explain her excellent English. Sweden's Carl XVI Gustaf, born six years later, missed the war completely but suffered tragedy of a very personal kind with the death of his father, Prince Gustaf Adolf, in an air crash when he was just nine months old.

It was not until he was seven that his German mother, Princess Sibylla, told him what had happened. Decades later, the King's sister Princess Birgitta, who was nine years his senior and so had felt the loss of her father more keenly, gave an interview in which she bemoaned the way their mother had handled the accident. "Children's questions were met with silence, children's anxiety and fear with the same silence," she said. "It was Mother's way of handling the situation, to handle living her life. Of course it was not good for us children. It would have been much better to be able to speak about Father's death."[14]

Born more than a decade before Carl XVI Gustaf, King Albert of Belgium and his elder brother, Baudouin, who ruled the country before him, had an especially tough childhood. First came the death of their mother, Queen Astrid, in the car crash in Switzerland in 1935; then came the Second World War, and a form of house arrest in Brussels; and then, following the Allied landings, deportation to Germany. For the last few months of the year, the boys were held together with their father and elder sister, Joséphine Charlotte, at a fort in Hirschstein in Saxony and then at Strobl in Austria. The presence of their father's new wife, Lilian Baels, who had had the first of three children by Léopold in 1942, further complicated matters. The end of the war meant their release – but not their return home. Faced with controversy over his role in the war, Léopold went into exile in Switzerland, where his three children continued their education in Geneva. Then, a few months before Baudouin's twenty-first birthday, his father abdicated and he became King – the youngest to ascend the throne in Europe since Queen Wilhelmina of the Netherlands more than half a century earlier.

The childhood of the future King Juan Carlos of Spain was also heavily influenced by his country's complicated political situation. He was born in Rome in 1938, where his grandfather King Alfonso XIII, father Don Juan and other members of the Spanish royal family had settled following the proclamation of the Second Spanish Republic seven year earlier. Juan Carlos's upbringing was to prove not to be the usual one of a royal exile, however. Instead, for the first decades of his life, he was caught up in a trial of strength between the royal family and General Francisco Franco, who was head of state after his forces won the Civil War.

Although determined to cling to power for his own lifetime, Franco tantalized the Borbóns by holding out the prospect of a restoration of the monarchy after he died. Crucially, however, he made clear that he – rather than the royal family itself – would decide who the next king would be. And as the years passed it became increasingly certain that this would not be Don Juan – whom Franco had come to detest – but rather his son, whom the dictator considered still young enough to be brought up in the ways of his regime.

Don Juan, who by then had moved from Rome to Estoril in Portugal to be closer to his home country, realized his son's claim to the throne would be strengthened considerably if he were educated in Spain. And so, in November 1948, a tearful Juanito, aged ten, was put on the overnight Lusitania Express, bound for a country in which he had not hitherto set foot. The discomfort he suffered was more than that of any small boy separated from his family. From the moment he arrived in Spain he was forced into a high-profile role that depended on fluctuating relations between his father and Franco's regime. While delegations of Royalists would come to fawn on him, he also had to come to terms with often savage attacks on his family in the official press. And then there were the meetings with Franco himself – and the fear of speaking out of turn. "When you meet Franco, listen to what he tells you, but say as little as possible," his father had warned him. "Be polite and reply briefly to his questions. A mouth tight shut lets in no flies."[15]

As Paul Preston, a biographer of Juan Carlos, has argued, the apparent equanimity with which the boy accepted that his father had effectively sold him into slavery for the sake of the dynasty was remarkable. "In a normal family, this act would be considered to be one of cruelty, or at best, of callous irresponsibility," he said. "But the Borbón family was not 'normal' and the decision to send Juan Carlos away responded to a 'higher' dynastic logic."[16]

It was just after celebrating his eighteenth birthday, during the time he was undergoing officer training at the Military Academy of Saragossa, that Juan Carlos was involved in a tragic episode that even today remains something of mystery. In March 1956, when the future king was back for the holidays at the family's Villa Giralda in Estoril, his younger brother, Prince Alfonso, then aged fourteen, died after being shot dead with a single bullet from a revolver. The official version, put out by the Spanish embassy in a communiqué, was that "while His Highness Prince Alfonso was cleaning a revolver last evening with his brother, a shot was fired hitting his forehead and killing him in a few minutes."

Rumours quickly began to circulate, however, that Juan Carlos had been holding the gun at the time it went off – although the various versions of what actually happened varied: Josefina Carolo, dressmaker to the future king's mother, for example, claimed the Prince had playfully pointed the pistol at his brother, unaware that it was loaded, and then pulled the trigger – remarkably irresponsible behaviour for an eighteen-year-old well into his stint of officer training. Bernardo Arnoso, a Portuguese friend of Juan Carlos, was also quoted as saying the Prince fired the pistol not knowing that it was loaded, but that the bullet ricocheted off a wall before hitting Alfonso in the face. Helena Matheopoulos, a Greek author who spoke with Juan Carlos's sister, Pilar, came up with a third and even more bizarre version of events: Alfonso, she claimed, had been out of the room and, when he returned, the opening of the door knocked Juan Carlos in the arm, causing him to fire the pistol.[17] Ironically, the pistol itself was said to have been a gift from General Franco.

The childhood of the Continent's coming generation of rulers has been very different. The Europe of the 1970s and 1980s in which they grew up was a peaceful place. In most cases they were also educated alongside other children, often at normal state schools – although with some exceptions. At the insistence of their French father, Crown Prince Frederik of Denmark and his younger brother Joachim spent the 1982–83 school year at the École des Roches, a boarding school in Normandy where the strict discipline proved something of a surprise for boys used to more relaxed Scandinavian ways. Crown Prince Philippe of Belgium, meanwhile, was obliged to split his education between French- and Dutch-speaking schools in order that he could be perfectly bilingual – a basic requirement for a future monarch of the linguistically divided country.

Yet none of them can be said to have had an ordinary childhood – and not only because of the wealth and status of their parents and the multiplicity of palaces and other homes in which they lived. It became clear to all of them from an early age that their parents had a job unlike almost any other: one that they performed twenty-four hours a day and seven days a week and that, in the case of the British royal family, would mean long foreign trips to far-flung corners of the Commonwealth on which their children would rarely be able to accompany them.

In some respects their position has not been so dissimilar from that of the children of American presidents. Yet there is a fundamental difference: thanks to the hereditary principle, royal children are in the public eye not only on account of the position that their father (or mother) occupies – but also because it is a role they will themselves later have to assume. The result is permanent scrutiny from the media that begins the moment when, just a few days old, they are produced for their first photo opportunity with their smiling parents outside the hospital. From then on they will become accustomed to a life in which the media will be keen to document their every move – from their first steps to their first boy- or girlfriend. If they make one mistake, they can count on a photographer being there to capture it.

Despite such pressures, Haakon for one appears to have had an idyllic childhood, spent at the country estate of Skaugum; his sole public duty was on 17th May, Constitution Day, when he would wave to the children's procession from the palace balcony. Elsewhere, however, distant relationships between parents and children have persisted. Denmark's Frederik has subsequently hinted that his childhood was far from happy. He and Joachim saw little of their parents; the two lived in a separate apartment at the top of the Amalienborg Palace, complete with bedrooms, a playroom and a dining room, where they were looked after by their nanny, Else Pedersen, who slept in her own room there.

In her controversial book, *1015 Copenhagen K*, which caused a stir when it was published in Denmark in 2007, Trine Villemann, a former royal reporter, described Margrethe as a distant woman who played little part in the rearing of her children. "It soon became clear to us all that she was not really that interested, not even in her own children, especially not when they were younger," claims one of the many unnamed former palace employees the author quotes.[18] For his part, Margrethe's husband Prince Henrik was a strict disciplinarian, who thought nothing of spanking his children when they did wrong. When the football-mad Frederik was looking for people to kick around a ball with, it fell to the bodyguards rather his father.

When Frederik was four – and his young brother three – there came what Villemann describes as one of the landmarks in their young lives: they were allowed to come down into the main part of the palace and eat dinner with their parents. As they grew up they did do so more often, but it was always by appointment, as if they were being granted an audience. It fell largely to Pedersen to assume the role of surrogate mother. Still a spinster in her mid-forties, she was an old-fashioned woman with a passion for good manners who became an emotional mainstay for the young princes. And, according to Villemann, it was Pedersen rather than his own mother whom Frederik would call from his boarding school in France on an almost daily basis to describe how unhappy he was.

Like Prince Charles before him, Frederik also developed a close relationship with his grandmother. As a young child he spent much of his time at Fredensborg, the royal residence north of Copenhagen; he and his brother would often walk across to Kancellihuset, the country house where Queen Ingrid lived. While she and Nanny Pedersen talked, the two boys would play.

By the time the princes were teenagers, however, it was decided they needed more of a male role model. So, in 1983, Major Carl Erik Gustaf von Freisleben, a Life Guards officer and equerry to the Queen, was put in charge of the boys, and three years later was appointed head of the Crown Prince's household. Freisleben, who had four children of his own, acted as a kind of replacement father, playing football and tennis with Frederik and Joachim and also helping them with their homework.

Hints about the strictness of Frederik's upbringing have not been confined to off-the-record comments from disgruntled courtiers whom Villemann interviewed for her book. The Crown Prince himself, in a speech at his parents' silver wedding anniversary in 1992, remarked poignantly: "There is an old Danish proverb which says chastise the one you love – and Father, let me assure you… we never doubted your love." As Frederik told the author Anne Wolden-Ræthinge, "It was a feeling of powerlessness which I often felt towards my parents. There was no question of two-way communication. It was just an order."

Alarmed, perhaps, at the picture being painted of his parents, the Prince seemed to backtrack a little in an authorized biography published to coincide with his fortieth birthday in 2008. In the book, Frederik and his brother denied that their father ruled them with an iron fist, but made clear that their traditional French-style upbringing had been more formal and involved greater distance between young and old than a more liberal Danish one. Not surprisingly, Frederik has also made great play of his intention to bring up his own children very differently. He and his wife Mary, who had a solidly middle-class upbringing in her native Tasmania, have made clear their determination to be modern, hands-on parents.[19]

In Belgium, Crown Prince Philippe, his sister Princess Astrid and brother Prince Laurent also had a less than conventional upbringing as a result of the collapse of their parents' marriage in the late 1960s – at the time when their father had just had a daughter, Delphine, by his mistress. Although Philippe was to some extent taken in hand by King Baudouin, his childless uncle, the situation undoubtedly weighed heavily on them. On one occasion, the servants even took them in for Christmas.

This was nothing, of course, compared to the emotional turmoil suffered by Prince William and Prince Harry. As children they were forced to suffer first the public disintegration of their parents' marriage and then their mother's death when William was fifteen and Harry was twelve. And then, in the full glare of publicity, they had to watch as their father pursued his relationship with Camilla Parker Bowles, the woman with whom he had betrayed their mother in the first place.

It would take a psychologist to determine the effect such an upbringing had on the princes, but it undoubtedly left its mark. In a speech in 2009 to mark Mother's Day at the Child Bereavement Charity, an organization for which the Princess of Wales had worked, Prince William spoke openly about the emptiness that he has felt since the death of his mother. "Losing a close family member is one of the hardest experiences that anyone can endure," he said. "Never being able to say the word 'mummy' again in your life sounds like a small thing. However, for many, including me, it's now just a word – hollow and evoking memories."

So what after school? At least among the Windsors, higher education took longer to catch on. The future Edward VII spent time at both Christ Church, Oxford, and Trinity College, Cambridge, but Prince Charles was the first member of the royal family to follow a proper bachelor's course and earn a degree. He was admitted to Trinity College, Cambridge, to read archaeology and anthropology,[20] but changed to history for the second part of his degree.

The Prince's status meant he necessarily received special treatment. When he arrived for his first day at the wheel of his red Mini, he was met on the pavement in front of the Great Gate of the college by Lord Butler, the master of Trinity. "It is the first time I have met a student here," Butler told reporters as he stood waiting several minutes for the prince to arrive.[21] Thereafter, however, the heir to the throne was treated as much as possible like the other students, eating with them at the scrubbed oaken tables in hall and sleeping in an ordinary three-room suite, sharing his toilet and bath with ten other students on the E staircase, where Sir Isaac Newton, Lord Macaulay and Thackeray had stayed before him. The only concession was a telephone in his room. The bodyguard who tailed him around town lived quietly in another part of the college.

These were the swinging Sixties, but they rather passed Charles by. Dressed most often in traditional tweeds and flannels or baggy cords and an old jacket, he preferred classical music to pop and by all accounts was not quick to make friends; his closest companions were his cousins. The Prince's happiest hours were spent performing in a series of comic revues; from childhood he had been a fan of the Goons, a long-running zany comedy show that was a forerunner of *Monty Python's Flying Circus* – so much so that he memorized many of their routines by heart. When it came to the final exams, Charles was awarded a respectable if not brilliant lower second-class degree. Yet it was not a bad achievement given the other distractions he had suffered: not only had he taken time out for state visits abroad, he also spent a term learning Welsh at the University College of Wales in Aberystwyth, to prepare for his investiture as the Prince of Wales in 1969.

Prince William is not particularly an intellectual, but by the time he came of age a university education had become so common that it would have looked odd if he had not applied, so he went to St Andrews, Scotland's oldest university. Prince Harry, whose academic results were not especially impressive, opted instead to join the army.

Charles's Continental counterparts have followed him to university, although more often they have studied political science or followed courses tailor-made to prepare them for their future role. Crown Prince Philippe of Belgium was the first in his family to go to university, studying for several months at Oxford before going on to Stanford, where he was awarded a Master of Arts in Political Science. Crown Princes Frederik and Haakon and Crown Princess Victoria also spent time in the United States – at Harvard, Berkeley and Yale respectively – as well as at universities at home. The only one not to study abroad was Willem-Alexander, who instead attended Leiden University in the Netherlands.

For the young princes, growing up has meant transition from schoolboy pranks to the more serious diversions available to the young, wealthy and privileged. Bars, restaurants and nightclubs have turned into their natural habitat – even if the periods of military service that they have all undergone provided some respite.

Willem-Alexander, for example, swiftly acquired a reputation as the enfant terrible of the Dutch royal family in the late 1980s and 1990s. Nicknamed Prince Pils for his beer-drinking, he became a familiar sight on the Amsterdam social circuit and became known for his penchant for high-performance vehicles and action-man sports. He was once fined for speeding after his car plunged into a canal. A fitness fanatic, he sparked outrage after running a race wearing a jacket advertising Marlboro cigarettes and trousers publicizing *Playboy* magazine.

As a student the Prince once famously excused himself from a Belgian state visit to revise for his exams, only to be spotted that afternoon on a racetrack. For a long time this was not offset by the adoption of any kind of public profile on serious issues. There were also some public-relations disasters worthy of the House of Windsor. In 1996, for example, when he took guests hunting on a royal estate, gamekeepers drove wild boar and deer past the royal Range Rovers to make it easier for elderly members of the party to shoot them. Usually loyal subjects were disgusted. More than seven thousand people sent faxes or letters of protest to the palace. "Highness, degrade yourself no more," screamed an advertisement taken out by animal-rights campaigners in leading newspapers. "The heavy responsibility you bear as our future king cannot be combined with spreading death and destruction among defenceless animals."

Sport was to prove Willem-Alexander's saving grace. By his late twenties it provided his main achievements, whether competing in the New York marathon or completing the Elfstedentocht, a gruelling one-hundred-and-twenty-mile skating race across the frozen canals of Holland. Willem-Alexander is not alone in his passion for sport: Frederik, the Danish Crown Prince, is a fanatical dinghy sailor, taking part in competitions across the world. Prince Albert II of Monaco has gone one better, representing his country five times in the bobsled at the Winter Olympics. Britain's Princess Anne was also an Olympian, forming part of the British equestrian team at the 1976 summer games in Montreal.

And then there have been the cars. As has been seen, car accidents have played a dramatic part in royal history, claiming the lives of Queen Astrid of Belgium and Britain's Princess Diana. (Princess Grace might also be added to the list, although she first suffered a stroke before crashing her car.) In August 1988, Crown Prince Frederik only narrowly avoided joining the list. He and two other friends were being driven by his younger brother, Prince Joachim, in a Peugeot 205 on a winding road near their parents' Château de Caïx in the south of

France. Suddenly Joachim, who had only recently gained his licence, lost control and crashed into a tree. Joachim escaped with only a few scratches, but Frederik and one of the friends were catapulted out of the car and into the River Lot. The Crown Prince was floating for several minutes unconscious before he was fished out and taken to hospital, suffering from a broken collarbone and in need of stitches for a deep gash in his forehead.

When news leaked of the accident, Queen Margrethe called a press conference at the castle to allow Joachim to explain what had happened. The Prince claimed he had been doing "only" sixty miles an hour – a high speed for such a narrow road – but although he did not face any legal penalties he received a serious telling-off from his mother. He had come perilously close to a nightmare scenario: if Frederik had died, not only would the Danes have been deprived of their future monarch, but his place would have been taken by the younger brother responsible for his death. The severity of the accident was revealed when a magazine published photographs of the wrecked car hidden under a tarpaulin at a local garage.

While Frederik and Joachim emerged unscathed from their car accident, Friso, the second son of Queen Beatrix of the Netherlands, was less fortunate when he and a childhood friend, Florian Moosbrugger, were buried by an avalanche while they were skiing in the Austrian resort of Lech in February 2012. Moosbrugger, owner of the Hotel Post, where the Dutch royal family traditionally spends its winter break, escaped without serious injury, thanks to the avalanche "airbag" he was wearing. The Prince, however, did not have one, and it took more than twenty minutes to dig him out from under the snow. Austrian doctors managed to resuscitate him, but the resulting oxygen starvation left him suffering from massive brain damage. Barring a miracle, the outlook for Friso, aged just forty-three, looked bleak – leaving a hole in the very heart of the Dutch royal family.

Although of a more trivial nature, there are other threats to young royals. Dating poses a tricky problem, especially for the young royal male: eminently eligible, the current generation of princes has enjoyed the pick of women – much as their father and grandfathers did before them. Even today, the prospect of a romance with a prince is enough to make many young women swoon.

Yet such romances these days are inevitably played out in full view of the media. While earlier royal lotharios such as Edward VII, Belgium's Léopolds or the Netherlands' Willems could indulge their passions largely hidden from the public gaze well into middle age, their successors have been pursued relentlessly by the paparazzi, much as if they were music or film stars. A snap of a new girl on the arm of a prince can be worth thousands of pounds to the photographer who snatches it – even if, as often turns out subsequently, she is merely an acquaintance rather than a new love.

For the prince himself, such attention, however unwelcome, is part of the job. It can be much tougher for the girl who has suddenly found her photograph splashed across the front pages. Our first sighting of her is often anonymous. But once she has been identified, it is open season on her. Friends are tracked down and questioned and her background probed; God forbid that there should be any past photographs, or worse, videos, that could be construed as embarrassing. These days, a Facebook page can be especially revealing. And then, with indecent haste, she suddenly finds herself treated as a possible future princess whose suitability is a legitimate matter for discussion. No Hollywood star's girlfriend has to put up with scrutiny such as this.

Despite such obstacles, however, love – or rather lust – has prevailed. Britain's Prince Charles, who came of age in the sexually freewheeling 1960s, blazed a path for the current generation, enjoying relationships with a number of women, something in which he was encouraged by his "Uncle Dickie" Mountbatten, who placed Broadlands, his grand country house in Hampshire, at his nephew's disposal. "I believe, in a case like yours, the man should sow his wild oats and have as many affairs as he can before settling down," Mountbatten advised Charles in one of many letters in February 1974.[22] (Mountbatten himself, by then in his seventies, had not allowed marriage to get in the way of his private life, indulging in a number of affairs with men as well as women.)

Charles did not fight shy of married women either – some, such as Dale "Kanga", Lady Tryon, were even married to his friends. Her husband, Lord Tryon, one of Charles's closest sporting companions, was apparently quite happy, like many aristocratic men before him, to find himself cast in the role of *mari complaisant*; Charles often dropped in at the pair's smart London home or was a guest at their fishing lodge in Iceland.

Amid this flurry of sexual partners was one constant: Camilla Shand, the daughter of Major Bruce Shand, a Second World War hero, and the Honourable Rosalind Cubitt, a society charmer. Appropriately enough, her great-grandmother, Alice Keppel, had been the favourite mistress of Edward VII. Accounts vary as to how Charles and Camilla first met, although it appears to have been at a hunt in the early summer of 1971. If the tabloid accounts are to be believed, Camilla's first words were: "You know, sir, my great-grandmother was the mistress of your great-great-grandfather – so how about it?" Yet this hardly rings true: far more plausible is another version in which Camilla looked at Charles's horse and declared, "That's a fine animal you have there, sir."

Their relationship quickly blossomed, and during the months that followed Charles and Camilla partied together in London at Annabel's, the Mayfair nightclub, or shared their passion for country pursuits. But duty called: in November 1972 the Prince was posted to the naval frigate HMS *Minerva*, which, the following February, was deployed to the Caribbean.

Despite their obvious feelings for one another, Charles was unable to commit to Camilla – probably because he realized that as a woman with a "history" she could be his mistress but never his wife. This did not lessen the blow he suffered when he went ashore in Antigua in April 1973 and learnt that the love of his life planned to marry Andrew Parker Bowles, a major in the prestigious Blues and Royals regiment. Their wedding, a grand society affair attended by the Queen Mother among others, took place two months later, while Charles was still at sea.

Yet Charles had to move on and find himself a bride: by 1980, he was past thirty, the age by which he had always said he was going to wed. But who would be the lucky woman? The basic formal requirements were not that onerous: the prospective princess of Wales and future queen could not be a Catholic or, with the memory of Edward VIII's abdication still fresh, a divorcee. However, there was another, more problematic requirement: while Charles's sexual exploits had been well documented by the media, his bride would have to be a virgin – or at least appear to be one. Such women were not easy to find in those post-pill and pre-AIDS days. Certainly, neither Camilla nor any of Charles's other conquests would have fitted the bill – all of which was to open the way for Diana Spencer.

* * *

Charles's Continental counterparts have, in most cases, shown the same predilection for glamorous young women. But it is one thing to date an underwear model: as many have found, the problems start when the relationship becomes serious. Just as in the past, some girls are seen as perfectly legitimate playthings for a royal fling – but certainly not as wife material.

Born in 1967, almost two decades later than Charles, Willem-Alexander was romantically linked with a number of glamorous women – among them Frederique van der Waal, a model and head of a lingerie company who happily posed for the cameras wearing nothing but the briefest of her own products. She was, as a result, considered highly unsuitable, and the Prince was "ordered" to end their affair. Or so the story went: van der Waal, who has gone on to a successful career and now lives in New York, later claimed the romance had been invented by the press. "He studied together with my brother in Leiden, and we certainly saw each other," she said. "But then it appeared in some ridiculous rag that that Beatrix had said I could never be queen because I had posed in my underwear. It was nonsense of course."[23]

In his late twenties, the Prince did embark on a serious relationship – with Emily Bremers, a dentist's daughter whom he met at Leiden University in 1994, when he was twenty-seven. Bremers, who worked for KLM Royal Dutch Airlines after her studies, was never officially recognized by the palace as the Prince's girlfriend. Not only was she a commoner, she was a Catholic – a major drawback.

Despite erroneous reports linking Willem-Alexander with Crown Princess Victoria of Sweden,[24] his romance with Bremers continued. And, as time passed, she seemed gradually to win acceptance in royal circles. In May 1998 she even accompanied the Prince to the wedding of his cousin Prince Maurits, fifth in line to the throne. The wedding was significant in itself: Maurits's bride, Marilène van den Broek, the daughter of a European commissioner, was both a commoner and a Catholic – a first for a member of the Dutch royal family. Indeed, royal watchers speculated that the official sanctioning of their union might open the way for Willem-Alexander to marry Emily, who appeared to be making her way into royal circles when she appeared at Queen Beatrix's sixtieth birthday celebrations that year.

It was not to be: that September, De Telgraaf reported the couple's romance was over. In fact, it was claimed, they had split up several months earlier, but kept their breakup under wraps in the hope they would sort out their problems. They didn't. The following year, the Prince, then thirty-two, declared that he would not marry for at least ten years – following the example of his father, who had waited until he was nearly forty.

Felipe, the heir to the Spanish throne, who is a year younger than Willem-Alexander, found that his love life came under equally close scrutiny. In his early adult years he went out with a number of glamorous women. One of his first serious relationships appears to have been in the late 1980s with Isabel Sartorius y Zorraquín de Mariño. Three years older than him, she had grown up in Madrid, lived in Peru and studied in Washington. She was the daughter of the Marquess de Mariño, Vicente Sartorius y Cabeza de Vaca, and Isabel Zorraquín. But the couple separated when their daughter was just eight. Her mother went on to marry Manuel Ulloa Elías, who was prime minister of Peru between 1980 and 1982, while her father wed Princess Nora of Liechtenstein, ensuring Isabel mixed with Europe's leading socialites.

The Prince, it was said, was besotted, but King Juan Carlos and Queen Sofía were dead against the relationship. Not only were her parents divorced, but the press linked some of her mother's friends to cocaine smuggling, although no proof was provided. She was also a commoner – and under a rule dating back to a royal ordinance made by Carlos III in the eighteenth century, anyone who wanted to marry a commoner had to be prepared to renounce the throne.

Apparently more serious was the Prince's relationship with Eva Sannum, a Norwegian student and part-time model whom he met in the late 1990s. The relationship, which lasted several years, raised eyebrows among monarchists who were convinced that Felipe, now in his thirties, should get on with doing his duty to preserve the fragile Borbón dynasty – that is, find a bride among the ranks of his fellow European royals and start a family. "It is obviously a matter of concern when the heir to the Crown is prepared to travel all the way to Oslo just to spend the weekend with a model," sniffed Jaime Peñafiel, Spain's most prominent royal expert, after photographs of the couple appeared. "This young woman has posed in bra and knickers, and bared her breasts on the catwalks. She cannot be the future bride of the Prince."

Their relationship endured, however, even though it was not until August 2001, four years after they first met, that Felipe and Sannum made their first public appearance together at the wedding of Crown Prince Haakon. Felipe, in full military regalia, and Sannum, wearing a light-blue silk evening dress, discreetly walked together into the great hall at the Norwegian royal palace where the party was being held. The wedding – and Sannum's especially sexy dress – may have been the final nail in the coffin of their relationship. Felipe confirmed to journalists that December that he and Sannum had decided to end their relationship "freely, with mutual accord and jointly". In his bachelor days, Norway's Haakon was also associated with a number of fashionable women, although usually from relatively high-placed families.

Crown Prince Philippe, heir to the Belgian throne, managed to keep his private life a little more discreet – but he too had his fair share of romances. The first love of his life appears to have been Barbara Maselis, the daughter of a cattle-food manufacturer from Roulers, whom he met while he was studying at secondary school in Zevenkerken in Loppem. Blonde and rather Scandinavian in appearance, she was intelligent, spoke at least three languages and, according to those who knew her, was not easily intimidated. They dated for three years: Philippe visited her at her parents' home in Roeselare or in the flat that she shared with her sister in Louvain, and she even came to the Château du Belvédère, where Philippe's mother and father lived.

Maselis's bourgeois origins remained a problem for the status-conscious Belgian royals and Philippe's father, the future King Albert II, put pressure on his son to end the union. "You are a prince of Belgium and you have an official future in our land," he reportedly told him. "I can see that Barbara is important to you, but you must try to put an end to it. There can be no talk of a wedding."[25]

Philippe appeared to have learnt his lesson. Even by the last decades of the twentieth century the Belgian royal family was still extremely particular – more so than other dynasties – about the social status of those whom its members married, and Philippe acted accordingly. Indeed, the list of women with whom it was claimed he had relationships in the years that followed read like a Who's Who of European aristocrats: among them was the Italian Countess Fiammetta de' Frescobaldi, once erroneously named as a girlfriend of Britain's Prince Charles.

The extent to which any of these were genuine romances is doubtful. As with other eligible young royals, it was enough for Philippe to be photographed with a woman for the press to start speculating about how soon they would marry. More serious, however, appeared to be his relationship with Countess Anna Plater-Syberg, a twenty-eight-year-old French woman of Polish origin, with whom he was photographed by *Point de Vue*, the French society magazine, in 1994 in Antibes on the Côte d'Azur. "Anna Plater-Syberg, the ideal fiancée for Philippe of Belgium," the magazine proclaimed on the cover of its edition that August.[26] The Belgian royal court went as far as to confirm the relationship, describing Plater-Syberg as a friend. But Philippe broke it up, and it was back to the speculation.

While Willem-Alexander, Felipe and Philippe appeared ready to give up their unsuitable girlfriends without complaint – at least in public – Denmark's Prince Frederik became embroiled in a more public struggle. His early adult years saw the usual romances – with Malou Aamund, for example, the slim blonde daughter of Suzanne Bjerrehuus, a television presenter and writer, who had appeared in a soft-porn movie during her youth. His first serious relationship, however, was in the mid-1990s with Katja Storkholm Nielsen, the daughter of Mogens Nielsen, chief executive of the company Risskov.

The pair had been acquaintances for several years. Both their fathers loved sailing and their children would bump into each other at events. Then, early in the summer of 1994, their friendship turned to romance; for the first time in his life, it seems, Frederik had fallen deeply in love.

It was a busy time for the Prince. He had to go away on military training and had already arranged to spend that autumn and winter in New York working at Denmark's United Nations mission. Despite such obstacles, their relationship flourished. Katja visited him in America and moved into his bachelor pad on the top floor of Christian VIII's mansion at Amalienborg. In January 1995 they went on holiday together in Mauritius.

Katja, with her fresh-faced beauty, easy laugh and common sense, was, according to Trine Villemann, a former royal reporter who tracked their romance in her book *1015 Copenhagen K*, the perfect partner for Frederik, and especially good at strengthening his self-confidence. "They were a team," one unnamed friend of the Crown Prince told Villemann. "They were brilliant at building each other up. There was togetherness and warmth between them, everybody could see that, and it gave him strength."[27] Villemann claims – without citing a source – that Frederik, now in his mid-twenties, even proposed marriage and Katja accepted.

But would Katja be embraced as a crown princess and a future queen? It certainly did not help that she had been working as a model – at one time even renting her own apartment in Milan, the fashion capital of Italy – and had done a few shots wearing expensive lingerie. Nor that her education had been relatively limited – although she was planning to start studying to become an art restorer.

The main problem was instead her nationality. The Danish monarchy continued to adhere to the tradition that members of the royal family should seek their spouses abroad. Frederik's mother, Queen Margrethe, had married a Frenchman and Margrethe's father, King Frederik IX, a Swede. Frederik's younger brother Joachim was poised to marry Hong Kong-born Alexandra Manley. Could Frederik fly in the face of such tradition?

The answer appears to have been "no". Although Villemann claims that his Swedish-born grandmother, Ingrid, with whom Frederik was close, approved of the union, his mother did not. The Queen effectively confirmed this veto in an interview a decade later. "When the boys were much younger, I let them know it would not be unwise if they married someone from another country," she said. "There is, and rightfully so, a long tradition in our family. Of course, there are always many difficulties, because of the language, and because the Danes are not always easy to please language-wise. But you come with what the British call 'no strings attached'. Of course, you have a past, but that past is not walking around in the streets among us."

Frederik was left in a difficult situation: he was not strong enough to challenge the family tradition, but nor did he break up with Storkholm immediately afterwards. Indeed, in the summer of 1996, during a summer holiday at the family's Château de Caïx, he introduced her to his grandmother – though not his parents. Soon afterwards, the Prince appears to have begun dating Maria Montell, a Danish pop singer. When Storkholm heard about the liaison, she ended their relationship – and did so publicly. In October that year her lawyer issued a statement declaring: "Katja Storkholm Nielsen would like to announce that her relationship with His Royal Highness, Crown Prince Frederik has been brought to an end."

Chapter 11

The Frog Who Turned into a Prince
and Other Fairy Tales

At least half a million cheering, flag-waving onlookers lined the streets of Stockholm on 19th June 2010 as Victoria, Crown Princess of Sweden, married Daniel Westling, her former fitness trainer. It was almost a decade since one of the most unlikely couples in modern European royal history had first met. Now the son of a provincial civil servant and a post-office worker had become HRH Prince Daniel, Duke of Västergötland, endowed with his own coat of arms and monogram.

Storkyrkan, the cathedral of Stockholm, close to the royal palace, was filled with nearly a thousand royals, dignitaries and friends from across Europe and beyond. Victoria wore a short-sleeved, pearl-white, off-the-shoulder gown with a gold diadem that Napoleon had given Joséphine and a veil that her own mother, Silvia, had worn when she married King Carl XVI Gustaf on the same day thirty-four years earlier. Her train was sixteen feet long. Daniel, in designer glasses with his hair slicked back, was in black tail coat and white bow tie.

Victoria, aged thirty-two, was beaming for most of the ceremony, at one point even winking at a member of the congregation. As Daniel, four years her senior, uttered the "*ja*" of the wedding vows, his eyes filled with tears as he turned to smile at his bride. Unusually for Sweden, Victoria chose to be given away by her father, to the consternation of many who considered such an Anglo-Saxon practice demeaning to women. Archbishop Anders Wejryd, who was presiding over the ceremony, was among those who had voiced concern over the breaking of a two-hundred-year-old Swedish tradition of "expressing equality between the spouses".

The service, which included a piece of choral music specially written by Benny Andersson of Abba, was short. And, after posing for photographs outside the cathedral, the couple set off in an open horse-drawn carriage in a procession through Stockholm, accompanied by mounted, blue-uniformed soldiers. The city was decked in flowers, blue-and-yellow flags and royal portraits.

When they reached Galärvarvet, a wharf on the Djurgården peninsula, the couple walked hand in hand down a blue carpet to the richly ornamented royal barge, Vasaorden. Still holding her bouquet, the bride waved to the crowd as eighteen sailors in their best dress uniforms rowed her and Daniel across the water to the royal palace. Eighteen Gripen fighter jets flew overhead in formation as the couple alighted at the steps leading up to the palace almost thirty minutes later. They were met by the King and Queen, who stood chatting with the groom's parents. A military band played.

This rather unlikely marriage marked the culmination of two weeks of celebrations dubbed "Love Stockholm 2010" that had begun on 6th June, Swedish National Day. The hype surrounding the Crown Princess's big day was enormous. For months, Sweden's newspapers, magazines and television had reported on every twist and turn in the preparations; Stockholm's hotels and restaurants were preparing for a bonanza; Arlanda airport had even been named "Official Love Airport" for the occasion. The city's chamber of commerce predicted the wedding would generate more than £8 million of extra revenue for local traders. The souvenir shops of Gamla Stan had long since filled with cups, mugs, fridge magnets and countless other items decorated with pictures of the royal couple.

Yet the souvenirs were not flying off the shelves quite as quickly as had been hoped, and some of the city's hotel rooms were empty. Two of the three special "wedding trains" laid on to bring spectators from the provinces were cancelled due to the lack of demand. Notes of dissent had begun to creep into the media – not least over the cost of the celebrations, estimated at twenty million kronor (£1.6 million), half of which was to be borne by taxpayers.

Yet such sentiments did little to dampen the mood that evening, as the happy couple presided over a sumptuous gala for six hundred guests in the staterooms of the royal palace. For many the high point was a speech by Daniel. Speaking confidently without notes and switching effortlessly between Swedish and English, he dispelled at a stroke any doubts about his ability to handle such big occasions. "I love you, Victoria, and I am proud that we are here together," he declared, calling his bride "princess of my heart". "And I am so happy to be your husband."

He recalled an early episode from their courtship when the future queen stayed up all night writing before an official trip abroad. "When I got up, I found thirty beautiful letters, addressed to me, one for each day she would be away," he said. He even managed a joke about his humble origins: drawing on the Grimm brothers, he told the story of a young man who "while perhaps not a frog, was certainly not a prince" who met a princess. "The first kiss did not change that," he continued, to laughter from the audience. "His transformation was not possible without the support of the wise King and Queen who had ruled the kingdom for many years and were full of wisdom and experience and had good hearts. They knew what was best and guided the young couple with a gentle hand, generously sharing all their valuable experience."

Daniel then led his bride onto the floor for the first dance, a perfectly executed waltz, while King Carl Gustaf followed with the groom's mother Eva, and Daniel's father partnered Queen Silvia.

In the early hours of the following morning, while the party was still in full flow, the couple slipped away to board a private jet belonging to Bertil Hult, one of Sweden's wealthiest businessmen and a friend of the King. It flew them to Tahiti and then on to one of the islands in French Polynesia, where a yacht was waiting for them.

Swedes, meanwhile, were left to ponder the newest addition to their royal family: they liked what they had seen – or rather, heard. *Aftonbladet* said the speech had "moved royals to tears and spread goosebumps over Swedes' arms around the whole country"; it was, the tabloid declared, "the moment he became our darling prince". An online poll on the website of its rival, *Expressen*, showed Daniel had become the country's second-most popular royal – beaten only by his wife.

Westling was something of a surprise as a royal consort, even though the Swedes had already had several years to get used to him. Victoria might have been expected to end up with one of what the Swedes call "brats" – the gilded youth from wealthy families who dress well, drive flashy cars and hang out in the bars, restaurants and clubs of Stockholm's upmarket Stureplan district.

Indeed, for several years the Crown Princess dated Daniel Collert, a "brat" par excellence, whom she met at school. Good-looking, rich and confident, Collert was an attractive catch. But his life had also been marred by tragedy: first his father died, then his mother, and he was brought up by his stepfather, Göran Collert, a wealthy banker.

When Victoria moved to America in 1998 to recover from the anorexia from which she suffered during her late teenage years, Collert followed her across the Atlantic, but by then their relationship was effectively over and they had become just friends. It was shortly after the Princess's return to Sweden that Westling came into her life – or rather she walked into his.

By royal standards, it was a curious way to meet your future husband. Victoria had been looking to join a gym and asked around for suggestions. Both Caroline Krueger, a close friend since childhood, and Victoria's younger sister, Princess Madeleine, recommended Master Training, an exclusive establishment near Stureplan, popular with Stockholm's smart set. With a restrictive membership policy and annual fee of more than £1,000, it was more like a private club than a fitness centre – in short, a place where even the heir to the throne could work out undisturbed. They also suggested a trainer: a young man named Daniel Westling.

Until then, Victoria had been mixing largely with "brats" like Collert: Westling was different, and not just because he worked in a gym rather than as a lawyer or in finance. For a start, he came not from one of the smart parts of Stockholm but instead from Ockelbo, a small town of six thousand or so people in central Sweden – a fact that was immediately clear to everyone as soon as he opened his mouth. His father was not a wealthy banker or industrialist, but worked for the local council, while his mother was employed by the post office. He dressed in jeans and baseball cap rather than smart designer wear, lived in a modest ground-floor flat and drove a little Alfa Romeo.

Yet, almost in spite of herself, Victoria came to fall for him. What had begun as a professional relationship turned into friendship – and then something more. Unbeknownst to all but members of her closest circle, she and Westling became lovers and she even started travelling back with him to Ockelbo. The locals appeared unfazed by their future queen's relationship with one of their own. And far from rushing to give the story to Sweden's gossip-hungry evening papers, they took pride in keeping their secret to themselves.

Just as the King's relationship with Silvia Sommerlath had been rumbled by the press thirty years earlier, so his daughter knew her secret would eventually come out. By May 2002 Johan T. Lindwall, a well-connected royal reporter from *Expressen*, Sweden's best-selling evening tabloid, had been tipped off about their relationship and, after warning the palace, wrote a story about it. By coincidence, Victoria was due to hold a news conference on another subject on the same day Lindwall's story appeared. This would have given her the perfect opportunity to deny the relationship – except she didn't. Asked about Westling, Victoria said only, "Daniel is a very good friend and is very close to me."

Confirmation of quite how close they were came that July at Krueger's twenty-fifth birthday party, held at a restaurant in the Stockholm harbour, hired especially for the occasion. The theme was Hawaiian: Victoria and Westling were there together but, conscious of the journalists camped around the venue, they knew they had to be discreet. Then, sometime after midnight, Victoria led Daniel to the dance floor – and they kissed. Unknown to them, a lucky photographer with a long lens on a boat in the harbour captured their clinch. The next afternoon the photograph was plastered over almost the entire front page of *Aftenposten* under the headline "The Kiss".

That day Victoria was due to fly to the Solliden Palace, the Swedish royals' summer residence on the southern island of Öland, to join her family for celebrations later that week to mark her own twenty-fifth birthday. As she walked onto the plane, her image stared back at her from the front of her fellow passengers' newspapers. That was nothing, however, compared with the discomfort that awaited her when she had to explain herself to her father.

The King, it seems, was not happy with her choice of Westling as a partner. "He was not what the King had imagined for his daughter," says Herman Lindqvist, a journalist turned popular historian who has got to know Victoria well after tutoring her on her country's past. "But when she met him she liked him, very much.

She wanted to keep things on a friendship level, but she couldn't control her feelings."[1]

The King wasn't the only one to have misgivings. Many of the palace officials, used to mixing in their narrow court circles, looked down on this boy from the provinces. So did some of Victoria's friends. However elite his gym, Westling was still a personal trainer. Stéphanie of Monaco may have married her bodyguard, but this was Sweden, not a tiny principality on the Mediterranean. And Victoria was going to be its next monarch. Comments began to appear in the Swedish press about Westling's poor English and lack of sophistication. Unprepared for the media attention, he made things worse by losing his temper with the photographers who began to follow his every move.

Victoria was not going to give him up, however, and Westling began gradually to win acceptance, being seen in public with the royal family and joining them at events – but it was a process that took several years. As he came more and more into the public eye, Westling was working on his image: the jeans were replaced by smart suits and the little Alfa Romeo by a Lexus. He was also becoming more confident in high society; his English improved. One of the country's leading public-relations companies started to give him advice and set up meetings with politicians and other prominent figures in Swedish society.

With every month that passed it increasingly became a matter not of whether the pair would marry but of when. In May 2008 Victoria and Westling appeared together at the fortieth birthday party of Crown Prince Frederik of Denmark, who is Victoria's second cousin, but they carefully avoided public displays of affection. The next month it was announced that Westling was going to rent a modest two-hundred-square-foot one-bedroom flat in Drottningholm, the royal estate outside Stockholm, paying just over £400 a month. Palace officials insisted that the Crown Princess would continue to live in the Sjöflygel wing of the palace, which was a few hundred metres away from Westling's new apartment in Pagebyggnaden, a house in the grounds.

The engagement was finally announced on 24th February 2009, with the wedding set for June the following year. Victoria's parents appeared to be reconciled to the prospect of having Westling as their son-in-law – not least, perhaps, because of the family's overarching need, like all dynasties, to have an heir. Their daughter, after all, was already into her thirties; breaking up with Westling and starting up with someone else anew could take time.

There was one more problem: although Westling seemed ostensibly fit and strong, he also suffered – unknown to the Swedish people – from a serious kidney complaint. That May, the Swedish royal court announced that he had been admitted to hospital and undergone a kidney transplant, with an organ donated by his father. The court claimed the need for a transplant had been known for a long time and the reason for the surgery was "a congenital but not inherited disease causing impaired renal function".

If Westling seemed an unusual choice of partner, he was positively conventional beside the woman that Crown Prince Haakon, Victoria's Norwegian counterpart, had married nine years earlier. Tall, blonde and statuesque, Mette-Marit Tjessem Høiby certainly looked like a princess; her background, however, was anything but the usual one for a future royal spouse – not least because she was a single mother.

Traditionally, Europe's royal houses have preferred the women who marry into their family to come "without a history". Mette-Marit had not just a history but living proof of it in the form of her son, Marius Borg Høiby, who had not only been born out of wedlock but had been fathered by a man, Morten Borg, with a conviction for possessing cocaine. Far from trying to gloss over her past, the royal couple confronted it head on. When Mette-Marit walked down the aisle of Oslo Cathedral on 25th August 2001, stunning in an ecru-coloured wedding gown of soft, thick crêpe with a twenty-foot veil, she was accompanied not just by three flower girls, but also by Marius, aged four, dressed in coat and tails.

In his wedding address, Gunnar Stålsett, the bishop of Oslo, praised the bride for setting an example in the way she had cared for her son. "You are beginning a new chapter, with the pages still unwritten," he said. "You do this with dignity. Today you are better equipped to understand others, young and old, who are in pain. Jesus says, 'He who is forgiven little, loves little.'"

So how had the heir to the Norwegian throne found himself such an unusual bride? The couple first met in July 1996 at the Quart Festival, a rock-music event in Kristiansand in southern Norway. Haakon had been staying with Morten Andreassen, one of the festival's organizers, whom he knew from his time in the navy. Andreassen, in turn, introduced him to Mette-Marit. The couple apparently clicked almost immediately, and they were soon seen dancing and laughing together. It has also been claimed they began a short but passionate summer romance.

The claim, if true, was extraordinary, for Mette-Marit was, at the time, pregnant with Marius, who was born the following January. Not that she was letting pregnancy slow her down. That autumn she appeared as a "flirt queen" on Lysthuset, a TV programme in which more than a hundred singles competed for a date with her.

Their backgrounds could have not have been more different. While Haakon was groomed from birth to be king, his bride grew up in more modest conditions in Kristiansand. Mette-Marit was born on 19th August 1973, the youngest of four children, to Sven O. Høiby, a journalist turned advertising copywriter, and his wife, Marit Tjessem. In 1984 her parents divorced. The three older children had already left home, but Mette-Marit was just eleven. She stayed with her mother in the family home, visiting her father every other weekend and on holidays. Although her parents' split was amicable, Mette-Marit took it badly.

Life went on, however. Mette-Marit grew into a pretty blonde teen-ager interested in music, boys and sport. Bored with life in Norway, she set off in 1990 for Australia for a year on a school exchange. She had hoped to be sent to Sydney, Melbourne or another big city, but ended up in Wangaratta, a dusty town of just 20,000 people in the state of Victoria. She nevertheless adapted quickly to Australian life, making friends and quickly losing her Norwegian accent.

Fitting back into life in southern Norway proved more difficult. One day she turned up to school with her head shaved; her school friends thought it was cool; her mother, predictably enough, was horrified. She also fell in love with a boy two years older than her who played in a party-loving local band. This meant alcohol and hashish, which she appeared to have tried for the first time.

Despite the hedonism, Mette-Marit passed her school-leaving exam in 1994. Shortly before, she had split with her musician boyfriend and taken up instead with John Ognby, a disc jockey from Lillestrøm in eastern Norway who was fifteen years her senior. Soon afterwards she moved in with him and was plunged into a life of wild parties,

although this time the drugs, including ecstasy, LSD and other hal-
lucinogens, were stronger than in her Kristiansand days.

Mette-Marit began to realize she had to move on. Her exam
results had not been that good, and she decided to take them again
at Bjørknes, a private grammar school in Oslo, where she moved in
with a girlfriend, who lived in the Grünerløkka part of town. Ognby
did not take separation easily: after allegedly making a number of
threatening telephone calls – for which she denounced him to the
police – he turned up in Oslo and threatened her with a knife on the
street. He was held for forty-eight hours before he was released. Their
intention, he said, had been to marry in Las Vegas; Mette-Marit had
already bought the rings.

It was shortly afterwards, while she was working as a waitress at
various cafés, that Mette-Marit met Borg and became pregnant by
him. She wanted to keep the baby and was strengthened in her resolve
by her mother, who had since remarried. Borg, too, promised to be
there for the baby, who was born on 13th January 1997 in Oslo's
Aker hospital.

At the 1999 Quart Festival, Haakon met Mette-Marit again. The
arrival of Marius had barely brought any stability to her life. After
living alone for a few months, in the summer of 1997 she moved in
with a new man – another disc jockey, this time ten years her senior –
but split from him the following spring and in early 1998 moved back
to Kristiansand with another boyfriend. This relationship, too, ended
after a few months. After spending a year at an engineering school in
Grimstad in southern Norway, she decided to give up and go back to
Oslo and study social anthropology. The problem was that she had
nowhere in the capital to live.

Fortuitously enough, Haakon did. Since his return from Califor-
nia, where he had been studying at Berkeley, he had been living in
a large bachelor pad at Ullevålsveien 7 in Oslo. He had fallen head
over heels in love with the woman he had first met three years earlier,
and, concerned at her plight, invited her to come and live there with
him. For the rest of that year Marius spent most of the time with his
grandparents in Kristiansand.

Initially, it seems, Haakon and Mette-Marit shared a flat – but
not a bed. Soon the relationship flourished. Even so, Haakon was
reluctant to tell his father, and Mette-Marit used to leave by the back

door. Norway is one of Europe's most liberal countries – but the Crown Prince knew what the press would nevertheless make of their relationship.

When Haakon finally summoned the courage to tell his father, Harald was understanding: his own relationship with Queen Sonja, a commoner, had been controversial during the 1960s. The question was: when should they tell the public? Birgitte Klækken, a journalist with the southern Norwegian newspaper *Fædrelandsvennen*, decided the question for them. For some time, she had been investigating rumours about the romance. On 29th December 1999 she broke the story.[2]

With their relationship now in the open, the couple embarked on a rapid damage-limitation exercise. They realized they had no chance of hiding Mette-Marit's past, but there was also the matter of various embarrassing private photographs and videotapes. One by one, Mette-Marit's friends handed them over, but there was concern there was still something out there.

The media, meanwhile, were investigating Mette-Marit's past. In April 2000 came the revelation that Borg had a past conviction for possessing cocaine. Crisis sessions in the palace followed: the following month, Haakon went on the offensive and gave an interview to NRK, the state television channel, in which he confirmed his relationship. "I have a girlfriend and her name is Mette-Marit," he declared. "The reason I have decided to go public now is that if I had been passive, my girlfriend, her son, her family, her friends and acquaintances could all have been dragged into this unnecessarily." In the interview the Crown Prince admitted his girlfriend had been a frequent visitor in the early Nineties to huge dances where drugs were often used, but insisted that was now a closed chapter.

Despite polls showing that his future subjects were less than enamoured of the relationship, Haakon persisted, and in September 2000 he, Mette-Marit and Marius moved into a flat in a smart but far from exclusive area just north of Oslo's city centre. The building was on a fairly busy road and had an overgrown front garden with a bus stop right outside and just a couple of discreet security cameras by way of protection. From there the Prince and his girlfriend, dressed in jeans and trainers, would go out to coffee bars, concerts and record shops like any other young couple. They even bought their furniture from Ikea.

And so it might well have continued, if there had not been pressure from Norway's Lutheran Church – of which Crown Prince Haakon is due one day to become head. And so, on 1st December 2000, after obtaining a green light from the prime minister, the King announced his son's engagement.

The following August, at a news conference three days before the wedding, Haakon expressed thanks that he had not been made to choose between love and the throne. Mette-Marit, meanwhile, made a heartfelt confession of her youthful indiscretions. "My adolescent rebellion was stronger than most," she said, holding back tears. "I was in an environment where we experimented and we went beyond the established norms." She did not deny suggestions of previous drug use, but insisted: "I have had experiences for which I have paid dearly. I would like to take this occasion to condemn drugs."

The news conference proved a masterstroke: from then on Mette-Marit's wild past ceased to be a story for the Norwegian media. There was one still problem though: her father, Sven O. Høiby. His career had gone downhill since the breakup of his marriage. While his daughter had moved in with the Crown Prince, Høiby, now in his mid-sixties, was living alone in a small flat in Kristiansand. He was also drinking heavily. For a woman hoping to become the next Queen of Norway, "Sven O.", as he became known, was a disaster waiting to happen – and a gift for the tabloid press.

Håvard Melnæs, an ambitious young journalist from *Se og Hør*, a celebrity magazine with a circulation of more than 400,000 copies a week and deep pockets, knew just how to exploit him. After news of Haakon's relationship with Mette-Marit broke, Melnæs had been given the job of trying to find her friends and family, and based himself down in Kristiansand for six months for the purpose. Past boyfriends were a particular target. Melnæs wanted photographs and stories and was happy to pay thousands of pounds for them – in cash, if necessary.

Almost a decade later, seated over a beer in the bar of the Grand Hotel on Oslo's Karl Johans Gate, Melnæs still seemed surprised by their willingness to cooperate. "I tracked down about ten to fifteen boyfriends, which, given she was twenty-seven, meant an average of one every six months," he recalls. All but one of them had a criminal record – mostly for drugs. Many of them, he claims, were ready to help the magazine in return for money – as too were many of the future Crown Princess's other friends. "The more people we paid off, the more copies we sold," he said.[3]

None of this could have prepared Melnæs for the experience of meeting Høiby. Melnæs had tried to contact him from Oslo but failed to find a telephone number, so he looked up his address in Kristiansand and went round to try his luck. After he had been standing several hours outside his apartment building, an elderly man, still distinguished and ramrod straight, appeared. Melnæs suggested they go for a coffee. Høiby proposed beer instead.

Later that evening they sat for four to five hours in Høiby's local bar, downing six or seven beers. Melnæs noticed a plastic bag he was carrying with him. It contained photographs of Mette-Marit – fifteen of them. "They were all innocent stuff: Christmas Eve, the first day at school, that kind of thing," Melnæs recalls. For a magazine that wanted to build up a picture of the future queen, they were worth a lot of money, which Melnæs was happy to pay. But Høiby, whose media background gave him an idea of how his daughter would be treated by the press, wanted something else: a story in *Se og Hør* painting his daughter in a positive light. Melnæs duly obliged. "I wrote the most positive story possible, even making up anonymous sources whom I quoted saying what a great future queen she would make," he says.

It was the beginning of a mutually beneficial friendship. Melnæs's bosses were so pleased with their new source they started to pay Høiby a retainer of 15,000 kroner (about £1,680) a month and provided him with a mobile phone so he could stay in touch. That was only the starting point: extra information or new photographs from his daughter's past would earn him more than £10,000. And now Høiby had a phone and was back in contact with friends and family, the information – and money – began to flow. "Over the first two years, we must have paid him 700,000 to 900,000 kroner [£78,000–100,000]," Melnæs recalls. "Lots of times it was black money – I used to carry the money in envelopes and hand it to him."

With the wedding approaching, Mette-Marit was faced with the problem of how to deal with the increasing embarrassment of her father. It is unknown whether she knew he was the source of all the photographs, but she realized he had to be brought under control. Initially it was not clear whether he would be allowed to come to the wedding. Eventually he received his invitation, although he was not permitted to accompany his daughter down the aisle. According to Melnæs – who had by then turned into a kind of surrogate son for Høiby – Mette-Marit also made her father sign an agreement pledging not to drink for the duration of the festivities.

Sven O. was left largely to his own devices: it was his "sponsors" at *Se og Hør* who not only paid for the four different suits he needed for the various formal wedding functions, but also financed his stay at the Grand Hotel, one of the most expensive in Oslo. They also gave him a pocket camera so he could take pictures of the wedding. "He was driven into our arms," says Melnæs. In the event he behaved himself (even though the camera was confiscated by a security guard).

The elevation of Sven O.'s daughter to Crown Princess had not solved his money problems – nor made him more reluctant to use the only means at his disposal of resolving them: the press. But the media's interests had changed since the wedding: the appetite for details of Mette-Marit's past life had faded. It was time for Sven O., hitherto an unnamed source, to become the story himself.

The result was his first on-the-record interview – with *Se og Hør*, of course – in which he talked frankly about his life. It was published under the headline: "I drink beer at nine in the morning". Sven O. was well paid for this too, but the money was soon gone, and he had to find other ways of cashing in on his new-found fame. He was also beginning to enjoy the attention.

Ever creative, Sven O. then announced he was going to write a book about his grandson, Marius. Haakon and Mette-Merit, who had both since gone to London to study, were horrified. It was announced that Sven O. would go to Britain for a "crisis meeting" with them. In the event the Crown Princess refused to see her father. The book was never written – nor was it clear it was ever going to have been. The important thing was it meant another story for the magazine, and more money for Høiby.

There was more embarrassment to come: in 2004 Sven O. went on tour with Sputnik, a veteran country-music singer. Also part of the act was Renate Barsgård, a stripper whose career, now she had reached her thirties, was on the way down. Sven O., in his late sixties, suggested they marry – which meant another exclusive for *Se og Hør* and a further four thousand or so pounds for Høiby. "It is strange that an old man like me could fall in love with a woman who is the same age as my youngest daughter," he told the magazine. "But it's true love."[4]

Even before the wedding took place, Sven called the magazine to say his young fiancée was pregnant. He was getting greedy, though, and claimed a rival publication was ready to pay 250,000 kroner (£28,000) for the exclusive. *Se og Hør* was ready to match that – but only if they could make sure the story was true. And so, since Melnæs was away, another reporter was dispatched from Oslo to meet Barsgård with a pregnancy-testing kit. She declined to take the test.

The wedding was still on track, and *Se og Hør* took control of the organization; it decided to hold the ceremony in a Norwegian embassy abroad, so the couple would not be recognized and the magazine would keep its exclusive. They chose The Hague, on the grounds that there were unlikely to be any Norwegian tourists around. The magazine paid for everything, including the rings, although Melnæs, who went along, was amused to see that Sven O. bought the cheapest ones possible – one for four euros and another for twelve euros – so he and his "bride" could keep as much money as possible for themselves. This didn't stop the Norwegian ambassador from congratulating the couple on their rings.

Se og Hør also had the rights for the couple's honeymoon in Thailand, but to Melnæs's relief it was a colleague from the magazine who went with them. "It was like a mental hospital," he says. "I never saw anyone as exhausted as my colleague when he came back. As for Sven O., he had stopped eating. It was just beer, gin and tonic and cigarettes."

Three months later, in June 2005, predictably enough, the unlikely couple announced they were divorcing – which meant another story and another 50,000 kroner fee (£5,600) for Sven O.

It was soon afterwards that Melnæs decided he had had enough of the magazine and left. To the embarrassment of his former employers, he decided to write a book about his experiences, with the ironic title *En helt vanlig dag på jobben* (*A Normal Day at Work*). Its contents were explosive. Those in the know had long suspected *Se og Hør* of employing dubious methods, but Melnæs's claims that the magazine had bought information not just from sources like Sven O. but also from police, banks, the civil service and other organizations provoked considerable hand-wringing.

"We had so many informers, it was like the Stasi," he claimed.[5] Others in the Norwegian media queued up to disassociate themselves from such methods. Despite protests from the magazine, Melnæs claimed he had got his facts right and was obliged to change only one word from the first to the second edition. In response to his revelations, a number of inquiries were set up. The book was itself turned into a film that opened in Norwegian cinemas in March 2010.

Sven O., meanwhile, had been edging towards a reconciliation of sorts with his daughter, despite the embarrassment he had caused her. It was to prove short-lived, however. In 2006 Sven O. was diagnosed with cancer. He died the following March at home in his apartment in Kristiansand – but still had the potential to cause problems even from beyond the grave. In November 2007, a biography written with his cooperation by Anette Gilje, a Norwegian journalist, was published.[6]

Among the guests at Haakon and Mette-Marit's wedding were Willem-Alexander, the Prince of Orange and heir to the Dutch throne, and his fiancée Máxima Zorreguieta. Máxima was born on 17th May 1971 in Buenos Aires to Jorge Zorreguieta and María del Carmen Cerruti. The generally accepted version of her background was that it was an affluent one – which seems to be confirmed by her education at the bilingual Northlands School, where the rich of Buenos Aires send their children, followed by the private Universidad Católica de Argentina.

The reality was different, according to Gonzalo Álvarez Guerrero and Soledad Ferrari, two Argentinian journalists who researched Máxima's life for an unofficial biography that appeared in 2009. The Zorreguietas lived in a fairly standard 1,290-square-foot apartment in the Barrio Norte part of Buenos Aires, while her father, far from being a wealthy landowner, began his working life as a customs officer, they found. When Máxima was born, her father was still married to another woman, by whom he already had three daughters. Because of Argentina's restrictive divorce laws, it was not until 1987 that he was finally able to marry her mother.[7]

If they could afford to pay their daughter's school and university fees, then it was only because they saved on everything else. Máxima repaid the investment: with her degree in economics, she worked in finance and in 1996 moved to New York, getting a job first at HSBC

James Capel Investment Management and then at Dresdner Kleinwort Benson.

Máxima and Willem-Alexander met in April 1999 at the Feria de Abril de Sevilla, an annual fortnight's festival in southern Spain during which the banks of the Guadalquivir River are covered with rows of *casetas* – individually decorated marquee tents – owned by prominent families, companies and other institutions. The official version has it that they met purely by chance, but Guerrero and Ferrari claim they were brought together by the matchmaking skills of Máxima's old school friend Cynthia Kaufmann, who had also moved to New York and met the Prince when he ran in the marathon there in 1992.

The Prince, still getting over the end of his four-year relationship with Emily Bremers, was immediately smitten. When he suggested going to New York to see her, she didn't say no – although she apparently said subsequently that when he turned up three weeks later, "I'd nearly forgotten what he looked like."

What began as a fling turned rapidly into a serious relationship. Over the next few months the Prince was to be a frequent visitor to the apartment at 225 West 20th Street that Máxima had until recently shared with Dieter Zimmermann, her former boyfriend. Máxima also visited the Netherlands. The Prince was soon ready to introduce her to his parents – a sensitive moment for anyone, particularly for the heir to the throne. That August Máxima was invited to join the royal family at Beatrix and Claus's house in Tavernelle near Florence; they also went to visit Willem-Alexander's grandfather, Prince Bernhard, at his villa in Porto Ercole.

It didn't take too long for the paparazzi to notice the glamorous new woman on Willem-Alexander's arm and by late August the story was out. Compared with Mette-Marit, whose existence was about to be revealed, Máxima seemed an ideal candidate to be a princess. Admittedly she was a commoner, but this no longer seemed a problem – and was perhaps even an advantage. In an increasingly secular age it also did not seem such a major drawback that she was Catholic, the religion of Holland's former Spanish masters. She made no secret that she liked to enjoy herself, but there was no history of drug use and, above all, no illegitimate child.

Yet, as with Mette-Marit, there was a problem with Máxima's father. As the Dutch media discovered within a few days, Jorge

Zorreguieta had progressed from humble beginnings in the customs service to become an under-secretary of agriculture in the military junta that ruled Argentina from 1976 to 1983, during which thousands of people disappeared or were killed – making him a potentially embarrassing father-in-law for a future Dutch Queen.

But what had Jorge Zorreguieta himself done? He claimed that as a civilian he had been unaware of what was going on during the dictatorship. Not everyone was convinced. And so, at the request of the Dutch parliament, Professor Michiel Baud, an expert on Latin American history, was charged with conducting an investigation into his past. Baud cleared Máxima's father of direct involvement in any of the atrocities, but concluded it was highly unlikely that a person in such a powerful position should have been unaware of what the regime was doing.

Concern about the union rumbled on. Beatrix, mindful of the criticism that had surrounded her engagement with Prince Claus more than thirty years earlier, stood by Willem-Alexander's choice. In November 2000, she hosted a dinner for her son's potential parents-in-law. And then, the following January, during her sixty-third birthday celebrations in Amsterdam's Stedelijk Museum, she gave her stamp of approval to the union, posing for photographs alongside the couple, who were appearing together in public for the first time.

Yet speculation was growing that Willem-Alexander might have to renounce the throne if he wanted to go ahead and marry Máxima – which would have meant his younger brother, Johan Friso, then aged thirty-two and working for Goldman Sachs in London, would have to take his place. Willem-Alexander did not make things any better with a rather clumsy defence of his father-in-law at a news conference in New York; members of the Dutch parliament described his comments as "painful" and "incomprehensible", while Wim Kok, the prime minister, said he had "asked him to keep quiet about the matter". A compromise was found: Kok sent Max van der Stoel, a former foreign minister, on a secret mission to meet Máxima's father and explain "that his presence at the wedding would be impossible". Zorreguieta agreed to stay away, as did his wife.

Matters moved more quickly than most observers would have predicted: on 30th March in a rare televised address, Queen Beatrix, accompanied by her husband, son and future daughter-in-law, announced Willem-Alexander's engagement and praised his fiancée as "an intelligent modern woman". At a news conference afterwards, Máxima, speaking in near flawless Dutch, said she abhorred the military regime and "the disappearances, the tortures, the murders and all the other terrible events of that time". As for her father, she said, "I regret that while doing his best for agriculture, he did so during a bad regime." That July, a joint session of the two houses of parliament gave their formal consent to the union, although fifteen of the 225 members voted against.

The wedding, held on 2nd February 2002 in Amsterdam, passed off without incident. After a civil ceremony at the Beurs van Berlage, a former bourse, the couple pronounced their vows in a Protestant ceremony at the Nieuwe Kerk, kneeling on a prayer stool specially made for the 1901 wedding of Willem-Alexander's great-grandmother, Queen Wilhelmina. The newly-weds then rode through the streets in the Golden Coach given to Wilhelmina by the city when she took the throne in 1898.

The only sign of dissent was a small group of demonstrators carrying placards that read "Where is my son?" – a pointed reference to the many young men who had "disappeared" during the junta's rule – but it was nothing compared to the riots that marred Beatrix's wedding in 1966. One of Máxima's first actions after the ceremony was to telephone her parents, who, according to the authors Guerrero and Ferrari, watched the ceremony on a television in a suite at the Ritz Hotel in London paid for by Beatrix.

Yet the controversy over Zorreguieta's past has never gone away completely: in November 2011, *Brandpunt*, a Dutch current-affairs programme, uncovered what it claimed was new evidence that the Princess's father was indeed aware of at least a few of the cases of atrocities against civilians. The Labour Party said that just as he had stayed away from his daughter's wedding, so he should be barred from attending Prince Willem-Alexander's coronation when he ascends the throne.

The year 2004 saw the weddings of two of Europe's crown princes, again both to commoners. On 14th May, as the strains of Handel's coronation anthem, 'Zadok the Priest', rang out in Copenhagen Cathedral, Crown Prince Frederik of Denmark married Australian Mary Elizabeth Donaldson. Eight days later, Prince Felipe de Borbón of Spain married Letizia Ortiz, a former television journalist.

Despite her lack of royal blood, Donaldson was in many respects the ideal bride. Born on 5th February 1972 in Hobart, capital of Australia's island state of Tasmania, she was the fourth child of John Donaldson, a Scottish-born mathematics professor at the University of Tasmania, and Henrietta, who had worked as secretary to the university's vice-chancellor. The parents, both from the little fishing village of Port Seton, east of Edinburgh, had been school friends and childhood sweethearts. They married aged just twenty-one in 1963, after John gained his bachelor's degree from the University of Edinburgh. Several months later they emigrated to Tasmania, to join the rest of John's family, who had relocated there already.

Mary's childhood, spent in Taroona, a few miles' drive from Hobart, was a comfortable suburban one. After school and at weekends, Morris Avenue, the street in which they lived, was filled with children of all ages who played together or went to the beach. Mary was especially close to her brother John, who was just eighteen months older than her.

After school Mary followed the rest of her family to the University of Tasmania, where her father was now dean of the science faculty; she took a bachelor's degree in commerce and law. Like many Tasmanians Donaldson found the island constricting and moved to the Australian mainland, first to Melbourne, where she got a job in advertising, as a trainee with DDB Needham. She was soon promoted and then moved onto Mojo Partners, where she became an accounts manager. Pretty, talented and ambitious, she seemed to have everything going for her: but then in November 1997 her mother, known as Etta to friends and family, died suddenly at the age of fifty-five from unexpected complications following a heart operation. Mary, just twenty-five, was devastated.

Six months later, Mary left Melbourne and after a few months' tour of Europe and America – including a spell in Edinburgh – took the next logical step for an energetic young Australian: she moved to Sydney, the country's largest city, where she was offered a job as account director in the local branch of Young & Rubicam. Soon after she moved to Love Communications, a major advertising agency.

Mary has said she saw herself eventually becoming managing director of such an international firm, but her life was changed for good by the Olympic Games, which opened in Sydney in September 2000. Politicians and heads of state from across the globe travelled to Australia for the ceremony; among them were Frederik and his younger brother Joachim.

That evening the princes decided to go out on the town with Bruno Gómez-Acebo, the nephew of King Juan Carlos of Spain. Their guides were Katya Tarnawski, an Australian friend of the Spaniard, and her sister Beatrice. Gómez-Acebo had said he would bring along two friends – but did not reveal they were the two Danish princes. Beatrice had assumed they would be Spanish athletes and called a friend, Andrew Miles, asking him to "bring some nice girls" to balance out the numbers. Among them was Mary, who was Miles's housemate.

The two groups met at the Slip Inn, a popular bar in Sussex Street, near the waterfront, where they ordered pizzas, beer and wine and chatted. Frederik was jet-lagged and burnt out after having just completed his pilot's training back home, but quickly seemed to hit it off with Mary, who was seated next to him. Quite when she realized the true identity of her partner is not clear, but after the party moved on later to Establishment, a trendy bar and restaurant a few streets away, the others noticed that the pair were deep in conversation. "When I left Establishment, they were still talking," Beatrice Tarnawski recalled later. "The next morning I talked to Andrew to evaluate the evening, and we concluded that something was afoot between Mary and Frederik."[8]

Frederik clearly had the same feeling and the next day, after far too little sleep, called her. "There was something special about this girl, I felt, and she was by no means discouraging when I called her," he recalled later. During the remaining weeks of the games, Frederik slipped away from his official functions to meet Mary several times, visiting her at the 1920s terraced house that she, Miles and other housemates rented at 20 Porter Street, near Bondi Beach. "I really felt she was a soulmate," he recalls. "I was attracted by Mary in all respects. She was fantastic. To begin with, it was all somewhat secretive, but very lovely. If one was to visualize it, it was almost like a moonlit summer landscape. A calm lake, ambient, there's a surface, but also depth."[9]

The Danish press followed Frederik's love life closely, but the journalists who had come to Australia to cover the Olympics were oblivious to the huge story unfolding under their noses – and the Prince was keen to keep it that way.

Frederik had to return home after the games, but he was determined to see Mary again. And so, just two weeks later, he flew back, halfway around the world, for what was billed as a five-week holiday to allow him to get to know better the country with which he had fallen in love during the games. In fact, it was Mary with whom he had fallen in love, and the couple spent much of the five weeks together, either at Porter Street or strolling in the city, hoping not to be spotted by a visiting Dane. Frederik got to know not just Mary but also her friends, who were struck by his down-to-earth manner.

During the following year, Frederik took the twenty-four-hour flight to Sydney at least five times; he spent much of the time with Mary in the city, but they also went on holiday together, on one occasion staying in a little cabin by the Queensland border and another time at a house on the coast just south of Sydney. Although a growing number of Mary's circle knew the identity of her lover, the Danish media were still none the wiser – much to Frederik's relief. "It was really good that the press didn't suss things out and that our love was able to unfold and develop," he told his biographers. "There were enough obstacles already. Not least the physical distance between us. But that year that passed before our deciding that something radical had to happen, we had to ourselves. It was an exciting time and an excellent test of how much we really wanted each other."

The frequency of Frederik's trips to Australia meant the secret was not going to keep much longer, however, and the Danish press began to suspect a romance lay behind his love for the country. In September 2001, the Danish gossip magazine Se og Hør published a cover story revealing, apparently much to Frederik's amusement, that he was going out with Belinda Stowell, who won gold for Australia in the sailing at the Olympics.

The next month, Frederik travelled again to Sydney to see Mary, staying for two weeks. After a relationship that had lasted thirteen months, they had come to a momentous decision: they couldn't continue living on opposite sides of the world; and, since he couldn't go and live in Australia, Mary would have to come to him, even though this would mean she would have to leave family, friends and job behind. By the time he left on 9th November, their minds were made up.

Three days later Mary got a first taste of her new life. Late that afternoon, as she was leaving her office at Belle Property, the estate agent where she was now working, she was confronted by Anna Johannesen, a reporter with *Se og Hør's* rival, *Billed-Bladet*, which describes itself as "Denmark's Royal Weekly Magazine". Johannesen had a simple question: "Are you going out with the Crown Prince?" "No comment," was Mary's reply. But the secret was out. Three days later, she was pictured in a tight red skirt and black blouse on the front of the magazine. The couple had enjoyed more than a year together undisturbed. Now their relationship was out in the open.

To Mary's horror and surprise, she found herself surrounded by photographers almost everywhere she went; an Australian freelancer was even employed to go through her rubbish bin in the hope of picking up an interesting snippet about her shopping habits. After a month, she gave up her lease on Porter Street and went to Paris to teach English, and then, in spring 2002, moved to Copenhagen.

The couple began to see more and more of each other, and Mary, who had got a job with Microsoft, built up a network of Danish girlfriends, who helped her to furnish the flat she moved into at Langelinie in Copenhagen, a few minutes' walk from Amalienborg, the main royal residence where Frederik was living.

Signs multiplied of the growing seriousness of their relationship: during Christmas that year Queen Margrethe was seen with the couple at a cinema in Aarhus, where they watched *The Lord of the Rings: The Two Towers*. Then in January 2003 the couple had their first public kiss – on the dock in Hobart, where Frederik was taking part in a sailing competition. It was only a peck on the cheek, but enough to create a sensation back home. Danish television showed it again and again, even in slow motion.

After keeping Mary – and the Danish public – waiting and waiting, Frederik finally proposed in September 2003 during a mini-break in Rome; going down on one knee and speaking in English, he asked if she would marry him. "You can't say no, you mustn't say no, you have to say yes," he told her. He wasn't disappointed.[10]

Later that day Frederik called Per Thornit, his chief of household, from Rome, telling him he could send out a press release announcing the royal engagement. The couple meanwhile had another four or five days to themselves, which they spent in a hotel on the Adriatic coast a few hours' drive from Rome.

The Queen gave her formal blessing to the union at a council of state on 8th October. Two hours later, after meeting members of the government for a champagne toast, the couple stepped out onto the balcony of the Amalienborg Palace and waved to the twenty-thousand-strong crowd below. That afternoon, at a press conference broadcast live on television, Danes were able to get a measure of the woman who was destined one day to be their queen.

While Mary Donaldson's past was blissfully free of complications, Letizia Ortiz, the future wife of Felipe, Prince of Asturias and heir to the Spanish throne, presented a serious potential problem: she was a divorcee. Divorce and royalty have long been incompatible – as Edward VIII's experience with Mrs Simpson showed – and the issue remained a particularly sensitive one in traditionally Catholic Spain. Divorce had not been permitted during the long years of Franco's dictatorship and even after it was legalized in 1981 it remained stig-matized, with many couples preferring instead to remain married but live apart. In the case of Letizia, however, the Spanish public appeared ready to forgive and forget.

The future Princess of Asturias was born Letizia Ortiz Rocasolano on 15th September 1972, the daughter of a journalist turned union leader, in the tranquil northern city of Oviedo. She went to La Gesta School there before her family moved to Madrid, where she attended the Ramiro de Maeztu High School.

Letizia appears to have decided early to follow her father into the media, studying journalism at the Complutense University of Madrid, where she obtained both bachelor's and master's degrees. After a brief spell in Guadalajara, Mexico, where she worked at the newspaper *Siglo XXI*, she returned to Spain and went into television, working for the Spanish version of Bloomberg and for CNN+.

During all that time Letizia had been having a relationship with Alonso Guerrero Pérez, a man ten years her senior whom she had first met while he was teaching literature at her high school. On 7th August 1998 at a simple civil ceremony in Almendralejo, Badajoz, they married. Their union did not last, and after just a year they broke up.

Letizia's media career, in the meantime, was taking off. In 2000 she moved to TVE, the Spanish state broadcaster, where she was given a mixture of increasingly prestigious reporting and presenting assignments, covering events ranging from that year's US presidential elections and the 9/11 attacks to the American invasion of Iraq, winning several awards for her work. Then in August 2003 she became the anchor of *Telediario 2*, TVE's daily evening news programme and the most viewed newscast in Spain.

By then her relationship with Felipe had already become serious. They had met at a dinner party at the end of the previous year in Galicia, in the north-west of Spain, where Letizia had been sent to cover the environmental disaster caused by the sinking in November 2002 of the *Prestige* oil tanker. Older than her by five years and, at 6'7", towering head and shoulders above her, the Prince was dark, dashing and blue-eyed; he was also single since breaking up in December 2001 with Eva Sannum, the Norwegian model.

Felipe's relationship with Letizia moved very quickly. The couple became closer in the spring of the following year, even though their meetings were interrupted by assignments such as her trip to Iraq. By September the Prince felt sure enough about their relationship to introduce her to his parents. Yet still the Spanish media knew nothing about her. Then on 1st November, out of the blue, the palace announced that Felipe was getting engaged to Letizia. The surprise was total: "I'm a journalist, I know how to shake people off," was how Letizia explained it to her colleagues.

The newspapers were enthusiastic: far from being seen as a disadvantage, Letizia's lack of a noble background appeared a strong point in her favour. The contrast with the royal origins of Felipe's mother, Sofía, a Greek princess, added to the modernizing feel. "The future queen is a Spanish woman who is very representative of our time: young, professional, a traveller, independent and with personal and professional experiences in common with millions of her compatriots," enthused *El País*.

Its right-of-centre rival, *El Mundo*, agreed: "The fact that the Prince has chosen a journalist whose face is very familiar is a sign of modern times," it said. Nor did it think her divorce should be an obstacle to their marriage. Spaniards seemed to agree: in a quick poll conducted by the newspaper, seventy per cent of respondents said they supported the marriage, with thirty per cent against. Five days later, Felipe formally asked for Letizia's hand in marriage, giving her a gleaming diamond and white gold ring before they came out to face hundreds of journalists at El Pardo Palace, just outside Madrid.

Despite the initial euphoric reaction to the announcement, there were concerns in the months that followed that the "wedding of the century", as the Spanish press were calling it, would be spoilt by discussion of Letizia's suitability. Aided by the conservative government of José María Aznar, the palace went to extraordinary lengths to suppress intrusions into the future princess's past: it was claimed that newspaper editors had been warned by authorities against publishing negative commentaries, while the divorce papers from her previous marriage were reportedly placed under twenty-four-hour guard in a 590-kg safe purchased specially for the purpose. This did not prevent some mildly embarrassing photographs emerging on the Internet, although there were doubts as to whether they were genuine. Some sites rather cruelly dubbed the future Princess of Asturias "*Putizia*", a combination of her name and *puta*, Spanish for whore, and speculated about her past sex life.

The damage was limited, however: her former husband, Guerrero, who was said to have been "briefed" by palace officials and even visited by the security services, made clear he was not going to sell stories about his past life with Letizia to the media – and when he was interviewed he confined himself to wishing the couple well. Such noble behaviour did not go unrewarded, especially when he began publishing books. The label "*El ex marido de la Princesa de Asturias*" ("The ex-husband of the Princess of Asturias"), which was inevitably attached to Guerrero's name, undoubtedly helped with publicity, even if he had to continue to fend off questions about his former wife whenever he appeared.

Felipe was also helped by the Catholic Church. Although not normally welcoming to divorcees, it was prepared to overlook Letizia's first marriage on the grounds that it had taken place in a register office – which meant there was no barrier to their getting married in the Catedral Santa María la Real de la Almudena in Madrid.

The mood changed on 11th March 2004, some two months before the date scheduled for the wedding, when Islamic terrorists attacked four packed commuter trains in Madrid, killing 191 people and injuring a further 1,700. The pre-wedding euphoria was replaced by shock and mourning. It also brought a political change: Aznar, who had tried to blame the attack on Basque separatists, lost the election three days later and was replaced by José Luis Zapatero, the Socialist leader.

Unlike Aznar, Zapatero was no royalist and, to general surprise, called for the rules of succession to be changed to put women on an equal footing with men – which was widely seen as an attack on Felipe, who has two elder sisters and owes his place as heir to male primogeniture. Other members of the newly resurgent left complained about the cost of the wedding, due to run into millions of pounds. Felipe cancelled two prenuptial parties, donating the money that would have been spent to the families of the victims of the bombings and towards the cost of a monument.

Set for 22nd May, it was the first royal wedding on Spanish soil since Felipe's great-grandfather, Alfonso XIII, married Victoria Eugenie of Battenberg in 1906. On that occasion, the bride and bridegroom narrowly escaped an assassination attempt by an anarchist with a bomb. This time, thankfully, amid heightened security, which involved twenty thousand police on patrol and the closing of airspace above the city, the wedding passed off peacefully – although it was marred by driving rain.

Despite the weather, tens of thousands of well-wishers turned out to line the streets of the Spanish capital, which was decked with flags and one million red-, yellow- and saffron-coloured flowers. The March bombings were not far from everyone's thoughts, however: royal guards sent by the couple placed a bouquet of white roses at a grove of potted olive and cypress trees that had been positioned outside Atocha station, one of the main targets of the attack, with a note saying: "Always in our memory, Felipe and Letizia."

The first half of the decade saw one more wedding of an heir to the throne, which was the most extraordinary of them all: that of Britain's Prince Charles and the great love of his life, Camilla Parker Bowles. Since the very painful and public collapse of the Prince's marriage to Diana and their divorce in 1996, there had been speculation about whether the Prince of Wales would ever marry Camilla. In the aftermath of Diana's death the following year, the answer was a definite "no". Camilla was already deeply unpopular. Now she was vilified by the British tabloid press, which was in the process of turning the dead Princess into a secular saint.

Charles was in no hurry, however, anticipating correctly that the passage of time would gradually make Camilla more acceptable to his future subjects. In June 2000, after years in which the Queen avoided meeting Camilla and pointedly did not invite her to royal functions, the two of them attended a party that Charles threw at Highgrove to celebrate the sixtieth birthday of ex-King Konstantinos of Greece, the younger brother of Queen Sofía of Spain. Their meeting, revealed the next day in the *Mail on Sunday*, had been kept secret until the last moment; the newspaper claimed that even Tony Blair, the prime minister, had not been told until the Queen arrived. So as not to push the matter, however, the monarch and her prospective daughter-in-law were seated far apart from each other during the lunch that followed. In a world in which protocol is everything, the choice of venue was deliberate. By meeting Camilla at Charles's house rather than at one of the royal palaces, it was noted, the Queen was signalling a desire to end the family rift, but without formally welcoming her son's girlfriend into the world of royalty.

The mood was changing – but only slowly and it was not until almost five years later that the announcement finally came: the couple would marry on 8th April 2005. In deference to the memory of the late Diana, however, Camilla would be known after the marriage not as the Princess of Wales, but as the Duchess of Cornwall. By royal standards this was to be a very low-key affair: as a divorcee, Camilla was barred from marrying Charles in the Church of England. (Charles was divorced too, but since his ex-wife had since died, he could have wed in a church.) The ceremony would be held instead at Windsor Castle, which would be temporarily designated a register office; the civil service would be followed by a blessing.

Things quickly started to go wrong – with a series of problems all eagerly seized on by the British tabloid press, who were still re-luctant to accept Camilla. The first problem was the venue: exami-nation of the small print of a law recently passed governing the use of non-standard buildings for weddings revealed that if the castle were licensed for the royal marriage it would have to be available for use by other couples for three years – which the royal family was understandably keen to avoid. The venue was quickly shifted to Windsor's Guildhall.

Then came the Queen's announcement that she would not attend the ceremony and only join her son for a "religious blessing" and party to be held in the castle. As supreme governor of the Church of England, she did not think it appropriate to attend a wedding not sanctioned by the Church.

Legal scholars also began to question whether it would be lawful for Charles and Camilla to marry in a civil ceremony, since members of the royal family were specifically excluded from the 1836 law that instituted civil marriages in England. Eventually, four unnamed legal experts ruled that the marriage would be lawful, although curiously it was later decided by the government that their advice would remain secret indefinitely because of its constitutional "sensitivity and significance".

The greatest blow, though, came completely out of the blue: on 2nd April, Pope John Paul II died and his funeral was set for six days later, clashing with the date chosen for Charles and Camilla's wedding. The Prince was left with no alternative but to postpone the marriage for twenty-four hours – not only would this allow him to attend the funeral, it would also avoid forcing Blair and other important guests from having to choose which event to attend. The press was not sympathetic. "What's the problem with waiting one more day?" demanded the *Sun*. "He's been keeping Camilla waiting for the past thirty-five years."[11] Souvenir sellers, meanwhile, faced a last-minute scramble to change the dates on their commemorative merchandise.

The sun was shining, though, as Camilla, dressed in an oyster-silk basket-weave coat and natural-straw hat, emerged from the Rolls-Royce that carried the couple to the Guildhall. Although the Queen and the Duke of Edinburgh stayed away, the other senior members of the royal family were there. Prince William and Camilla's son Tom Parker Bowles were the witnesses.

The contrast with Charles and Diana's wedding in 1981 could not have been greater. Then, an estimated six hundred thousand people had lined the streets to watch the couple travel to and from St Paul's. This time, there were just twenty thousand on the streets of Windsor. More than thirty years after their romance began, the Prince had finally married the woman he loved. According to guests, the Queen made a speech at the reception in which she told how "proud" she was of her son on his wedding day, and wished him and his new wife well.

If Charles's second wedding was low key, that of Prince William to Kate Middleton on 29th April 2011 was anything but; up to a million people – thousands of whom had camped out for one or more nights – lined the streets as Kate set off with her father aboard the Queen's Rolls-Royce Phantom VI limousine for Westminster Abbey from the Goring Hotel in Belgravia, where she had spent her last night as a single woman.

William, who had been given three new titles to mark the occasion – Duke of Cambridge, Earl of Strathearn and Baron Carrickfergus – was waiting at the altar, dressed in the red tunic of the Irish Guards infantry regiment, the uniform of his highest military rank. When the couple emerged just over an hour later, now man and wife, to more bells and cheering from the crowd in Parliament Square, Kate, the middle-class girl now to be known as Her Royal Highness the Duchess of Cambridge, looked entirely composed, but William seemed a little nervous.

For commentators in the British media, the contemporary feel to the day's proceedings was in sharp contrast to the rather unreal, fairy-tale atmosphere of Charles and Diana's wedding. "There was traditional pomp, pageantry and protocol aplenty, nostalgia and sentiment, but also a new and different air to this wedding – more relaxed, less reverent, more personal and natural," wrote the *Times*. "Even the balcony kiss was brief and artless, followed by a princely blush. To make it seem sufficiently schmaltzy, television editors felt obliged to slow down the footage. Where Charles and Diana seemed almost overwhelmed by the sheer scale and majesty of their nuptials, Wills and Kate (to restore their rightful monosyllables) seemed merely joyful."[12]

Part of the difference between the two events was attributable to the enormous changes in British society in the intervening three decades. Yet it also appeared a reflection of the determination of the couple to put their personal stamp on proceedings rather than allow themselves to be bullied by the palace establishment.

Although the couple's every move remained a matter of fascination to the press, Kate seem to be spared the excessive media intrusion faced by Diana three decades earlier. Matters were helped by the fact that she and William began married life in a cottage on the Welsh island of Anglesey, where he continued his posting as a search-and-rescue helicopter pilot for the Royal Air Force – which, to the fury of the Argentinian government, included a six-week stint in the Falkland Islands starting in February 2012. Even so, this did not prevent the occasional royal complaint against paparazzi who overstepped the mark.

When Kate celebrated her thirtieth birthday in January 2012 – at a suitably quiet dinner for friends and family – the occasion was marked by stories in the British press praising the way she had taken to her new role. St James's Palace announced that she had accepted honorary positions with four charities that deal with a range of issues, including tackling drug addiction and helping young people. The four, chosen out of hundreds of applicants, reflected her "personal interests in the arts, the promotion of outdoor activity, and supporting people who are in need of all ages, especially young children". The announcement drew comparisons with Diana and her work with charities that helped AIDS victims and removed landmines from conflict zones.

As far as the British press was concerned there was only one more thing that Kate needed to do: produce an heir, and what better year to do so than 2012, the year of the Queen's jubilee? In an apparent attempt to encourage her, the February edition of *Tatler* even ran a cover photograph of the Duchess accompanied with the words: "Kate (What to expect when you are expecting)". Whether she would do her royal duty remained to be seen.

Chapter 12

Playing the Waiting Game

When Crown Prince Frederik of Denmark celebrated his fortieth birthday in May 2008, he did so in style. Some 140 guests joined the heir to the throne and his wife Mary for the party in the Orangery of Fredensborg Palace. Friends sang songs in his honour, and even Mary chipped in. When a group of five of them formed an ad-hoc boy band, the Crown Prince joined them on stage on harmonica. Later they all moved to a marquee erected in the garden behind Chancellery House, where a band played and drinks were served with ice brought specially from Greenland. It was not until five a.m. that the last guests finally left.

It was, by all accounts, a hell of a party, and came at the end of a week of celebrations begun on Frederik's birthday itself, when crowds braved dismal weather to gather outside the Amalienborg Palace to catch a glimpse of the Crown Prince and the rest of the family in their familiar spot on the balcony. Among them were his two-year-old son Christian and daughter Princess Isabella, who had recently turned one and was making her first appearance on the balcony wearing a pink dress and cardigan – and a somewhat bemused expression.

Frederik had plenty to celebrate: a beautiful wife, two children and, of course, all the comforts that come from being born into a royal family. Looking back on his life, he could also boast of a highly successful few years in the military during which, through sheer grit and determination, he had qualified as a member of the elite Frømandskorpset (Frogman Corps) and took a tour of duty on the Sirius Patrol, a military dog-sled patrol servicing the northern Greenland coast under some of the most extreme weather conditions on earth.

But now that Frederik had reached an age when his contemporaries in the world of business, banking or the law were moving to the high point of their careers, what precisely was his role in life? A passionate yachtsman, the Crown Prince travelled the world taking part in competitions, but far from bringing him kudos, it looked to some rather more like having fun than hard work. There was growing concern too at the lavishness of his lifestyle, which appeared to be confirmed by royal accounts published the following May showing that he and Mary had overspent their 16.5-million-kroner budget by 2.1 million – which would have to come out of Frederik's "personal savings". In the couple's worst blowout to date, all categories of expenditure rose, from payments to staff to "court expenses" (read clothes, make-up, parties), "administrative expenses" and the cost of the upkeep of their palace. Such was the overspend that in February the pair cut five from their staff of thirty.

It is a question that could be asked not just of Frederik but of every other heir to a European throne. What is it like to be born into a job that you know you will not be able to fulfil until your father – or, in Frederik's case, your mother – dies? Once your formal education is out of the way, how do you prepare further? And how else do you spend the time until then, knowing that your every decision and action will be scrutinized and judged for your entire life in a way that almost no one else in your country has to endure?

In the days when kings ruled rather than reigned there were plenty of tasks, often military in nature, to keep a crown prince busy. Long after kings ceased to lead their armies into battle, it remained acceptable for their sons and heirs to do so. Often the heir to the throne was also plotting against his father – although in Europe, at least in the past few hundred years, none have gone so far as to attempt to overthrow him. Relatively low life expectancy also meant crown princes succeeded to the throne earlier.

There were some glorious exceptions, however, most notably in Britain, where the adult years of the future George IV – first as the Prince of Wales and then as Prince Regent – at the end of the eighteenth and the beginning of the nineteenth century passed in a haze of womanizing and extravagant spending that turned him into one of the most reviled British royals of all time, before he finally became king at the age of fifty-seven. A century later his great-nephew, the future

Edward VII, followed a similarly hedonistic course, not acceding to the throne until he was fifty-nine.

Both men, by temperament, clearly enjoyed food, drink and the company of beautiful women, and had the time and money (albeit largely borrowed) to pursue their passions. In Edward's case, at least, there was another explanation for his dissolute behaviour: his mother Queen Victoria had never been much impressed by his intellect or application and was unwilling to give him any part in affairs of state during his long wait to succeed her. Without such a role he had nothing to do apart from pursue his own pleasure, which in turn further diminished his reputation in the eyes of his mother.

Recent years have provided fewer role models, whether positive or negative, for the current generation of crown princes and princesses. The problem for Britain's Queen Elizabeth II – just twenty-five when King George VI died – and Carl XVI Gustaf of Sweden, who was twenty-seven when he succeeded his grandfather, was a lack rather than a surfeit of time to prepare for the job. Juan Carlos of Spain was thirty-seven when he came to the throne, but his apprenticeship during Franco's dictatorship was a very specific one and of little relevance to his son, who came of age in a democratic Spain. Albert II of Belgium, by contrast, at fifty-nine was far older when he succeeded his childless brother, Baudouin – but it would be wrong to say he had spent his life preparing for the role. Once it became clear his brother was not going to have children, it was expected that the throne would pass directly to Albert's son, Philippe.

Margrethe and Beatrix, who became queens in their early thirties and early forties respectively, had more time to prepare – although young children also provided something of a sense of purpose to their lives. The most relevant example perhaps is that of King Harald of Norway, who did not accede to the throne until he was fifty-three. In September 1957, when he was twenty, he started attending meetings of the Council of State, and the following year served as regent in his father's absence for the first time. Like many royals, he had a passion for yachting – which he was able to pursue at the highest level – representing Norway at the Olympics in 1964 and 1968 and continuing to take part in many international competitions.

* * *

There is general acceptance these days that members of the royal family should earn – or at least be seen to be earning – their keep. For that reason, in most countries, when the monarch-to-be is deemed to have come of age, he will become a member of a council or other advisory body and also be prepared to act as a regent in case of the monarch's ill health – as Norway's Crown Prince Haakon did, for example, for more than four months starting in November 2003, while King Harald was being treated for cancer, and again for another two months from March 2005 when his father was recovering from heart surgery. And then there are all the ceremonial duties that the king or queen doesn't have the time or inclination to undertake and other representational functions to perform.

This alone is unlikely to satisfy the demands of the young monarch-in-waiting who wishes actually to do something with his or her life. Yet choosing an appropriate activity can be difficult, and they will be driven by different motives from any other young person setting out onto the job market. For a start, it is not about money: the heirs to Europe's thrones all receive generous allowances. Nor do they have to worry about where they live: their families each have several palaces at their disposal.

So what would be the ideal royal job? Ideally, the crown prince or princess should be involved in activities that benefit the nation as a whole rather than serve their own self-interest or that of a narrow group of society. It must also not be something that could be considered political. For that reason, staying on in the armed forces beyond the initial couple of years or so deemed de rigueur can be the ideal solution. Spells in the diplomatic service, involvement in overseas aid projects or perhaps working for the European Union can be useful – except in the case of Britain, where it would be doubtless be greeted with outrage by the more Eurosceptic wing of the media.[1]

As the oldest of the Europe's monarchs-in-waiting, Prince Charles's experience is instructive. He has had four decades of adult life to try to define what it means to be heir to the throne – and also in which to face controversy when he is perceived to have overstepped the mark. It has been a mixed picture.

Concern for the natural world has long loomed large in his thinking; he had already embraced environmentalism and sustainability when his fellow European heirs to the throne were all still at school. He has also long since progressed from merely expressing concern to concrete action. In 1986 – the year that saw him mocked after telling a television interviewer he talked to his plants – his Duchy Home Farm went organic, at a time when few people even knew what that meant, and in the early 1990s he began to warn of the dangers of global warming. The Prince brought his ideas together in the autumn of 2010 with the publication of *Harmony*, a book and film project expounding his vision of life, which drew comparisons with Al Gore's *An Inconvenient Truth*. He has also rightfully won praise for his charity work, especially with the Prince's Trust, which has worked with more than six hundred thousand people aged thirteen to thirty since he founded it in 1976.

Yet while Charles has enjoyed the undoubted satisfaction of seeing many of his environmental ideas become mainstream, he has become criticized for his advocacy of homeopathy and was roundly mocked by the British media in 2010 when he declared himself proud to be considered "an enemy of the Enlightenment".

Most controversial have been his various assaults on modern architecture, which made headlines in 1984, when he described a proposed extension to London's National Gallery as "a monstrous carbuncle on the face of a much-loved and elegant friend". Keen to put his ideas into action, he began in 1988 to develop Poundbury, an addition to the ancient town of Dorchester, built in a traditional style that he loves, but which many contemporary architects despise as pastiche.

For critics, Charles crossed the line of acceptable behaviour in 2009 over his opposition to a £3-billion redevelopment of Chelsea Barracks. The project, financed by Qatari Diar, the investment arm of the gas-rich emirate's ruling family, was effectively torpedoed by the Prince's behind-the-scenes lobbying of Sheikh Hamad bin Jassim bin Jaber Al Thani, a cousin of the Emir, who is prime minister and head of the company. Embarrassingly for Charles, the full extent of his involvement was revealed the following year, when the developers Christian and Nick Candy, who have made a fortune marketing expensive flats to the world's super-rich, took the Qataris to court demanding £81 million for what they described as breach of contract – and won.

Many Londoners undoubtedly shared the Prince's opposition to the scheme and like him would have preferred a more traditional building. Yet there was clearly a broader constitutional issue at stake. Apologists for the Prince, who appeared on television to defend him, claimed rather disingenuously that Charles was entitled to express his opinion "like anyone else" – dodging the rather obvious point that inviting the Emir round to tea, as the Prince had done, would not have been an option open to his subjects, regardless of their views on the project.

Critics, however, saw this as clear misuse of the influence that Charles automatically enjoys as part of his role. For Paul Richards, a former special advisor to the Labour government, it was merely the latest episode of surreptitious interference by the Prince, who over the years had written countless trademark "stiff letters" to ministers about political issues, whether on his own behalf or in the name of one of the twenty charities, foundations and campaigning groups he has established. Only a few have ever been published.

"Unlike his predecessor as Prince of Wales, Edward VII, he has not occupied his time shooting grouse, collecting stamps and smoking twelve cigars a day," Richards wrote in an article in the *Mail on Sunday* a few days after the judge's ruling. "In some areas, such as environmentalism, Charles has been ahead of the pack. In others, like homoeopathy, he has been dismissed as a 'quack'. Nevertheless, there's something disturbing and unconstitutional about it all." The only solution, Richards suggested, was to publish all of Charles's written interventions. The result could be a lucrative book, he added, tongue in cheek: "The Prince would make enough royalties to fund his campaigns for potteries in Kabul, more loft insulation and organic eucalyptus shampoo, for decades to come."[2]

Although considerably younger, Charles's Continental counterparts have also had plenty of time to appreciate the contradictions inherent in their role – although they have faced up to their challenges in different ways. Helping his nation's businesses, perhaps by leading trade delegations abroad, has been important for Felipe, heir to the Spanish throne, who has made many official visits to Europe and Latin America as well as to countries in the Arab world, the Far East and Australasia. He has also played a very active role in the promotion of Spain's economic and commercial interests and of the Spanish language and culture in foreign countries. He frequently presides at economic and trade fairs held by Spain abroad. Like Frederik, Felipe is a keen competitive yachtsman.

Climate change has also emerged as an area of special interest for heirs to the throne: at the end of May 2009, Frederik was joined by Victoria of Sweden and Haakon of Norway on a five-day visit to Greenland, where they took part in research seminars with environmental experts, visited the shrinking Ilulissat glacier and studied the impact of global warming on local people. That December Frederik also played a part, alongside his mother, in the ultimately abortive Copenhagen summit on climate change.

In a newspaper interview three months later, Frederik underlined the role that royals, not as bound by short-term thinking as politicians, can play in raising awareness of the issue. "Greenland is a wonderful country," he said. "But you can see the changes. I was most impressed by the visual things; that you can see what's happening there. I think it's important for me to have a message for other people from that, to convince the broader population that there are changes happening and that we are making the change."[3]

In the years before he succeeded his father Rainier, Prince Albert of Monaco also developed an interest in the environment. The two men travelled together to the Earth Summit in Rio de Janeiro in 1992, where the parent treaty to the Kyoto protocol was signed. Albert went on to visit the North Pole in 2006 and the South Pole in January 2009, which he reached only after a two-day cross-country ski trip through wind and fog and temperatures of −40°C. In 2006, the year after his father's death, he founded and became the chairman of the Prince Albert II of Monaco Foundation, which focuses on climate change, the search for renewable energies and many other environmental issues.

Haakon too has gone beyond environmentalism to become a global activist of sorts on a variety of issues relating to the developing world, from combating poverty to the battle against HIV-AIDS, and has taken part in the World Economic Forum in Davos. He regularly speaks to youth groups about the need for dignity, self-respect and involvement.

Willem-Alexander, putting his bar-hopping youth behind him, has successfully reinvented himself as an expert on water management. Prince Pils has become Prince Water. The subject is an appropriate one for the future king of a country whose fate is so closely linked to the sea. The reclaiming of land has made a huge contribution to

Dutch agricultural production, but floods have been the cause of its most serious natural disasters – such as the one in 1953 that killed 1,835 people and left 72,000 homeless. Water – or, more often, the lack of it – is also a major problem for large swathes of the developing world.

Sport – provided it is in the service of the nation as a whole – can also be useful, but there are unexpected pitfalls there too, as Frederik found when he announced in October 2006 his desire to become a member of the International Olympic Committee (IOC). The committee already counted a number of royals in its ranks – among them Willem-Alexander, Prince Albert II of Monaco, Grand Duke Henri of Luxembourg and Britain's Princess Anne. Yet Frederik's aspiration to join them prompted a tirade of criticism from royalists and republicans alike. According to Danish critics, the IOC was not only corrupt but by its nature political, especially over its willingness to turn a blind eye to human-rights abuses in member states. By becoming a member of the committee, it was argued, Frederik would make the Danish royal family complicit in such abuses. The timing was unfortunate in that the controversy coincided with a referendum in June 2009 on changing the rules of succession, which in turn provoked a broader media debate about the monarchy. The Prince ignored his critics and that October joined anyway.

Such was the strength of feeling, however, that Jacques Rogue, the committee's Belgian president, issued a statement making clear the Crown Prince would not be obliged by his new role to take a stand on politically sensitive subjects. "Living in a monarchy myself, I understand quite well the problematic position, but we will never ask the Danish Crown Prince to do something which conflicts with his institutional role," said Rogge. "If the Crown Prince ends up in a conflict of interest, he can simply abstain from voting."[4]

While the controversy was a relatively rare one for Frederik, Philippe, heir to the Belgian throne, has faced a much rougher ride from his country's press. His problems began at the beginning of the 1990s, when he was in his early thirties. Although often seen at the side of his childless uncle, King Baudouin, and with his own home and staff, the Prince increasingly became the subject of criticism. He was reproached for his timidity and awkwardness in public, and despite studying at Trinity College, Oxford, and gaining an MA in political science at Stanford, found it difficult to shake off accusations of being an intellectual lightweight. A change in rules of succession in 1991 to allow women to sit on the Belgian throne prompted negative comparisons of him with Astrid, his charming and popular younger sister.

The sudden death of Baudouin two years later brought matters to a head. Although Philippe's father Albert was next in line to the throne, he was already fifty-nine, and many royal watchers expected him to step aside in favour of his thirty-three-year-old son. It did not happen, and Albert himself instead became king. Those close to Philippe claim it came as a serious blow to him. Embarrassingly for the Prince, the fact he was passed over was seized on by critics – rightly or wrongly – as a further sign that he was not considered fit for the job.

In the years since, Philippe has fought back hard to try to improve his reputation. In 1996 the palace took the unusual step of arranging informal meetings with journalists to allow him to explain his projects, aspirations and the way he saw his role. The next morning, most newspapers carried pictures of the Prince alongside headlines such as "Philippe is the true successor" and "Prince Philippe will be king". Mathilde, whom he married three years later, has also been a considerable asset: the Princess has impressed with the effectiveness with which she has carried out her role and has consistently topped the royal popularity polls.

Yet the various slurs have continued. Further fuel was added to the fire by the publication in 2003 of a book that again raised the possibility of Philippe not taking the throne: in this version, attributed to an unnamed vice-premier in the outgoing administration, his sister Astrid would become regent on the death of her father until Philippe's daughter, Princess Elisabeth, was old enough to reign in her own right.[5]

Being Belgium, such criticisms have inevitably been coloured by the language question: there were suggestions that the Prince is somehow more Francophone than Dutch, despite his recruitment of a number of Dutch-speaking advisors and the decision to send Elisabeth and her brothers Prince Gabriel and Prince Emmanuel to nursery and primary school at the Dutch-language Sint-Jan Berchmans in Brussels.

Philippe has generally borne such criticism in silence, but in 2007, after a particularly virulent burst of attacks in the Flemish media, he cracked. Spotting Yves Desmet, editor of the daily *De Morgen* and

Pol Van Den Driessche, an editor from VTM television and one of those behind the 2003 book, at a New Year's reception, he allegedly warned them he could have them banned from the palace if they continued writing negative stories about him. "You have to show me respect. I am the Crown Prince and will become the next king, so the press should not be critical of me," the pair quoted him as saying.[6] Philippe's words backfired badly: Guy Verhofstadt, the prime minister, was dragged into the row and called Philippe's remarks "inappropriate". The palace, meanwhile, issued a statement saying all reporters and media remained welcome there.

In one of another crop of books about the Belgian royals published in 2009 to coincide with Albert and Paola's fiftieth wedding anniversary, Kathy Pauwels, a leading Belgian royal watcher, claimed that Philippe was unhappy that his father, unlike his counterparts elsewhere in Europe, has not done enough to prepare his son for the throne.

Chapter 13

Spares and Spouses

Ari Behn, the son-in-law of King Harald V of Norway, is a difficult man to categorize. If you believe some of the accounts in the country's tabloids and celebrity magazines, he is the *enfant terrible* of the royal family and a Scandinavian Jack Kerouac: a hard-drinking writer whose ventures into the seedier side of life have turned him into a threat to the monarchy. Oh, and his wife Princess Märtha Louise has been accused of cashing in on her status with various commercial ventures that have included, most recently, a school where people can be taught to get in touch with their "inner angels".

It is hard to reconcile all this with the man I meet in the lobby bar of the Continental Hotel in the centre of Oslo, a short walk from the Royal Palace. In his late thirties, Behn is wearing a stylish black suit and sports a neatly trimmed beard flecked with grey. He is not drinking bourbon, but rather a glass of white wine, followed by tea. So much for the comparisons with Kerouac or Hunter S. Thompson. Behn is softly spoken and friendly. Unfortunately, Märtha Louise is not with him.

I am pleasantly surprised that Behn has agreed to see me at all after I ring him out of the blue; his relationship with the media is often uncomfortable, largely because of the controversy usually caused by the comments he makes when interviewed. Establishing a role after marrying into any royal family is difficult for anyone, says Behn, but especially so for men, even in twenty-first-century Norway, one of the most progressive countries in Europe.

"If you're a woman, it's as if you have been chosen and picked up," he tells me. "But as a man, you're the seducer. That's part of the whole thing, even in Norway now. But like it or not, the people have to deal with it." His profession further complicates things: "I have to go out there and speak freely. It's what writers have to do," he continues. "It's a balance between being prince consort and a writer. It's impossible, a challenge that I have to master... I don't have trouble with people attacking me; the only trouble I have is with not being able to talk back. That's what really frustrates me."

Behn first became known in 1999 at the age of twenty-seven, following the publication of his first collection of short stories, *Trist som faen (Sad as Hell)*. Well received by the critics, the book sold more than a hundred thousand copies, a runaway best-seller by Norwegian standards. He followed with a series of short television films that touched on prostitution and cocaine use in Las Vegas.

But then he rather deviated from the script: returning from America to Norway in late 2000, Behn fell in love with Märtha Louise, at the time second in line to the throne after her younger brother, Haakon. They met not in a fashionable bar or club but over tea at Behn's mother's house. His mother, Marianne Solberg Behn, had got to know the Princess while they were both studying a course on the Rosen method, a form of alternative medicine based on massage.

Märtha Louise's relationship with Behn was revealed in March the following year by the newspaper *Dagbladet*. At the time the Norwegian media was full of revelations about the wild youth of Haakon's fiancée Mette-Marit, whom the Crown Prince was due to marry that August. As if that weren't controversial enough, another colourful figure in the form of Behn, described by one commentator as a "bouncer's nightmare", was now set to join the Norwegian royal family. After the news broke, Behn left suddenly for a few weeks – to Timbuktu. He and Märtha Louise got engaged in December 2001 and married at Nidaros cathedral in Trondheim in May the following year.

Märtha Louise was born in 1971, the first child of the future King Harald and Queen Sonja. Norwegian law did not allow a woman to become queen regnant, and although the rules were amended in 1990 to give equal rights to men and women, the change – unlike in Sweden – was not made retrospectively. And so it was her younger brother Haakon who was destined to become the next monarch.

As a young woman she had a passion for showjumping – an appropriate hobby for a princess, although eyebrows were raised when

Stein-Erik Hagen, one of the richest men in Norway, gifted her two horses. They were raised again when the King was guest of honour at the opening of Hagen's shopping centre in Latvia.

Märtha Louise's private life was also beginning to provoke controversy: she reportedly had a series of liaisons with eligible – and not so eligible – men, several of them sports personalities: Britain's Prince Edward is said to have tentatively attempted a romance with her in 1990. Then in 1994 she was accused of having an affair with Philip Morris, a married English showjumping star almost twice her age. She was named in Morris's subsequent divorce at the insistence of his wife Irene, who worked as a clerk in an Asda supermarket in Chester, and was spared an appearance in court only after lawyers acting for her father successfully argued she was entitled to diplomatic immunity. A series of disastrous relationships followed, including one with a New Zealand showjumper.

And then along came Behn. Talking to reporters several days before the wedding, the Princess shrugged off suggestions that her choice of partner was denting support for the Norwegian monarchy – reminding them of how many of her compatriots had frowned when her father had himself married a commoner more than thirty years earlier. "We're keeping a tradition going," she said.

Before her marriage Märtha Louise took a controversial decision: she would not rely on a state allowance but would instead pay her own way by setting up an entertainment company. The government stopped paying her at the beginning of 2002; her father also ruled that she would lose her title of Royal Highness from the beginning of February. She did, however, retain her place in the succession.

The Princess's commercial activities initially largely consisted of reciting folk tales and singing with well-known Norwegian choirs. Then in 2004 she published her first book, *Hvorfor de kongelige ikke har krone på hodet* (*Why Kings and Queens Don't Wear Crowns*), a children's story about the founders of Norway's current dynasty; it was accompanied by a CD of her reading it aloud. In October that year, she and Behn went to live in New York.

Märtha Louise wanted her daughters to be educated in Norway, however, and she and Behn returned home after only a short time. Soon afterwards she was plunged into controversy again after the announcement in 2007 that she was starting a new alternative-therapy centre that would draw on an ability to talk to angels that she had acquired while working with horses. Students at the centre – swiftly nicknamed the "angel school" by the Norwegian press – would learn to "create miracles" in their lives and harness the powers of their angels, which she described as "forces that surround us and who are a resource and help in all aspects of our lives". Märtha Louise said she wanted to share her "important gift" with other people – or at least those prepared to pay an annual fee of 24,000 kroner for the three-year, part-time course.

The palace insisted it had nothing to do with the venture, but some churchmen were horrified, especially because of her father's role as symbolic head of the Evangelical Lutheran Church. Some suggested she be excommunicated. Jan Hanvold, a televangelist, accused the Princess of "blasphemy" and called her "an emissary from hell".

Undaunted, Märtha Louise went one step further: by publishing a book, *Møt din skytsengel* (*Meet Your Guardian Angel*), expounding on her theories. The press were scathing, but the Norwegian public seemed fascinated and it became a best-seller, and was translated into both Swedish and German. During a promotional tour of Germany in May 2010, Märtha Louise declared in a magazine interview that being in touch with her own angel helped her with her royal work. "Only through conversations with angels did I find my role as a member of the royal family," she declared. Asked what her parents thought of her interest, she declined to answer.[1]

Märtha Louise's activities and the accusations of "cashing in" on her royal connections are part of a much broader question: what is – or should be – the function within Europe's royal families of "the spare"? As we have seen in the previous chapter, it is difficult enough to find an appropriate role for the heir to the throne. What of their siblings, who are really little more than an insurance policy?

On the simplest level, the role of a "spare" is to be precisely what the name suggests: the second, third or fourth child of a monarch stands ready to step in if those before them in the line of succession are somehow disqualified from taking the throne. This was more important in the days of high infant mortality, but even in recent times many "spares" have gone on to become kings or queens. In Britain, three of the six most recent monarchs – Victoria, George V and George VI – owed their place on the throne to the death of the more direct heir or abdication. Belgium's Albert II is a second son who became king only because of the premature death of his brother; his namesake, Albert, who reigned in the first part of the twentieth century, was merely the second son of the third son of Léopold I, the founder of the dynasty.

More recently, there was speculation, at a time when the furore over Crown Prince Haakon of Norway's choice of bride was at its height, that he might cede his place to Märtha Louise. There was similar talk in the Netherlands over Crown Prince Willem-Alexander's relationship with Máxima, with suggestions he might step aside in favour of his younger brother Friso. In neither case did it happen.

But what if the crown passes seamlessly from monarch to crown prince or princess? What can the "spare" do other than watch him- or herself slide further and further down the list of succession as the heir to the throne produces children? And if it's difficult enough for the spares, what about their husbands and wives?

Royalty is like a family business, which means there is always work for everyone, whether it's addressing conferences, opening factories or attending cultural events. These are unlikely to be the most glittering or attractive of occasions, however, and the spares do not have any formal role in the ceremonial side of monarchy. Furthermore, as seen in Chapter Five, the second sons and daughters enjoy considerably less generous financial arrangements than the heir – even though they benefit from the use of palaces and other perks that come from being part of a royal family. Not surprisingly, Märtha Louise is not the only one of them to have been embroiled in controversy.

The British royal family has had its share of troublesome "spares", exemplified most colourfully in the late eighteenth and earlier nineteenth centuries by the eight younger brothers of the future George IV (or rather the six who survived to adulthood), whose womanizing and financial problems made them a constant source of despair to their father; not, admittedly, that their elder brother behaved any better during his years as prince of Wales and prince regent.

Seen in that way, the present queen's younger sister Margaret Rose, born in August 1930 at Glamis Castle, her mother's ancestral home in Scotland, was continuing something of a family tradition. The difference in character between the two sisters was apparent from an early age: Elizabeth was serious and conscientious – Margaret, four years her junior, was naughtier and an attention-seeker. Their father George VI neatly summed up the contrast between his two daughters: the first was his pride and the second his joy.[2]

As a beautiful young woman with an eighteen-inch waist and vivid eyes, Margaret quickly established herself as a feature of high society in the years immediately after the Second World War, often appearing in the press at balls, parties and nightclubs. She was a gift for the gossip columnists – much as Diana was to be three decades later. Then, when she was just twenty-one, her father the King died. While her elder sister, now queen, moved into Buckingham Palace, Margaret and her mother went to live in Clarence House, where she became surrounded by a group of rich and largely titled young men who became known as the "Margaret Set".

In those years, Margaret was linked with no fewer than thirty-one eligible young bachelors. Yet the photographers who covered her twenty-first birthday celebrations at Balmoral in August 1951 were disappointed that the only pictures they got of her were while she was out riding with Group Captain Peter Townsend, her father's equerry, who was seventeen years her senior. Little did they know what was really going on.

Margaret had got to know the dashing former fighter pilot in 1947 during a visit with her parents and sisters to southern Africa on which Townsend had been her chaperone. Despite their age difference their friendship turned to romance. Then in 1953 Townsend, who after the King's death had become comptroller of the Queen Mother's household, proposed marriage. Margaret accepted. Townsend was a war hero, and his exploits, which included a prominent role in the Battle of Britain, made him look like suitable partner. Yet there was also one, apparently insurmountable problem: he was divorced with two small children.

Memories of the abdication crisis of 1936 were still fresh, and Queen Elizabeth's coronation was set for 2nd June, after which she planned to set off on a six-month tour of the Commonwealth. The establishment lined up against Margaret, while the Queen, not wanting to stand in the way of her younger sister's happiness, asked her to wait a year. In the meantime Townsend was transferred from the Queen Mother's household to the Queen's own, and then on to Brussels.

As in 1936, public opinion was deeply divided. One newspaper, *People*, claimed a marriage between Margaret and a divorcee such as Townsend would be "unthinkable" and "fly in the face of Royal and Christian tradition".[3] Others were less judgemental, not least because there was considerably less at stake than there had been seventeen years earlier. Margaret, unlike her uncle, was not the monarch, and now that her elder sister had two children, Charles and Anne, she was never likely to become queen.

Two years later, Townsend returned from exile. The Princess was now twenty-five and so no longer bound by the Royal Marriages Act of 1772, which previously obliged her to seek her sister's permission before marrying. Yet the conventions of the state and the Church of England still placed obstacles in her path. In October 1955 Margaret finally made her choice: in a statement she announced she was choosing her royal role over Townsend. "I have been aware that, subject to my renouncing my rights of succession, it might have been possible for me to contract a civil marriage," she said. "But mindful of the Church's teachings that Christian marriage is indissoluble, and conscious of my duty to the Commonwealth, I have resolved to put these considerations before others."

It is impossible to do anything more than speculate whether such a union would ultimately have succeeded. What is not in doubt, however, is that it marked Margaret's life for good. In the years that followed, she had her share of affairs; then in February 1960 she got engaged to Antony Armstrong-Jones, a fashionable young photographer who was part of the bohemian crowd with whom she mixed. The pair had met regularly at his tiny flat in Rotherhithe, south-east London, for intimate dinners, but the press, who were following the Princess's private life, were taken completely by surprise. Margaret had apparently accepted his proposal after learning from Townsend that he intended to marry Marie-Luce Jamagne, a Belgian heiress half his age who bore "more than a passing resemblance to the Princess".[4]

Margaret's wedding, held that May in Westminster Abbey, was the first British royal wedding to be broadcast on television, attracting as many as 300 million viewers across the world.[5] Margaret dazzled in her dress designed by Norman Hartnell. The couple honeymooned in appropriately grand style: setting off on a six-week cruise of the Caribbean aboard the royal yacht *Britannia*. As a wedding present Colin Tennant, the 3rd Baron Glenconner, gave Margaret a plot of land on his private Caribbean island, Mustique, where she was later to spend a considerable amount of time. This was the swinging Sixties, when the stuffy conformism of an earlier age was replaced by a more liberal spirit, and London, home of the Beatles, Mary Quant and the Mini, seemed the centre of the world. Margaret and Armstrong-Jones, ennobled as the Earl of Snowdon, played their part in this new world perfectly, becoming prominent members of the party scene. They also had two children: David, Viscount Linley, in 1961 and Lady Sarah in 1964.

But despite the passion they felt for each other, cracks soon became apparent in their marriage, especially after Snowdon began to disappear for long foreign assignments after being taken on as a photographer for the *Sunday Times* magazine. It was while he was away on such a trip, to India, that Margaret embarked on what was reportedly her first extramarital affair, with her daughter's godfather Anthony Barton, a Bordeaux wine producer. In the years that followed, Margaret was associated – rightly or wrongly – with yet more well-known names, including the actor David Niven. More fanciful were suggestions (unproven) of flings with Mick Jagger, the actor Peter Sellers and Keith Miller, an Australian cricketer. John Bindon, a cockney actor who had spent time in prison, sold a story to the *Daily Mirror* boasting of a close relationship with Margaret. While the veracity of his claim was debatable, it further damaged her reputation.[6]

This was nothing compared to what was to happen next. In September 1973 Colin Tennant hosted a house party in Scotland at which Margaret met a young man named Roddy Llewellyn, whose father Harry was an Olympic showjumper. At just twenty-five, he was seventeen years younger than Margaret. In the months that followed, Llewellyn became a frequent visitor to Les Jolies Eaux, the holiday home the Princess had built for herself on Mustique – which, according to a television documentary aired after her death, became the centre of wild parties and drug-taking. In February 1976 a picture of the couple in bathing costumes on the island was published on the front page of *News of the World*. Margaret, by then forty-five, was portrayed as the predatory older woman and Llewellyn as her toy-boy lover. The following month the Snowdons publicly acknowledged that their marriage was over.

The contrast with the staid but thoroughly commendable home life of Margaret's older sister could not have been greater. Willie Hamilton, a Labour MP and one of Britain's few out-and-out republicans, described the Princess as "a monstrous charge on the public purse". The last vestiges of sympathy that Margaret had enjoyed for putting royal duty above her relationship with Townsend faded, and there were calls to end her entitlement to payments from the Civil List.

In July 1978 her divorce was finalized. It was the first divorce of a senior member of the British royal family since Henry VIII – but not, as we have already seen, the last. Indeed, it could be argued that by breaking up with Snowdon Margaret paved the way for the divorces more than a decade later of her nephews Charles and Andrew and niece Anne.

While Snowdon married his assistant Lucy Lindsay-Hogg just five months later, Margaret remained single. She and Llewellyn, who went on to become a successful landscape gardener and designer, remained close for several years, and stayed as friends for the rest of her life. When he told her he was to marry Tatiana Soskin, an old friend, she approved, even hosting a luncheon party for them on the announcement of their engagement.

Margaret, however, was beginning to suffer from increasingly ill health. In January 1985 she had part of her left lung removed and, starting in 1998, she suffered a series of strokes, which ultimately brought her to her death four years later. She was seventy-one. In accordance with her wishes, the ceremony was a private one for family and friends; among the mourners was her mother, who died six weeks later. Although Margaret carried out her share of royal duties, it is difficult to avoid the impression of a wasted life. As the writer Gore Vidal, an acquaintance, once wrote: "She was far too intelligent for her station in life".

While Margaret gave in and chose duty over love when it came to Townsend, several of her Continental counterparts in the 1950s, 1960s and 1970s chose instead to follow their hearts. Changing social attitudes meant they were increasingly willing to challenge the rules – especially when it came to marriage – even if it meant losing their privileges and place in the line of succession.

As was seen earlier, in Sweden two of the children and the sole nephew of King Gustaf VI Adolf, who reigned from 1950 until 1973, had to give up their places in the succession after they chose brides deemed unsuitable. In Norway King Harald's two sisters also attracted criticism by marrying commoners. Purely in dramatic terms, however, none of these cases could compare with the war of words that erupted in Netherlands in the 1960s over the marriage of Princess Irene, the younger sister of Queen Beatrix, the current Dutch Queen.

While studying Spanish in Madrid in the early 1960s, Irene, then in her twenties, fell in love with Carlos Hugo of Bourbon-Parma, the eldest son of Xavier, Duke of Parma, the Carlist pretender to the throne of Spain. The union was problematic on various levels: not only was Carlos Hugo a Roman Catholic, he was Spanish, a representative of Holland's old enemy, and also close to General Franco, who was not remembered fondly by the Dutch for the support he had given Hitler.

Irene's handling of the difficult situation in which she found herself was anything but delicate: in the summer of 1963 she secretly converted to Catholicism. The first the Dutch public – or even her own family – knew about it was when a photograph appeared on the front page of an Amsterdam newspaper showing the Princess kneeling at a Mass in the Roman Catholic Church of Los Jerónimos in Madrid, provoking outrage among Protestants and a constitutional crisis back home.

What followed bordered on farce. Desperate to stop a marriage that would have been a political disaster, Irene's mother Queen Juliana sent a member of her staff to Madrid to persuade the Princess to think again. It seemed to work, and the Queen went on Dutch radio to announce that her daughter had agreed to cancel her engagement and was returning home. When the plane that was meant to be carrying the Princess arrived at Amsterdam's Schiphol Airport, however, she was not on board, and Queen Juliana and her husband, Prince Bernhard, were supplied with a Dutch military plane to go to Spain to retrieve their daughter. The government was losing patience, however, and threatened to resign en masse if Juliana dared set foot on the soil of the old enemy – something no monarch from the House of Orange had done before. The royal trip was cancelled.

Princess Irene finally flew home early the next year, accompanied by Carlos Hugo, and went into an immediate meeting with the Queen, prime minister Victor Marijnen and three top cabinet ministers. Irene insisted on pressing ahead with the marriage, even pouring further salt into the wound when she and her fiancé had an audience with Pope Paul VI and attended a Carlist rally in Spain. That April the couple married in the Basilica di Santa Maria Maggiore in Rome. No member of the Dutch Royal family or any Dutch diplomatic representative were present.

The Queen and Prince Bernhard watched the ceremony on television, until a power cut prevented them from seeing the exchange of vows. Irene, second in line to the throne, was stripped of her right to succession, because she had failed to obtain the approval of the States-General, the Norwegian parliament, and agreed to live outside the Netherlands. She continued to cause embarrassment for the royal family by becoming active in her husband's political cause, but over time they drifted away from right-wing ideology and became part of the international jet set.

The couple had four children, but the marriage ended in divorce in 1981. Irene later returned to the Netherlands, and in 1995 published her book *Dialoog met de natuur* (*Dialogue with Nature*). In it she outlined her philosophy that human beings are alienated from the natural world; the Dutch media were more interested in passages that recounted conversations the Princess claimed to have had with trees and dolphins – not with angels, like Märtha Louise of Norway.

Irene's younger sister Marijke, who from 1963 had decided to be known by her second name Christina, also caused controversy with her marriage – to Jorge Pérez y Guillermo, a Cuban refugee and social worker whom she met while teaching at a Montessori school in New York. They married in 1975, but only after the Princess converted to Catholicism and renounced her – and her children's – right to the Dutch throne. They too divorced, in 1996.

Consolation for Queen Juliana was no doubt provided by her third daughter, Princess Margriet, who in 1967 married Pieter van Vollenhoven, a fellow student at Leiden University, who went on to have a suitably worthy career as a professor of risk management and chairman of a number of transport- and safety-related committees. Four children and more than four decades later, they remained married, with van Vollenhoven turning into a respected figure with quasi-royal status.

* * *

The intervening years had led to more liberal attitudes towards who is – and who is not – a suitable marital partner for a prince or princess, but it has not made life easier for "spares" and their spouses – as demonstrated vividly in Britain by the travails of Prince Charles's three younger siblings. These days, Princess Anne, born in 1950, is frequently described by the media as the most hard-working royal, as a result of the more than five hundred official engagements she carries out each year. Yet in her youth, when she was pursuing an international showjumping career that included an appearance at the 1976 Olympics in Montreal, she was renowned for her grumpy outbursts; one of the most famous was at the 1982 Badminton Horse Trials when she shouted "naff off" at photographers trying to take her picture after she fell off her horse at a water jump.

As Anne herself admitted, her temper almost got her into more serious trouble in 1974, when a twenty-year-old man with mental-health problems and armed with a gun tried to kidnap her and hold her ransom for £2 million as she was being driven back to Buckingham Palace after attending a charity event in nearby Pall Mall. Anne, who dived out of the car door, was unhurt, but the kidnapper shot and wounded two police officers, a driver and a journalist who tried to follow them in a taxi. "I nearly lost my temper with him, but I knew that if I did, I should hit him and he would shoot me," Anne told police officers. Royal security was stepped up considerably thereafter.

While Anne has gradually metamorphosed over the years into a national treasure, her younger brother Andrew, the Duke of York, born in 1960, has seen his personal and professional life come under rather stronger scrutiny. He has struggled to carve out a role for himself since he stepped down from the Royal Navy in 2001 after twenty-two years of service, and has faced criticism for his extravagant lifestyle: in 2007, for instance, he was dogged by accusations over his expenses in his role as ambassador for British Trade International (BTI), which that year came to £436,000. Potentially more damaging have been the business and personal contacts that Andrew has cultivated with senior figures in countries such as Libya, Kazakhstan, Azerbaijan and Turkmenistan. Following the emergence of pro-democracy movements in the Arab world and the civil war in Libya, the Prince's relations with some of the region's less savoury characters looked rather too friendly – and too personal.

Before all of this, however, Andrew was forced to endure negative newspaper coverage over the break-up of his marriage to Sarah Ferguson, the Duchess of York, whom he wed in July 1986. Although the Duke and Duchess agreed on an amicable separation in March 1992, any hopes of reconciliation were dashed that August when the *Daily Mirror* published surreptitiously taken photographs of John Bryan, the Duchess's American financial advisor, in the act of sucking on the toes of a topless Sarah while they were on a Caribbean holiday together. She divorced Andrew in May 1996 but, despite remaining on good terms with her ex-husband as well as sharing custody of their daughters Beatrice and Eugenie, the Duchess was left with large debts: she reportedly owed between £3 and £4.2 million. The revenue-raising activities in the years that followed – including writing children's books and an attempt to launch a media career in the United States – ended in failure. Her difficulties were compounded in May 2010 by the notorious "Fake Sheik" scandal, in which Sarah was recorded by a tabloid newspaper offering access to Prince Andrew, in his capacity as an official British trade envoy, in return for £500,000.[7]

Prince Edward, born in 1964, does not have the same wealthy foreign friends as his elder brother, and of Queen Elizabeth's four children he is the only one not to have divorced. This does not mean, however, that he has been spared criticism. In Edward's case this focused initially on his wife Sophie Rhys-Jones, who became Countess of Wessex on their marriage in 1999. Suspicions began to grow that Sophie, who had made her career in public relations, was trading on her royal connections in order to win business for her firm, RJH Public Relations, something that was apparently confirmed by another stunt by the *News of the World*'s "Fake Sheik", who this time posed as a wealthy Arab with a leisure complex in Dubai, which he wanted Sophie's company to promote.[8] In the days that followed, newspapers were filled with stories of crisis meetings. According to their accounts, the royal family was divided over what to do next: while Edward's father the Duke of Edinburgh was angry that the press seemed to be dictating the agenda yet again, Prince Charles and his sister Anne argued that their brother and his wife should make a choice between their business activities and their royal status and privileges – which were considerable.

The affair also inevitably focused attention on Edward's own activities, which had already begun to cause embarrassment. The Prince had resigned his Royal Marines commission in 1987 to pursue a career in the performing arts, eventually setting up his own television production company, Ardent, which as well as making a loss year after year caused controversy by filming at St Andrews University, where Prince William was studying, in defiance of an agreement that the second in line to the throne should be allowed to pursue his studies free of media intrusion. Prince Charles was reported to be "incandescent with rage", and a few days later the company announced it would stop making films about royalty. In March the following year, Edward and Sophie announced they were permanently stepping down from their business roles. The official reason was to support the Queen during her Golden Jubilee, but given that their decision was a permanent rather than a temporary one, no one was convinced. "Few were surprised when Prince Edward announced that his career in TV was over," commented the *Guardian*. "The only mystery was how it had lasted so long."[9]

The current generation of Continental "spares" have also run into problems. In the Netherlands, Prince Friso (born Johan Friso in 1968, but the "Johan" was dropped in 2004), the second son of Queen Beatrix, could not have foreseen the trouble that lay ahead when he met a glamorous young woman named Mabel Wisse Smit in 2001 while working at Goldman Sachs in London.

When the couple's engagement was announced just over two years later, it seemed like a match made in public-relations heaven. Wisse Smit, a former Balkans expert at the United Nations, and long-running head of the Brussels office of financier George Soros's Open Society Institute, was vetted by the Dutch secret service and approved as a suitable bride. For the Prince the union had the added benefit of quashing persistent rumours about his sexuality – which had become so prevalent that an official announcement was made in 2001 denying he was homosexual.

Before long however it emerged that Mabel had some rather awkward skeletons in her closet. It was bad enough that her previous lovers included Muhamed Sacirbey, the former ambassador of Bosnia-Herzegovina to the United Nations, who was by that time incarcerated in New York's Metropolitan Correctional Center, where he was fighting attempts by the Bosnians to extradite him on charges of misappropriating public funds. Even more embarrassing were claims she had also had a relationship with Klaas Bruinsma, one of the most notorious figures in the Dutch mafia.

The Dutch press's interest was understandable. Bruinsma, born into a wealthy brewing family, had become an infamous underworld boss with links to drug trafficking and a series of murders. One of his victims was found embedded in concrete; his legs and penis had been cut off before he was killed. Bruinsma himself was gunned down in 1991 at the age of thirty-seven after a late-night drinking session at the Amsterdam Hilton ended in an argument.

Wisse Smit had initially told Jan Peter Balkenende, the prime minister, that she had "vaguely" known Bruinsma for a short time in 1989 when she was a student, after meeting him through their shared love of sailing – but had broken off contact with him when she discovered how he earned his money. Bruinsma's former bodyguard, Charlie da Silva, alleged in an interview with Dutch television however that their relationship went far beyond that – and indeed, that the gangster had been smitten by her, so much so that she was the only woman he had allowed on board his yacht.

The scandal that became known as Mabelgate was underway. And, as the press continued to dig, Prince Friso finally admitted in October 2003 that he and his fiancée had been less than forthcoming about her contacts with the mafia boss. Balkenende, visibly perturbed, went on television to announce that his cabinet would not submit the couple's marriage to parliament for its approval, a prerequisite for maintaining Friso's position in the succession to the throne. Mabel, he claimed, had given "false and incomplete information", adding: "Trust has been violated... there is no remedy for untruths."

Friso, third in line to the throne, had to choose between his official position and Mabel. He chose Mabel. Their wedding in April 2004 in Delft was described rather cruelly by the Dutch press as a B-rated affair. Although the Queen and other members of the Dutch royal family attended, there were few representatives from other royal houses. In a televised interview shown earlier in the week, the couple admitted making public-relations mistakes.

Until his horrific skiing accident in February 2012, Friso inhabited a curious halfway house, like his aunts Irene and Christina (and two of Margriet's sons, Pieter-Christiaan and Floris, who both made what were deemed unsuitable marriages in 2005). They and their respective spouses are still entitled to call themselves His (or Her) Royal High-ness and Prince or Princess.[10] However, although still part of the *Koninklijke familie* (royal family), they are not considered members of the *Koninklijk Huis* (royal house). Thus Friso did not appear on formal occasions – on Prinsjesdag, for example, he did not join his mother and two brothers on the balcony of the Noordeinde Palace in The Hague to wave to the crowds below. This does not prevent the Dutch media taking almost as much interest in Friso and his wife as they do in other members of the family – so much so that his Alpine disaster was turned into a national tragedy.

No other European prince or princess has been obliged to renounce his or her rights to the throne, but some have certainly endured problems of their own, including relentlessly hostile press coverage. Prince Laurent, second son of King Albert II of Belgium, has suf-fered especially badly – even more so than his elder brother Philippe. As a young man he struggled with his studies – or so claimed Rudy Bogaerts, the head of a private school in Uccle, who tutored him for eight years. "In one of the first lessons Laurent asked what a half plus a half was," Bogaerts said in an interview with the news magazine *Humo*. "He didn't know it."[11]

The Prince's passion for cars was also to get him into trouble. The owner of several Ferraris, he was said to be especially fond of racing the TGV train along the stretch of motorway between the Belgian border and Paris. Belgian foreign-ministry officials became used to having to take care of speeding tickets that had been issued in France, elsewhere in Europe and even in America. On one occasion, Laurent was reportedly pulled over by a female state trooper outside Washington. "You can't do this to me: I'm the prince of Belgium," he protested. "Yeah," the policewoman is said to have replied. "And I'm the Queen of Sheba."[12]

And then there were the inevitable stories of relationships with unsuitable women – and the seemingly permanent financial difficul-ties. Denied a civil-list payment until 2001, when he was thirty-seven, and forced to rely on handouts from his parents, Laurent was paid instead through the IRGT, the Institut Royal pour la Gestion Durable des Ressources Naturelles et la Promotion des Technologies Propres (Royal Institute for the Sustainable Management of Natural Resources and the Promotion of Clean Technology), an organization he founded in 1994.

Not surprisingly, many Belgians believed the real reason behind the government's decision in 1991 to change the rules to allow women to succeed to the throne was to make it more unlikely that Laurent would ever become king. Before the change he was third in line behind his father and elder brother, but ahead of his elder sister Princess Astrid, to succeed his childless uncle Baudouin. He has since dropped down to twelfth place and, with time, will go down further still.

Laurent's reputation improved following his marriage in April 2003 to Claire Combs, an Anglo-Belgian property surveyor who was born in Bath and grew up in Wavre, outside Brussels. But speculation continued about the poor state of his finances. Matters appeared to become more serious in December 2006, when the Prince's name surfaced in connection with a corruption scandal centring on claims that Belgian naval funds had been used to refurbish Villa Clémentine, the home in Tervuren, outside Brussels, he shares with Claire and their three children. The following month, after his father signed a special Royal Decree, Laurent was subpoenaed, questioned by the police and appeared in court, where he declared he had no reason to suspect the funding of the renovations was illegal. Although Laurent was a witness rather than a defendant, it was a first for a senior member of the Belgian royal family – and an embarrassment for the palace. The Belgian media reported that Albert barred his son from royal functions for four months as a sign of his displeasure.

Laurent survived the crisis, but the criticisms continued. The Prince, according to his former advisor Noël Vaessen, a retired colonel sentenced to two and half years in jail for his role in the fraud, was "obsessed" with spending money and buying cars, and during the 1990s had spent most of the annual allowance, which currently stands at close to €300,000, on expensive watches, clothes and going out. The following year members of parliament demanded a cut in Laurent's civil-list allowance after it was claimed he had used government money to buy a €1 million villa in Italy.

In Sweden, by contrast, Crown Princess Victoria's younger brother Carl Philip and their glamorous younger sister Madeleine had for a long time a gentler ride with the press, not least because both became involved in long-term relationships at a relatively early age: Madeleine with Jonas Bergström, a lawyer, and Carl Philip with Emma Pernald, who worked in public relations. In August 2009, six months after her elder sister's engagement, it was announced that Madeleine too was going to get married: although no date was set, it was expected to be in late 2010 or early 2011.

As Victoria's own wedding, scheduled for June 2010, approached, however, things started to go wrong with both her siblings' relationships. Carl Philip had broken with Pernald after ten years, and in early 2010 was reported to be having an affair with Sofia Hellqvist, a glamour model who had appeared on *Paradise Hotel*, a reality television show, and posed topless for photographers with a python draped artistically around her body. An invitation to the palace to meet Carl Philip's parents seemed out of the question.

Then, in what was potentially even more damaging for the palace, reports began to appear that all was not well with Madeleine's relationship either. At the Princess's side for eight years, Bergström, with his upper-class background, successful career and good looks, had seemed the ideal royal spouse – much more suitable, in the eyes of some, than Victoria's own fiancé Daniel Westling. Yet suddenly the couple stopped being seen together in public and the Swedish tabloids began to fill with stories of Bergström's "double life" and hedonism.

Asked in April what was going on with her daughter, Queen Silvia said the wedding was being postponed, but insisted "everything is OK". Not everybody – least of all the tabloid royal watchers – were convinced. Their doubts grew even stronger after the Norwegian weekly *Se og Hør*, which had done so much to delve into the past life of Crown Princess Mette-Marit before her marriage, published an interview with Tora Uppstrøm Berg, a twenty-one-year-old Norwegian student and former handball player who claimed to have slept with Bergström during a trip he made without Madeleine to the ski resort of Åre in April the previous year.

A few days later it was official. An hour after Madeleine left Stockholm on board a plane bound for New York, where she was due to spend several weeks working for the World Childhood Foundation, a children's charity founded by her mother, came an announcement from the palace that she and Bergström had "made a joint decision to go separate ways".

Royal engagements are serious affairs and not normally broken off. While the Swedish media went into a frenzy, it was left to King Harald of Norway to make what was probably the most apt comment. "It's good that the breach is now and not after the wedding," he said.

Madeleine remained in America and, with time, the relentless press attention on her private life began to fade. When she attended her elder sister's wedding that June, looking glamorous in a blue chiffon dress and a diamond tiara, she was accompanied not by a new love but by her brother, Carl Philip. She is since said to have found love with Chris O'Neill, an American financier.

Elsewhere in Europe, Prince Joachim, the second son of Queen Margrethe II of Denmark, has also been obliged to cope with some harsh newspaper coverage after the collapse of his first marriage to Alexandra, his Hong Kong-born first wife, who had become a favourite with the Danes – not least because of the speed with which she learnt their difficult language. His reputation appeared restored after he married Marie Agathe Odile Cavallier, a glamorous Parisienne twelve years Alexandra's junior, in May 2008. The marriage of Infanta Elena, the eldest daughter of King Juan Carlos of Spain, also broke down after just over a decade. She and her husband, who had two children, stopped living together in November 2007; their divorce was finalized in January 2010.

Elena's younger sister, the Infanta Cristina, faced problems of a different character: in late 2011 her husband, Iñaki Urdangarin, the Duke of Palma de Mallorca, a former Olympic handball player turned businessman, became embroiled in a scandal involving the alleged embezzlement of large amounts of public money from the Nóos Institute, a non-profit foundation that he headed for several years. That December, as the case rumbled on and the damage to the monarchy grew, the palace took the unusual step of announcing that Urdangarin would no longer take part in official ceremonies involving the royal family.

Chapter 14

Letting in the Light

Kathy Pauwels, the chic blonde forty-something presenter of the Belgian television programme *Royalty*, is having a good week. The day I meet her at the studios of VTM, the main Flemish commercial station, she has made the front pages of the Belgian newspapers. After some sleuthing, she has discovered that King Albert II has spent €1.5 million on buying two apartments and some garages in a luxurious complex in Ostende. Rumours had been flying for some time about the purchase, but Pauwels has managed to come up with the evidence: official documents naming the purchaser of the apartments as "king of the Belgians, Albert II Felix". VTM ran it on the evening news, and this morning the papers are eagerly following up her scoop.

The story comes at a sensitive time for the Belgian royal family. It is September 2009 and the credit crunch is at its height. In his annual address to the nation on the eve of Belgian National Day on 21st July, Albert has described the crisis as raising "questions over the increasing materialism" of society. Yet in the weeks since he has rather lost his footing on the moral high ground after it emerged he has spent €4.6 million on a new yacht. And now yet another expensive purchase has been revealed.

It is only Thursday and Pauwels is not yet sure whether she and her small team will try to follow up the story for *Royalty*, which goes out for half an hour every Sunday at six p.m. Even without it the programme's several hundred thousand viewers – not bad given a total Flemish population of six million people – can rely on the usual mixture of stories about the royal family and their counterparts elsewhere in Europe. Among other items will be an interview with Princess Astrid, the second child of King Albert II, on her twenty-five years of marriage, and a report from over the border in the Netherlands, where it is Prinsjesdag. The tone this week, as always, will be critical rather than fawning – not surprising given that the programme was edited until a few years ago by Pol van den Driessche, now a senator, who has made no secret of his republican views.

Pauwels likes to feel she brings the same qualities to the job as in her previous role as a news reporter. But she admits it can be a difficult balancing act: if she goes too far in criticizing the royal family, she risks upsetting the ardent monarchists in her audience, many of them middle-aged women.

A few miles away across Brussels, Anne Quevrin, an elegant dark-haired woman several years older than Pauwels, is also hard at work on her programme about royalty, *Place Royale*, which is broadcast at eight o'clock on Saturday night on RTL, the main French-language commercial station, drawing an audience of 600,000.

Belgium may have only one king but, thanks to the country's division along linguistic lines, it has two of almost everything else – and that includes programmes on royalty. The difference is more than just one of language. Quevrin has a rather more respectful attitude to her subject. Her show, the first of its type in Europe, was launched in 1994, following the death of King Baudouin the previous year. A former political reporter, she believes her viewers want to see images of the lives of the royal family at work and has little time for "negative reports" about apartments or other such scandals. "What business of ours is what the King spends his money on?" she asks. "Our aim is to strengthen the institution of monarchy." For that reason, *Place Royale* does not use paparazzi pictures and, unlike *Royalty*, it refrained from interviewing Delphine Boël, the King's illegitimate daughter, the revelation of which in 1999 became a major news story. Indeed, Boël has only featured in her programme once – and that was when she was inadvertently caught on camera near Prince Laurent. Quevrin ceased presenting *Place Royale* the year after we met, but the programme's attitude to royalty remained respectful.

The two programmes clearly know their respective audiences: their differing approaches reflect the divergence in attitude towards the royal family in the two parts of Belgium. While polls show the French speakers in the south are overwhelmingly in favour of monarchy, the Dutch-speaking north is more critical.

Yet it also reflects a more general paradox at the heart of all reporting of royal affairs, one that has become acute in the modern multimedia age. Are members of the royal family to be treated as part of a celebrity culture, whose foibles are to be ruthlessly exposed to the world? Or does their constitutional role mean they must be accorded more dignity than we would give to Madonna, Paris Hilton or Lady Gaga? And what of the institution itself? Should the media question the continued existence of monarchy or confine their criticism to the effectiveness or not with which members of the royal family carry out their duties?

This is not just a matter of deference: it can also have implications for the newspapers, magazines, TV shows or websites that feature the activities of the various royal families. Royalty is unlike celebrity in one important respect: while new singers, film stars and reality-show contestants can be easily replaced by others when we tire of them, royals are more permanent: only a few of them come along every generation. There is only one heir to the throne: devalue the brand too much and we risk killing the goose that lays the golden egg.

Matters were simpler in the days before mass media, when the only image the overwhelming majority of the population saw of their ruler was on a coin, statue or the occasional portrait. With the publication of pamphlets and newspapers came the first royal news – and also the beginnings of what was to become a love-hate relationship between palaces and the press.

In early nineteenth-century Britain, King George III was responsible for one of the first moves towards modern royal media management. Irritated at erroneous reports about movements by himself and his family, he instituted the Court Circular, an official record of royal en-gagements still published today. This did not prevent him from being cruelly lampooned by the caricaturists of the day, however.

His son, who succeeded him as George IV in 1820, was an even more attractive target for the fledgling media because of his lavish spending and sexual peccadilloes during his long period as Prince of Wales and then Regent. A further dimension was provided by his disastrous marriage to Caroline of Brunswick. In a foretaste of Princess Diana's behaviour almost two centuries later, the then

Princess of Wales was ready to make use of the press to get her side of the story into the public domain. Angry at being denied access to their daughter Charlotte, Caroline wrote a complaining letter to her husband and, when he didn't respond, had it published on 10th February 1813 in the *Morning Chronicle*. In it she begged her husband to pity "the deep wounds which so cruel an arrangement inflicts on my feelings... cut off from one of the very few domestic enjoyments left to me... the society of my child". The tactic worked – at least as far as winning over public opinion; prints and even cups and plates were made and sold in Caroline's honour. It didn't prompt her husband, however, to allow her access to their daughter. Their battle went on, much of it in print.

The newspapers continued to adopt the same critical tone towards George IV even after his death in 1830. The obituary in the *Times* was characterized by a savagery that would be unthinkable in the case of a modern-day monarch. "There never was an individual less regretted by his fellow creatures than this deceased king," the newspaper wrote. "What eye has wept for him? What heart has heaved one throb of unmercenary sorrow?"

Elsewhere in Europe, other monarchies were also having to come to terms with the might of the press. Soon after coming to power, Louis Philippe, France's citizen king, came under fierce criticism from his country's newspapers for "betraying" the revolution of 1830 that had brought him to the throne. An extra visual dimension was provided by the invention of lithography, which made it much easier and quicker to reproduce images. This encouraged the emergence of caricatures, which were often savage; the King became a favourite target and was depicted as a pear. Indeed, so closely did Louis Philippe become identified with the fruit that the smallest image of a pear was immediately understood by readers as referring to him. The inevitable clampdown on caricatures as well as the written word swiftly followed.

In newly created Belgium, by contrast, the newspapers continued to operate with a freedom rare in the rest of the Continent. Thanks to his years in Britain, Léopold appreciated the power of the press and, rather than trying to curb it, set out to manipulate it. In 1831, shortly after coming to the throne, he secretly founded his own newspaper, *L'Indépendant*, which backed the Catholic Party, and during the twelve years that followed he pumped in 40,000 francs a year to cover its losses. Then in 1858 he provided another 200,000 francs to found *L'Écho du Parlement*, which supported the other main group, the Liberals.[1]

This did not prevent other newspapers from being critical – especially of Léopold's colourful private life. Articles started appearing in the newspapers in 1847 about his relationship with his young mistress, Arcadie Meyer. To stop its diffusion, the King began to bribe journalists to avoid such subject matter. The British ambassador reported to London that Léopold gave up to 125,000 francs in "hush money" a year to "scurrilous papers".[2]

Léopold II, his son and successor, also paid journalists to buy more favourable coverage; indeed, he spent so much money on the practice that Adrien Goffinet, his loyal aide-de-camp, warned him to hide all the accounts of the Civil List carefully so they would "never fall into the hands of the enemy or of revolutionaries, thereby revealing that you subsidized newspapers and paid pensions to journalists".[3]

The King was obliged to step up his efforts considerably after reports of the atrocities carried out by his agents in the Congo at the end of the nineteenth century began to circulate in Europe and America through letters from Protestant missionaries. The tactics he had employed to build his private empire were sharply criticized in both British and American newspapers and also in pamphlets such as 'King Leopold's Soliloquy', written in 1905 by Mark Twain. Their judgement coloured in part by payments from the King, Belgian newspapers from the Liberal *Le Soir* to the Catholic *Le XXe Siècle* fought back with articles that blamed such critical foreign reports on British agents who were bitter that they had been beaten to the Congo by the Belgians.

Trying to win over the foreign press necessitated a more sophisticated approach. Showing an early understanding of the dark arts of public relations, Léopold set up a secret press bureau that provided journalists with information favourable to his activities and commissioned public statements of approval from big names of the day. Embarrassingly for the King, however, the bureau's existence was revealed to the world by the *New York American* after a few years of its clandestine operations.

In the last years before Léopold's death in 1909, the media focus shifted to his private life, as had been the case with his father before him. The socialist newspaper *Le Peuple* was especially savage, seizing on his relationship with his last mistress, Blanche Delacroix. "The King no longer stoops to prostitution, like his associates, in wild outbursts of sensuality and lasciviousness: prostitution climbs to meet the King," wrote Jules Lekeu on 19th July 1906, in the first of a series of articles. "To megalomaniac financing and building, the King now adds megalomaniac debauchery, and this debauchery is founded on plunder and on crime."[4]

Although British newspapers remained just as free as their Belgian counterparts to criticize the monarchy through all these years, they often exercised considerable self-restraint, as was shown as late as 1936 by the way they covered – or rather didn't cover – the events leading to the abdication of King Edward VIII.

The American newspapers relished the story of his romance with Wallis Simpson, reporting the various twists and turns in their relationship, and couldn't understand why their British colleagues remained so quiet. When Lord Beaverbrook, whose ownership of the *Daily Express* made him the most powerful press tycoon of Fleet Street, arrived by ship in Manhattan during the crisis, reporters demanded to know why his and the other British papers had not printed the story. "You are the censor!" cried one reporter. "Who? Me?" Beaverbrook replied. But even so, as *Time* magazine put it, "the entire British Press continued unanimously to ostrich".[5] When American newspapers and magazines with stories about the romance were imported into Britain, the relevant columns were blacked out and whole pages torn out.

Then, suddenly, on 3rd December 1936, as the crisis was reaching its height, the British press suddenly broke their silence. The catalyst was a bizarre one: in a speech to a Church conference Alfred Blunt, the appropriately named Bishop of Bradford, had talked about the King's need for divine grace – which was interpreted, wrongly as it turned out, by a local journalist in the audience as a reference to the King's affair. When his report was carried by the Press Association, the national news agency, the British newspapers took it as the signal they had all been waiting for: they could now report the affair.

The *Daily Mirror*, for example, filled its pages on 3rd December and the days that followed with stories of crisis meetings at the palace, pictures of Wallis Simpson and the opinions of men and women in the street. "They have much in common," began its gushing profile of the royal couple. "They both love the sea. They both love swimming. They both love golf and gardening. And soon they discovered that each loved the other."

Under the headline "Six Months of Rumours" the newspaper also looked at how speculation about the relationship had spread since Mrs Simpson's name appeared as a guest at a dinner hosted by the King at St James's Palace that May. Tellingly, it also felt the need to justify to its readers why it – and the rest of Fleet Street – had been sitting on the story for so long. "We have been in full possession of the facts, but we resolved to withhold them until it was clear that the problem could not be solved by diplomatic methods," it claimed. "This course we took with the welfare of the nation and the Empire at heart. Such is the position now that the nation, too, must be placed in possession of the facts." There were echoes of this same self-restraint – initially, at least – on the part of the British press a decade and half later when rumours started to circulate that Edward VIII's niece, Princess Margaret, was having an affair with the divorced Peter Townsend.

The willingness of the American papers to tread where the British were reluctant to follow exemplified a broader tendency still true today. When reporting on the activities of members of the royal family of their own country, the media often hold back, whether out of respect for the institution or because of a more pragmatic realization of the need to keep on good terms with them: step too far and they risk being denied precious access to events or having other privileges withdrawn. This mutual dependency is similar to that which exists between the media and Hollywood actors and pop stars. There is far less at stake, however, when dealing with foreign countries' royals, which opens the way to more aggressive and often downright fictional reporting – as demonstrated by the imaginative royal coverage of the more downmarket German magazines.

The invention of radio, cinema and television presented new challenges for the monarchies across Europe, especially since their arrival coincided with a greater democratization of society and a reduction in the deference of old. The various royal courts were far from passive actors and began to adapt to this new age. On Christmas Day 1932 George V began what was to turn into a national tradition: the annual radio broadcast to the nation. Seated at a desk under the stairs in Sandringham, the elderly monarchy read out words written for him by Rudyard Kipling, the great imperial poet and author of *The Jungle Book*. "I speak now from my home and from my heart to you all, to all my peoples throughout the Empire, to men and women so cut off by the snows, the desert or the sea that only voices of the air can reach them, men and women of every race and colour who look to the Crown as the symbol of their union."

The broadcasts, which were mildly, but not overly, religious in tone, were intended to cast the monarch in the role of head of a great family, that spanned not just the United Kingdom but also the Empire (or Commonwealth, as it is today). This was made explicit by his son George VI in his first Christmas speech of 1937. "Many of you will remember the Christmas broadcasts of former years when my father spoke to his peoples at home and overseas as the head of a great family," the newly crowned King declared.

That George VI had made the speech at all was an achievement in itself: despite working for more than a decade with Lionel Logue, his Australian-born speech therapist, he still loathed public speaking. In 1936 there hadn't even been a speech: his elder brother, Edward VIII, had abdicated just two weeks earlier, and the new King did not yet feel ready to address his subjects. And even when he gave his speech the next Christmas, he made clear it was a one-off, and didn't repeat it in 1938. Following the outbreak of war, however, he realized the importance of this annual ritual for boosting morale and reluctantly spoke to the nation again – and indeed every 25th December for the rest of his life. After her accession in 1952, his daughter, the present Queen, continued what was by then a well-established tradition.

By that time Britain was well into the television age. When Elizabeth was crowned in 1953, the now elderly Winston Churchill, back for his final stint as prime minister, did not want to allow the television cameras into Westminster Abbey out of fear it would impose an intolerable burden on the young monarch. His cabinet unanimously agreed. The Queen's position was not so clear. According to the official version of events, she overruled them, insisting that the event be televised. Robert Lacey, the respected royal biographer, by contrast, suggests she was initially opposed but changed her mind after an outcry by the newspapers.[6] In any case the cameras were admitted into the Abbey, for the first time in its history, allowing an estimated twenty million viewers to watch the mammoth outside broadcast, transmitted from 10.15 a.m. to 5.20 p.m.

It was an undoubted success – even if the man in charge of the television cameras who was meant to press the "censor" button to prevent any too intrusive close-ups during the ceremony got carried away by the occasion and failed to do so. The viewers will have thanked him for it. Nor was it only people in Britain who were able to enjoy the spectacle. Since satellite link-ups had yet to be invented, Canberra jet bombers were used to fly film recordings of the day's events to America and Canada.

The televising of the coronation not only enhanced the new Queen's popularity, it also provided a boost for the young BBC. Almost overnight the number of licence-fee holders who provided its revenue doubled to three million. Equally importantly, the public-service broadcaster had established itself as the medium on which to watch great public events – preferably narrated by Richard Dimbleby, whose whispering delivery became synonymous with royal coverage.

The relationship between these two great British institutions had begun, and from the beginning the BBC played the role of a loyal subject. In the late 1950s the Corporation banned from its airwaves the writer Lord Altrincham after he provoked a controversy by suggesting in an obscure journal that the Queen's court was too upper-class and described her style of speaking as "a pain in the neck". The same fate befell another critic, Malcolm Muggeridge, who compared the lives of the royal family to a soap opera. Both men were obliged to state their cases on ITV, the new commercial service, instead.

For the time being at least, the Christmas speech was confined to radio, but in 1957 the Queen was seen as well as heard for the first time. Such a development was far from automatic, however. Although she agreed to have cameras in the Abbey, it was quite another thing to have them intruding on her family Christmas – since, like its radio equivalent, the television version was to be broadcast live. Again, however, the palace had to bow to the inevitable, not least because the spread of television ownership had caused the ratings for her radio broadcast to dip alarmingly. In the event the broadcast proved a resounding success: sixteen and a half million people watched the three p.m. broadcast. From then on, watching – rather than just seeing – the Queen became an important part of Britons' Christmas Day ritual.

Europe's other royals also give speeches during the holiday season, although in Denmark and Norway it is on New Year's Eve. In both cases this is in effect a continuation of a tradition begun during the Second World War, when their then rulers made rousing speeches to their respective nations from exile in London.

As Europe entered the media age, other events began to be televised – especially royal weddings, starting with that of Prince Rainier of Monaco and Grace Kelly in 1956 – which, as seen earlier, was a true media sensation. The audiences, meanwhile, soared. The marriage of Princess Margaret to Antony Armstrong-Jones in 1960, also in Westminster Abbey, attracted an estimated three hundred million viewers worldwide. That number had risen to five hundred million by June 1976 when King Carl XVI Gustaf of Sweden married Silvia Sommerlath.

Then in July 1981 came the biggest one of them all: the wedding of Prince Charles and Lady Diana Spencer. It was taken for granted that when Diana died sixteen years later, the television cameras should not only follow her funeral procession through London but also broadcast the service from inside Westminster Abbey. The marriage of Crown Prince Victoria of Sweden to Daniel Westling in June 2010 was also a major spectacle; Prince William's marriage to Kate Middleton in April 2011 was even bigger still.

Churchill, with his opposition to the televising of the coronation, was wrong: the ability of people to follow royal occasions – both joyful and sad – on television did the royal brand no harm. It soon became clear, however, that such set-piece events would not be enough to satisfy the demands of the modern media, who were increasingly keen to portray members of their respective royal families as flesh-and-blood humans rather than as mere symbols. Conveniently, this coincided with a move by the various dynasties to portray themselves as the leading family of the nation.

In Britain this process had already begun in the late 1920s, when the young Princess Elizabeth became a media star, with newspapers and magazines on both side of the Atlantic keen to publish stories and photographs – often with the encouragement of the royal family, which appreciated their publicity value. Extraordinarily, the third birthday of baby "Lilibet", as Elizabeth was known in the family, was considered an important enough occasion to earn her a place on the cover of *Time* magazine on 21st April 1929 – even though her father, at that stage, was not even heir to the throne.

Other royal families were pursuing a similar course: after the birth of the future Queen Beatrix in 1938, her father Prince Bernhard supplied the Dutch newspapers with his own photographs of her, which appeared on the front pages. He also shot some amateur movie footage of his daughter's first steps, which was turned into a film, *Ons prinsesje loopt* (*Our Princess Walks*), which was a box-office hit when it came out at cinemas the following year.

In Denmark, Queen Ingrid, the Swedish-born wife of King Frederik IX, also had a keen appreciation of the importance of public relations for the monarchy. The couple's marriage in 1935 had been one of the major media events of the day. After her husband came to the throne in 1947, Ingrid, by then the mother of three young daughters, strove to make the Danish monarchy more media-friendly and shift attention away from the King alone to the royal family as a whole. Danish newspapers and magazines began to fill with photographs of the family; cosy gatherings turned to public-relations events. The Queen even gave permission to Ebba Neergard, her *hofdame* (lady-in-waiting), to publish a book of private photographs of the three princesses.

One of the more unusual fruits of the Danish royal family's media strategy was a special unrehearsed children's radio programme in 1949 that allowed an estimated one million listeners to eavesdrop on Frederik's tea with Ingrid and their children. During the show the King could be heard telling Margrethe, the future Queen, who was a few months short of her ninth birthday, to take her feet off the table. His children, Frederik told his interviewer, were "as charming as anyone else's" but they could also be very noisy on occasion, "so that sometimes you feel you could strangle them". He also gave an insight into his working life, with its rounds of meetings with ministers, public audiences and daily signings of documents. "Sometimes I work late, but when one has a charming wife and charming kids, there is no reason for complaint," he concluded.[7]

This merely whetted the appetite for more ambitious fly-on-the-wall television documentaries, which have become commonplace across Europe in the past few years. One of the most notable was

Richard Cawston's *Royal Family*, a programme made by the BBC to accompany the investiture of Prince Charles as Prince of Wales in July 1969. In the most famous scene he and the family are seen having a barbecue beside a loch at Balmoral, their Scottish home. While Prince Charles mixes salad dressing, Prince Philip grills the sausages. In another scene, Prince Charles is playing the cello when a string snaps, hitting his younger brother Edward in the face. The family are shown eating lunch and decorating their Christmas tree; the Queen even visits a shop.

The project had been prompted by demand from broadcasters from across the world for footage of the Prince ahead of his inauguration. Given that Charles, at that early stage in his life, had not actually done very much, it was decided instead to make a film that looked more broadly at monarchy and its role. It also appears to have coincided with a desire by the royal family to show themselves in public amid criticism from some commentators who saw them as out of step with the more liberal atmosphere of the 1960s.

According to one account by a former courtier who had a small part in the film, Prince Philip was a driving force behind the project, which he hoped would reveal quite how much his wife and the rest of the family did for the nation. "We were saying, 'Hey fellers, this is the Queen,'" the courtier said. "This is a year in the life of the Queen. And it isn't all gilt coaches and Rolls-Royces, balls and banquets and champagne. It's bloody hard work, and this film reveals what sort of hard work it is."[8] In other words, it was all about people involved in running a family business, but doing so with a sense of humour and fun.

For Cawston, one of the most serious problems was being allowed to film some of the scenes. "Get away from the Queen with your bloody cameras," Philip barked at him during the Balmoral barbecue. An even greater obstacle was the reluctance of the family, whose public comments were traditionally confined to reading carefully prepared speeches, to allow their unscripted conversations to be recorded.

The programme went to the heart of the delicate balancing act that the royal family faced: trying on the one hand to allow enough access to give an insight into their lives while showing enough restraint to "to preserve the mystique". Just in case it all went wrong, the palace was promised a right of veto – although it didn't need to exercise it.

It was still a high-risk strategy, as David Attenborough, who was at the time the BBC's director of programmes, pointed out to Cawston in appropriately anthropological terms. "You're killing the monarchy, you know, with this film you're making," he said. "The whole institution depends on mystique and the tribal chief in his hut. If any member of the tribe ever sees inside the hut, then the whole system of the tribal chiefdom is damaged and the tribe eventually disintegrates."[9]

Milton Shulman, television critic for the *Evening Standard*, expressed similar sentiments. "Is it, in the long run, wise for the Queen's advisers to set as a precedent this right of the television camera to act as an image-making apparatus for the monarchy?" he asked. "Every institution that has so far attempted to use TV to popularize or aggrandize itself has been trivialized by it."[10]

In terms of ratings, *Royal Family*, broadcast first on the BBC and repeated a week later on ITV, was a great success: as many as two-thirds of the population are believed to have watched one or other of the two screenings, an extraordinary figure even for an era when there were just three television channels. So what of its longer-term effects on the monarchy? In one sense, by allowing the cameras to record them in such informal moments the royal family were blurring the distinction between the public and private, which effectively paved the way for the more invasive and personalized reporting of their lives that has followed. As one contemporary observer put it, the sight of Prince Philip cooking sausages meant that thereafter people would want to see and hear everything. Even so, it would be going too far to blame the programme alone for the public-relations disasters that befell the Windsors in the 1990s.

Surprisingly for such a significant film, it has not been shown again since. Researchers are allowed to view it, but only with prior permission from Buckingham Palace. Other royal documentaries are allowed to use only short clips – although not of the celebrated barbecue scene (even though snippets of it have popped up on YouTube). When the National Portrait Gallery put on an exhibition, *The Queen: Art and Image*, to mark the Diamond Jubilee, it was allowed only a ninety-second extract.

Other television films setting out to show the everyday life of the royal family have followed in Britain and elsewhere in Europe. In Denmark, Jacob Jørgensen, head of JJ Film, a production company, appeared to break new ground in 1995 with *Årstider i kongehuset* (*The Seasons of the Royal Family*) a series of four sixty-minute films that tracked a year in the life of the royal family and their staff. JJ Film has made something of a speciality of such shows and has produced more than twenty films featuring the Danish royals, establishing a close relationship with the family. Quite how close this relationship was became clear when it emerged that Jørgensen's cameraman son Martin fell for Alexandra, the wife of Prince Joachim, the younger of the Queen's two sons, after apparently meeting during the making of one of the programmes. Alexandra was divorced in 2005 and married her new love, who is fourteen years her junior, in March 2007.

In Sweden meanwhile the Bernadotte dynasty's two hundredth anniversary in 2010 was marked with a six-part documentary entitled *Familjen Bernadotte*. To make the programmes, Gregor Nowinski, a documentary film-maker, was given unprecedented access to the royal family, following them at work and play for two years and conducting a number of in-depth interviews.

While most such projects appear to have been well received, there was one notable exception: an execrable one-off version of the popular slapstick game *It's a Knockout*, organized by a twenty-three-year-old Prince Edward in June 1987 in what was his first foray into television. The programme raised more than a million pounds for various royal-backed charities, but many traditionalists were appalled by the sight of Edward, Princess Anne and the Duke and Duchess of York presiding over competitions between various film, television and sports stars, including John Travolta, Rowan Atkinson and Meat Loaf – all of them dressed in medieval costumes. The programme did not do much for Edward's reputation: at a news conference afterwards, the Prince asked the journalists present what they had thought of the show. The response was nervous laughter, prompting an angry Edward to storm out.

While members of the British royal family proved reluctant to hold themselves up to such ridicule again, there were plenty of others prepared to do it for them. In the early 1960s the popular television programme *That Was the Week That Was*, presented by a young David Frost, lampooned the royal family along with other parts of the establishment. *Private Eye*, launched in 1961, responded to the royal family documentary by referring to them by working-class nicknames: the

Queen became Brenda, Prince Charles was nicknamed Brian and the Diana character, when she came on the scene later, named Cheryl. This was taken a step further in the 1980s by *Spitting Image*, which cruelly parodied the royal family. Prince Charles was shown talking to flowers, Prince Philip was portrayed as a buffoon always in naval uniform, and the Queen Mother, who elsewhere in the media had long since attained the status of national treasure, was generally seen with a bottle of Gordon's Gin in one hand and a copy of the *Racing Post* in the other. In Sweden, meanwhile, *Hey Baberiba*, a comedy-impressions show launched in 2005, included a regular strand, "Familjen", in which actors impersonated members of the country's royal family.

Many in Europe's palaces would probably have been happy to confine themselves to various televised set-piece engagements and the occasional documentary, but by the 1980s the media, especially in Britain, wanted more. It was provided for them by Diana Spencer. For newspaper and magazine editors, not just in Britain but across the world, her arrival was a godsend. She was young and beautiful, and inclusion of her image on a cover was bound to boost circulation.

Diana's Cinderella-like transformation from ordinary young woman about town to princess was something with which readers could identify – even if, as the daughter of an earl and a member of one of Britain's grandest families, she had never been quite as "ordinary" as the media liked to portray her.

The protracted – and very public – collapse of her marriage to Charles during the 1990s provided even more stories, many of them fed to the press by the couple themselves. The tradition in Britain, as elsewhere in Europe, had hitherto been that royal brides – however unhappy with their partners – kept their feelings to themselves. Diana was not ready to abide by that rule, however, and chose instead to follow the example of Caroline of Brunswick. The results were equally disastrous: Diana's secret cooperation with Andrew Morton, which in 1992 produced *Diana: Her True Story*, chronicling the misery of her marriage – suicide attempts and all – prompted Charles to tell his version of events in an authorized book and television interview with the broadcaster Jonathan Dimbleby two years later. This, in turn, led Diana to retaliate in November 1995 with her notorious *Panorama* interview with Martin Bashir, in which she memorably declared:

"There were three of us in this marriage, so it was a bit crowded." As if that were not enough, even one of Diana's lovers, James Hewitt, a dashing staff captain in the Life Guards, weighed in with *Princess in Love*, a steamy account of his relationship with the Princess written, according to many, in a style reminiscent of Barbara Cartland. The revelations proved great box office: some twenty-one million Britons – almost half the adult population – tuned in to watch Diana pour out her heart to Bashir – but, taken together, they constituted an unedifying spectacle that dealt a serious blow to the image of the British monarchy.

Diana's death in August 1997, appropriately enough while being pursued by the paparazzi, heralded the third and final act in the tragedy – and generated even more press coverage. The fatal car accident in a tunnel in Paris and the various conspiracy theories that followed were the source of a flood of stories that continued for years.

Diana proved a difficult act to follow – especially for the British media. Princes William and Harry made good copy, although their respective girlfriends, Kate Middleton and Chelsy Davy, could not initially fill the gap left by the demise of the princes' mother. Kate has necessarily moved to centre stage since her engagement and marriage. Yet both the national mood and attitude of the media have changed in the intervening years, and there has been no return to the reporting frenzy that accompanied Diana's every move. William, understandably enough, has grown up with a strong suspicion towards the media, and has resisted strongly any attempt to turn Kate into a twenty-first-century version of his mother.

For her part, the Duchess has quickly demonstrated a flair for handling the media, dealing well with the relentless attention – and pressure. Her first speech, delivered on 19th March 2012 at the opening of a hospice in Ipswich, run by one of "her charities", was roundly pronounced a success.

The activities of foreign princes and princesses, on the other hand, have been greeted with indifference in Britain, apart from a small number of hard-core royalists. The Monégasque royal family are the exception: the Grimaldis had been entertaining readers, listeners and viewers since Prince Rainier married Grace Kelly in 1956, neatly merging the worlds of royalty and show business. By the 1980s the colourful love lives of their daughters Caroline and Stéphanie were the source of rich pickings. Yet their appeal too has faded in recent years, although Caroline's children, Andrea, Charlotte and Pierre, now in their twenties and with a series of high-profile relationships behind them, have started to take their place.

The Continental monarchies watched the obsessive media attention that Diana generated with a mixture of bemusement and relief at how much quieter things were at home in comparison. Yet by the mid-1990s attitudes were beginning to change, as a new generation of royals came of age. Philippe, Willem-Alexander, Frederik, Haakon, Felipe and Victoria were young, glamorous and attractive to young readers, especially once they started to enjoy themselves socially and fall for members of the opposite sex. *Paris Match*, of course, had been charting the ups and downs of the love lives of Europe's royals for years. Given that France had no royal family of its own, it had followed everyone else's – starting with the Grimaldis. Across Europe, other magazines and the newly emerging "lifestyle" sections of newspapers started to follow its lead.

Royals were portrayed as celebrities whose private lives were worthy of the same treatment as those of pop singers or television or film stars. Magazines such as ¡Hola!, *Bunte* or *Oggi* still used the posed photographs and photo opportunities arranged by the palaces, but supplemented them with informal images of the royals at play taken by paparazzi, who were generously paid for their exclusives. For readers wanting a more reverent approach there were specialist royal magazines such as Britain's *Majesty* or the Dutch *Vorsten Royale*. The pictures are formal ones; the stories describe engagements carried out by members of the various royal families or talk about their jewellery, palaces or history. Their selling point is that they provide an "insider's" – or maybe that should be courtier's – view of what goes on behind the walls of the royal palace.

Britain's *Majesty*, founded in 1980, sums itself up thus on its website: "Every month *Majesty* gives its readers a colourful insight into the privileged lives of the royal families of the world. Personalities, lifestyles and fashion are all captured in exciting features and stunning photographs. *Majesty* records all the important royal engagements and takes an in-depth look at the dramatic history of Britain's monarchs. Month by month it builds into a beautiful and authoritative collection."

Within the countries that are still monarchies, interest is necessarily concentrated on the national royal family, with foreign ones playing a supporting role. The German media, with a voracious appetite for royalty but like the French no ruling family of their own, have simply adopted everyone else's instead: the Swedish royal family has come to enjoy a special role, though, thanks to German-born Queen Silvia – "*unsere Königin*" ("our Queen"). This fascination was reflected in the huge coverage the German media gave to Crown Princess Victoria's wedding in June 2010.

The changing relationship between royalty and magazines over recent decades is well illustrated by the transformation of Sweden's *Svensk Damtidning*, a glossy women's magazine that sells 140,000 copies a week. Back in the 1950s, when King Carl XVI Gustaf and his four elder sisters were growing up, it used to publish sweet photographs of the royal children. Over the following decades, however, the royals were only a relatively small part of their coverage. That suddenly changed in the mid-1990s following the revelation that Crown Princess Victoria was suffering from anorexia.

Karin Lennmor, the magazine's editor-in-chief, had previously assumed her readership was composed of middle-aged or older women. Now she found a new generation of young girls who identified with the twenty-year-old Princess and wanted to read about her and her friends. "Victoria became a trendsetter: where she went, where she went on vacation, the kind of labels she would buy," Lennmor recalls.[11] So the magazine was revamped with the strapline "*Den Kungliga Veckotidningen*" ("The Royal Weekly") and a little crown on its cover, and began to follow the Princess and her younger siblings, Carl Philip and Madeleine, who were also beginning to make their way in the world.

Inevitably, the emphasis is on the positive, so when the magazine's journalists heard in early 2010 of problems in Princess Madeleine's relationship with her fiancé, Jonas Bergström, they did not print them. Instead it was the Norwegian magazine *Se og Hør* that effectively precipitated the break-up by publishing the claims of the Norwegian woman who said she had slept with him.

Alongside such magazines there are also television programmes. While Belgium has *Royalty* and *Place Royale*, Dutch television has *Blauw Bloed*, a weekly show running since 2004 in which host Jeroen Snel presents a mixture of news and history about both the country's own royal family and the other European ones. Snel also co-hosts a quiz programme, *De grootste Royaltykenner van Nederland* (*The Greatest Royalty Expert in the Netherlands*), in which contestants compete to answer obscure questions about the Dutch royal house.

Such programmes are not a permanent fixture elsewhere in Europe, although in Sweden, in the three months preceding the marriage of Crown Princess Victoria in June 2010, SVT, the main state television channel, screened *Det kungliga bröllopet* (*The Royal Wedding*), in a one-hour, prime-time slot every Monday evening. The show, presented by Ebba von Sydow, a former magazine editor, drew audiences of up to one million people with a mixture of footage of past royal events and reports on everything from the pastry chef charged with making the wedding cake to the groom Daniel Westling's home town of Ockelbo.

As in Britain, much of the reporting has concentrated on the glitz, the history and ceremonial of monarchy or else on the private lives of royals. Yet some newspapers have mounted serious investigations into royal activities – and especially into the background of the prospective crown princesses who emerged in the late 1990s – with dramatic results: Mette-Marit, for example, was obliged to come clean about her previous drug use, while Máxima's father, Jorge Zorreguieta, had to keep away from his daughter's wedding following revelations of his role as a minister in the country's former ruling military junta. Interest has continued since the weddings, with the media seizing on suggestions that their unions might be anything less than happy or, in the case of Mary's marriage to Frederik, the Crown Prince of Denmark, hinting at the reappearance of old flames.

Even more far-reaching were, as we have seen, the Dutch media's investigations into the past of Mabel Wisse Smit, which forced Prince Friso to renounce his claim to the throne when he married her. While the methods used were, in most cases, conventional journalistic ones, there have also been examples of the kind of tabloid techniques used by Britain's *News of the World* and *Daily Mirror* – as shown most graphically by Håvard Melnæs and other reporters at the Norwegian gossip magazine *Se og Hør* in their investigations into Mette-Marit's past.

For the Belgian media, interest came from a different quarter. During his forty-two-year reign, the devoutly religious King Baudouin and his wife Queen Fabiola had provided the press with little to get their teeth into. The accession in 1993 of his younger brother Albert, whose marriage had been a much stormier affair, was to be more fruitful for them – including the revelation of the existence of the King's love child in 1999. The speed with which the Belgian media identified and tracked down Delphine Boël was impressive.

However loud the criticism of individual members of the royal families, Europe's media devote little space to the questioning of the institution of monarchy and its continued relevance in the twenty-first century – and republican groups must fight hard to get any coverage at all. Andrew Marr's high-profile three-part television series, *Diamond Queen*, broadcast on BBC 1 in February 2012, was distinctly hagiographical in tone. As two observers of the British media scene have argued, the media tends to depoliticize and trivialize the monarchy in favour of a relentless focus on the activities of the royals as family members.[12] Such a focus tends to squeeze out a broader debate about monarchy as a whole. Yet it is impossible to separate the two completely. As has been shown on plenty of occasions in Britain and elsewhere, popular unhappiness with the behaviour of individual royals can spill over into a decline in support for the institution.

Such coverage is also an inevitable by-product of the blurring of monarchy with celebrity that has become common even in the more heavyweight newspapers. Politicians frequently complain that too much emphasis is put on personality rather than on policy. Yet with members of the royal family there is no policy to discuss – quite the opposite: in contrast to their eighteenth- and nineteenth-century predecessors, who still ruled as well as reigned, modern-day monarchs are at pains not to involve themselves in the political process or do so only according to carefully circumscribed rules. The result is to leave only the personal for the media to report.

The palaces have responded in different ways to the new demands placed upon them – especially when it comes to interviews. Britain's Queen Elizabeth, for example, does not give interviews; nor did her parents before her. The only time her mother gave one was when, as Lady Elizabeth Bowes-Lyon, she became engaged to her "beloved Bertie", the future King George VI. She talked to a journalist about her engagement ring and said how she enjoyed tennis and hunting – all of which proved too much for the palace, which reminded her that such openness was not appropriate. She never spoke to the newspapers again.

The Scandinavian monarchs have been far more accessible: Sweden's Carl XVI Gustaf frequently talks with journalists, especially during royal trips. Margrethe II of Denmark has not confined herself to her many appearances in documentaries: she frequently gives newspaper and television interviews and has even cooperated with the authors of books; in the most recent one, published in April 2010 to coincide with her seventieth birthday, she reflected among other things on her childhood, her family and her role as head of state. In the unlikely event that Britain's Queen agreed to such a publication, it would be seized upon by royal watchers desperate for an insight into her views. In Denmark, by contrast, reviewers complained that their Queen had already spoken so extensively about herself that she had little new left to say.

Denmark is also unusual in that Prince Henrik, the Queen's French-born husband, published a book of his own, *Destin Oblige*, in 1996. In it he writes of life both before and after he became prince consort – and does so with considerable frankness. Indeed, it is impossible to imagine, say, Prince Philip, talking so openly about the problems he has faced since marrying into the royal family. For many years the Danish royal couple also used to invite journalists to their chateau in the south of France, where they answered questions in an informal setting. In 2009 the event was cancelled. No official reason was given, but some at the palace clearly believed the royal family were in danger of becoming overexposed.

The heirs to the throne and other members of the royal families are far more willing to give newspaper or television interviews – especially at the time they become engaged, when they will typically give a press conference or television interview jointly with their partner. In Britain, the ritual of the pre-wedding interview was initiated by Princess Anne and Mark Phillips before their marriage in 1973. Sometimes the subject matter can be tough – such as when Mette-Marit of Norway was forced to reveal her past as a drug-user. Equally memorable was the interview Prince Charles gave with Diana Spencer before they married in 1981 when, asked if he was in love, the heir to the throne replied "whatever that is" – the words were to be quoted against him long afterwards. (Diana, by contrast, had replied, "Of course.") Undaunted, Charles has continued to talk to journalists, often on favourite subjects such as architecture and the environment. His Continental counterparts have often followed suit. Prince William and Kate Middleton observed the tradition when they announced their engagement.

Such interviews are inevitably soft in tone. Those members of a royal family who agree to subject themselves to an interview are largely spared the tough questions that politicians or business leaders routinely endure. Strict rules also apply during coverage of royal visits and events: certain occasions are intended purely as opportunities to film and take photographs – not to ask questions. Occasionally, however, a journalist will challenge such protocol, as happened in Belgium in August 2009, at the height of the controversy over King Albert and Queen Paola's new yacht. During a fête at the Palace of Laeken to celebrate their fiftieth wedding anniversary, the royal couple were challenged over the purchase by Christophe Deborsu, a journalist for Belgian television. And why not, retorted Queen Paola. "We find that it is terribly unjust... especially since we've had yachts since our marriage, that is to say for fifty years. We have always had them. We started with a little boat measuring two metres... no, five metres."

Albert himself said nothing, apparently stunned by such a breach of etiquette. Pierre-Emmanuel De Bauw, the palace spokesman, complained afterwards that it was forbidden for journalists to try to pose questions when the microphones were on. For Belgian royal watchers, the fact that the journalist concerned was from the traditionally more royalist French-speaking part of the country rather than the more republican Flanders was significant.

This remains the exception, though. Most interactions with royalty are characterized by a form of deference and an acceptance of the ground rules set by the palace. It is almost as if those interviewing them – like members of the public who go weak at the knees after a royal encounter – cannot entirely free themselves from the feeling that they are mere subjects and must behave accordingly in the presence of their rulers. Even the most experienced television interrogators are not immune: when Christiane Amanpour, the veteran foreign correspondent, interviewed Haakon and Mette-Marit in October 2009 on CNN, she gave them a considerably gentler ride than she would have done a politician.

Media coverage of royalty in Britain in particular has acquired an extra dimension thanks to a small number of courtiers and other royal officials who have been tempted, usually by the prospect of considerable financial reward, to publish inside accounts of life within the palace. Most notorious of them all was Marion Crawford, who spent fifteen years as a governess to the young Princesses Elizabeth and Margaret. After she retired in 1949 at the age of forty, Crawfie, as she was known, was asked by the American magazine *Ladies' Home Journal* to write articles or a book about them.

Crawfie asked the Queen, who at a meeting told her she should say "No no no to offers of dollars for articles about something as private & precious as our family", and offered instead to help her find a new teaching post.[13] Crawfie initially appeared to comply, but the lure of the money on offer was too great and she went ahead with the project. Her account boosted the circulation of the *Ladies' Home Journal* by half a million and was also published in Britain by *Women's Own* and in book form. After years on a meagre royal salary, Crawfie became a very rich woman indeed: she was paid £30,000 for world rights by her British publisher George Newnes and another $6,000 for its serialization in the United States in *Ladies' Home Journal*.

The contents of the book were innocuous enough and painted a fairly touching portrait of royal life. Indeed, the publishers even sent a manuscript to the palace and agreed to remove certain inaccuracies pointed out to them. But that was not the point as far as the King and Queen were concerned. The former governess was guilty of the worst kind of breach of trust – and "doing a Crawfie" thereafter became the term used for betrayal. For the palace, she had become a "non person".

Crawfie nevertheless continued to write – or at least have people write under her own name. Her career came to an abrupt end in 1955, however, when an article was published under her name describing the Trooping the Colour ceremony and the Ascot races, even though both had been cancelled that year because of a strike. Crawfie retired to her native Scotland, to a cottage close to Balmoral Castle, but no member of the royal family ever visited; when she died in 1988 neither the Queen, the Queen Mother nor Princess Margaret sent a wreath.

The death of Diana – and the massive market for books about her – brought forth a crop of latter-day Crawfies; among them was Paul Burrell, her former butler. His autobiographical book, *A Royal Duty*, published in 2003, denounced by Prince William and Harry as "a cold and overt betrayal" of their mother, was an international best-seller and launched him on a second career based largely on cashing in on his royal past. This included everything from appearing on television reality and game shows to launching his own "Royal Butler" range of furniture, rugs and wine, aimed largely at buyers in America, which became his home for several years.

Such "insider" memoirs have been rarer elsewhere in Europe – one of the few exceptions being a book by Jesper Lundorf, the former bodyguard of Crown Prince Frederik, in which, among other things, he discusses the time he spent training with him in the elite Frømandskorpset.

Europe's royal families have generally responded to such intrusions into their privacy either by journalists or former associates in silence, refusing to confirm or deny what is reported. Occasionally, though, they will let slip their real feelings. In a speech at dinner in aid of sick and impoverished journalists in May 1930, the future King George VI reflected on the huge media attention his young family was attracting. "I owe a rather special debt of gratitude to the gossip columns of our newspapers for, if I am in doubt as to what is happening in my own home, I need only turn to the gossip in the *Daily Wonder* and I find all the information I require," he said.[14]

While George VI seemed amused rather than angered by the attention, tempers can sometimes flare – as famously happened during a royal photo opportunity in the Swiss Alps in March 2005, a few weeks before Prince Charles married Camilla. Asked by Nicholas Witchell, the BBC's royal reporter, whether he was looking forward to the wedding, Charles gave a sarcastic reply before turning to his sons and saying softly, "These bloody people. I can't bear that man. I mean, he's so awful, he really is… I hate these people." Unfortunately for Charles, his comments were picked up, leaving his communications director to insist the Prince "doesn't have contempt for the media".

Sometimes, though, the media will be perceived to have gone just too far – prompting a royal response. In Britain, injunctions such as the one against the account and photographs of palace life published in the *Daily Mirror* in November 2003 after one of its reporters, Ryan Parry, managed to get employed for two months as a footman are relatively rare. Such is the media's acknowledgement of its reliance on cooperation with the palace than it can be brought into line with a warning – as happened when the newly married Princess Diana was pregnant with her first child and could not leave Highgrove, their country estate in Gloucestershire, without being photographed. "The Princess of Wales feels totally beleaguered," Michael Shea, the Queen's press secretary, complained. "She has coped extremely well, she has come through with flying colours. But now the people who love her and care for her are anxious at the reaction it is having."[15]

Almost two decades later there were fears that Kate Middleton, yet to become engaged to Prince William, could suffer similar harassment. In December 2009, as the royal family prepared to celebrate Christmas at their Sandringham estate, the Queen issued a strong warning to newspapers not to publish paparazzi pictures of the royal family.

Middleton herself was reported in February 2010 to be in line to receive at least £10,000 in damages, plus substantial legal costs, after threatening to sue a photographer and two British picture agencies over photographs taken of her while she was playing tennis at Christmas 2009 – even though the pictures were taken from a public place with a camera with a normal rather than a telephoto lens and were published only in Germany and not in Britain. The claim rested on privacy law, a rapidly developing area that draws on the European Convention on Human Rights.

A precedent was set by the European Court of Human Rights, which ruled in June 2004 that photographs published by Germany's *Bunte*, *Neue Post* and *Freizeit Revue* showing Princess Caroline of Monaco skiing, horse-riding, sitting in a café and playing tennis with her husband Prince Ernst August of Hanover infringed her privacy. The "Caroline ruling", which had significant implications for the tabloid media across Europe, overturned a German decision dating from 1999, which said that as a public figure she had to accept being photographed in public.

Princess Caroline's legal action was only one of many by Monaco's royals, whose colourful lifestyle has increased media interest. That October her five-year-old daughter Alexandra was awarded a record €76,693.78 in compensation from the German supreme court after two magazines, *Die Aktuelle* and *Die Zwei*, published paparazzi pictures of her when she was a baby. Years earlier, in 1996, Caroline had been awarded 180,000 Deutschmarks (£77,000) after the magazine *Bunte* was found to have made up an interview with her and €102,000 from another scandal sheet, *Gala*, in 2001.

Acting for Caroline was Matthias Prinz, one of Germany's most high-profile media lawyers, whose father Günter, ironically enough, was editor of the tabloid *Bild Zeitung* for most of the 1970s and 1980s. In an interview with the news magazine *Der Spiegel* in 2009, Prinz rejected suggestions he was stifling freedom of expression. The situation faced by Caroline when she moved to the French village of Saint-Rémy after the death of her second husband Stefano Casiraghi was "catastrophic", he said. He recalled a visit there in 1992, counting as many as twenty paparazzi outside the front door and another fifteen outside the school, attended by her three children, in the hope of getting shots of them.[16]

Prinz has also acted for the Swedish royal family over the many legal actions it has pursued – most dramatically in December 2004, when he sued Klambt, one of Germany's biggest magazine publishers, over what he claimed were 1,588 made-up stories, including more than five hundred front-page "exclusives". Among them were claims the King had been unfaithful with a mystery blonde and that the Queen had been suffering from cancer but was cured by a miraculous wristband. The reaction of Rudiger Dienst, a Klambt executive, who called himself a "repentant sinner" and vowed not to print any more inaccurate stories, was revealing. "We have learnt our lesson," he said. "We admit that we may have embellished some reports, but we have done nothing different to other tabloids. This kind of reporting has been going on for fifty years, and I don't understand why all of a sudden the Swedish royal family are taking action against us now."

In a further royal legal victory, a Hamburg court in July 2009 ordered another German publishing house, Sonnenverlag, to pay Sweden's Princess Madeleine €400,000 in damages for fabricating stories about her – including erroneous claims she was pregnant. The Princess pledged to give the money to charity.

The Dutch royals have also often had recourse to the courts – largely, again, in cases against German publications. In 1968, Prince Bernhard, the husband of Queen Juliana, became the first member of the country's royal family to take legal action against a gossip magazine after *Neue Welt* published a report claiming that his daughter Princess Irene had had an abortion. It took three years, but the Prince eventually won and was awarded the equivalent of over £40,000 damages, which he donated to the Red Cross.[17]

Other members of the Dutch royal family followed suit, especially Bernhard's son-in-law, Prince Claus, whose own relationship with the press got off to a difficult start after he was "outed" in May 1965 by Britain's *Daily Express* as the man in the life of the future Queen Beatrix, despite a request by the palace to give the couple a little more time together out of the limelight. Claus went on to pursue several cases successfully against the press – including one over claims by *Privé* magazine in 1985 that Crown Prince Willem-Alexander, still just eighteen, had spent a night in the Amsterdam Hilton with an unknown woman.[18] Other legal actions followed – the last of which the Prince won just days before his death in 2002.

Willem-Alexander has enthusiastically taken up the baton, especially after the beginning of his relationship with his future wife, Máxima. The couple have been especially determined to prevent publication of what they consider intrusive pictures of their three daughters, Catharina-Amalia, Alexia and Ariane. Nor is it just mass-market magazines such as *Privé* or *Shownieuws* that have come into conflict with the palace. In August 2009 the royal family won a legal battle with Associated Press, the American news agency, after it sent its clients photographs of Crown Prince Willem-Alexander and his family on holiday in Argentina. In weighing freedom of expression against the right of privacy, a Dutch court ruled that members of the royal family, while they take the risk of media scrutiny when performing their public duties, do have an expectation of privacy in their personal lives.

Such cases, though, are relatively rare given the sheer amount of royal reporting – a reflection of the fundamental interdependence of royalty and the media. While the various royal families may find some of the coverage of their lives intrusive, they would be even more concerned if the media simply stopped covering them at all. With their function these days largely a representational one, it would be a first step towards irrelevance and possibly extinction.

For the media, meanwhile, the royals are a useful source of material to fill newspapers or television programmes. Hence the often pragmatic deals struck between the two: official royal trips are carefully orchestrated to provide photographers and cameramen the shots they need. In the case of the British royal family this principle is extended to some private holidays too, such as when Prince Charles goes skiing with his sons: photographers are granted a photo opportunity in return for agreeing to leave them in peace for the rest of the time. An extreme example of such an arrangement was the agreement between the palace and the British media over Prince Harry's deployment to Afghanistan – significantly, it was an American website rather than the British media that broke the embargo.

Illuminating is the example of the *Independent*, which, when it was launched in 1986, vowed to ignore royal stories. Andreas Whittam-Smith, who edited the newspaper for its first eight years, claimed later to have had a private bet with himself that a successful newspaper could manage without royalty. He lost, however, and after a time the *Independent* abandoned its stance and began to report the Windsors' activities like other newspapers. "For good commercial reasons, national newspapers as a whole cannot any longer manage without daily coverage [of the royal family]," Whittam-Smith concluded in 2000. "The doings of the various members of the House of Windsor provide the raw material for the most powerful of narrative forms – invented as it was by television, drawing its inspiration from nineteenth-century novels – the soap opera. A large cast is essential."[19]

Other newspapers and magazines elsewhere in Europe have come to a similar conclusion. In Denmark *Ekstra Bladet*, a strident tabloid, has been a fierce critic of the monarchy – but this has not prevented it from running plenty of stories about both its country's royal family and royalty elsewhere. The Danish edition of the weekly magazine *Se og Hør* has also proved itself as enthusiastic a pursuer of the royals as its Norwegian namesake; curiously, the magazine is owned by the same media group as *Billed Bladet*, a pro-royalty weekly, and both are run out of the same spectacular building on the Copenhagen waterfront. The motivation appears largely commercial: targeting both monarchists and republicans means they have the whole market covered.

The last years of the twentieth century and the first decade of the twenty-first brought a new challenge – and opportunity: the Internet. The British royal family has been a pioneer, setting up its website in the late 1990s following the arrival of a new press chief, Simon Lewis. The site (www.royal.gov.uk) has grown enormously since, and offers a huge mixture of news, history, photographs and information as well as clever features such as an interactive map that allows you to find royal visits past and present in your area. Since October 2007, there has been a "Royal Channel" on YouTube, which as of April 2012 has 465 professional-quality videos and boasts more than thirty-six million views. Then in November 2010 it was announced that the British monarchy was to get its own page on Facebook. Unlike her subjects, however, the Queen would not be accepting friends or, it was assumed, writing her own entries. It was nevertheless a success: more than 40,000 people rushed to "like" the Queen an hour after the page was launched – although some went on to post abusive comments, many of them about her daughter-in-law Camilla, the Duchess of Cornwall.

The other royal families also have websites of their own, although they are less comprehensive and professional than the British one, notably the Belgian (www.monarchie.be) and Spanish (www.casareal.es) sites. But they too are becoming more sophisticated. In May 2009 the Dutch royal family followed the British by setting up their own YouTube channel, which includes both contemporary material and clips dating back to the enthronement of Queen Wilhelmina in 1898. Those curious about the activities of Norway's Crown Prince Haakon and Crown Princess Mette-Marit, meanwhile, can follow their activities on Twitter. Some of the entries, the palace claims, are even written by the royal couple rather than by their spin doctors: "kph" at the end means Haakon, "kpm" stands for Mette-Marit and "kpp" denotes a joint effort. They also have their own Facebook page.

Many of the websites of Europe's newspaper and television channels have set up separate royal sections – in a reflection of the popularity of such news with readers. *Hello!* magazine's website, for example, has not just news and photographs but also background information such as family trees and descriptions of palaces.

Countless stand-alone websites and networks have also sprung up – some fairly professional and well-funded affairs, others little more than one-person blogs written from some of the more unlikely locations on earth. Some do little more than collect together links to stories on mainstream media, while others run forums and chatrooms for readers interested in royalty across the world to ask each other questions or share ideas. One of the most comprehensive, www.royalforums.com, which has more than 30,000 registered members and presumably many more casual users, has a bewildering variety of chatrooms, links and discussion strands covering royal families past as well as current, not just in Europe but also in Africa, Asia and Latin America.

And then there are the more personal blogs, some of which are both well written and learned. For anyone interested in the Scandinavian monarchies, one of the best is undoubtedly the blog written by Trond Norén Isaksen, a young Norwegian historian who is the author of several books and many articles on different aspects of monarchy (trondni.blogspot.com). Exhibiting an extraordinarily detailed knowledge of his subject, Isaksen (who writes in perfect English) reflects on royal news and also runs often critical reviews of the latest royal literature. Equally serious but very different in tone is crossoflaeken.blogspot.com, which describes itself as "dedicated to the Catholic monarchs of Belgium, and other topics of historical, cultural, human, political and religious interest". Belgium's monarchs – especially Léopold III – have a chequered history, but the writer portrays them as martyrs.

There are also a few quirky or more light-hearted blogs – one of the oddest of which is madhattery.royalroundup.com, which features photographs of different members of royal families in hats and tiaras, the more exotic the better. "My goal here is always to entertain," writes Ella Kay, the American-based author. "This is primarily a blog about silliness – I have a healthy respect for the British royals and royals around the world, and I do not intend to belittle. It's about frivolous fashion and nothing more than that, really." Kay, a teacher who developed her love for all things royal during a semester spent abroad in England as a student, also runs a more serious blog, www.royaltywithellakay.com.

Chapter 15

Vive la République

On an unusually warm Saturday in June, the heirs of Oliver Cromwell are sitting in a rented room in a building behind Euston station in London listening to speaker after speaker denounce the British monarchy. They have gathered here for the annual conference of Republic, an organization with the mission of "campaigning for a democratic alternative to the monarchy". To call Republic a mass movement would be an exaggeration: although the organization claims 1,500 members, a mere hundred or so have turned up today. They are predominantly male, middle class and over fifty.

The discussions are calm and largely devoid of passion, although the atmosphere livens up when Geoffrey Robertson, one of Britain's best-known human-rights lawyers, presents a glowing tribute to Cromwell and the men who tried and executed King Charles I in 1649. The French revolutionaries of 1789 also come in for praise. His audience are not about to man the barricades themselves, however. If this is all the support the republicans can muster, then the Queen – or Elizabeth Windsor as they prefer to call her – has little to fear.

The high point of the day's debates is a discussion about the "meddling" of Prince Charles and the way he uses the influence that comes with his position to lobby for his pet causes. Charles is good news for republicans. While few can fault his mother's behaviour as Queen, her son and his apparent disregard for the convention of royal neutrality can annoy people. One of the speakers, Peter Jenkins, an architect, says he has been drawn into republicanism by the Prince's campaign against modern architecture. David Colquhoun, a professor of pharmacology at University College, London, is outraged by the way the heir to the throne lends respectability to some of the wackier forms of alternative medicine. "The influence he has exerted has been consistently malign," he says.

Others present complain about the cost of the monarchy and oppose any proposals to increase the Queen's Civil List at a time when other government spending is being cut back. There is talk too of the bad behaviour of some members of the royal family: it is only a few weeks since Sarah Ferguson has been trapped by the "Fake Sheik" from *News of the World*.

For Graham Smith, Republic's full-time campaign manager, the issue is far more fundamental than that: the monarchy is a serious obstacle to the modernization of the British political system and to the abolition of such historical anomalies as an unelected House of Lords and the highly secretive Privy Council. "Some reformers dismiss monarchy as a decorative bauble," says Smith. "But it's the central pillar of our feudal constitution."

The argument has acquired a particular resonance following the general election of May 2010, the first in more than thirty years not to give a single party a majority of seats in the House of Commons. The price that David Cameron, the Conservative leader, had to pay in order to become prime minister was to promise the Liberal Democrats, the country's third party, a reform of Britain's first-past-the-post electoral system. Although voters went on the following April to reject change in a referendum, constitutional reform was back on the agenda, and some hoped this could lead to discussion of the role of the monarchy. The uncertainty that followed the election has also focused attention on the powers of the Queen – or rather what was seen as her determination not to be involved in politics, leaving Britain alone among Europe's democracies in not having a figure, whether a monarch or an elected president, steering the coalition-building process.

It is ironic that Britain, the country with the most deeply entrenched and best-known monarchy in Europe, and probably the world, should have been the first to try republicanism. Indeed, the eleven years between the execution of Charles I and the restoration of his brother Charles II in 1660 are not generally considered a good advertisement for republican rule. However admirable the motives of many who backed him, Cromwell did not prove himself a model democrat, dissolving parliament when it did not agree with him. By having himself appointed Lord Protector for life and naming his ineffectual son Richard to succeed him after his death, Cromwell became a king in all but name.

The Restoration appeared to close the door for good on republicanism: the men who brought Charles I to trial were themselves hanged, drawn and quartered after his brother climbed the throne; such was the desire for vengeance that Cromwell's body was exhumed the following year on the anniversary of the King's execution and his severed head displayed on a pole outside Westminster Hall for the next twenty-four years.

Yet republicanism has lived on in Britain in the centuries since in radical circles, at times winning broader appeal – usually in response to bad behaviour on the part of monarchs. One such point was during the last years of the eighteenth and early years of the nineteenth century, when George IV's antics as Prince of Wales and Prince Regent added to the unpopularity of the Hanoverians. The arrival on the throne of his niece Victoria in 1837 gave the monarchy a boost that was to last for several decades – but this was to be undone following the premature death of her husband Albert in 1861. Consumed with grief, Victoria largely withdrew from public life, plunging the British monarchy into one of its most serious crises since the Civil War.

By the late 1860s ministers were beginning to express increasing concern about the invisibility of the Queen, who was spending most of her time at Osborne House on the Isle of Wight or at Balmoral in Scotland, and in February 1870 flatly refused a request to open parliament. Such reticence was perhaps understandable: when she had made a rare public appearance the previous year to open the new Blackfriars Bridge over the Thames, her carriage was booed as she drove down the Strand. Matters were not helped by the private life of her eldest son, the Prince of Wales, who was required to give evidence in an unsavoury divorce case in February 1870. The *Times* reflected broader exasperation with the Queen's behaviour when it said the time had come for her to stop devoting her life to mourning her late consort and "think of her subjects' claims and the duties of her high station, and not postpone them longer to an unavailing grief".

After the overthrow of Napoleon III and the declaration of a French republic in September 1870, republican clubs sprung up across Britain. In a loudly cheered speech to the House of Commons that November, Sir Charles Dilke, a radical member of parliament, declared the cost of the royal family had jumped to a million pounds a year – ten times the income of the President of the United States, as another speaker put it – and this was "chiefly not waste but mischief". "The republic must come, and at the rate at which we are moving, it will come in our generation," Joseph Chamberlain, a future President of the Board of Trade, wrote to Dilke the following year.

Britain was not to become a republic, however, although the boost the monarchy received came from an unexpected quarter: on the day that the *Times* reported Dilke's speech, the Prince of Wales fell ill with typhoid fever, the same disease that had killed his father. Dilke pressed on with his meetings, but with the heir to the throne's life in danger the popular mood shifted radically. When he gave a speech at the Bolton Temperance Hall on 30th November 1871, royalists tried to storm the building and proceedings degenerated into a pitched battle between the two rival camps. It was a similar story a few days later in Derby. Then on 14th December, the tenth anniversary of Albert's death, came the announcement that the Prince of Wales was recovering.

In public-relations terms, this was a golden opportunity for Victoria and the monarchy: heeding the advice of her hated prime minister, William Gladstone, the Queen agreed to a public thanksgiving service for her son's recovery to be held on 27th February 1872 in St Paul's Cathedral. And she insisted that "the show", as she called it, should be done properly: dressed in black, but with a white feather in her bonnet, she travelled through London in an open landau drawn by six horses. The crowds went wild.

When Dilke's motion came to a vote in a stormy House of Commons the following month, it was crushed by 276 votes to two. The result was greeted with cheers and laughter in the chamber. Dilke's argument proved so convincing, mocked the *Manchester Guardian*, that "he carried with him into the lobby only just so many followers as he could have carried away with him inside a cab". In retrospect, as Vernon Bogdanor, the British constitutional expert, has pointed out, the 1870s were to prove the high-water mark of republicanism.

An important factor in the monarchy's continued survival in the decades since has been the attitude of the Labour Party, which began to emerge at the end of the nineteenth century and by the middle of the twentieth century had supplanted the Liberals as the main anti-Conservative party. When the Labour conference debated the monarchy in 1923, republicanism was defeated by 3,694,000 votes to 386,000. A republican motion in the House of Commons in December 1936 in the aftermath of the abdication of Edward VIII won only five votes.

Elsewhere in Europe, the end of the nineteenth century and the rise of organized labour and social democracy also led to a growth in republicanism that identified monarchy with the forces of reaction. In Sweden, the Social Democratic Party even made abolition of the monarchy part of its programme when it was founded in 1889 and has retained its commitment ever since. But although the party has been in power for much of the time since the 1930s, its leaders have always found something else more pressing to do – not least because of fear of upsetting their working-class supporters, who have always been rather fond of their kings. "Certainly I am a republican," declared Tage Erlander, who was Social Democrat prime minister of Sweden from 1946 until 1969. "But that does not mean that I want a republic."

The Swedish monarchy was certainly stripped of its political power in the 1970s, but at least it survived. As has been noted, it has tended to be military defeat and the disruption to society it caused rather than the success of republican parties at the ballot box that has done for monarchy in those European countries that have become republics during the last century.

Most of Europe's monarchies – even Luxembourg's – have at least one campaigning group which, like Britain's Republic, is committed to getting rid of the king or queen. They have websites, hold meetings and congresses and publish newsletters and magazines setting out their cause. Sometimes they even get together – as happened during Crown Princess Victoria of Sweden's wedding in June 2010, when the local republican association invited its counterparts from the six other main monarchies to meet in Stockholm to form an Alliance of European Republican Movements.

All such groups are small, however; their leadership is often little more than a handful of enthusiasts, while membership is in the low thousands. And despite their dedication to the republican cause, they receive little attention from the media. Some, such as the Swedish Republican Association, include individual politicians among their ranks. The majority of the mainstream political parties, including those on the centre left, tend to support the status quo, however. Only small fringe parties, such as those on the far left or those devoted to "green" issues, tend to be committed to republicanism, and even for them, abolition of the monarchy is low in their list of priorities behind other more pressing social and economic concerns.

This is partly pragmatism; in most cases the constitutional procedures needed to transform a country from monarchy to republic are so complicated and require such large parliamentary majorities as to make them virtually impossible to implement in peacetime. Yet the continuation of monarchy is due to more than just inertia or to the much-voiced horror at the prospect of having a party politician – or even worse, a celebrity – elected to the newly created role of president. A modern-day constitutional monarch, by appearing to be impartial, above political party and not representative of any particular class or ethnic or linguistic group, is also perceived by many Europeans as a symbol of national unity. The Swedish example is instructive: the removal of the King from the formal political process during the 1970s did not turn out, as the republicans had hoped, to be the first step towards abolition of the monarchy. Instead it seemed actually to strengthen his position by removing a major source of criticism.

National unity is not seen everywhere as positive, however – certainly not by many in Belgium, where the monarchy remains one of the few common elements in a country divided between Dutch and French speakers. The extent of separatist feeling in Flanders, the northern part of the country, was shown by the results of the parliamentary elections of June 2010, in which the New Flemish Alliance, which advocates the dissolution of Belgium, emerged as the strongest party in parliament.

For Flemish separatists, the monarchy has become synonymous with the hated Belgian state, and they have waged a campaign to identify the royal family with the Francophone south. Their view was summed up by Mario Danneels, the young author who achieved notoriety after revealing the existence of King Albert's love child in 1999. In a postscript to his polemical second book, *Les Traumatisés du trône*, published eight years later, he wrote: "Not only is the royal family

French-speaking in origin, but also, over the past decade, it has given the impression of having chosen, almost openly, the French-speaking camp and of having been on its guard against the Flemish community. Under the circumstances, Flanders feels estranged from its royal family. It has turned its back on it because it intuitively perceives that is what some members of the royal family have done towards Flanders."

The irony of such sentiments will not be lost on those who recall that during the 1950 plebiscite on the fate of Albert's father Léopold III, it was the Flemings who voted overwhelmingly for his return, while a majority of French-speakers were against him. Yet care should be taken in analysing the results of that vote: if the Flemings voted for the King it was not because they perceived him as one of them. At the time, theirs was the poorer, more rural, more conservative and more Catholic part of the country – all of which translated into support for the monarchy. More heavily industrialized Wallonia, by contrast, was the power base of the left, which was traditionally more sceptical about monarchy. There was another more sensitive explanation, too: while the French-speakers had resisted the Nazis, some of the Flemish had a more equivocal relationship with the occupying forces, making them less quick to judge their King.

More than half a century later, the situation has changed, and not just because economic – and with it political – power has shifted from the south, mired in post-industrial decline, to the more economically vibrant Flanders which has found itself better placed to prosper in the global economy of the twenty-first century. In today's Belgium almost everything is seen in terms of the language question. Danneels is not alone among the Flemings in viewing the royal family as representing the French-speaking community. No matter that the perceptions don't quite match reality: as one commentator – Francophone, of course – pointed out, the royal family is more Flemish now than at any time before, with Dutch speakers forming a majority of the King's advisors. In such matters, however, perception can be every bit as important as reality.

Any move towards the break up of Belgium would be watched closely elsewhere in Europe, especially in Spain, where there are also links between separatism and republicanism. Advocates of independence in the northern Catalan and Basque regions resent the royals as representatives of the centralizing Spanish state. Underlying this is the more fundamental question of how deeply rooted monarchy is in Spain, which has had two republics and four decades of right-wing dictatorship under General Francisco Franco during the last century and a half – a very different experience from the continuity enjoyed by Europe's other surviving monarchies. Indeed, it was only after Juan Carlos's successful facing-down of the attempted military coup of 1981 that the monarchy won wide acceptance – prompting the oft-repeated claim that Spaniards are not monarchists but rather Juancarlists. Just as many Britons wonder how Prince Charles will fare once he succeeds his mother, so many of Prince Felipe's future subjects question the extent to which he will be up to the job.

The year 2007 proved an especially turbulent one for the Spanish monarchy: Catalan separatists burnt pictures of the King during his visit to the region, and a controversy erupted when two cartoonists were fined under a rarely used law against "damaging the prestige of the Crown" after they published a cartoon of Prince Felipe having sex on the cover of the satirical magazine *El Jueves*. There were questions too about the cost of the monarchy.

The King responded in August by appointing an auditor to scrutinize the spending of the royal family – which is kept hidden from the public by law. Juan Carlos also took the unprecedented step of attempting publicly to justify his role as head of state, claiming that he had contributed to the "longest period of stability and prosperity under democracy in Spain".

The situation has calmed somewhat in the years since, but even minor incidents can be seen as disproportionately damaging. The divorce of the King's eldest daughter Elena, announced in February 2010 – a first for the Spanish royal family – sparked fierce debate, as did the court appearance two years later of his younger daughter Cristina's husband, Iñaki Urdangarin, in connection with a multi-million-euro corruption case. Then, that Easter, Elena's thirteen-year-old son, Froilán, shot himself in the foot with a shotgun, even though by law in Spain you must be at least fourteen to handle a gun. The incident was reminiscent of the accidental killing of the King's younger brother, Alfonso, in March 1956 by a stray revolver bullet.

Juan Carlos's personal popularity has been dented by accusations of meddling – his public admission of concern at the slowness with which the country is recovering from recession and decision to hold talks with trade-union officials and bankers have held him open to accusations that he is venturing onto political territory. There was worse to come: the King's claims he could not sleep because of the plight of Spain's young unemployed began to sound hollow after it emerged in April 2012 that he had been on an expensive elephant-hunting trip in Botswana, allegedly financed by a wealthy Arab businessman. The trip, which came to light only after Juan Carlos broke his hip and had to be rushed home for emergency surgery, provoked widespread anger and prompted calls for him to resign from his honorary presidency of the Spanish branch of the World Wildlife Fund. The King was then forced to make a public statement to the television cameras as he left Madrid's San José hospital. "I'm very sorry," he said. "I made a mistake. It won't happen again."

Republicanism is not such a powerful force elsewhere in Europe, but there is a sense in which support for monarchy is not absolute but instead conditional on the behaviour of the royal families. While a relatively small number of out-and-out republicans object on principle to an unelected head of state, most people seem prepared to tolerate the continuation of monarchy under certain conditions: namely that members of the royal family behave themselves and are seen to provide taxpayers with good value for money.

The emphasis on personalities rather than the institution means popular support also follows a certain cycle. Generally, the longer a king or queen is on the throne the more his or her ratings will rise; familiarity seems to lead to contentment rather than contempt – unlike with politicians. The birth of an heir will provide a boost, as will the arrival on the scene of a glamorous boy- or girlfriend followed by a royal marriage – provided that he or she is deemed suitable, that is. That being said, young people seem in most cases less passionate about monarchy as an institution than their parents or grandparents.

The monarchy has experienced many such swings in its popularity in Scandinavia, a tendency documented by the many polls on the subject. In Norway, for example, the monarchy's approval rating surged past ninety per cent in the late 1980s before dropping below sixty per cent (and to just forty-nine per cent in the capital) a decade later. The decline was due partly to revelations about the colourful past of Mette-Marit, the future Crown Princess. It was compounded by an outcry over the cost of a six-year renovation of the royal palace, which came in at 400 million kroner, against an original budget of just 150 million kroner. This prompted suggestions that the hitherto somewhat parsimonious royal family were, in the words of Carl-Erik Grimstad, a former deputy head of the household turned royal critic, "spending money like drunken sailors".

The royal ratings had bounced back to sixty-seven per cent by April 2010, helped in part by Mette-Marit's impressive performance as a crown princess, which bodes well for her future role as queen. The average Norwegian republican, says Grimstad, is "male, middle-income, university-educated and urban". "Indifference is the greatest danger to the monarchy," he believes.[1] The country's Socialist Left Party has pledged itself to raise the question once every four years (every parliament) of whether the country should change to a republic. The motion is always defeated by a large majority, however – in the last vote, in 2010, by 125 to seventeen.

In Denmark, by contrast, polls suggested the popularity of the royal house grew through the 1970s, 1980s and 1990s from between seventy and seventy-five per cent to between eight-five and ninety per cent – due, in part, to the arrival of an attractive young queen. The fading of class divisions and a decline in traditional antagonism on the part of the left-wing parties also helped the monarchist cause. A referendum in June 2009 on changing the rules of succession to give equal status to male and female heirs turned, to almost everyone's surprise, into a broader debate about the monarchy. The controversy helped ensure that turnout easily passed the minimum forty per cent threshold – although some, especially in Copenhagen and other cities, heeded calls by republicans to stay away or hand in blank voting slips. The change itself was approved with an eight-five per cent majority. Polls suggest the effect of the vote was to reduce support for monarchy, although not substantially.

Queen Margrethe II's seventieth birthday in April 2010 brought another wave of polling. She herself had little to worry about: her personal approval rating was well above eighty per cent, with Crown Prince Frederik and Crown Princess Mary a few points behind. Support for the Queen's unpopular consort, Prince Henrik, slumped to just 24.8 per cent, however – down from 41.8 per cent in 2004. Danish voters also appeared to back constitutional changes that would reduce the Queen to a figurehead like her Swedish counterpart: a majority wanted the prime minister to be appointed by the speaker of parliament rather than the Queen, and more feel that the Queen should not have to continue to give her assent to legislation than those who support the current system.[2]

Royalists appear to have more cause for concern in Sweden – or at least so it seemed in the months leading up to the wedding in June 2010 of Crown Princess Victoria and Daniel Westling. A poll on the King's sixty-fourth birthday that April showed just fifty-eight per cent support for the monarchy, down from eighty-five per cent in 2000. Support for a republic, meanwhile, climbed to twenty-eight per cent, up from twelve per cent ten years earlier.

The decline was not an entirely steady one: the royal cause suffered as a result of some remarks made by the King during a visit to Brunei, generally regarded as a gaffe, but support picked up again as a result of his response to the 2004 Christmas tsunami, which claimed the lives of five hundred and fifty Swedish holidaymakers in Thailand. Perversely, though, it began to fall again as the royal wedding approached.

Dashing the hopes of republicans, the wedding itself, however, appears to have produced a boost for the monarchist cause. An opinion poll carried out immediately after the ceremony showed seventy-four per cent in favour of the monarchy; in another in November, they received a sixty-nine per cent positive rating.

Republican views are nevertheless held by a surprisingly large number of members of parliament – and are not confined to the Social Democrats, the Left party and the Greens. There are also some republicans among parliamentarians from the centre-right parties too. Yet the Social Democrats do not look any more likely to try to translate the commitment to republicanism in their party programme into action now than they did during the decades in which they dominated politics.

Indeed, the Social Democrats in particular appear to see republicanism as unpopular with their key supporters, and during occasional parliamentary votes on abolishing the monarchy they support the status quo. Hillevi Larsson, a Social Democrat member of parliament who used to be the head of the Republican movement, recalls one such vote. Told by her party whips to vote to keep the monarchy, she protested that this would sit awkwardly with her work for the republican movement. She was eventually allowed to vote according to her conscience, but only after appealing to a higher body within her party.[3]

Support for the monarchy in post-war Britain has also had its ups and downs, but when there has been criticism it has generally been of individuals and of their behaviour rather than of the institution itself. The furore that surrounded Lord Altrincham's remarks on Queen Elizabeth II's style in 1957 was dwarfed by the controversy over the private lives of first the Queen's younger sister Margaret, and then later by the collapse of the Queen's children's marriages. Criticism of the cost of monarchy – and the extent to which taxpayers are getting "value for money" – has also surfaced from time to time. All this came together in the Queen's *annus horribilis* of 1992; in the years that followed, the battle between Prince Charles and Diana provided further fuel for republicans.

Or rather it would have done if there had been sufficient republican-minded people in political life to exploit it. One of the few exception was Willie Hamilton, who in the years after becoming a Labour member of parliament in 1950 branded the Queen "a clockwork doll", labelled Princess Margaret "a floozie", called Prince Charles "a twerp" and described Princess Anne as "plain". It was no coincidence that Hamilton came from Scotland – which, much like Spain's Basque or Catalan regions, has long been more republican than the rest of the country. Yet Hamilton remained something of a curiosity, and after his retirement from parliament in 1987 no one stepped forward to succeed him.

Tony Blair proved just as staunch a monarchist as his Conservative predecessors, skilfully saving the royal family from the public-relations disaster it brought on itself through its mishandling of the death of Princess Diana a few months after he came to power. Not so his wife Cherie, who reportedly refused to curtsy to the Queen when they met in private, although she did so reluctantly in public. Nor were all of his political allies as supportive as him of the monarchy. But when Mo Mowlam, the cabinet minister, caused an outcry in 2000 by suggesting the royals should move out of Buckingham Palace and calling for a nationwide debate on whether Britain should be a monarchy or a republic, Downing Street responded by declaring the prime minister was "one hundred per cent a supporter of the monarchy".

However embarrassing the headlines for individual members of the royal family in the 1990s, it would be difficult to argue that the monarchy as an institution was ever seriously at risk, even during the week immediately after Diana's death, when hysteria appeared to seize hold of the country and a poll commissioned by the American TV network ABC, which featured extensively in the film *The Queen*, showed nearly one in four in Britain thought the country would be better off without the monarchy. Within a few weeks, however, it had recovered again quickly – just as was the case, albeit to a lesser extent, after events such as "Sophiegate" or during the run-up to Prince Charles's marriage to Camilla Parker Bowles. In the same way, the boost provided by Prince William's marriage in April 2011 looks likely to have been only a temporary one. Indeed, polls by Ipsos MORI showed support for the monarchy running at a remarkably constant sixty-nine to seventy-two per cent between 1993 and 2006 (dipping only briefly to sixty-five per cent in April 2005), while backing for a republic varied between fifteen and twenty-two per cent.[4]

This is despite what sometimes seems almost like disdain for the monarchy among Britain's largely London-based liberal intelligentsia, who see it as old-fashioned and in need of modernization, and who feel affronted – and even embarrassed – by the continued popular support that the royal family enjoys in the country as a whole. A case in point was the Golden Jubilee of 2002, which many on the left were keen to write off in advance as a likely non-event – but which turned out to be a mass outpouring of enthusiasm. "We need to face up to the facts," admitted a leader in the *Guardian*. "The Queen's Jubilee celebrations of 2002 have been in every respect more successful than either the organizers had feared or the critics had hoped." That being said, the newspaper still insisted that the enthusiasm witnessed on the streets had been for a "good person" and not for "a lousy system".[5]

Equally telling had been the furore that ensued three months earlier when the BBC newscaster Peter Sissons wore a burgundy rather than black tie as he reported the death of the Queen Mother at the age of 101 – apparently after being told by his editor "not to go overboard. She's a very old woman who had to go sometime".[6] The scale of the turnout for her funeral was another surprise for those same members of the metropolitan intelligentsia.

The Dutch monarchy has also experienced similar swings in its popularity – though again within a fairly narrow range: the reign of Queen Beatrix's mother Juliana was marked by the crisis of 1956 brought about by her relationship with the pacifist faith healer Greet Hofmans and, two decades later, by the accusations that her husband, Prince Bernhard, had taken a $1 million bribe from the Lockheed aircraft corporation. And then, as has been seen, there were the unfortunate marriages: of Juliana's daughters in the 1960s and, more recently, of her grandsons Crown Prince Willem-Alexander and Prince Friso.

While monarchists elsewhere in Europe are a largely unorganized force, the Dutch monarchy enjoys the support of a network of grassroots organizations known as Oranjeverenigingen (Orange Unions). Some four hundred of them are brought together under the group known as De Bond van Oranjeverenigingen (Association of Orange Unions). Yet these are no mere royal lackeys. The federation's chairman, Michiel Zonnevylle, a former civil servant and now mayor of the town of Leiderdorp in the west of the Netherlands, speaks out when he feels members of the royal family are not behaving according to the high standards expected of them – as he did in October 2009 when there was an outcry over Crown Prince Willem-Alexander's decision to buy a villa in Mozambique.

The property had been promoted as a development project that would benefit the local community, but rumours of corruption persisted. Such a purchase also seemed inappropriate at a time when the economic crisis meant many ordinary Dutch were having to tighten their belts. In an interview with *de Volkskrant*, one of the country's leading newspapers, Zonnevylle weighed into the row. "It is very unfortunate to choose such a poor country as Mozambique, particularly if you do it out of considerations of privacy," he said. "I think prime minister Jan Peter Balkenende and Queen Beatrix should talk about this. And I would really value the project being abandoned."[7]

A parliamentary debate on royal finances a few days later in October 2009 provided fuel for the royal-bashers. Mozambique, inevitably, was on the agenda. But so too were the allowances. The discussion even widened to take in calls for the Dutch monarchy to have its role reduced to a purely ceremonial one, as in Sweden. Jan Peter Balkenende, the prime minister, rejected this proposal outright, however, saying "it would be detrimental to the monarchy". He did, however, agree to calls by the Labour and Socialist parties to curb expenses for private flights by the royal family, which in 2008 had reached €600,000. In future, it was announced, only the Queen, her successor and his wife would be allowed to make claim. That was as far as he would go. In any case, Willem-Alexander had got the message: shortly afterwards he announced he was pulling out of the Mozambique project. In January 2012 the government announced that the Prince had finally sold the villa for a symbolic sum, after failing to find a private buyer.

Despite such occasional hiccups, the Dutch monarchy remains extremely popular: a poll conducted for a live television debate in October 2011 found seventy-five per cent of the people still support the monarchy, with more than fifty per cent of them satisfied with the institution in its current form. A substantial minority – twenty-six per cent – however, wanted the House of Orange reduced to a purely ceremonial institution. This followed criticism not just from the left and the centre, but also from Geert Wilders' Freedom Party (PVV), which has been especially critical of the considerable influence given to the Dutch monarch by the country's constitution in choosing a prime minister.

Barring war or revolution – neither of which look likely in today's Europe – it is difficult to conceive of circumstances that would lead to the removal of any of the continent's monarchies any time soon – with one proviso: the British monarch's continued position as head of state of fifteen Commonwealth countries outside the United Kingdom including Australia, New Zealand and Canada looks less secure. For Britons, the monarchy is a symbol of national unity – for many in these countries, known as the Commonwealth Realms, the Queen is a vestige of historic subordination to the "mother country", which no longer seems appropriate in the twenty-first century.

In 1993 Australia's Labour premier, Paul Keating, who had shocked the British tabloid press the previous year by daring to put his arm around the Queen, committed his party to a referendum on the monarchy by the end of the century. In November 1999 the vote finally took place: voters were asked whether they wanted to replace the Queen as head of state with a president.

Opinion polls in the years before the vote had suggested a majority in favour of a republic. Yet when it came to the referendum, only

45.13 per cent voted "yes", compared with 54.87 who wanted to leave things as they were. So what changed?

A crucial role was undoubtedly played by the proposed method for selecting the new president. Rather than have a directly elected head of state as in, say, France, which inevitably would have led to a fundamental change in the functioning of the country's Westminster-style political system, it was proposed that the new president be appointed by parliament – leaving the "yes" camp open to accusations that the change was undemocratic and would turn Australia into a "politicians' republic". For this reason, even some of the more radical republicans voted "no" – better stick to the status quo with the chance of another vote further down the line than move to a flawed model, they argued. Moderate republicans were outraged.

A decade later, Australians are still waiting for another vote. It is difficult to avoid the conclusion that it would have been far fairer to have asked voters simply if they were in favour of a republic, and only if they had voted yes then decide, perhaps through another referendum, on how to elect the president.

In New Zealand, by contrast, there is little agitation for ending the role of the monarchy, although even here support is far from overwhelming: John Key, leader of the centre-right National Party, who became prime minister in November 2008, has said he is not convinced a republic will be a big issue in the short term – although he does believe it is "inevitable" in the end. Politicians were given a chance to have their say on the issue in April 2010 after a private member's bill proposed by Keith Locke, a member of the Green party and an ardent republican, was put to the vote. It was defeated at its first reading by sixty-eight votes to fifty-three. The monarchist cause appeared to have been given a boost by a visit to New Zealand that January by Prince William, who, delivering his first major speech, officially opened the country's Supreme Court building dressed in a traditional Maori cloak.

At the time of writing, there is no sign of a rerun of the Australian vote or of referendums in any of the other countries where the Queen still reigns. That may change when she dies. There seems little doubt that support for the institution of monarchy in these countries has been bolstered considerably by support for the Queen herself, and the dedication she has shown to her job for almost six decades. Charles will not automatically enjoy such popularity, at least initially, providing Australian republicans and those elsewhere with a golden opportunity to push for change. Quite how they – or those in the other Commonwealth Realms – would succeed in jumping over all the constitutional hurdles that would stand in the way of turning their country into a republic remains to be seen.

In Canada, meanwhile, monarchists and republicans have been locked in debate over the institution of monarchy since before the country's confederation in 1867. Opinion polls have showed support for the monarchy has varied over the years, although – not surprisingly – republican feeling is stronger in French-speaking Quebec than it is in the English-speaking provinces. As in Australia and New Zealand, however, Prince Charles appears to enjoy considerably less support than his mother, suggesting his succession may provide opponents of monarchy with the opportunity for which they have long been waiting. Here, too, a visit by Prince William in July 2011 – this time accompanied by his new wife – was of great help to the monarchist cause.

Chapter 16

A Reign without End

The year is 2052, and with his seventieth birthday approaching on 21st June, King William V of the United Kingdom of England and Wales is coming under increasing pressure to abdicate. Formal retirement dates have long since been abolished as ageist, but seventy is still the age at which most people choose to end their working life; so why should kings, even ones as popular as William, be any different?

Blame his father, Charles, who did not become king until he was almost seventy because of his own mother's conviction that it was God's will that she should remain on the throne until she died. When that moment came, plunging the country into a period of mourning not seen since the death of Princess Diana, there was speculation that Charles might step aside in favour of his son, to spare him the frustration of such a long apprenticeship. It was not to be. After spending his entire adult life as Prince of Wales, Charles was determined to have a crack at the top job.

Charles's reign was not a success, however. It got off to the worst possible start when both Australia and New Zealand chose his accession to hold referendums on transforming themselves into republics: despite a passionate and highly organized campaign by the monarchists, the republicans won. While both countries mourned the passing of Queen Elizabeth, there was little enthusiasm for a third King Charles.

Charles never managed to recover from this initial blow to his prestige. True, his subjects were surprisingly amenable to the idea of a Queen Camilla – which had not seemed likely when he had married her back in 2005. Charles's problem was a more fundamental one:

after a lifetime in which he had never been shy about expressing his opinions, he found it difficult to adapt to the strictly apolitical role that his mother had carried off so well.

Responsibility lay in great part with Charles's advisors, who encouraged him to adopt a more interventionist role – the British people would warm to a monarch who made his views known, they argued. For Charles it was also a matter of conscience: he continued to feel strongly about certain issues and did not see his elevation from prince of Wales to king should prevent him from speaking out about them.

And so the letters written in his characteristic spidery hand continued to land on the desks of the great and the good – usually achieving the desired effect. Then he went too far: it emerged that he had been lobbying behind the scenes to try to block a massive wind-farm project – one of his principal *bêtes noires*. The newly elected Labour government, which had a surprisingly large number of avowed republicans among its leading members, cried foul. With a constitutional crisis looming, Charles decided it best to abdicate "for reasons of health" in favour of William.

William, who was forty-five when he came to the throne, with Queen Catherine at his side, did much to restore confidence in the monarchy. He had spent most of his working life in the RAF and, although expressing the requisite interest in the environment and the developing world, did not share his father's passions. He also won respect for the dignity with which he accepted both the loss of Northern Ireland – which was peacefully united in a federation with the Republic in the south – and the secession of Scotland. Now, though, it was time for him to step aside.

The British monarchy was not alone in having undergone – and survived – serious challenges; so too had its Continental counterparts. In Scandinavia, falling support for the monarchy after the accession first of King Haakon of Norway and then of King Frederik of Denmark led both countries to adopt the Swedish model: while both monarchs remained head of state of their respective countries, they no longer played any part in the political process, although both men, accompanied by their ever popular wives, continued to carry out their remaining official duties with skill and enthusiasm.

The Swedes themselves went one stage further: after a surge of republican support put the future of the monarchy in question, a constitutional commission was set up, as it had been in the 1950s. The result, after a number of years of careful deliberation, was a character-istic compromise: out of respect for Queen Victoria, no change would be made as long as she was on the throne, but her successor would no longer be head of state – this role would instead be assumed by the speaker of parliament. For its advocates, such a solution would provide the best of both worlds: the palaces and pageantry remained, but the last remnant of the monarch's historic political role would go. Critics wondered what the point was: opinion polls suggested growing support for eliminating the monarchy completely and throwing open the royal palaces entirely to tourists.

The Dutch monarchy survived such pressures, helped by the support given by the ever loyal Orange Unions. So, surprisingly, did the Span-ish royal family, thanks to King Felipe, who was able to demonstrate that his compatriots were real royalists and not mere *Juancarlistas*.

The Belgian royal house was not so fortunate: by the time the Wal-loons and Flemings had finally hammered out the terms of their "vel-vet divorce", neither of the two independent countries that emerged from its ruins could find much use for a king. The dynasty founded by Léopold I in 1831 never lived to see its two hundredth anniversary.

Making any long-term political prediction is hard enough – and that is especially the case when it comes to the fate of monarchy. In the past, as we have seen, military defeat and the resulting upheaval have been the most common reasons for the end of monarchy – whether directly, as in the case of Germany, Austria and Russia during the First World War – or indirectly, as in the case of Italy, where Vittorio Emanuele III's close relationship with Mussolini helped the republi-can cause to victory in the referendum of 1946. The transformation of the monarchies of Eastern Europe into people's republics under the watchful eye of Stalin should be seen in the same category. The revolution that swept away the monarchy in Portugal in 1910 was an exception in that it happened in peacetime – although, as in Nepal, it followed a regicide: the shooting two years earlier of King Carlos I and his son Luís Filipe as they travelled in a carriage through Lisbon.

But what of those monarchies that have survived, which have been the main focus of this book – to what do they attribute their success and what clues does this provide to their future?

Flexibility on the part of monarchs and their acceptance of the gradual transformation of their countries over the course of the centuries from absolute to constitutional monarchies has been important – even if it was a far from linear process and, in most cases, the kings (and queens) did not give up such powers without a struggle. Being on the winning side during the First and Second World Wars (or at least, in the case of Spain and Sweden, not being on the losing side) has also helped – even if Nazi occupation left a problematic legacy, especially in the case of Belgium, where Léopold III only saved the monarchy by abdicating in favour of his son, Baudouin, who was too young to be tainted by accusations of collaboration. By contrast, Queen Wilhelmina of the Netherlands and King Haakon VII of Norway helped the monarchist cause by their championing of the national resistance from exile. In Britain, George VI's apparent determination to share the suffering of his subjects ensured that the house of Windsor emerged strengthened from the war – even if the toll the conflict took on the King's health was widely blamed for his premature death just seven years later.

Strength of character has played an equally important part in more recent years in the case of Juan Carlos of Spain, who has had more of an impact on his country and the life of its subjects than any of his peers in other realms. The King's refusal to follow the path laid down for him by Franco after he came to the throne in 1975 has ensured that Spain has turned into a modern constitutional monarchy rather than a republic – which surely would have been the eventual result if he had instead sided with the forces of reaction. Juan Carlos also displayed considerable personal courage when he smothered the attempted military coup of 1981. As time has passed, however, gratitude for his extraordinary achievements has faded and given way to concern about the King's love life and lapses of judgement such as his controversial Botswanan elephant safari in April 2012.

None of the Spanish monarch's contemporaries have been confronted with such an existential challenge. Nor can we be certain that they would have reacted with the same determination. Yet they are widely perceived to have performed their jobs well, rarely putting a foot out of line and acting as symbols of permanence and national unity, particularly at times of crisis. This has been especially true of Queen Elizabeth, who has towered over post-war Britain, enjoying huge personal popularity largely untouched by the criticisms heaped on her children.

Surveying Europe's monarchies at the beginning of the second decade of the twenty-first century, the overall impression is one of continuity. Republicanism remains a minority interest. Republicans insist polls suggest support for the monarchy is "soft" – that is, it would only take a dramatic event or major error of judgement on the part of a monarch to bring about a rapid shift in opinion polls. Yet this seems unlikely.

But what of the next generation, the current crop of crown princes and crown princesses who will gradually take their places over the next few years? During their late teenage years and twenties, the men among them demonstrated an all-too-predictable predilection for long-legged blonde models of varying degrees of unsuitability. Yet one by one they have settled down. As we have seen, their partners were in almost every case controversial – with the exception of Philippe of Belgium's choice of the aristocratic Mathilde d'Udekem d'Acoz. Yet their marriages, as far as it is possible to judge, have been successful. Crown Princess Mette-Marit, who spent part of her youth steeped in Norway's drug-fuelled party scene, is now equally at home attending conferences or meeting foreign heads of state. No one seems unduly worried any more about what Máxima of the Netherlands' father knew or didn't know during the Argentinian dictatorship of the 1970s, nor are they concerned about the short first marriage of Letizia of Asturias.

Prince Charles, half a generation older than Philippe and a full generation older than Victoria, also appears settled with Camilla, although a newspaper report by one of Britain's more influential royal watchers in 2010 suggested the couple were leading separate lives: Camilla, it was claimed, so disliked the starchy formality of royal life at Highgrove, her husband's Gloucestershire home, that she was spending increasing amounts of time at Ray Mill, her own country house in Gloucestershire, sixteen miles away. The report followed repeated claims in the British media, usually sourced to anonymous courtiers, that Camilla does not show the required enthusiasm for her royal duties – prompting one former senior aide to the Prince of Wales to label her "the laziest woman to have been born in England in the twentieth century".[1]

There was no suggestion that Charles and Camilla would separate, let alone divorce; if anything, a return to the style of relationship they enjoyed when both were married to other people may actually suit them. Yet the British public will never worship Camilla the way they did Diana. Nor is she likely to enjoy the same popularity as her Continental counterparts when her husband eventually becomes king.

The marriage of Prince William and Kate Middleton, and the enthusiasm with which it was received, also inevitably revived suggestions that Charles should stand aside in favour of his son, especially since by the time the Queen dies, William might even already have children of his own. An opinion poll for the *Sunday Times* published after the announcement of their engagement found a majority of people thought he would make a better king than his father; some forty-four per cent thought Charles should make way for William, against thirty-seven per cent who thought the usual rules of succession should apply.

William's aides promptly stepped in to quash such speculation: the Prince, they said, had "no desire to climb the ladder of kingship" prematurely. Nor did he share his late mother's view, expressed during her Panorama interview in 1995, that the role of king would bring "enormous limitations" to Charles. He is very close to his father and incredibly supportive of him and his work as the Prince of Wales. "Both of them will let nature take its course. There is no suggestion from anywhere within the institution that a generation will be skipped."[2]

Marriage is not enough, of course. In a hereditary monarchy, an heir – and a spare – must also be produced to guarantee the succession. Charles led the way: Prince William was born within eleven months of his father's marriage to Diana; Harry followed just over two years later. One by one, Europe's crown princes and princesses have followed Charles's example: Haakon and Felipe each have two children, Willem-Alexander has three, Philippe and Frederik each have four and, in February 2012, Crown Princess Victoria gave birth to a girl, Estelle.

It is not clear whether Prince Albert of Monaco (who as a prince regnant rather than heir does not, strictly speaking, belong in this list) will meet the dynastic requirement to produce a legitimate heir to add to the two (or more) illegitimate ones he has already fathered.

His relations with his wife Charlene seem so bad, however, that there are doubts that he will do his duty.

For Europe's various monarchs in waiting, it is also important to demonstrate that they will be capable of fulfilling the role that they will one day assume. This is like no other job application, however: judgement as to whether they are performing as heir is very much a subjective one and, in any case, even if they do badly there is no precedent for removing them.

Their record has been mixed, with Prince Charles's use of his position to promote his various pet causes considered by critics as bordering on the unconstitutional. Yet it would be wrong to exaggerate the impact of this on Charles's standing with the population as a whole. While anathema to republicans, such interventions – especially the Prince's campaign against modern architecture – appear to go down well with a large section of the British public who share his views, at least if the letters pages of the national newspapers are a reliable guide.

The current European heirs have also faced their ups and downs – although it is difficult to avoid the impression that their travails have been worsened by tabloid journalists keen to stir up a controversy: while Willem-Alexander of the Netherlands bowed to opposition to his plans to build his luxury villa in Mozambique, Frederik of Denmark persisted in his decision to stand for membership of the International Olympic Committee. Most serious of all have been the doubts long expressed about the suitability of Philippe of Belgium as king – something that has been exploited by Flemish separatists in their campaign for an independent republic.

Such criticisms are due in part to the challenge of carrying out the "non job" of heir to the throne and the difficulty of finding activities that are perceived as useful to society without being overtly political or giving the impression of "cashing in". It is in many respects a thankless task – which, as Charles's example shows, seems to become more difficult with each year that passes. It is one thing for a twenty-five-year-old crown prince to be seen to be devoting himself full time to preparing to be king; by the time he reaches his forties, when most of his contemporaries are near the peak of their careers, it begins to look absurd.

The problem has been exacerbated by a combination of increased life expectancy and the relatively early age at which the current monarchs – the three queens, in particular – had their children, which looks set to condemn their heirs to many more years of waiting.

The solution is an obvious one: abdication. In the Netherlands, both Queen Juliana and Queen Wilhelmina did just that, strengthening rather than weakening the Dutch monarchy in the process, and settling into a perfectly respectable royal retirement. The same has been true in Luxembourg. The experience was a less happy one in Britain – with the departure of Edward VIII in 1936 – and in Belgium – when Léopold III stood down in favour of his son Baudouin in 1951. Yet these were *enforced* rather than voluntary abdications, and however traumatic for those involved, and for the country as a whole, the monarchy survived the temporary crisis that accompanied them; indeed, as an institution, it was strengthened: George VI was undoubtedly a better wartime monarch than his elder brother would have been, while Baudouin became a well-loved figure during his forty-two-year reign.

It is time for Europe's monarchs to consider such a course, starting with Beatrix of the Netherlands. Willem-Alexander is already into his mid-forties, several years past the age when both his mother and grandmother became queen. What is holding Beatrix back, now she has her seventieth birthday behind her? And what of the other monarchs – what, apart from lack of historical precedent, is preventing them from following suit?

As we have seen, a combination of circumstances has ensured that all of them – with the exceptions of Norway's Harald and Albert II of Belgium – came to the throne relatively early in life. Yet this should not mean that they are unable to appreciate the inevitable frustration felt by their children during their long wait. Some may cling to the notion of a monarch as someone who has been anointed by God to serve their country until death, but in an increasingly secular age it is not a point of view that is widely shared by their subjects. Indeed, opinion polls in most countries – with the exception of Britain, where doubts persist about Prince Charles's suitability for the role – show support for the idea of the current monarchs stepping down in favour of the next generation. For many, a king in early middle age with a glamorous wife and young children is an appealing prospect.

Regardless of when they eventually take over, however, the next generation will be inheriting an institution that has proved remarkably resilient and has repeatedly defied predictions of its demise. Since the upheavals that followed the Second World War, only one European nation, Greece, has become a republic, while Spain moved in the opposite direction. If anything, Europe's monarchies looked more firmly entrenched today than they did fifty years ago.

Monarchy is still going strong elsewhere in the world too, whether in Japan, Thailand or the Gulf states. In Cambodia, the former King Norodom Sihanouk was returned to his throne in 1999 and went on to help heal the wounds inflicted on society during the bloody years of Khmer Rouge domination. King Jigme Singye Wangchuck of Bhutan won plaudits by modernizing his once isolated country and steering it towards its first truly democratic elections. But then there is Nepal, where in 2001 a drunken Crown Prince Dipendra went on a shooting spree, assassinating his father, King Birendra, and eight other members of the royal family, before turning the gun on himself. Although Dipendra's younger brother Gyanendra became king, his reign proved a disaster and in May 2008 Nepal was declared a federal democratic republic. A repetition of the bloodbath seen in Kathmandu seems unlikely, although it is not yet clear what will be the eventual impact of the pro-democracy movement that emerged in the Arab world in early 2011 on some of that region's monarchies.

The point is, quite simply, that monarchy – at least in the constitutional form found in Britain and elsewhere in Europe – actually works. When it comes to national cohesion, there is much to be said for a system in which the head of state is truly above politics rather than identified with one or other party. This was particularly the case during the Second World War and has also been so during more recent times of crisis: when Queen Elizabeth visited the victims of London's 7/7 bombings in July 2005 or King Carl XVI Gustaf led national mourning for the Swedes who died in the Thai tsunami the previous Christmas, they did so as representatives of the entire nation. Admittedly, respect for the institution of presidency ensured that Americans of all political persuasions rallied around George W. Bush in the aftermath of the 9/11 attacks on New York and Washington, but his military response soon divided the nation again.

The monarch continues to play this same unifying role during peacetime. The political parties may be at war over policy, but the king or queen floats above it all. When Queen Elizabeth leads mourning at the Cenotaph on Remembrance Sunday, she does so not just as the representative of the nation but also as someone without any responsibility for having sent the latest generation of young men and women to their deaths in Iraq and Afghanistan. The same is true of her Continental counterparts. In those countries – including Britain – where monarchs still open their countries' parliaments, they do as effective symbols of the impartiality of the state.

Even more importantly, a monarch represents continuity. While presidents come and go every four or five years, the king or queen remains as an enduring symbol of unity and a national emblem that transcends the inevitable short-termism of politicians forced to think in terms of their next election.

The strength of continued support for monarchy is also partly attributable to the sticky problem of how best to select an alternative head of state and define his or her role – as was shown by the 1999 referendum in Australia. During the debate in Sweden in the 1960s and 1970s over removal of the monarch's political power, some argued there was no need to have a head of state at all: the role of meeting and greeting foreign presidents could instead be fulfilled by the speaker of parliament. Indeed, Switzerland, for example, does not have a head of state as such: the function is instead performed by the seven-member ruling National Council, but such is the peculiarity of the country's political system that it doesn't have a prime minister either.

Switzerland apart, nations feel the need for a head of state. But should he or she be directly elected by the people or indirectly by the parliament? And should the president be an executive one or merely a figurehead? Replacing kings and queens regnant with a powerful political president such as the French or American one would be a massive constitutional change for Britain and Europe's other monarchies, with their long traditions of parliamentary democracy. By definition, they would also be divisive figures, elected by only part of the nation. The alternative of a German- or Italian-style figurehead president is scarcely more appealing: typically former politicians, selected as a result of a process of horse-trading between the political parties, they rarely command the same respect at home as a monarch. Their profile abroad is also considerably lower: how can you compare the international prestige of Queen Elizabeth with that of President Giorgio Napolitano of Italy or Germany's Joachim Gauck (who only found himself in the job at all after the resignation of his predecessor over a corruption scandal)?

Considering the alternatives, it is no wonder that a constitutional monarchy can seem appealing to those living within one. A negative justification, certainly – but no less persuasive because of it. Furthermore, this appeal looks set to endure, provided the next generation of monarchs handle their role as deftly as their parents have done, adapting with the times and finding new ways of maintaining their relevance to their changing societies. After all, if something isn't broken, why replace it?

In 1948, King Farouk of Egypt famously declared, "The whole world is in revolt. Soon there will be only five kings left – the king of England, the king of Spades, the king of Clubs, the king of Hearts and the king of Diamonds." Farouk was right, at least about one king: himself. Four years after his pronouncement, he was forced to flee his country in great haste, leaving behind all his possessions, including an impressive collection of pornography.[3] Sixty years later, however, the other European monarchs are still on their thrones. Most – if not all – will still be there another sixty years from now.

ACKNOWLEDGEMENTS

Given the extent of the ground that I had to cover in writing this book, I have drawn on many books and other published sources in a variety of languages. As part of my research, I have also been privileged to speak to officials from the various royal courts, both on and off the record, who have shared with me their valuable insights.

A number of other people have also helped me. Among them have been Nina Berglund, Elisabet Carlsson, Nina Eldh, Carl-Erik Grimstad, Hillevi Larsson, Karin Lennmor, Herman Lindqvist, Johan T. Lindwall, Jesper Lundorf, Herman Matthijs, Håvard Melnæs, Annemor Møst, Kathy Pauwels, Anne Quevrin, Gitte Redder, Magnus Simonsson, Pol Van Den Driessche and Michiel Zonnevylle – to name just a few.

I owe special thanks to Trond Norén Isaksen, the Norwegian historian, who made use of his encyclopaedic knowledge of European royalty to identify and correct some factual errors in the first draft, and to Vernon Bogdanor, my former politics tutor at Brasenose College, Oxford and now Research Professor at King's College London's Institute for Contemporary History, who read the chapter on politics and made some useful suggestions for improvement. If any mistakes have nevertheless made it through into the book, then that is entirely my fault. Thanks also to Phil Robinson, for drawing the family tree.

I would also like to thank my agent, Andrew Nurnberg of Andrew Nurnberg Associates, for initiating the project, which began as a book aimed at French readers, Alessandro Gallenzi and Elisabetta Minervini at Alma Books for taking on this, the English edition, and Alex Middleton for his careful and sensitive editing.

NOTES

INTRODUCTION

1 Although curiously the united Germany was a federal state, and Bavaria, Württemberg and Saxony continued to have their own kings (and other states their own dukes and grand dukes) until 1918.

2 It fell just short of the seventy-two years (1643 to 1715) notched up by Louis XIV of France and the seventy years (1858–1929) of Johann II, Prince of Liechtenstein.

3 Arguably, this list should also include the Vatican – which can be characterized as an elective monarchy – and Andorra, ruled by the Bishop of Urgell and the President of France, who, in his capacity as Prince of Andorra, is the only monarch elected at regular intervals by voters in another country.

4 When the fifteen Commonwealth countries over which the British monarch reigns are added, the figure passes 220 million.

CHAPTER 1

1 The family's name was formally changed to Windsor in 1917, at the height of the First World War, from Saxe-Coburg-Gotha (prompting George V's cousin, Kaiser Wilhelm II of Germany, to joke that he looked forward to seeing Shakespeare's play *The Merry Wives of Saxe-Coburg-Gotha*).

2 *En Kongelig Familie* [*A Royal Family*], Nordisk Film, 2004.

3 There were rumours, though, that he had been poisoned. Count Axel von Fersen, reputed to have been a lover of Queen Marie Antoinette of France, was suspected of the murder and was lynched during the funeral procession.

4 This title, rather than "king of Belgium", was chosen to emphasize the new monarchy's link with the people rather than the territory; it also worked better in Latin: the Dutch king had already taken the name *Rex Belgii*, leaving the Belgians with *Rex Belgarum* instead.

CHAPTER 2

1 John Lindskog, *Royale rejser – Bag Kulisserne Hos De Kongelige* [*Royal Travels – Behind the Scenes with the Royals*] (Copenhagen: Documentas, 2009).
2 Georgios's son, Konstantinos, who succeeded him, abdicated twice – first in favour of his second son, Alexander, who died three years later of sepsis brought on by monkey bites, and then in favour of his eldest son, Georgios, who, in what was becoming something of a Greek habit, was deposed but then allowed to return.
3 *Billed-Bladet*, no. 6, 2010.
4 Failure to do so could mean a repetition of the split between Luxembourg and the Netherlands in 1890, when Grand Duchy's succession laws prevented it from accepting Wilhelmina as its sovereign.
5 Unlike in other European countries, the Belgian monarch does not automatically accede to the throne upon the death or abdication of his predecessor, but only after taking the oath – which in the case of Albert II, the current king, happened nine days after the death of his brother Baudouin.

CHAPTER 3

1 In 1642, King Charles I entered the Commons chamber and attempted to arrest five members. The Speaker famously defied the King, refusing to tell him where they were hiding.
2 *Nottingham Evening Post*, 24th November 1998.
3 Vernon Bogdanor, *The Monarchy and the Constitution* (Oxford: Clarendon Press, 1995), p. 1.
4 Ibid., p. 1.
5 'Nick Clegg "Propped Up" Gordon Brown to Seal Tory Deal: Insider Account Reveals Lib Dems Never Wanted Coalition with Labour', *Mail on Sunday*, 14th November 2010.

6 Margaret Thatcher, *The Downing Street Years* (London: HarperCollins, 1993), p. 18.

7 Interview with the author, April 2012.

8 Jörgen Weibull, 'The Power of the Crown', in Gösta Vogel-Rödin, ed., Paul Britten Austin, trans., *The Bernadottes: Their Political and Cultural Achievements* (Lidköping: Läckö Castle Foundation, 1991), p. 40.

9 'Prince Hans-Adam II: Liechtenstein's Future as a "Clean Tax Haven"', *New York Times*, 31st August 2000.

CHAPTER 4

1 The Queen's real birthday is 21st April, but the weather at that time is not considered reliable.

2 'Being Queen Is Just What I Do', *Sunday Telegraph*, 5th January 2003.

3 The Swedish king retained the position, at his own request, after the Church of Sweden was formally separated from the state on 1st January 2000.

4 Interview with the author, Copenhagen, September 2009.

5 *BBC News*, 28th February 2008.

CHAPTER 5

1 'Your (Commuter) Carriage Awaits! Thrifty Queen Catches Ordinary Passenger Train on her Journey to Sandringham for Christmas', *Daily Mail*, 17th December 2009.

2 Walter Bagehot, *The English Constitution* (1867; New York, NY: Oxford University Press, 2001), pp. 49–50.

3 Marion Crawford, *The Little Princesses* (London: Odhams Press, 1950), p. 40.

4 Sarah Bradford, *Elizabeth: A Biography of Her Majesty the Queen* (London: Heinemann, 1996), p. 358.

5 Robert Lacey, *Royal: Her Majesty Queen Elizabeth II* (London: Little, Brown, 2002), p. 189.

6 'Revealed: The Battered Table That Carries Tea, Toast, Jam (and Mismatched Crockery) for the Royal Breakfast in Bed', *Daily Mail*, 26th October 2009.

7 Horatio Clare, 'The Moral of the Queen's Breakfast Tray', *Daily Telegraph*, 27th October 2009.

8 'The Real Elizabeth II', *Daily Telegraph*, 8th January 2002.

9 Jeremy Paxman, *On Royalty* (London: Penguin, 2006), p. 275.

10 'Mystery over Prince Charles and his Boiled Eggs Deepens', *Mail on Sunday*, 24th September 2006.

11 'I Need More Public Cash to Repair Palaces, Says Queen', *Daily Telegraph*, 5th July 2011.

12 The military budget, by contrast, had been voted annually and controlled by parliament, under a system finalized in 1698, limiting the King's ability, should he be so tempted, to use the army for internal repression.

13 Phillip Hall, *Royal Fortune: Tax, Money and the Monarchy* (London: Bloomsbury, 1992), p. 8.

14 Ibid., p. 11.

15 Robert Rhodes James, *Albert Prince Consort* (London: Hamish Hamilton, 1985), p. 143.

16 Hall, op. cit., p. 45.

17 The reason for such a convoluted arrangement became clear only several years later: like many of her subjects, the Queen was trying to cut her tax bill. Treating these payments as costs meant she could offset them against any tax she owed.

18 'Cameron Gets on Board "Inspirational" Royal Yacht Plan', *Financial Times*, 16th January 2012.

19 'Queen Shares the Pain with Pay Freeze to 2015', *Sunday Times*, 4th December 2011.

20 'Prince Charles's Income up by £1m', *Guardian*, 28th June 2011.

21 'Anti-monarchy Group Says British Royals Costs Taxpayer 5 Times Palace's Official Figure', Associated Press, 23rd June 2011.

22 Interview with the author, 9th November 2009.

23 Interview with the author, 10th November 2009.

24 *Ekstra Bladet*, 26th January 2009.

25 Herman Matthijs, *Overheidsbegrotingen* [*Public Spending*] (Bruges: Die Keure, 2009).

26 Interview with the author, September 2009.

27 'Le Vlaams Belang veut contrôler les dépenses royales et princières' ['Vlaams Belang Want to Control Royal and Princely Expenses'], *Le Vif*, 14th May 2008.

28 'Koning Albert wil zelf meer transparantie' ['King Albert Wants to Increase Transparency'], *Knack*, 19th August 2009.

29 Interview with the author, September 2009.

30 'Belgian Royals Latest to Join Austerity Drive', *Guardian*, 9th January 2012.

31 'The World's Richest Royals', *Forbes*, 17th June 2009.

32 *Wall Street Journal*, 6th December 1999.

33 Paul Belien, *A Throne in Brussels: Britain, the Saxe-Coburgs and the Belgianization of Europe* (Charlottesville, VA: Imprint Academic, 2005), p. 42.

34 Federico Quevedo and Daniel Forcada, *El negocio del poder. Así viven los políticos con nuestro dinero* [*The Business of Power. So Politicians Live with Our Money*] (Madrid: Altera, 2009).

CHAPTER 6

1 Thomas Sjöberg, Deanne Rauscher and Tove Meyer, *Carl XVI Gustaf: Den motvillige monarken* [*Carl XVI Gustaf: The Reluctant Monarch*] (Stockholm: Lind & Co., 2010).

2 'Camilla Henemark fick skandalboken' ['Camilla Henemark Received Scandalous Book'], *Expressen*, 6th November 2010.

3 Peter Wolodarski, 'Kungen: Tredubblade insatser' ['The King: Tripled Efforts'], *Dagens Nyheter*, 31st May 2011.

4 Jaime Peñafiel, *Juan Carlos y Sofía: Retrato de un matrimonio* [*Juan Carlos and Sofía: Portrait of a Marriage*] (Madrid: La Esfera de los Libros, 2008), quoted in 'Code of Silence Broken as New Book Reveals Popular King as a Don Juan', *Times*, 12th January 2008.

5 Pilar Eyre, *La soledad de la Reina* [*The Solitude of the Queen*] (Madrid: La Esfera de los Libros, 2012).

6 Mario Danneels, *Paola: van la dolce vita tot koningin* [*Paola: From la Dolce Vita to Queen*] (Leuven: Uitgeverij Van Halewyck, 1999).

7 Crawford, op. cit., p. 59.

8 Nicholas Davies, *Elizabeth: Behind Palace Doors* (London: Mainstream Publishing, 2000), p. 70.

9 *De stem van de koningin* [*The Voice of the Queen*], Één, 6th June 2006.

10 *De Morgen*, 21st May 2005.

11 'Albert had duobaan met "de patron"' ['Albert had a job share with "the boss"'], *De Standaard*, 11th April 2009.

12 'The King's Place in My Art', *Times*, 17th April 2008.

13 Delphine Boël, *Couper le cordon* [*Cut the Cord*] (Brussels: Wever & Bergh, 2008).

14 Paul Preston, *Juan Carlos: Steering Spain from Dictatorship to Democracy* (London: HarperCollins, 2004), p. 154.

15 'Family Reunion', *Time*, 13th September 1954.

16 *Época*, 22nd March 1993.

17 'Royalty: My Son, the Prince', *Time*, 28th December 1962.

18 'The Netherlands: Woman in the House', *Time*, 13th May 1946.

19 'Queen Wilhelmina Wore the Pants', *Milwaukee Journal*, 8th September 1955.

20 Henri de Monpezat, *Destin oblige* (Paris: Plon, 1996), p. 24.

21 Per Egil Hegge, *Harald V: En Biographi* [*Harald V: A Biography*] (Oslo: N.W. Damm & Søn, 2006).

22 Interview with the author, 10th November 2009.

23 Hegge, op. cit.

24 Annemor Møst, *25 lykkelige år: Kong Harald og dronning Sonja i hverdag og fest* [*Twenty-Five Happy Years: King Harald and Queen Sonja in Their Daily Lives and Celebrations*] (Oslo: Schibsted, 1993), p. 158.

25 Interview with the author, 10th November 2009.

26 Møst, op. cit. p. 158.

27 Norbert Loh, *Silvia von Schweden: Eine deutsche Königin* [*Silvia of Sweden: A German Queen*] (Munich: Droemer, 2003), p. 55.

28 Margaret of Connaught died at the age of thirty-eight and Gustaf VI Adolf then married Louise Mountbatten, elder sister of Prince Philip's influential "Uncle Dickie".

CHAPTER 7

1 Alison Weir, *King Henry VIII: King and Court* (London: Jonathan Cape, 2001), p. 403.

2 Christopher Hibbert, *George IV, Prince of Wales 1762–1811* (Newton Abbot: Readers Union, 1973), pp. 14–19, 23–24.

3 Kate Williams, *Becoming Queen* (London: Hutchinson, 2008), p. 6.

4 Valérie de Montfort, *Les plus belles anecdotes historiques sur la famille royale* [*The Best Historical Anecdotes about the Royal Family*] (Brussels: Jourdan Éditeur, 2007), p. 27.

5 Belien, op. cit., pp. 75–76.

6 Ibid., p. 77.

7 de Montfort, op. cit., p. 52.

8 Belien, op. cit., p. 77.

9 Ibid., p. 93.

10 Ibid., p. 94.

11 'A Queen's Unhappy Life: Misery of the Late Marie-Henriette of Belgium Revealed in Letters', *New York Times*, 5th October 1902.

12 'Holland's Queen', *New York Times*, 26th September 1897.

13 Lord John Hervey, *Some Materials towards Memoirs of the Reign of King George II*, Vol. I (London: Eyre & Spottiswoode, 1931), p. 42.

14 Belien, op. cit., p. 78.

15 *Pall Mall Gazette*, 10th, 11th April 1885, quoted in Belien, op. cit., p. 102.

16 Munthe later became well known as the author of *The Story of San Michele*, an autobiography that became one of the first truly international best-sellers after it was published in 1929.

17 John D. Bergamini, *The Spanish Bourbons: The History of a Tenacious Dynasty* (New York, NY: G.P. Putnam's Sons, 1974), p. 108.

18 Gerard Noel, *Ena: Spain's English Queen* (London: Constable, 1984), pp. 238–40.

19 Eleanor Herman, *Sex with the Queen: 900 Years of Vile Kings, Virile Lovers and Passionate Politics* (New York, NY: William Morrow, 2006), p. 137.

20 Half a century later the jar was discovered by Catherine the Great on a dusty shelf in a back room of the palace, alongside another containing the head of Mary Hamilton, one of Peter's own lovers, whom he had also beheaded. Although struck by how well both were preserved, the Tsarina did the decent thing and had them both buried.

21 Joan Haslip, *Catherine the Great* (New York, NY: G.P. Putnam's Sons, 1978), p. 353.

22 Bergamini, op. cit., p. 229.

23 Herman, op. cit., p. 252.

24 Tor Bomann-Larsen, *Folket: Haakon og Maud* [*The People: Haakon and Maud*] Vol. II (Oslo: Cappelen, 2004).

25 Reuters, 14th October 2004.

26 Odd Arvid Storsveen [book review], *Historisk Tidsskrift*, No. 1, 2005, pp. 130–41.

CHAPTER 8

1 'Globespotters; London: A Fashion Biography', *New York Times*, 18th April 2010.
2 'The Girl in White Gloves', *Time*, 31st January 1955.
3 Pascal went on to have a fling with Gary Cooper before marrying Raymond Pellegrin, another actor – by whom she had a daughter.
4 'The Prince and the Papers', *Time*, 23rd January 1956.
5 In fact, the celebrated courtesan was said to have been the lover of no fewer than six crowned heads of state – also including Britain's King Edward VII and Tsar Nicholas of Russia.
6 Christian de Massy and Charles Higham, *Palace: My Life in the Royal Family of Monaco* (New York, NY: Atheneum, 1986), p. 12.
7 *Madame Figaro*, 13th August 1994.
8 'Royals Seek Lower Profile at Monaco Birthday Bash', Reuters, 2nd January 1997.
9 'Swimmer Tells of Dream Date with Prince Charming', *Sunday Times* [South Africa], 1st July 2001.
10 David Isaacson, 'SA "Blondie" Laughs Last', *Sunday Times* [South Africa], 24th June 2010.
11 'Prince Albert Finally Settles Down and Ends Monaco's 30-Year Wait for a Monarch's Wedding', *Daily Mail*, 24th June 2010.

CHAPTER 9

1 'Bernhard zakenprins (1911–2004)' ['Bernhard, the Businessman Prince (1911–2004)'], *De Groene Amsterdammer*, 3rd December 2004.
2 William Hoffman, *Queen Juliana: The Story of the Richest Woman in the World* (New York, NY: Harcourt Brace Jovanovich, 1979), p. 69.
3 'Die Gesundbeterin' ['The Faith Healer'], *Der Spiegel*, 13th June 1956.
4 Hoffman, op. cit., p. 214.
5 *Newsweek*, 5th April 1976.
6 Hermione Hobhouse, *Prince Albert: His Life and Work* (London: Hamish Hamilton, 1983).
7 'The Queen's Husband', *Time*, 21st October 1957.

8 de Monpezat, op. cit., pp. 231–32.

9 *BT*, 3rd February 2002.

10 Annelise Bistrup, *Margrethe* (Copenhagen: Politiken Bøger, 2005).

11 Trine Villemann, *1015 Copenhagen K: Mary's Dysfunctional In-Laws* (Burnham, UK: Andartes Press, 2008), p. 74.

12 Gyles Brandreth, *Philip and Elizabeth: Portrait of a Marriage* (London: Century, 2004), pp. 253–54.

13 Davies, op. cit., p. 118.

14 Ibid., p. 118.

15 'The Crown Jewel', *Sunday Telegraph*, 11th November 2007.

16 Ibid.

17 'Prince Phillip's Secret Letters to the Showgirl', *Mail on Sunday*, 20th December 2008.

18 http://trondni.blogspot.com, 28th March 2010.

19 *Aftenposten*, 29th August 2008.

CHAPTER 10

1 Gyles Brandreth, *Charles and Camilla: Portrait of a Love Affair* (London: Century, 2005), p. 140.

2 Ibid., pp. 122, 126.

3 Ibid., p. 129.

4 J.M. Ledgard, 'The Man Who Would Be Useful', *Intelligent Life*, Autumn 2008.

5 Brandreth, *Charles and Camilla*, op. cit., p. 141.

6 *Time*, 20th March 1964.

7 Brandreth, *Charles and Camilla*, op. cit., p. 140.

8 'Britain's Prince Charles: The Apprentice King', *Time*, 27th June 1969.

9 Crawford, op. cit., p. 16.

10 Ibid., p. 28.

11 'The Netherlands: Woman in the House', *Time*, 13th May 1946.

12 Hoffman, op. cit., p. 37.

13 Ibid., p. 55.

14 *Aftonbladet*, 1st December 2005.

15 Preston, op. cit., p. 49.

16 Ibid., p. 1.

17 Ibid., p. 101.

18 Villemann, op. cit., p. 17.
19 Gitte Redder and Karin Palshøj, *Frederik: Kronprins af Danmark* [*Frederik: Crown Prince of Denmark*] (Copenhagen: Høst & Søn, 2008).
20 This was despite obtaining only two A levels, at a time when at least three were the norm – and not especially good grades at that: a B in history and a C in French.
21 'The Princely Life', *Time*, 20th October 1967.
22 Tina Brown, *The Diana Chronicles* (London: Century, 2007), p. 86.
23 *De Gelderlander*, 30th October 2004.
24 Willem-Alexander himself once declared the only princesses he fancied were the Princess of Wales and Stéphanie of Monaco.
25 *De Standaard*, 11th October 2007.
26 *Point de Vue*, 30th August 1994.
27 Villemann, op. cit., p. 170.

CHAPTER 11

1 Interview with the author, April 2010.
2 'Kronprinsens nye kjærlighet' ['The Crown Prince's New Love'], *Fædrelandsvennen*, 29th December 1999.
3 Interview with the author, 9th November 2009.
4 'Norwegian Crown Princess's Father Weds Former Stripper', Associated Press, 11th March 2005.
5 Håvard Melnæs, *En helt vanlig dag på jobben* [*A Normal Day at Work*] (Oslo: Kagge, 2007).
6 Anette Gilje, *Sven O. Høiby: Et portrett* [*Sven O. Høiby: A Portrait*] (Oslo: Glydendal, 2007).
7 Gonzalo Álvarez Guerrero and Soledad Ferrari, *Máxima: Una Historia Real* [*Máxima: A True Story*] (Buenos Aires: Editorial Sudamericana, 2009).
8 Gitte Redder and Karin Palshøj, *Mary, Kronprinsesse af Danmark* [*Mary: Crown Princess of Denmark*] (Copenhagen: Høst & Søn, 2004), p. 28.
9 Ibid., p. 169.
10 In the traditional manner, he had already written a long letter to Mary's father, asking for her hand – though with the added proviso that, even if he said no, he would still propose.
11 'Papal Path', *Sun*, 28th July 2007.

12 'They Sealed It with Kisses and a Surprise Drive: William and Kate Marry', *Times*, 30th April 2011.

CHAPTER 12

1 It is also not an option in Norway, which is not a member of the EU.
2 Paul Richards, 'Secret Web of the Black Spider Prince', *Mail on Sunday*, 26th June 2010.
3 'Europe's Royals as Climate Activists', *Financial Times*, 27th March 2010.
4 'IOC Won't Pressure Prince Politically', *Copenhagen Post*, 16th September 2009.
5 Brigitte Balfoort, Barend Leyts and Pol Van Den Driessche, *Albert II, 10 jaar koning* [*Albert II: Ten Years as King*] (Leuven: Van Halewijck, 2003).
6 Associated Press, 25th January 2007.

CHAPTER 13

1 'Märtha Louise von Norwegen, Interview mit einem Engel' ['Märtha Louise of Norway, Interview with an Angel'], *Bunte*, 5th May 2010.
2 Noel Botham, *Margaret: The Last Real Princess* (London: Blake Publishing Ltd, 2002), p. 9.
3 Christopher Warwick, *Princess Margaret: A Life of Contrasts* (London: Carlton Publishing Group, 2002), p. 190.
4 Ibid., p. 223.
5 Ibid., pp. 229–30.
6 Ibid., p. 255.
7 'Fergie "Sells" Andy for £500k', *News of the World*, 23rd May 2010.
8 Mazher Mahmood, *Confessions of a Fake Sheik* (London: HarperCollins, 2008), p. 261.
9 'It's a Royal Cock-Up', *Guardian*, 5th March 2002.
10 Under the rather arcane rules that govern royal titles, there has been some downgrading of their status, however: Friso is no longer a Prince of the Netherlands and his daughters are countesses rather than princesses.
11 'Op zijn achttiende vroeg hij me wat "een halve plus een halve" was. Hij wist dat gewoon niet' ['When he was eighteen, he asked me what "a half plus a half" was. He really didn't know'], *Humo*, 24th December 2001.

12 'The Global Class: Royal Flush', *International Herald Tribune*, 4th April 2002.

13 Belien, op. cit., p. 55.

CHAPTER 14

1 Belien, op. cit., p. 67.

2 Ibid., p. 95.

3 Neal Ascherson, *The King Incorporated: Léopold II in the Age of Trusts* (London: George Allen & Unwin, 1963), p. 262.

4 'Unprivate Lives', *Time*, 23rd November 1936.

5 Lacey, op. cit., p. 179.

6 'Royal Teatime', *Time*, 24th January 1949.

7 Richard Tomlinson, 'Trying to Be Useful', *Independent*, 19th June 1994.

8 Bradford, op. cit., p. 45.

9 Ibid., p. 166.

10 Interview with the author, April 2010.

11 Neil Blain and Hugh O'Donnell, *Media, Monarchy and Power* (Bristol: Intellect, 2003).

12 'The Forgotten Royal Nanny', *Daily Express*, 30th July 2011.

13 *Pittsburgh Press*, 13th December 1936.

14 Associated Press, 14th December 1981.

15 'Wie wichtig ist Ihnen die Wahrheit, Herr Prinz?' ['How Important to You Is the Truth, Mr Prince'?], *Der Spiegel*, 6th March 2009.

16 Carla Joosten, *Het Koningshuis in een notendop* [*The Royals in a Nutshell*] (Amsterdam: Uitgeverij Bert Bakker, 2006), p. 109.

17 Ibid., p. 110.

18 Andreas Whittam-Smith, 'Debate the Monarchy's Future, but It Will Change Nothing', *Independent*, 11th December 2000.

CHAPTER 15

1 Interview with the author, October 2009.

2 Poll by Rambøll/Analyse Danmark, published in *Jyllands-Posten*, 4th, 14th April 2010.

3 Interview with the author, April 2010.

4 Peter Whittle, *Monarchy Matters* (London: The Social Affairs Unit, 2011), p. 55.
5 'A Spectacular Jubilee', *Guardian*, 5th June 2002.
6 'How BBC Bosses Ordered Me to Downplay the Queen Mother's Death', *Daily Mail*, 24th January 2011.
7 'Prins moet weg uit vastgoedproject' ['Prince Must Leave Real-Estate Project'], *de Volkskrant*, 5th October 2009.

CHAPTER 16

1 'Why Charles and Camilla Are Now Living Such Separate Lives', *Daily Mail*, 29th June 2010.
2 'Prince William: Let My Father Become King', *Sunday Telegraph*, 28th November 2010.
3 In exile in Rome, he indulged his passion for fine eating, growing to more than 130 kilos and dying at the age of forty-five, appropriately enough, over a meal in a restaurant.

SELECT BIBLIOGRAPHY

ARTICLES

'Albert had duobaan met "de patron"' ['Albert had a job share with "the boss"'],
   De Standaard, 11th April 2009

'Anti-monarchy Group Says British Royals Costs Taxpayer 5 Times Palace's
   Official Figure', Associated Press, 23rd June 2011

'Being Queen Is Just What I Do', *Sunday Telegraph*, 5th January 2003

'Belgian Royals Latest to Join Austerity Drive', *Guardian*, 9th January 2012

'Bernhard zakenprins (1911–2004)' ['Bernhard, the Businessman Prince (1911–
   2004)'], *De Groene Amsterdammer*, 3rd December 2004

'Britain's Prince Charles: The Apprentice King', *Time*, 27th June 1969

'Cameron Gets on Board "Inspirational" Royal Yacht Plan', *Financial Times*,
   16th January 2012

'Camilla Henemark fick skandalboken' ['Camilla Henemark Received Scandalous Book'], *Expressen*, 6th November 2010

Clare, Horatio, 'The Moral of the Queen's Breakfast Tray', *Daily Telegraph*,
   27th October 2009

'Crown Jewel, The', *Sunday Telegraph*, 11th November 2007

'Die Gesundbeterin' ['The Faith Healer'], *Der Spiegel*, 13th June 1956

'Europe's Royals as Climate Activists', *Financial Times*, 27th March 2010

'Family Reunion', *Time*, 13th September 1954

'Fergie "Sells" Andy for £500k', *News of the World*, 23rd May 2010

'Forgotten Royal Nanny, The', *Daily Express*, 30th July 2011

'Girl in White Gloves, The', *Time*, 31st January 1955

'Global Class: Royal Flush, The', *International Herald Tribune*, 4th April 2002

'Globespotters; London: A Fashion Biography', *New York Times*, 18th April
   2010

'Holland's Queen', *New York Times*, 26th September 1897

'How BBC Bosses Ordered Me to Downplay the Queen Mother's Death', *Daily Mail*, 24th January 2011

'I Need More Public Cash to Repair Palaces, Says Queen', *Daily Telegraph*, 5th July 2011

'IOC Won't Pressure Prince Politically', *Copenhagen Post*, 16th September 2009

Isaacson, David, 'SA "Blondie" Laughs Last', *Sunday Times* [South Africa], 24th June 2010

'It's a Royal Cock-Up', *Guardian*, 5th March 2002

'King's Place in My Art, The', *Times*, 17th April 2008

'Koning Albert wil zelf meer transparantie' ['King Albert Wants to Increase Transparency'], *Knack*, 19th August 2009

'Kronprinsens nye kjærlighet' ['The Crown Prince's New Love'], *Fædrelandsvennen*, 29th December 1999

Ledgard, J.M., 'The Man Who Would Be Useful', *Intelligent Life*, Autumn 2008

'Le Vlaams Belang veut contrôler les dépenses royales et princières' ['Vlaams Belang Want to Control Royal and Princely Expenses'], *Le Vif*, 14th May 2008

'Märtha Louise von Norwegen, Interview mit einem Engel' ['Märtha Louise of Norway, Interview with an Angel'], *Bunte*, 5th May 2010

'Mystery over Prince Charles and his Boiled Eggs Deepens', *Mail on Sunday*, 24th September 2006

'Netherlands, The: Woman in the House', *Time*, 13th May 1946

'Nick Clegg "Propped Up" Gordon Brown to Seal Tory Deal: Insider Account Reveals Lib Dems Never Wanted Coalition with Labour', *Mail on Sunday*, 14th November 2010

'Norwegian Crown Princess's Father Weds Former Stripper', Associated Press, 11th March 2005

'Op zijn achttiende vroeg hij me wat "een halve plus een halve" was. Hij wist dat gewoon niet' ['When he was eighteen, he asked me what "a half plus a half" was. He really didn't know'], *Humo*, 24th December 2001

'Papal Path', *Sun*, 28th July 2007

'Prince Albert Finally Settles down and Ends Monaco's 30-Year Wait for a Monarch's Wedding', *Daily Mail*, 24th June 2010

'Prince and the Papers, The', *Time*, 23rd January 1956

'Prince Charles's Income up by £1m', *Guardian*, 28th June 2011

'Prince Hans-Adam II: Liechtenstein's Future as a "Clean Tax Haven"', *New York Times*, 31st August 2000

'Prince Phillip's Secret Letters to the Showgirl', *Mail on Sunday*, 20th December 2008

'Prince William: Let My Father Become King', *Sunday Telegraph*, 28th November 2010

'Princely Life, The', *Time*, 20th October 1967

'Prins moet weg uit vastgoedproject' ['Prince Must Leave Real-Estate Project'], de Volkskrant, 5th October 2009

'Queen Shares the Pain with Pay Freeze to 2015', *Sunday Times*, 4th December 2011

'Queen Wilhelmina Wore the Pants', *Milwaukee Journal*, 8th September 1955

'Queen's Husband, The', *Time*, 21st October 1957

'Queen's Unhappy Life, A: Misery of the Late Marie-Henriette of Belgium Revealed in Letters', *New York Times*, 5th October 1902

'Real Elizabeth II, The', *Daily Telegraph*, 8th January 2002

'Revealed: The Battered Table That Carries Tea, Toast, Jam (and Mismatched Crockery) for the Royal Breakfast in Bed', *Daily Mail*, 26th October 2009

Richards, Paul, 'Secret Web of the Black Spider Prince', *Mail on Sunday*, 26th June 2010

'Royal Teatime', *Time*, 24th January 1949

'Royals Seek Lower Profile at Monaco Birthday Bash', Reuters, 2nd January 1997

'Royalty: My Son, the Prince', *Time*, 28th December 1962

'Spectacular Jubilee, A', *Guardian*, 5th June 2002

'Swimmer Tells of Dream Date with Prince Charming', *Sunday Times* [South Africa], 1st July 2001

'They Sealed It with Kisses and a Surprise Drive: William and Kate Marry', *Times*, 30th April 2011

Tomlinson, Richard, 'Trying to Be Useful', *Independent*, 19th June 1994

'Unprivate Lives', *Time*, 23rd November 1936

Weibull, Jörgen, 'The Power of the Crown', in Gösta Vogel-Rödin, ed., Paul Britten Austin, trans., *The Bernadottes: Their Political and Cultural Achievements* (Lidköping: Läckö Castle Foundation, 1991)

Whittam-Smith, Andreas, 'Debate the Monarchy's Future, but It Will Change Nothing', *Independent*, 11th December 2000

'Why Charles and Camilla Are Now Living Such Separate Lives', *Daily Mail*, 29th June 2010

'Wie wichtig ist Ihnen die Wahrheit, Herr Prinz?' ['How Important to You Is the Truth, Mr Prince'?], *Der Spiegel*, 6th March 2009

Wolodarski, Peter, 'Kungen: Tredubblade insatser' ['The King: Tripled Efforts'], *Dagens Nyheter*, 31st May 2011

'World's Richest Royals, The', *Forbes*, 17th June 2009

'Your (Commuter) Carriage Awaits! Thrifty Queen Catches Ordinary Passenger Train on her Journey to Sandringham for Christmas', *Daily Mail*, 17th December 2009

BOOKS

Ascherson, Neal, *The King Incorporated: Léopold II in the Age of Trusts* (London: George Allen & Unwin, 1963)

Bagehot, Walter, *The English Constitution* (1867; New York, NY: Oxford University Press, 2001)

Balfoort, Brigitte, Leyts, Barend, and Van Den Driessche, Pol, *Albert II, 10 jaar koning* [*Albert II: Ten Years as King*] (Leuven: Van Halewijck, 2003)

Belien, Paul, *A Throne in Brussels: Britain, the Saxe-Coburgs and the Belgianization of Europe* (Charlotteville, VA: Imprint Academic, 2005)

Bergamini, John D., *The Spanish Bourbons: The History of a Tenacious Dynasty*, (New York, NY: G.P. Putnam's Sons, 1974)

Bistrup, Annelise, *Margrethe* ([Denmark]: Politiken Bøger, 2005)

Blain, Neil, and O'Donnell, Hugh, *Media, Monarchy and Power* (Bristol: Intellect, 2003)

Boël, Delphine, *Couper le cordon* [*Cut the Cord*] (Brussels: Wever & Bergh, 2008)

Bogdanor, Vernon, *The Monarchy and the Constitution* (Oxford: Clarendon Press, 1995)

Bomann-Larsen, Tor, *Folket: Haakon og Maud* [*The People: Haakon and Maud*] Vol. II (Oslo: Cappelen, 2004)

Botham, Noel, *Margaret: The Last Real Princess* (London: Blake Publishing Ltd, 2002)

Bradford, Sarah, *Elizabeth: A Biography of Her Majesty the Queen* (London: Heinemann, 1996)

Brandreth, Gyles, *Charles and Camilla: Portrait of a Love Affair* (London: Century, 2005)

Brandreth, Gyles, *Philip and Elizabeth: Portrait of a Marriage* (London: Century, 2004)

Brown, Tina, *The Diana Chronicles* (London: Century, 2007)

Crawford, Marion, *The Little Princesses* (London: Odhams Press, 1950)

Danneels, Mario, *Paola: van la dolce vita tot koningin* [*Paola: From la Dolce Vita to Queen*] (Leuven: Uitgeverij Van Halewyck, 1999)

Davies, Nicholas, *Elizabeth: Behind Palace Doors* (London: Mainstream Publishing, 2000)

de Massy, Christian, and Higham, Charles, *Palace: My Life in the Royal Family of Monaco* (New York, NY: Atheneum, 1986)

de Monpezat, Henri, *Destin Oblige* (Paris: Plon, 1996)

de Montfort, Valérie, *Les plus belles anecdotes historiques sur la famille royale* [*The Best Historical Anecdotes about the Royal Family*] (Brussels: Jourdan Editeur, 2007)

Eyre, Pilar, *La soledad de la Reina* [*The Solitude of the Queen*] (Madrid: La Esfera de los Libros, 2012)

Gilje, Anette, *Sven O. Høiby: Et portrett* [*Sven O. Høiby: A Portrait*] (Oslo: Glydendal, 2007)

Guerrero, Gonzalo Álvarez, and Ferrari, Soledad, *Máxima: Una Historia Real* [*Máxima: A True Story*] (Buenos Aires: Editorial Sudamericana, 2009)

Hall, Phillip, *Royal Fortune: Tax, Money and the Monarchy* (London: Bloomsbury, 1992)

Haslip, Joan, *Catherine the Great* (New York, NY: G.P. Putnam's Sons, 1978)

Hegge, Per Egil, *Harald V: En Biographi* [*Harald V: A Biography*] (Oslo: N.W. Damm & Søn, 2006)

Herman, Eleanor, *Sex with the Queen: 900 Years of Vile Kings, Virile Lovers and Passionate Politics* (New York: William Morrow, 2006)

Hervey, Lord John, *Some Materials towards Memoirs of the Reign of King George II*, Vol. 1 (London: Eyre & Spottiswoode, 1931)

Hibbert, Christopher, *George IV, Prince of Wales 1762–1811* (Newton Abbot: Readers Union, 1973)

Hobhouse, Hermione, *Prince Albert: His Life and Work* (London: Hamish Hamilton, 1983)

Hoffman, William, *Queen Juliana: The Story of the Richest Woman in the World* (New York, NY: Harcourt Brace Jovanovich, 1979)

James, Robert Rhodes, *Albert Prince Consort* (London: Hamish Hamilton, 1985)

Joosten, Carla, *Het Koningshuis in een notendop* [*The Royals in a Nutshell*] (Amsterdam: Uitgeverij Bert Bakker, 2006)

Lacey, Robert, *Royal: Her Majesty Queen Elizabeth II* (St Ives: Little, Brown, 2002)

Lindskog, John, *Royale rejser – Bag Kulisserne Hos De Kongelige* [*Royal Travels – Behind the Scenes with the Royals*] (Copenhagen: Documentas, 2009)

Loh, Norbert, *Silvia von Schweden: Eine deutsche Königin* [*Silvia of Sweden: A German Queen*] (Munich: Droemer, 2003)

Mahmood, Mazher, *Confessions of a Fake Sheik* (London: HarperCollins, 2008)

Matthijs, Herman, *Overheidsbegrotingen* [*Public Spending*] (Bruges: Die Keure, 2009)

Melnæs, Håvard, *En helt vanlig dag på jobben* [*A Normal Day at Work*] (Oslo: Kagge, 2007)

Møst, Annemor, *25 lykkelige år: Kong Harald og dronning Sonja i hverdag og fest* [*Twenty-Five Happy Years: King Harald and Queen Sonja in Their Daily Lives and Celebrations*] (Oslo: Schibsted, 1993)

Noel, Gerard, *Ena: Spain's English Queen* (London: Constable, 1984)

Paxman, Jeremy, *On Royalty* (St Ives: Penguin, 2006)

Peñafiel, Jaime, *Juan Carlos y Sofía: Retrato de un matrimonio* [*Juan Carlos and Sofía: Portrait of a Marriage*] (Madrid: La Esfera de los Libros, 2008), quoted in 'Code of Silence Broken as New Book Reveals Popular King as a Don Juan', *Times*, 12th January 2008

Preston, Paul, *Juan Carlos: Steering Spain from Dictatorship to Democracy* (London: HarperCollins, 2004)

Quevedo, Federico, and Forcada, Daniel, *El negocio del poder. Así viven los políticos con nuestro dinero* [*The Business of Power. So Politicians Live with Our Money*] (Madrid: Altera, 2009)

Redder, Gitte, and Palshøj, Karin, *Frederik: Kronprins af Danmark* [*Frederik: Crown Prince of Denmark*] (Copenhagen: Høst & Søn, 2008)

Redder, Gitte, and Palshøj, Karin, *Mary, Kronprinsesse af Danmark* [*Mary: Crown Princess of Denmark*] (Copenhagen: Høst & Søn, 2004)

Sjöberg, Thomas, Rauscher, Deanne, and Meyer, Tove, *Carl XVI Gustaf: Den motvillige monarken* [*Carl XVI Gustaf: The Reluctant Monarch*] (Stockholm: Lind & Co., 2010)

Thatcher, Margaret, *The Downing Street Years* (London: HarperCollins, 1993)

Villemann, Trine, *1015 Copenhagen K: Mary's Dysfunctional In-Laws* (Burnham, UK: Andartes Press, 2008)

Warwick, Christopher, *Princess Margaret: A Life of Contrasts* (London: Carlton Publishing Group, 2002)

Weir, Alison, *King Henry VIII: King and Court* (London: Jonathan Cape, 2001)

Whittle, Peter, *Monarchy Matters* (London: The Social Affairs Unit, 2011)

Williams, Kate, *Becoming Queen* (London: Hutchinson, 2008)

INDEX

Casiraghi, Charlotte (daughter of Caroline, Princess of Hanover): 300
Casiraghi, Pierre (son of Caroline, Princess of Hanover): 300
Casiraghi, Stefano (second husband of Caroline, Princess of Hanover): 172, 309
Castlemaine, Lady (mistress of Charles II): 151
Cath, Bodil (Danish journalist): 190
Catharina-Amalia, Princess of the Netherlands (daughter of Willem-Alexander, Prince of Orange): 77, 310
Catherine I (tsarina of Russia 1725–27): 162
Catherine II (Catherine the Great, tsarina of Russia 1762–96): 11, 35, 38
Catherine of Aragon (wife of Henry VIII): 75
Catherine of Braganza (wife of Charles II): 151
Catherine Pavlovna of Russia (wife of Wilhelm I of Württemberg): 149
Catherine, Duchess of Cambridge (Kate Middleton, wife of William, Duke of Cambridge): 40, 72, 83, 253, 293, 299, 305, 308, 332, 336
Cawston, Richard (British broadcaster): 295–96
Chamberlain, Joseph (British politician): 317
Charlemagne (king of the Franks 768–814 and Holy Roman Emperor 800–814): 35
Charlene, Princess of Monaco (Charlene Wittstock, wife of Albert II of Monaco): 167, 175–79, 337
Charles I (king of England 1624–49): 43, 49, 54, 314–16
Charles II (king of England 1660–85): 34, 49, 54, 95, 151, 315
Charles X (king of France 1824–30): 11
Charles, Prince of Belgium (brother of Léopold III and regent 1944–50): 24
Charles, Prince of Wales (son of Elizabeth II): 33, 45, 70–72, 75, 82, 88, 90–91, 94, 97, 101, 117, 138, 150, 152, 198, 200–3, 212, 214–15, 218–20, 222, 250–53, 258–60, 271, 273, 276, 278, 293, 295, 298, 304–5, 307, 311, 314, 321, 325–26, 329–32, 335–38
Charlotte (grand duchess of Luxembourg 1919–64): 46

Charlotte Frederikke, Duchess of Mecklenburg-Schwerin (wife of Christian VIII of Denmark): 149
Charlotte, Duchess of Valentinois, Princess (daughter of Louis II of Monaco): 38, 171–72, 174
Charlotte, Princess of Belgium (daughter of Léopold I of the Belgians): 37, 153
Charlotte, Princess of Wales (daughter of George IV and wife of Léopold I of Belgium): 22, 73, 110, 146–47, 153, 158, 287
Charlotte, Queen Consort (Charlotte of Mecklenburg-Strelitz, wife of George III): 144, 160
Charteris, Lord (British courtier): 193
Chatto, Lady Sarah (daughter of Princess Margaret): 272
Chazal, Pierre (Belgian statesman and lover of Marie Henriette of Austria): 148
Chrétien, see von Eppinghoven, Arthur
Christian IX (king of Denmark 1863–1906): 15–16, 28, 36–37, 142, 156, 196
Christian VII (king of Denmark 1766–1808): 159
Christian VIII (king of Denmark 1839–48): 16, 36, 149, 151, 223
Christian X (king of Denmark 1912–47): 17, 58
Christian, Count of Rosenborg (son of Knud, hereditary prince of Denmark): 39
Christian, Prince of Denmark (son of Frederik, Crown Prince of Denmark): 39, 255
Christian, Prince of Hanover (son of Prince Ernst August of Hanover): 128
Christina, Princess of the Netherlands (Maria Christina or Marijke, daughter of Juliana and sister of Beatrix of the Netherlands): 183, 275, 279
Churchill, Lady Randolph (Jeanette "Jennie" Jerome, mother of Winston Churchill and mistress of Edward VII): 157
Churchill, Winston (British prime minister 1940–45, 1951–55): 19, 89, 157, 192, 291, 293
Claire, Princess of Belgium (Claire Combs, wife of Prince Laurent of Belgium): 281
Claret, Arcadie (married name Arcadie Meyer, mistress of Léopold I of the Belgians): 152–53, 155

Matheopoulos, Helena (Greek author): 210

Mathilde, Duchess of Brabant, Princess (Mathilde d'Udekem d'Acoz, wife of Prince Philippe, Duke of Brabant): 124, 140, 263, 335

Matthijs, Herman (Belgian academic): 103–4

Maud, Princess of Wales (queen consort of Norway and wife of Haakon VII): 25, 106, 134, 164–65, 195, 197

Maugham, William Somerset (British author): 30

Maurits, Prince of Orange-Nassau (cousin of Willem-Alexander, Prince of Orange): 220

Máxima, Princess of the Netherlands (Máxima Zorreguieta, wife of Willem-Alexander, Prince of Orange): 51, 77, 106, 117, 198, 239–42, 269, 302, 310, 335

Maximilian I (emperor of Mexico 1864–67): 37, 43

McCloskey, Matthew (American publisher): 172

McLean, Roderick (would-be assassin of Queen Victoria): 44

Meat Loaf (American musician): 297

Meeûs, Ferdinand (Count de Meeûs d'Argenteuil, Belgian industrialist): 110–11

Melnæs, Håvard (Norwegian journalist): 235–39, 302

Mette-Marit, Crown Princess of Norway (Mette-Marit Tjessem Høiby, wife of Haakon, Crown Prince of Norway): 26, 198, 231–37, 239–40, 266, 282, 302, 304–5, 312, 322–23, 335

Metternich, Klemens von (Austrian statesman): 23, 147

Meyer, Frédéric (husband of Arcadie Claret): 152

Meyer, Georges-Frédéric (illegitimate son of Léopold I of the Belgians): 153

Michael, Prince of Kent (cousin of Elizabeth II): 76

Michael, Princess of Kent (Baroness Marie-Christine von Reibnitz, wife of Prince Michael of Kent): 76

Middleton, Carol (mother of Catherine, Duchess of Cambridge): 83

Middleton, Kate, see Catherine, Duchess of Cambridge

Middleton, Michael (father of Catherine, Duchess of Cambridge): 83

Mihai (king of Romania 1927–30): 13

Miles, Andrew (former flatmate of Mary, Crown Princess of Denmark): 244

Milland, Ray (British actor): 168

Miller, Keith (Australian cricketer): 272

Mons, William (lover of Catherine I of Russia): 162

Montell, Maria (former girlfriend of Frederik, Crown Prince of Denmark): 224

Moore, Roger (British actor): 179

Mordaunt, Harriet (mistress of Edward VII): 158

Mordaunt, Sir Charles (husband of Harriet Mordaunt): 158

Morris, Irene (wife of Philip Morris): 267

Morris, Philip (British showjumper): 267

Morton, Andrew (British author): 298

Møst, Annemor (Norwegian journalist): 99, 135

Mountbatten, George, Marquess of Milford Haven (uncle of Prince Philip): 118

Mountbatten, Louis, 1st Earl Mountbatten of Burma ("Uncle Dickie", uncle of Prince Philip): 118–20, 192, 218

Mountbatten, Victoria (maternal grandmother of Prince Philip): 118

Mowlam, Mo (British politician): 325

Muggeridge, Malcolm (British journalist): 292

Munthe, Axel (Swedish psychiatrist and lover of Queen Victoria of Sweden): 159

Mussolini, Benito (Italian head of state 1922–43): 12, 333

Napoleon I (emperor of the French 1804–14, 1815): 18–20, 41, 225

Napoleon III (emperor of the French 1852–70): 12, 23, 37, 44, 87, 142, 317

Neergard, Ebba (lady-in-waiting to Ingrid of Sweden): 294

Newton, Sir Isaac (British scientist): 214

Nicholas Alexandrovich, Tsarevich of Russia ("Nixa", son of Alexander II of Russia and brother of Alexander III of Russia): 142

Nielsen, Katja Storkholm (former girlfriend of Frederik, Crown Prince of Denmark): 223–24

Phillips, Mark (former husband of Anne, Princess Royal): 45, 304
Phillips, Peter (son of Anne, Princess Royal, and Peter Phillips): 83
Pierre, Duke of Valentinois, Prince (Pierre de Polignac, father of Rainer III of Monaco): 171
Pieter-Christiaan van Vollenhoven, Prince of Orange-Nassau (son of Princess Margriet of the Netherlands): 279
Pilar, Duchess of Badajoz, Infanta (sister of Juan Carlos I of Spain): 210
Pinelli, Pierre (lover of Princess Stéphanie of Monaco): 173
Pius VII (pope 1800–23): 41
Pius IX (pope 1846–78): 37
Pius X (pope 1903–14): 155
Plater-Syberg, Countess Anna (former girlfriend of Prince Philippe, Duke of Brabant): 223
Ponsonby, Sir Frederick (British courtier): 93
Potemkin, Gregory (lover of Catherine II of Russia): 163
Preston, Paul (British historian): 210
Princip, Gavrilo (killer of Archduke Franz Ferdinand of Austria): 43
Prinz, Günter (German journalist): 309
Prinz, Matthias (German lawyer): 309
Puigmoltó y Mayans, Enrique (Spanish soldier and possible father of Alfonso XII): 164

Quant, Mary (British fashion designer): 272
Quevrin, Anne (Belgian journalist): 285

Ragnhild, Princess of Norway (daughter of Olav V of Norway and sister of Harald V of Norway): 133
Rainier III (prince of Monaco 1949–2005): 29–30, 34, 39, 72, 166–72, 261, 293, 299
Rasmussen, Louise (wife of Frederik VII of Denmark): 160–61
Rasputin (Russian mystic): 19
Razumovsky, Alexei (lover of Elizabeth of Russia): 163
Reid, Sir Alan (British courtier): 91
Repossi, Alberto (jeweller, owner of Repossi Joailliers): 178
Richard III (king of England 1483–85): 36, 77

Richard, Duke of York (son of Edward IV): 140
Richards, Paul (British former special advisor): 260
Rim, Merwan (French actor and lover of Princess Stéphanie of Monaco): 174
Robertson, Geoffrey (British-Australian lawyer): 314
Robinson, Mary (mistress of George IV): 144, 146
Roosevelt, Eleanor (wife of Franklin D. Roosevelt): 89
Roosevelt, Franklin D. (president of the United States 1933–45): 89
Roosevelt, Theodore (president of the United States 1901–09): 131
Rose, Helen (American costume designer): 72
Rosenbaum, Tibor (Swiss banker): 185
Rossellini, Robertino (son of Roberto Rossellini and lover of Caroline, Princess of Hanover): 172
Rossellini, Roberto (Italian film director): 172
Rotolo, Tamara (lover of Albert II of Monaco): 174
Rubens, Peter Paul (Flemish artist): 141
Rutte, Mark (Dutch politician): 66

Sacirbey, Muhamed (former boyfriend of Princess Mabel of Orange-Nassau): 278
Safra, Edmond (Lebanese financier): 154
Safra, Lily (wife of Edmond Safra): 154
Saltykov, Count Sergei (lover of Catherine II of Russia): 163
Sannum, Eva (former girlfriend of Felipe, Prince of Asturias): 221–22, 248
Sarah, Duchess of York (Sarah Ferguson, also "Fergie", former wife of Prince Andrew, Duke of York): 277, 297, 315
Sarkozy, Nicolas (French president 2007–12): 179
Sartorius y Cabeza de Vaca, Vicente (Spanish bobsledder): 221
Sartorius y Zorraquín de Mariño, Isabel (former girlfriend of Felipe, Prince of Asturias): 221
Schiffer, Claudia (German model): 167
Sellers, Peter (British comedian and actor): 272